Mergers and Acquisitions

Rajinder S. Aurora
Senior Lead—Academics
Future Innoversity
Mumbai

Kavita Shetty
Management Consultant
Mumbai

Sharad R. Kale
Management Consultant
Mumbai

OXFORD
UNIVERSITY PRESS

OXFORD
UNIVERSITY PRESS

Oxford University Press is a department of the University of Oxford.
It furthers the University's objective of excellence in research, scholarship,
and education by publishing worldwide. Oxford is a registered trade mark of
Oxford University Press in the UK and in certain other countries.

Published in India by
Oxford University Press
YMCA Library Building, Jai Singh Road, New Delhi 110001, India

ISBN-13: 978-0-19-806451-0
ISBN-10: 0-19-806451-9

Typeset in Baskerville
by iPlus Knowledge Solutions Private Limited, Chennai
Printed in India by Repro India Ltd

Dedicated to the loving memory of

My father Shriram Gurudittamal Aurora

Who never lived to see me being a part of the knowledge revolution and touching so many lives.

Rajinder S. Aurora

My mother Purnima Changotra

My friend, philosopher, and guide in the true sense—may her soul rest in peace.

Kavita Shetty

My wife Neelima Sharad Kale

The vacuum she has left behind shall remain forever—may her soul rest in peace.

Sharad R. Kale

Foreword

Mergers and acquisitions (M&As) have become almost an everyday phenomenon in the business world. Companies involved in M&As aim at attaining growth and enhancing their competitive strengths by joining together.

In the context of the growing use of M&As as a strategic tool, the present book, written by eminent authors with extensive corporate exposure and intensive understanding of the subject, is indeed a welcome addition to the existing body of literature on the subject.

The book is comprehensive in its coverage, dealing not only with the legal and accounting processes but also with the organizational and human resource (HR) issues arising in the wake of M&As.

The effort made by the authors in punctuating the text with a number of examples and introducing contemporary cases adds further value to the book, and makes it equally useful for both corporate users and management students.

I have great pleasure in recommending the book to practitioners, academicians, and student readers.

Prof. Y.K. Bhushan
Senior Advisor & Head, IBS Mumbai
Vice Chancellor, ICFAI University, Meghalaya

Preface

The corporate world is undergoing a sea change and throwing up new issues and challenges every day. Organizations have been growing in size, becoming global, and diversifying into new areas. They are quite often confronted with cultural, social, and regulatory changes that impact the entire dimension of their operations. The challenges posed by the changing environment need strategies that have never been tried before. The changing environment and the resultant unfamiliar surroundings often lead to collapse of companies. While this does not happen in every case, it has often caused turmoil both within and outside the company.

Economies such as India opted for the New International Economic Order and adopted liberalization, privatization, and globalization rather reluctantly. However, it turned out to be a blessing in disguise for India, as the country's real potential was realized thereafter. Indian companies, which had often been targets of mergers and acquisitions (M&As), reversed the trend and started acquiring other companies both in India and abroad. Foreign entities that were thought to be corporate raiders suddenly became acquisition targets of their Indian counterparts.

The last decade has seen numerous M&As, which have often forced organizations to adopt special strategies for tiding over the pressures generated by this trend. Mergers and acquisitions were once looked upon as a phenomenon confined to the USA, but today that is no longer the case; M&As have become a global phenomenon. They represent the most critical of all the business strategies being pursued to attain growth and expansion. It is no wonder then that business schools across the globe have started focusing on the study of M&As as a very important component of management education. This enables management graduates to understand the basics of M&As and evolve appropriate strategies on joining the industry. It is, therefore, important that managers get clear, complete, and up-to-date insights into issues pertaining to M&As.

About the Book

Mergers and Acquisitions is an effort to fulfil the needs of future and practising managers in getting appropriate insights into this complex subject. The book addresses both conceptual issues and their practical applications. It gives an in-depth explanation of the concepts, processes, issues, and pitfalls involved in M&As and corporate restructuring using a lucid style. It further elaborates them with appropriate examples and well-researched case studies. It also discusses the legal and accounting angles of M&As, and the human resource and integration issues involved.

This book is based on extensive research and will be an important tool in helping readers understand the finer details of the subject and evolve a successful M&A strategy.

Pedagogical Features

The book presents information in a standardized and student-friendly format, so that the content flows seamlessly from one concept to another. Each chapter contains a list of learning objectives, followed by an introduction, discussions on relevant topics, a conclusion, and a summary. For quick understanding and easy reference, the key terms used in the chapters have been summarized at the end of each chapter with brief definitions.

The book also contains the following:

- Numerous examples to help students relate to the terms used
- Relevant case studies and solved examples
- Concept review questions at the end of each chapter
- Assignments to improve students' understanding and involvement
- Appendices to highlight the legal documents necessary for M&As

Some of the key features of the book are as follows:

- Exhaustive coverage of all topics, especially the introductory ones
- Solved examples to provide a better understanding of accounting issues
- Numerous examples for understanding concepts
- Case studies that deal with Indian companies
- Comprehensive case studies at the end of the book, covering more than one issue each

Coverage and Structure

The book is divided into nine chapters. Each chapter captures the different aspects of corporate restructuring, especially M&As.

Chapter 1, Corporate Restructuring, deals with the framework of corporate restructuring, its reasons, types, and barriers, and strategies involved.

Chapter 2, Takeovers, highlights the concept and forms of takeover, the types of takeover defence, benefits and disadvantages of takeovers, the takeover code, and the procedure for takeover.

Chapter 3, Mergers and Acquisitions, covers the concept, genesis, and types of M&As, difference between mergers and acquisitions, motives behind M&As, value drivers, difficulties encountered, processes involved, and ways and means of financing. It also provides an insight into M&As on the domestic front.

Chapter 4, Due Diligence, explains the concept of due diligence; its need, types, and process; and parties involved. It also discusses due diligence reporting, reasons for failure of due diligence, methods for avoiding failure, and requirements for making an effective due diligence team.

Chapter 5, Legal Issues in Mergers and Acquisitions, covers all the legal provisions pertaining to M&As, such as Provisions of Companies Act, 1956; SEBI (Buyback of Securities) Regulations, 1998; SEBI (Substantial Acquisition of Shares and Takeovers), 1997; Listing Agreement norms; SEBI (Delisting of Securities) norms; corporate governance issues; Provision of Income Tax Act, 1961; Foreign Exchange Management Act (FEMA), 1999; and Competition Act, 2002.

Chapter 6, Valuation and Accounting Issues, deals with the concept of valuation, factors considered for valuation, different methods of valuation, difficulties in valuing companies, and basic accounting.

Chapter 7, Post-merger Issues, provides insights into the concept of integration, tools used for integration, post-merger growth strategies, and human resources angle of M&As.

Chapter 8, Cross-border Acquisitions, discusses the concept of cross-border acquisition (CBA), need for CBA, its benefits and problems, and the need for integration.

Chapter 9, Alternatives to Mergers and Acquisitions, explores various alternatives to M&As, including divestitures, strategic alliances, and internal development, reasons why these strategies are explored by companies, and their advantages and disadvantages.

The chapters are followed by four case studies, which cover several aspects relating to M&As, and five appendices, which give the format of the legal documents necessary for M&As.

While the textual content and cases address all issues relating to M&As, the dynamic nature of the business environment necessitates continuous update of content and information. In view of this fact, readers must remember that the examples and cases referred to in the book are time-sensitive. The success stories of today may become poor examples of tomorrow. Similarly, the failures of today have the potential to become leading examples of tomorrow. We, therefore, request the readers to look at the examples, especially those of entities that may be struggling today or do not exist anymore, merely as tools for understanding concepts.

Acknowledgements

We would like to acknowledge the support and inputs of our families and friends, whose motivation made this onerous task a pleasant learning experience for us. While we express our sincere gratitude to all of them, we shall not list them here as they are too numerous to name.

We also express our sincere gratitude to the editorial team of Oxford University Press, without whose help we would not have been able to complete this book.

We have referred to a large number of books, journals, research papers, and other publications, and listed them at the end of each chapter. The sole responsibility for errors and omissions (if any) in the book lies with us.

We invite suggestions from managers, faculty, researchers, and students, to improve the contents of the book further and make it more relevant to users.

Rajinder S. Aurora
Kavita Shetty
Sharad R. Kale

Brief Contents

Detailed Contents

CASE STUDIES

APPENDICES

1

Corporate Restructuring

LEARNING OBJECTIVES

After studying the chapter, you will be able to understand

- the concept of corporate restructuring
- the framework of corporate restructuring
- the reasons for restructuring, barriers to restructuring, types of restructuring, and strategies for restructuring
- the strategic options in corporate restructuring
- the conditions to be fulfilled by a company going in for a buyback
- the concept and types of leveraged buyouts (LBOs)
- the reasons behind growing unpopularity of LBOs
- the concept of management buyouts

1.1 INTRODUCTION

The global economy is undergoing major transitions and paradigm shifts. As a result, several corporate giants of yesteryears are either disappearing or undergoing massive restructuring exercises. Restructuring is the modern mantra of survival. While very little can be done with regard to permanent closure of business, the strategy of restructuring is an attempt to revive the operations of the entity and make it profitable once again. In addition, expansion of markets hitherto unknown to many entities can be profitably milked with the help of a partner who knows the tide, and can help new entrants sail through with ease. Mergers and acquisitions (M&As) are looked upon as instruments of successful corporate restructuring and fulfilment of corporate goals.

In the era of liberalization and globalization, entities compete in unfamiliar markets. In addition, the protection provided by high tariffs and other trade barriers are no longer available, making it difficult for an entity to yield a steady output of goods, services, and even profits year after year. Managers have to continuously work towards improvements in the quality of goods and services produced, reduction in costs, and maintenance of output prices at competitive levels.

Change is inevitable, and the magnitude and speed of change differs from case to case. Under normal circumstances, change in the work environment occurs in a gradual and predictable manner. As such, enough time is available to assess the impact. On the contrary, when change assumes the velocity of a hurricane, routine tinkering with policies, structure, and managerial practices is of no use. In such a scenario, organizations need to adopt a result-oriented approach that not only keeps the organization on course, but also enables it to target new destinations and new heights of achievement. The change approach adopted 'to ring out the old and ring in the new' should be in tune with the circumstances and the environment. It is thus important to note that restructuring is a continuous process driven by corporate vision.

1.2 CONCEPT OF CORPORATE RESTRUCTURING

The concept of restructuring focuses on change. The Oxford Dictionary (2007) defines restructuring as 'giving a new structure, to rebuild/rearrange'. Taking a cue from this definition, one can say that corporate restructuring is a structured decision-making exercise undertaken to evaluate the current endowments of a company by fine-tuning the available skills, machinery, and technology to meet the challenges of tomorrow.

Restructuring is a corporate management term that stands for the act of partially dismantling or otherwise reorganizing a company to make it more efficient and therefore more profitable. It generally involves selling off portions of the company and making drastic staff reductions. Restructuring is often undertaken as part of a bankruptcy or takeover by another firm, particularly a leveraged buyout (LBO) by a private equity firm. It may also be done by a new CEO hired specifically to effect difficult and controversial decisions required to save or reposition the company.

Different authors present different views on the concept of corporate restructuring. Let us examine some views:

- Corporate restructuring refers to a broad array of activities that expand or contract a firm's operations or substantially modify its financial structure or bring about a significant change in its organizational structure or internal financing (Chandra 2007).
- Corporate restructuring is the reorganization of a company to attain greater efficiency and to adapt to new markets (www.financialdictionary.com).
- Corporate restructuring refers to liquidating projects in some areas and redirecting assets to other existing or new areas (Weston et al. 2005).

At its most general level, the term corporate restructuring can and has been used to mean almost any change in operations, capital structure, and/or ownership that is not part of the firm's ordinary course of business (Marshall et al. 2004).

1.3 CONCEPTUAL FRAMEWORK

Liberal doses of restructuring have sparked off a series of academic deliberations into the phenomenon of corporate restructuring. A closer look at the concept of restructuring reminds one of what Alfred P. Sloan Jr once said, 'The strategic aim of a business is to earn a return on capital and if in any particular case, the return in the long run is not satisfactory, then the deficiency should be corrected or the activity abandoned for a more favourable one.'

Bowman and Singh (1997) are of the opinion that the current spate of restructuring exercises is induced by the simultaneity of changes in the product and the capital markets. According to them, changes in the product markets stem largely from domestic and foreign competition, accelerated technological change, and the competitive pressures faced in the global markets. Changes in capital markets, on the other hand, originate from new debt instruments, new tolerance for increased level of debt in the capital structure of the firm, and institutional innovations and aggressiveness.

Muller (1988) argues that the changing culture and image of the company are the most important rationale influencing restructuring. He also states that the human dimension is imperative in any such exercise.

Donaldson (1994) has systematically chronicled the instances in corporate America where takeover bids have forced a company to restructure to ward off hostile takeover threats.

Gibbs (1993) expressed the view that corporate restructuring is needed under three conditions: the presence of free cash flow, ineffective corporate governance, and the threat of takeover.

Finally, Bethel and Liebeskind (2007) argued that shareholders often exert influence over managers and press for restructuring the business.

If one tries to analyse the restructuring models, the basic question that remains is, what are the factors that one should study, to position the organization to achieve the intended objectives? Various models and theories have been propagated in this regard. Some models look only at the internal factors, others only at the external factors; some combine these perspectives and others look for congruence between various aspects of the organization being studied. There is no unanimity on the factors that a company needs to study for effective positioning in the market.

1.4 McKINSEY 7S MODEL

Keeping in mind the complex nature of the restructuring process, McKinsey undertook a study towards the end of the 1970s. The main objectives were to diagnose the causes of original problems and to formulate programs for improvement. This framework came to be known as McKinsey's 7S framework for restructuring. Developed in the early 1980s by Tom Peters and Robert Waterman, two consultants working at McKinsey & Company, the 7S model is based on the premise that there are seven internal aspects of an organization that need to be aligned, if the organization has to be successful.

The 7S model can be used in a wide variety of situations where an alignment perspective is useful:

- Improving the performance of a company
- Examining the likely effects of future changes within a company

- Aligning departments and processes during a merger or acquisition
- Determining how best to implement a proposed strategy

The McKinsey 7S model involves seven interdependent factors, which are categorized as either 'hard' or 'soft' elements. 'Hard' elements are easier to define or identify and the management can directly influence them. These are strategy statements, organization charts, reporting lines, formal processes, and IT systems. They include strategy, structure, and systems.

'Soft' elements, on the other hand, are more difficult to describe, less tangible, and often more influenced by culture. However, the soft elements are as important as the hard elements for the organization to succeed. The soft elements include shared values, skills, style, and staff.

Figure 1.1 depicts the interdependency of the elements and indicates how change in one affects all the others.

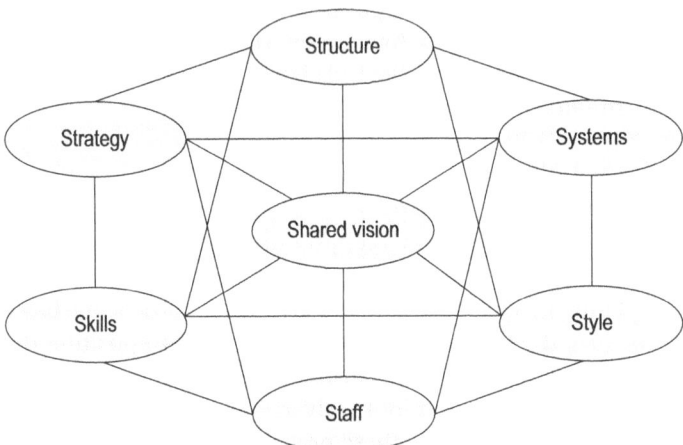

Figure 1.1   McKinsey 7S model

Let us look at the elements in brief:

Strategy   Every entity wants to be 'one up' on its competitors. It has to evolve plans that will help to attain its newly-defined objectives and help to maintain and build competitive advantage in the markets that are getting increasingly competitive.

Structure   Structure represents the way an organization is structured, and depicts the reporting relationships. Effective functioning requires an appropriate organizational structure that would have clearly defined relationships. A good structure is one that facilitates smooth flow of information across levels.

Systems   While goals are the guiding light in an entity, they need to be pursued in an effective and efficient manner. It is important that every individual knows the daily activities to be performed. Thus, systems represent the activities and procedures that employees across hierarchies should engage in to get the job done.

Shared values Every entity has/propagates certain values and culture that are effectively built into the system. These get reflected in the corporate culture and the general work ethics of individuals. Also known as 'superordinate goals', these are the core values of the company and are evidenced in the way the entity responds to environmental changes and ethical dilemmas.

Style This deals with the style of leadership adopted by the leader of the team. To a great extent, the success of an entity depends on the quality of leadership. An organization where the leader 'walks the talk' attains its objectives with greater ease, for a leader successfully inspires his team and allows the work culture and values to percolate to all the strata in the organization.

Staff While inspiring leadership is a key to success, the ultimate attainment of goals and objectives depends on the employees and their general capabilities. Every organization recruits the best available human resource. Recruitment is not just about hiring the right employees. An important mantra for success is the ability to retain and groom human resource, to enable them to adapt to the changes with ease and remain focused. Thus, a successful HR policy calls for the following:

- Right person for the right job
- Right policies to retain talented and skilled employees
- Right and regular training and grooming
- Right strategy for getting rid of deadwood

Skills This deals with the actual skills and competencies of the employees working for the company. Very often, this is misinterpreted as skills possessed by employees at the time of recruitment. While skills are critical to performance, regular and continuous upgradation is necessary to ensure that they are in tune with the prevailing practices and meet the requirements of the environment.

The 7S model is based on the fundamental theory that an organization can perform well when all the seven elements are aligned and mutually reinforcing. The model is very important in the modern business environment. It helps to identify what needs to be realigned to improve performance and how to maintain alignment (and performance) during change. The change could relate to restructuring, introduction of new processes, organizational merger, introducing new systems, change of leadership, and so on. The model can be used to understand how the organizational elements are interrelated. It is also helpful in assessing the impact of changes in one area on the other areas. For example, to analyse the current situation point A and the proposed future situation point B, one needs to identify the gaps and inconsistencies between them. Once these are identified, it is a matter of adjusting and tuning the elements of the 7S model to ensure that the organization works effectively and attains the desired objectives.

This adjustment and tuning of the different elements of the organization is not as easy as it seems to be. This is where the 7S model proves beneficial. It helps the organization ask the right questions, although the answers to these questions may be elusive. It is here that the organization needs to bring together the right knowledge, skills, and experience.

One could consider some sample questions pertaining to each element. These questions need to be supplemented with specific situational questions based on circumstances and accumulated organizational wisdom. Some of the sample questions for each element are as follows:

Strategy

- What is our strategy?
- How do we intend to achieve our objectives?
- How do we deal with changes in customer demands?
- How do we deal with competitive pressure?
- How do we adjust strategy for environmental issues?

Structure

- What is the hierarchy?
- How is the company/team divided?
- How do different departments coordinate their activities?
- How do the team members organize and align themselves?
- Where are the lines of communication—explicit and implicit?
- Is decision making and controlling centralized or decentralized? Is this as it should be, given what we are doing?

Systems

- What are the main systems that run the organization? (Consider financial and HR systems as well as communication and document storage.)
- Where are the controls and how are they monitored and evaluated?
- What are the internal rules and processes used by the team to stay on track?

Shared values

- What are the fundamental values that the company/team has been built on?
- What are the core values?
- How strong are the values?
- What is the corporate/team culture?

Style

- How participative is the management/leadership style?
- How effective is the leadership?
- Do employees/team members tend to be competitive or cooperative?
- Are there real teams functioning within the organization or are they just nominal groups?

Staff

- What are the positions or specializations represented within the team?
- What are the positions that need to be filled?
- Are there gaps in the required competencies?

Skills

- What are the strongest skills represented in the company/team?
- How are skills monitored and assessed?
- Are there any skill gaps?
- What is the company/team known for doing well?
- Do the current employees/team members have the ability to do the job?

Once these questions have been listed, the organization evolves a matrix to ascertain whether the elements are in alignment with one another.

- The organization can start with shared values and ascertain whether they are consistent with the structure, strategy, and systems.
- If they are not, what needs to change so that the organization can reach the desired objectives?
- Next, the organization needs to look at the hard elements to ascertain whether these support each other.
- If they are not mutually supportive, changes needed are to be identified.
- Finally, the organization can analyse the soft elements to determine whether these support the desired hard elements or not.
- If they do not support the hard elements, the organization needs to identify the changes required.

After adjusting and aligning the 7S, one needs to constantly re-analyse the elements to understand how a change in one element impacts the other elements and what further adjustments are needed to align them. As this process continues, deficiencies get highlighted and performance improves.

1.5 REASONS FOR RESTRUCTURING

The entire debate on the corporate restructuring process brings to focus the following basic reasons that compel companies to opt for restructuring.

1.5.1 Change in Fiscal and Government Policies

Changed fiscal and governmental policies such as deregulation/decontrol have led many companies to tap new markets and customer segments. A few sectors have been hit hard by the withdrawal of government patronage as they have to look after their own financial requirements and at the same time face competition from powerful global giants. To prepare themselves to survive in the changed business environment, companies have to pursue restructuring so as to adapt their structure to the new challenges and meet their financial requirements.

1.5.2 Liberalization, Privatization, and Globalization

Liberalization, privatization, and globalization have changed the rules of the game. The only way to survive in the changed business environment is to change the way business is conducted. These three factors have compelled companies to restructure their operations because only the most cost-effective producers can survive in the present global markets. In addition, these three stimuli have given rise to a whole new set of laws and regulations. Survival has become a function of adapting to these stimuli.

1.5.3 Information Technology Revolution

Information technology (IT) has become the lifeline of modern business enterprises. Most of the business is carried out using modern tools of communication and IT. Information technology drives corporate performance. Companies have to adopt and adapt to the ever-changing IT environment, by tweaking their organizational structure. In addition, a lot of investment flows into creating an appropriate IT infrastructure, including familiarizing people working in the organization with the tools of IT. This obviously calls for a major restructuring in the operations of the enterprise.

1.5.4 Concept of Customer Delight

The competitive global environment has brought to the fore the new concept of 'customer delight', which states that only those companies that can understand and fulfil the needs and expectations of the customer shall survive. Modern customers are knowledgeable, clear about their needs and expectations, and are increasingly demanding and very often unpredictable about their consumption habits. The changing customer profile has intensified competition and companies have to reshape their activities to survive in business. Many giants of yesteryears have been forced out of the market or have merged with another company, for either they were reluctant, or very slow to change. Some companies have undergone major restructuring processes to survive. For example, General Motors, Lakme, Tata Oil Mills Company (TOMCO), Premier Automobiles, and Mahindra and Mahindra have changed to satisfy the needs and expectations of the customers.

Figure 1.2 shows how successful companies deliver value.

1.5.5 Cost Reduction

Customers not only expect quality products, but also affordable prices. Companies have to make continuous efforts to reduce costs and improve quality. Quite often, companies resort to downsizing—one of the tools of corporate restructuring—to become cost-effective. In a perpetually changing competitive environment, there is no place for inflexibility, an obsession with activity rather than results, bureaucratic functioning, and high overheads. Cost reduction and cost control are the new mantras of success.

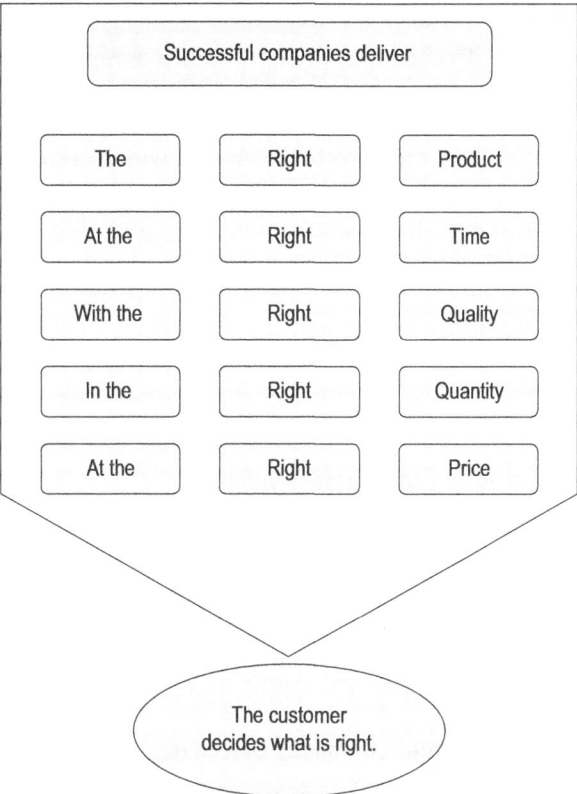

Source: Siemens Limited Case, *'Customer is the King; Restructuring is Change'*, AIMA, New Delhi, 23 August 1997
Figure 1.2 Value delivery by successful companies

1.5.6 Divestment

Many companies have either divisionalized their operations into smaller businesses, or have sold off units or divisions that do not have a strategic fit with the business. Divestment is often done to get out of activities that do not add value to the business, or sometimes destroy value. It is also a way of releasing capital resources that have been blocked in activities where the company does not enjoy core competency or competitive advantage. For example, Larsen and Toubro's (L&T) sale of L&T Cement, Tata's exit from Tata Oil Mills Co. (TOMCO), etc.

1.5.7 Improving Bottom Line

The basic business objective shall always be maximizing profits. It is the only way to keep all the stakeholders happy. To achieve it, companies have to narrow down the gap between the attainable and the attained. Restructuring becomes necessary to realize the full potential of the company.

1.5.8 Core Competencies

Prof. C.K. Prahalad's concept of core competency also results in restructuring. Core competency is a specific factor that a business perceives to be central to its functioning. It provides recurring consumer benefits, is not easy for competitors to imitate, and can be leveraged widely across many products and markets. A core competency can be technical—a reliable process, a close relationship with customers and suppliers, product development and/or culture, such as employee dedication. The concept is integral to the strategic vision of the company as it provides the fundamental basis for the provision of added value.

Core competencies are the collective learning in organizations, involving coordination of diverse production skills and integration of multiple streams of technologies. Core competencies often provide impetus for many companies to restructure.

1.5.9 Enhancing Shareholder Value

Every company aims at enhancing shareholder value. This is necessary for the capital inflows to continue. Shareholders shy away from companies that do not provide adequate returns. Such companies cannot execute their growth plans and stagnate, resulting in further decline in returns and erosion of shareholder value. When a company is not able to generate adequate returns, restructuring can bring about effective allocation and use of resources.

1.5.10 Incompatible Company Objectives

When company objectives are no longer compatible with the current portfolio, restructuring is planned. Decline in demand, high competitive pressures, and quicker product-line obsolescence signify such incompatibility. Such companies face a declining revenue and market share, and difficulty to survive.

1.5.11 Evolving Appropriate Capital Structure

Companies that are either over-capitalized or under-capitalized opt for restructuring. The process helps the company to evolve a balanced capital mix. It not only minimizes the cost of capital, but also increases earnings.

When companies expand their operations, the capital base grows and the capital mix changes. This also affects the cost of capital. The capital requirements change during different stages of the organizational life cycle and the capital mix often becomes inappropriate and unbalanced. Therefore, companies adopt restructuring to evolve an appropriate financial structure and achieve reduction in the cost of capital.

1.5.12 Consistent Growth and Profitability

The expectations of customers have changed over the years. Today, they demand quality at a reasonable price. They do not mind spending, but always look out for products that offer value for money. This aspiration of the customers is not unwarranted, as customer is the king. To meet customer expectations, companies have to adopt improved production techniques and effective cost control measures. If a company is not ready for this change, it should restructure its operations so that these objectives can be achieved.

1.5.13 Environmental Changes

The business environment in which companies operate is prone to changes. This, very often, results in changes such as decline in demand, increased competitive pressures, quicker product obsolescence, increasing stakeholder expectations, changed legal framework, and increasing need for innovation. These changes are often drastic, and more often than not render the company's present set of objectives incompatible with the changed business environment, leading to failure to meet the stakeholders' expectations. This forces the company to initiate restructuring, to attain compatibility between company objectives and the environment.

1.5.14 Meeting Investors' Expectations

Every company requires regular and steady inflow of capital to pursue its organizational objectives. Investors provide the required capital but expect safety of their investment and ever-increasing returns. If the company fails to meet investors' expectations, investors shy away from the company. Keeping this in mind, companies need to take steps that will increase returns. This goal is often pursued by restructuring the operations of the company.

1.5.15 Resolving Conflict

Companies often experience conflict between the management and the shareholders' perception of the prevailing state of affairs. The management often perceives that all is well with the company, whereas shareholders think otherwise. To resolve this conflict, companies often initiate restructuring.

1.5.16 Transferring Corporate Assets

Companies often have assets that they are unable to use efficiently. They choose restructuring to transfer their assets to a more efficient user. The efficient user may be its own division/segment or another company. This transfer benefits the company by making the operations cost-effective and by increasing the company's returns.

1.5.17 Bifurcating Business

There is a common belief that the sum of returns of two businesses is often greater than that of a single entity. This happens as bifurcation results in increased efficiency due to a focused approach. Companies often opt for restructuring with the aim to bifurcate the company into two or more entities so that it can achieve the objectives of increased returns.

While these arguments indicate that restructuring generates positive results, it may not always be true. The success or failure of the process of restructuring depends on factors such as management approach, core competencies present, prospect of the existing line of business, prospects of the proposed line of business, coordination between various functional heads, communication initiated, etc. Organizations should not let the fear of failure prevent restructuring, for death then becomes inevitable.

1.6 BARRIERS TO RESTRUCTURING

Companies often opt for restructuring to attain the benefits mentioned so far. However, the process is never a smooth ride. The process may also involve a number of impediments.

1.6.1 Inadequate Commitment from Top Management

This is one of the biggest barriers to restructuring. Managers are quite unsure about the outcome of the process, and the support needed from the top management is often missing. In addition, they often go by the dictum, 'What is in it for me?' When the change process does not get the support of the top management, the process often fails.

1.6.2 Resistance to Change

The managerial mindset of resisting change is another barrier to the process of restructuring. Managers resist change mainly because they are never taken into confidence before initiating the process. This instils fear in their mind and they feel that the only possible outcome of the process would be downsizing and loss of jobs. When managers resist change, the employees working under them follow suit. It is, therefore, necessary to have an open dialogue with the managers and employees about the need and reasons for initiating restructuring.

The employees should expect the following changes:

- Changed work environment
- Unfamiliar technology
- Cost-cutting measures resulting in layoffs
- Stringent performance targets

These elements create a fear psychosis and result in resistance to change.

1.6.3 Poor Communication

Poor communication is another hurdle in the process of restructuring. The top management often fails to communicate the reasons and objectives of the restructuring process. This activates the grapevine, which results in prejudice and negativity among the employees. Making changes without communicating with the people who implement the changes at the operational level and are likely to be affected the most sabotages the restructuring effort. Research shows that companies that communicate with their employees about the proposed restructuring, more often than not, face no resistance to the process.

1.6.4 Absence of Requisite Skills

Restructuring is more a science than anything else. People who need to initiate this process should be familiar with the processes and methodology involved. Companies often do not hire the services of experts as they consider it a routine internal matter, and think everybody is capable of carrying out the task. This approach results in failure to carry out the process in a professional manner, and the objectives are never attained.

1.6.5 Scepticism

Quite often, people in charge of the restructuring exercise show scepticism about the outcome of the process. As a result, the process is never executed effectively. The negativity with which the process is carried out spells disaster for the organization and the desired objectives remain on paper.

1.6.6 Failure to Understand Benefits of Restructuring

Restructuring is carried out to attain the objectives of cost reduction and proper allocation of resources. Employees often look at it as an attempt to get rid of workforce. Though some deadwood may be sacrificed, it may not be the ultimate aim of the process. The stakeholders need to understand that it is wiser to sacrifice deadwood than jeopardize the whole company and its employees. The process of dealing with redundancy should be gradual and provide for smooth exit of employees. Rather than enforcing compulsory retirement, voluntary retirement options for people expected to be laid off and golden handshakes for surplus staff is more fruitful in gaining employee acceptance. The key is to keep the communication channels open with the stakeholders on the course of action intended to be followed by the company.

1.6.7 Lack of Resources

The total process of restructuring is time-consuming and resource-intensive. Business entities often look upon it as a natural process and hence do not earmark resources for the process. For example, if the company proposes to lay off certain employees, they need to be adequately compensated, for which financial provisions have to be made. Absence of such provisions is bound to create a financial strain on the company and even invite legal proceedings at times. Therefore, it is advisable to evolve a clear plan of restructuring, which ascertains and provides for adequate resources to facilitate smooth completion of the process.

1.6.8 Organizational Workload

Failure to anticipate the effects of restructuring on organizational workload often acts as a barrier. Employees are likely to perceive restructuring as a pretext to reduce workforce and transfer the workload of those laid off to those who continue to retain their jobs. The labour leaders interpret it as a case of workforce exploitation and hence instigate workers against restructuring.

1.6.9 Non-adherence to Time Schedule

The process of restructuring calls for strict adherence to time schedules. Failure to stick to the scheduled timeframe results in cost increase, increased legal hassles, and failure to attain planned objectives, among other things. Hence, it is critical to ensure that the company moves into the renewal or revitalization phase without delays.

1.6.10 Lack of Clear and Visible Leadership

A strong and formidable leadership is of prime importance to lead the process of restructuring. Absence of clear and visible leadership results in vague, ambiguous environment and misdirects the entire process.

1.7 KEY ELEMENTS OF RESTRUCTURING PROCESS

Corporate restructuring involves assessing the value addition and value annihilation caused by different business divisions (Blatz et al. 2008). To complete the analysis, the following variables are studied.

1.7.1 Portfolio Management

This element aims at determining how each business division fits into the overall business strategy of the company. This exercise involves evolving strategies to position the company in a competitive environment and ascertaining the impact of strategic decisions on the contribution of the company. Portfolio management is concerned with the potential of the redefined strategy on achieving synergy in goals and objectives.

1.7.2 Corporate Functions

Analysing corporate functions involves determining the extent of centralization or decentralization adopted by the company and its impact on the day-to-day functioning of the entity. The purpose of this analysis is to identify and adopt the most cost-effective organizational structure.

1.7.3 Operational Performance

The basic objective of this analysis is to determine the amount of available reserves and channelizing the same in restructuring activities. The objectives sought to be attained may be revenue growth, cost reduction, and improving the liquidity position of the company.

1.7.4 Value Structure

This element focuses on achieving optimized linkages of existing locations and competencies. It decides whether the company should pursue vertical integration or forward integration. The purpose of the assessment is synergy utilization, cost reduction, and improved utilization of available technical know how.

The aforementioned variables of the restructuring process revolve around four key elements—customer focus, core business processes, cross-functional teams, and IT. Unless these are taken care of, the process falters.

Customer Focus

Customer focus—on both internal customers and external customers—is one of the key business compulsions of today's environment. If the top management fails to commit itself to offering better and improved customer service, survival of the business is near impossible. Customer focus is the driving force of any restructuring exercise. Companies need to capture, cultivate, cosset, coddle, and ultimately captivate the customer for survival (Kuriakose 1997).

The strategy for success for a restructured entity is 'don't just sell, satisfy; don't just satisfy, pamper; don't just pamper, charm your customers'. Satisfied customers bring rich dividends. They form a loyal customer base, which leads to repeat business, increased market shares, higher revenues, and better returns (Kuriakose 1997).

Core Business Processes

The process of restructuring should always involve identifying the core competencies of the organization. As stated above, it is about deciding what the company is good at and focusing on the strengths to attain the business goal. Once the core competencies are identified, achieving customer delight becomes easier and the processes become logical and efficient.

Cross-functional Teams

Once the core competencies are identified, the available manpower should be reorganized around the core competencies. The change process can succeed only when people in the company show commitment, coordination, and competence. To attain the best results, teams need to be empowered to think, interact, use judgment, and make decisions. One should remember that empowered teams do not need bosses; they need facilitators and enablers.

Information Technology

Companies pursuing restructuring should focus on IT, which is one of the most crucial components of the restructuring process. It facilitates paperless work, just-in-time (JIT) applications, online manufacturing, i.e., manufacturing using enterprise resource planning (ERP), etc. Care should be taken that before replacing systems, the thought process should be changed, so that people do not resist change.

1.8 TYPES OF CORPORATE RESTRUCTURING

Restructuring is a strategic process that provides companies with the much needed launching pad to improve their performance and profitability. However, the objective to improve performance does not always ensure success. While results have been mixed, companies have often found new direction and drive to perform. Restructuring can be carried out in any one of the following lines.

1.8.1 Financial Restructuring

Financial restructuring involves changes in the capital structure and capital mix of the company to minimize its cost of capital. It deals with infusion of financial resources to facilitate mergers, acquisitions, joint ventures (JVs), strategic alliances, LBOs, and stock buyback. It is to be noted that all these initiatives depend on availability of free cash flows, takeover threats faced by the company, and concentration of equity ownership.

Companies opt for financial restructuring for the following reasons:

- Generate cash for exploiting available investment opportunities
- Ensure effective use of available financial resources
- Change the existing financial structure to reduce the cost of capital
- Leverage the firm
- Prevent attempts at hostile takeover

1.8.2 Portfolio Restructuring

Portfolio restructuring involves divesting or acquiring a line of business perceived peripheral to the long-term business strategy of the company. It represents the company's attempt to respond to the market needs without losing sight of its core competencies.

Portfolio restructuring involves the following:

- Restructuring as a result of some strategic alliance
- Responding to the shareholders' desire to downsize and refocus the company's operations
- Responding to some outside board's suggestion to restructure
- Responding to strategies adopted as a response to exercising call or put options

1.8.3 Organizational Restructuring

Organizational restructuring is a strategy designed to increase efficiency and effectiveness of personnel through significant changes in the organizational structure. It is a response to changes in the business and related environments. Such restructuring takes the form of divestiture and acquisitions.

1.9 STRATEGIES FOR RESTRUCTURING

Organizations differ in terms of work culture and value systems. There can be no single standardized restructuring strategy that will help all organizations attain their restructuring objectives. In view of this fact, the following restructuring strategies have been evolved.

1.9.1 Hardware Restructuring

When the structure of the organization is redefined, dismantled, or modified, the restructuring is termed hardware restructuring.

The focus of hardware restructuring is on the following elements:

- Identifying the core competencies of the business to pursue the growth objectives
- Flattening the organizational layers to improve organizational responsiveness towards planned strategies
- Initiating downsizing to reduce excess workforce, so that overheads can be reduced
- Creating self-directed teams that do not wait for instructions and guidance, and practice autonomy in functioning
- Benchmarking against the toughest competitors so that best practices are adopted

1.9.2 Software Restructuring

Software restructuring involves cultural and process changes to establish a collaborative environment that facilitates growth and restructuring.

Software restructuring focuses on the following:

- Adopting an open and transparent communication mechanism, whereby the strategy is communicated to all levels of the organization without any difficulty
- Building a culture of guidance and coaching
- Building an environment of trust, so that individuals are assured of all support in carrying out their tasks
- Raising the aspiration levels of individuals, commonly referred to as 'stretch' in management terminology
- Empowering people and encouraging decentralized decision making
- Helping individuals develop foresight, that is, understanding changes and getting ready for the anticipated changes
- Training people to accept new ideas and challenging assignments

1.10 STRATEGIC OPTIONS IN CORPORATE RESTRUCTURING

An organization that is passing through a bad patch needs to restructure its operations to get rid of the existing inefficiencies. The restructuring process requires certain strategies. The strategies adopted are expected to lead to the following results:

- Improve operations
- Alter the relative strength of the organization to face competition
- Facilitate creation of competitive advantage
- Provide better customer satisfaction

- Generate profits in a free market economy
- Help the organization differentiate itself from competitors
- Ensure that it delivers value to the customers

Figure 1.3 highlights the strategic options available to the organization to initiate the process of restructuring.

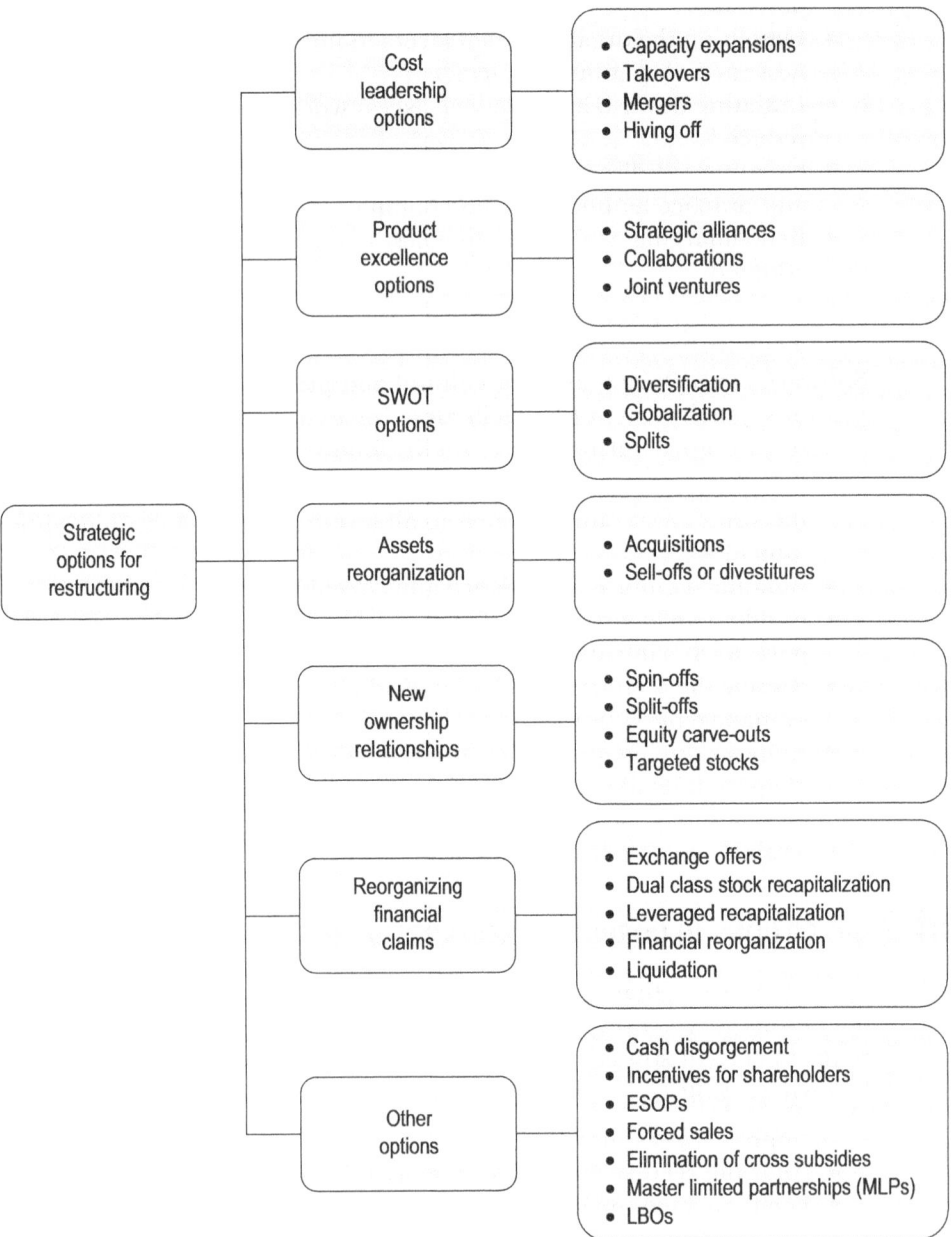

Figure 1.3   Strategic options for corporate reorganization

1.10.1 Cost Leadership Options

Some strategic options for corporate reorganization are termed cost leadership options, as they focus on reduction in the overall cost, resulting in rise in profits. The different strategies under this group are given in Fig. 1.3.

Capacity Expansion

This strategy involves expansion in the production capacity, resulting in higher trading volumes and hefty margins. This strategy works when the market is starved for goods and services, and gleefully accepts all the output. For example, during 2008, Holcim commissioned 1.5 million tonnes of cement capacity group-wide. By the end of 2008, Holcim also had capacity expansion projects underway involving 25.9 million tonnes. By the end of 2011, plant expansions and new facilities will have increased group capacity to around 218 million tonnes of cement (Holcim Group 2009).

But capacity expansion is a mixed blessing because if the cost of expansion is not kept under control, it can exceed the profitability. It can also result in excess capacity as competition increases. For example, steel and cement.

Takeovers

In takeovers, the ownership and consequently the right of management stands transferred from one company to another without dissolution of the existing unit (More details in Chapter 2). Takeovers can be friendly or hostile.

Friendly takeovers are those where the current owners agree for the transfer of the business at a mutually acceptable share price. For example, Ashok Leyland by Hindujas, German telecommunications and engineering group Mannesmann AG by UK-based mobile phone group Vodafone AirTouch, and GoodKnight by Godrej.

Hostile takeovers, on the other hand, involve acquiring the controlling number of shares without the concurrence of the existing controlling interest. For example, Kwality ice creams by Hindustan Unilever (HUL), and Ahmedabad Electric Company by Bombay Dyeing.

While takeovers have merits and demerits, one cannot contradict the fact that they provide fast growing companies an easy and quick solution for the acquisition of the much needed capacity.

Mergers

Mergers involve the coming together of two or more companies and pooling of resources for the purpose of achieving certain common objectives (More details in Chapter 3). Mergers presumably result in a bigger, more cost-effective, and efficient new entity. The new entity might assume the name of one of the merging entities or may assume a new name altogether. For example, merger of Lipton and Brooke Bond into Brooke Bond India Limited (BBIL), which was subsequently merged with HUL.

Mergers are also used as an effective tool for reviving sick or potentially sick units. For example, merger of Hyderabad Allwyn with Voltas.

Hiving Off

Hiving off is a process wherein an existing company sells a particular division to reduce unproductive expenditure. It also helps an entity to reap the benefits of core competencies, competitive advantage, and optimum capacity. Examples are the hiving off of the yarn division of Modern Woollens to Modern Threads, Dollops of Cadbury to HUL, Kissan and Dipy brands of UB Group to HUL, and Dr Reddy's, Sun Pharma, Ranbaxy, and Nicholas Piramal hiving off their R&D divisions.

1.10.2 Product Excellence Options

The strategies adopted here focus on improving the profitability of the company by changing the product mix and product quality.

Strategic Alliances and Collaborations

Strategic alliances represent a long-term agreement between two or more entities to co-operate with each other in specific areas of interest (see Chapter 9 for more details). Some areas of common interest include access to new technology, product range, and markets. A big advantage of strategic alliances is that they do not involve investment of funds in the share capital of the entities and neither do they involve any changes in the hierarchies of the participating companies. For example, strategic alliance between Wipro and IBM, whereby Wipro will market and integrate in India IBM's wide range of server and storage products such as pSeries (UNIX servers), xSeries (Intel-based servers), iSeries, and zSeries. In addition, IBM's full portfolio of storage products covering Enterprise Storage Systems (ESS), Linear Tape Open (LTO), Network Attached Storage (NAS), and iSCSI products also will be offered.

Similarly, Bridge Mobile Alliance is a business alliance of eleven major mobile companies in Asia and Australia. Members include Singtel (Singapore), Airtel (India), AIS (Thailand), CSL (Hong Kong), CTM (Macau), Globe (Philippines), Maxis (Malaysia), Optus (Australia), SK Telecom (S. Korea), Taiwan Mobile (Taiwan), and Telkomsel (Indonesia) (Membrillera et al. 2009).

Joint Ventures

A joint venture is generally a technical and financial collaboration either in the form of greenfield projects, takeovers, or alliances with existing companies (Nabhi 1997).

Joint ventures may take any one of the following three forms:

- Two parties, which may be individuals or companies, one of them non-resident or both residents, incorporate a company in India. The business of one party is transferred to the company and as a consideration, shares are issued by the company and subscribed by that party. The other party subscribes for the shares in cash.

- Alternately, the two parties subscribe to the shares of the JV company in an agreed proportion, in cash, and start a new business.
- The promoter shareholder of an existing Indian company and a third party, who/which may be an individual/company, one of them non-resident or both residents, collaborate to jointly carry on the business of that company and its shares are taken by the said third party through payment in cash (Sheth Associates 2003).

Joint ventures are preferred because they facilitate transfer of technology, quality improvement, efficiency, and productivity. Joint ventures are very common in automobile, customer electronics, telecommunications, insurance, IT, and engineering sectors. For example, Motorola's JVs in India will develop telecom and IT applications and solutions with Tech Mahindra and Wipro Technologies. The JV with Tech Mahindra, known as Canvas M, will focus on developing a variety of mobile IT solutions, including end-user applications, content services and frameworks for delivery and management. The JV with the IT services arm of Wipro Ltd., known as WMNetServ, will provide outsourced telecom services to public and private network operators. Some other examples of JVs in India include Hero–Honda, Tata Motors–Fiat, Bharti–Wal-Mart, Modi–Xerox, Godrej–GE, and HDFC–Standard Life.

1.10.3 SWOT Options

These are strategies that focus on a given element of SWOT. The purpose behind such restructuring is to exploit the strengths and opportunities prevalent in the market.

Diversification

Diversification is a strategy whereby a company enters different product or market segments to increase market penetration. The main objective behind diversification is to exploit the new avenues available and add to the group profits.

Diversification is a mixed blessing. While some companies succeed, others are often forced to re-evaluate their decisions. Companies fail to achieve the desired results because they enter areas where they do not have core competencies and competitive advantage.

Some of the well known groups that have diversified into unchartered waters include Godrej, Tata, the Anil Dhirubhai Ambani group, the UB group, Larsen and Toubro, and the Bharti group.

Globalization

This is a trend where companies set up businesses in other countries. The trend is on the rise since the Indian economy has been liberalized. Many Indian companies from the power, telecommunications, financial services, entertainment, and consumer products industries have gone global.

Some well-known examples include the Taj group, TCS, Infosys, Bharti group, Tata group, Mukesh Ambani group, Wipro, and Ranbaxy.

Splits

Splits involve the breaking up of a business into independent entities to exploit opportunities of growth, raise capital, achieve efficiency, and derive taxation benefits. Splits also provide benefits of synergy, competence, and revival.
Splits can be of two types:

- In the first type, the existing unit is broken up and a number of units are regrouped in viable subgroups. Here, the success of the new subunits cannot be safeguarded. Example: Bajaj group, Reliance group
- In the second type, the assets of the entity are regrouped on a rational basis to ensure future success of the new subunits. Example: Tata group

1.10.4 Assets Reorganization

An organization's assets can be reorganized by acquisitions or by divestitures. Let us now discuss these methods of reorganizing assets.

Acquisitions

Acquisitions represent purchase of new entities to utilize the existing strength and capabilities or to exploit the untapped or underutilized markets. It is also carried out to grow in size and prevent possibilities of future takeover attempts. Example: Tata Steel's decision to acquire Corus.

Acquisitions are also looked upon as a way of moving from industries/markets with unfavourable outlook to industries/markets with more favourable opportunities. For example, Airtel's efforts to acquire companies abroad.

Sell-offs or Divestitures

Sell-off or divestiture is an attempt to come out of a product segment or sector to adjust the operations to the changing economic and political environments. These are voluntary decisions implemented to attain shareholder wealth maximization.

Divestitures are resorted to for the following reasons:

- Dismantling conglomerates
- Abandoning one's core business
- Changing the group's strategic focus
- Adding value by selling the entity to a company that could exploit opportunities more effectively
- Making huge investments that are beyond the company's capacity
- Harvesting the past success
- Discarding unwanted segments and generate resources for acquiring new businesses
- Warding off takeover attempts
- Fulfilling statutory requirements
- Reversing past buyout mistakes

1.10.5 New Ownership Relationships

These strategic options result in change of ownership of the entity, which is expected to add value to the entity and result in improvement in profitability.

Spin-offs

In a spin-off, a company creates a subsidiary whose shares are distributed on a pro-rata basis to the shareholders of the parent company to generate positive returns.

Schipper and Smith (1983) conducted a study on the effects of spin-offs and found that they generate 2.84% abnormal returns to the parent company. A similar study by Hite and Owers (1984) concluded that the abnormal returns were 3.8%. They also found a positive relation between the size of the spin-off and the announcement effect. Both the studies concluded that there was no negative effect on the bondholders.

Similar results were also found by Copeland, Lemgruber, and Mayers (1987) who conducted an extended study on the subject. The study measured the market performance of spin-offs and their parent company for three years following the completion of the spin-off. They found that the mean return during the three-year period was 76%. The study also concluded that such firms were more actively involved in takeovers, which often generated abnormal returns compared to normal returns by other firms in the industry.

Other examples of spin-offs are Marriott Corporation's decision to spin off Marriott International, Kodak's decision to spin off Eastman Chemical, etc. (Finegan 2010).

Split-ups

Split-ups represent a restructuring process, where companies split themselves into two or more parts. Split-ups have some common reasons:

- The company wants to reduce the business risks.
- A certain sector is facing intense competition.
- The valuation of the core business would improve.
- The unit that is split is making continuous losses.
- The split-up would allow the company to focus on key sections/products.

Some famous examples of split-ups are National Medical (later auctioned to Hercules) and Allegis Corporation, Dole Foods' decision to split off Castle & Cooke, Sears' decision to split off Dean Witter, Quaker Oats' decision to shed Fisher-Price Toys, etc. (Finegan 2010).

Equity Carve-outs

An equity carve-out is a process whereby an IPO of a portion of the common stock of a wholly owned subsidiary is offered to raise resources. Equity carve-outs are also known as 'split-off IPOs'. This process initiates trading in a new and distinct set of equity claims on the assets of the subsidiary.

An equity carve-out can result in the following changes:

- It helps in restructuring the operations of the assets.
- It helps in establishing a public value for the operations of the subsidiary.
- The subsidiary publishes separate financial reports on its operations.
- The flow of information on the subsidiary has a positive impact on the operations.
- It facilitates evaluation of the performance of the subsidiary independently.
- It helps the employees get performance-linked incentives.
- It facilitates sale of the subsidiary to an outsider.

Targeted Stock

Under targeted stock, an entity's operations are split into two or more common equity claims, but the businesses remains wholly owned segments of a single parent. Here, the targeted stock is regarded as common stock of the consolidated company, and not that of the subsidiary.

In targeting stock, the voting rights and dividends are based on the relative values of each target stock segment. However, the liquidation rights are in proportion to the relative market values of each target stock segment.

Target stock segments generate the following benefits:

- The financial markets value different businesses based on their own performance.
- It increases the ability of the parent company to raise capital.
- Each target stock segment can be offered incentives based on their individual performance.
- There is no change in the management of the segments.
- The operating synergies are maintained.

1.10.6 Reorganizing Financial Claims

This strategy involves bringing about changes in the financial claims of the stakeholders. The stakeholders are motivated to accept the change only when the exchange offers them greater market value than that of the existing securities.

Exchange Offers

An exchange offer provides one or more classes of security and the right or option to exchange part or all of their holdings for a different class of securities of the entity. To induce the security holders to accept the exchange offer, the terms of exchange offered involve securities of a greater market value than the existing securities. The average life of the offer is about seven weeks.

Exchange offers are subject to certain conditions:

- Specification of the maximum number of securities that are offered in exchange
- Specification that the exchange offers are contingent upon acceptance by a minimum number of securities to be exchanged

Exchange offers may generate positive or negative returns. It is generally observed that exchange of debt and preferred stock for common stock generates positive returns and vice versa.

Dual Class Stock Recapitalization

Under this head, the entity creates a second class of common stock that carry limited voting rights and usually preferential claim to the entity's cash flows. This is done by distributing limited voting shares on pro-rata basis to the existing shareholders. Such stocks usually carry higher rates of dividend.

In most entities having dual class stock, the founding families have control over the entity, as they own stock of the company. The second class stock is offered to outsiders. Such companies do not generally face takeover threats as they are closely held entities. The shares are owned by family members or close relatives and friends, and only a small fraction of the total capital floats in the market.

Leveraged Recapitalization

A firm that is low levered is often vulnerable to takeover by an entity that is seeking to recapture the tax benefits of debt capital. On the other hand, a high levered entity does not often find bidders, as prospective bidders are reluctant to face the task of returning the firm to leverage ratios that are closer to industry norms.

Leverage decisions represent potential for value enhancement or defence against acquisition. Leverage recapitalization often results in operating improvements. The large overhang of debt stimulates the management to improve operations for generating sufficient cash flows to repay the debt.

The market response to announcements of leveraged recapitalization depends on whether the action is proactive or defensive. Proactive action aims at improving the performance of the entity, whereas defensive actions are initiated in response to actual takeovers or possible takeover bids.

Financial Reorganization

Entities facing financial distress usually adopt financial reorganization. Financial distress is a condition where the liquidation value of the firm's assets is less than the total face value of the creditor's claims.

Financial reorganization may take any one of the following forms:

Out of court procedure   Here the entity is either liquidated or continues with its operations. If the operations continue, a part of the equity claim may be substituted with debt or the maturity of the debt may be postponed. The idea behind this strategy is to provide time to the entity to improve its performance and stabilise earnings.

Merger with another firm   This involves merging of the firm in financial distress with a financially healthy entity. Research indicates that takeover of firms facing financial distress is likely to be more successful than takeover of firms whose operating performance is poor. Though there is no concrete evidence that takeover always helps restructure a distressed entity, it certainly is the best option under the given circumstances.

Formal legal proceedings   This process involves adoption of legal procedures to restructure a distressed entity, such as referring the case to the Board for Industrial and Financial Reconstruction (BIFR) under Indian laws for reconstruction.

Liquidation

Liquidation is the last option available to the entity. It involves initiating bankruptcy proceedings. Here, all the assets are discarded and all the liabilities are repaid, after which the entity ceases to exist. Liquidation may be voluntary or involuntary.

1.10.7 Other Options

There are also options that are general in nature and do not fit into the categories discussed so far. However, this does not take away the crucial role they play in the process of corporate restructuring.

Cash Disgorgement

The basic objective of business is to utilize financial resources effectively and generate wealth in a more assured and rapid manner. Cash disgorgement is the principle where accumulated cash resources of a business are spent or reinvested effectively. Having cash but not being able to use it defeats the purpose, for the entity is missing out on profitable investment opportunities or might be spending cash frivolously on things that are not necessary (Childers 2009).

Just sitting on cash with no interest earnings or low interest earnings makes no sense. The company should identify and adopt ways of using the resources productively to attain long term wealth accumulation objectives.

A company's capital structure includes both equity and debt. When a company borrows, it has to manage its resources in such a way that it is able to repay its debt on a regular basis by channelizing surplus cash. This obligation may prevent a company from reinvesting its surplus cash in new projects or profitable opportunities.

Whenever a company comes across projects and acquisitions that make business sense from a long-term wealth accumulation perspective, it should explore the possibilities of investing in such projects. If the surplus cash is being utilized for repaying debt, there is no harm in pursuing expansion through new capital. This is advisable because the proposed investment plan is put to test at the market. A positive market feedback provides an insight into the risk involved in the project and reiterates the manager's confidence in going ahead with it. It also encourages managers to shun their discretionary approach to investment, and ensures that available resources are put to proper use.

While we have stressed on two major options, let us list out all the options available to a company for cash disgorgement:

Repayment of debt A company that has debt in its capital structure should utilize the available surplus cash to repay the debt. Debt repayment would reduce the interest burden of the company and also free its assets from existing mortgages/claims.

Buyback of shares The company can also utilize the surplus cash for buying back its common stock from the open market. Buyback reduces the number of shares floating in the market and leads to rise in the prices of the floating stock.

Partnerships The company can also explore the option of reinvesting its cash flows by entering into partnerships/strategic alliances/JVs. Such arrangements require limited investment but can generate good long-term returns.

Dividends A company can also disgorge cash by paying increased dividend. No company likes to cut the dividend rate once it has been raised. Increased dividend payment is interpreted positively by the market as a commitment to pay the same or higher rate of dividend in future. Of course, one needs to ensure that future cash flows stay healthy so that company is not forced to cut dividend.

Employee Stock Option Plans

Employee stock option plans (ESOPs) are contracts between a company and its employees that give employees the right to buy a specific number of the company's shares at a fixed price within a specified period of time.

If an employee is granted the option to purchase 1,000 shares of the company's stock at the current market price of ₹50 per share, called the 'grant' price, he can exercise the option at ₹50 per share. The exercise price would typically be equal to the price when the options are granted. Employee stock option plans allow employees to exercise their options after a specified number of years or when the company's stock reaches a certain price. If we assume that the stock price increases to ₹200 per share, and the employee exercises his option to buy 1,000 shares at ₹50 per share and then sell the stock at the current market price of ₹200.

The basic objective of ESOP is to motivate employees to perform better and thus help improve shareholder value. Employee stock option plans create a strong sense of belongingness and ownership among the employees, apart from bringing them financial gains. They can be done in two ways:

Creating a special purpose vehicle Here, a trust or special purpose vehicle (SPV) is formed and the company issues shares or options to the trust. The trust is required to pay for these shares and needs funds for the same. To ensure that the SPV has funds to buy the options, the company may either give soft loans from its own funds or can allow the trust to raise loans through other sources to meet its financial requirement.

In case the trust decides to raise funds through loans, the company acts as a guarantor to the lender. The trust acquires the shares/options required. Subsequently, when the employees purchase the shares, they pay the necessary amount to the trust for the same. The funds so generated are used by the trust to repay its loans.

Giving options directly to employees Here employees showing extraordinary performance are offered shares directly. The selection of the employees is based on their personal and performance criteria:

- Performance of the employee as indicated by the annual performance appraisal
- Minimum period of service
- Present and potential contribution of the employee
- Other factors deemed to be relevant for the success of the company

Every employee is not offered an equal number of options. The same is determined taking into consideration the grade, level to which the employee belongs, years of service, salary drawn, etc. The variables are determined on the objective the company wants to attain through the ESOP.

Employee stock option plans can be of different types depending upon the objectives that the company wants to achieve. The most common forms of ESOP include the following:

Employee stock option scheme Under the employee stock option scheme (ESOS), the company grants an option to its employees to acquire shares at a pre-determined price at a future date. The employees eligible under the scheme are free to acquire shares within the period stipulated. Once the shares are acquired, employees are free to dispose them subject to lock-in period, if any. Here the price at which ESOS is offered—exercise price—is lower than the prevalent market price so that employees find the offer attractive and take benefit of the same.

Employee stock purchase plan Employee stock purchase plans (ESPP) are very popular among listed companies, where the employees are given the right to acquire shares of the company immediately and not at a future date as in ESOS. The shares are again offered at a price lower than the prevailing market price to make the scheme popular.

The scheme has certain built-in restrictions such as lock-in period and hence shares cannot be sold during the period. In addition, the employee should continue to work with the employer for a specified number of years after the allotment of the shares.

Share appreciation rights/phantom shares In the share appreciation rights (SAR)/phantom shares scheme, the employees are not offered or allotted any shares of the company. Instead, they are given an incentive or performance bonus based on the appreciation in the value of shares between two specified dates. The basis of this scheme is that the increase in the value of shares is attributed to the improved performance by the employees and so they need to be suitably rewarded.

The Companies Act (1956) states that stock options can be issued only after getting approval of the shareholders by a special resolution. In case of a private company, stock options can be issued under the approval by the board of directors and the approval of the shareholder is not mandatory.

Employee stock option plans also have tax implications both for the employer and the employee. Until recently, the difference between the cost of the share to the employees and market value on the date on which an employee got the share would be treated as perquisite and taxed in addition to capital gains tax payable by the employee on sale of those shares.

After the removal of the perquisite tax, the employee is not required to pay tax on the difference in the cost of share and its market value. However, the capital gains tax is still payable under the changed rules.

The SEBI norms say that the company allotting ESOP can treat the amount as an expense and account for the same accordingly. However, there is still no clarity whether the amount accounted as expense will be allowed as deductible expense by the income tax authorities.

Forced Sales

The capital structure of a company includes both equity and debt. When debt exceeds equity, the entity becomes high leveraged and often finds the debt load intolerable. To manage the situation, the company often decides to sell unrelated and underperforming assets and businesses. This is called a forced sale.

It is a simple case of 'fit' and 'focus' for the buying and selling entity. It helps the selling entity to divest unrelated activities and helps the management to focus on the remaining business divisions that offer better growth opportunities.

While the assets may be unrelated and underperforming for the company selling them, they may be worth much more to the buying entity. As such, the assets are sold for a value greater than the value they represent for the selling company.

Forced sales should not be construed as failure of the selling entity. It represents a true case of reaping the benefits of past successful investments and good management. It also helps the company to eliminate unwanted layers in the organizational structure and speed up the decision-making process.

Organizational Imperatives

'Cash is king' is a common organizational imperative. It again draws us towards the capital structure, which includes debt and equity. Having a proper blend of equity and debt is crucial as it offers flexibility and balance to the capital structure and also brings down the overall cost of capital.

While payment of dividend is not mandatory, the overall cost of capital is very high. This fact is often overlooked by the company and reality dawns when the earnings start declining.

Debt, on the other hand, carries a fixed rate of interest that has to be paid whether the company earns profits or incurs losses. Confronted with debt, the management has to make untiring efforts to improve the earnings of the company. Since debt carries an obligation, there is no room for inefficiencies and mistakes. The management has to ensure that adequate cash surplus is generated to pay the interest and principal amount regularly. To prevent default in payment of debt-related liability, the management needs to avoid mistakes and eliminate inefficiencies. It is imperative for the company to generate cash, hence the dictum 'Cash is king'.

Elimination of Cross Subsidies

A company often has numerous divisions/departments, each specializing in specific products and services. All the divisions are expected to create value by exploiting available opportunities. However, all the divisions do not create value. Some divisions incur losses and destroy value. Such departments are able to continue because the profit-making divisions absorb the losses of the loss-making divisions/departments. As a result, the consolidated bottom line of the company remains 'black'. The process where profit-making divisions facilitate continuation of loss-making divisions is called cross subsidization.

The element of cross subsidy can be identified by valuing the assets and the business separately and ascertain which is more valuable. When the assets that support a business are worth more than the business itself, it indicates that the assets have alternative use and are not being fully exploited and utilized. Once this is identified, the company should start looking at alternatives whereby the assets can be deployed more effectively to create value.

Buyback of Shares/Tender Offers

Tender offer is a public offer made by a potential acquirer to purchase some or all the shareholders' shares in a company. The price at which these shares are offered to be purchased is higher than the current market value of the shares. It is assumed that the premium would induce the shareholders to show willingness to sell their holdings.

The acquirer offers to purchase the shares at a premium because it allows him to acquire control over the company. The sellers obviously are interested in the offer as it helps them to earn significant profits on their holdings. Tender offers have to be made within a stipulated time frame, subject to a minimum and maximum number of shares. If a company comes out with a tender offer to purchase shares of a company for say ₹150 per share, the prevailing market price of the shares may be ₹120. This means that the tender offer has been made at a premium of ₹30 per share. In the tender offer, the minimum number of shares has been stated as say, 50 and the maximum at 500 shares. Accordingly no seller would be able to sell less than 50 shares or more than 500 shares through the tender offer.

Tender offers may be friendly or unfriendly. When the acquirer fulfils the legal provisions for the tender offer and expresses his desire to purchase the shares with the endorsement of the company, the offer is friendly. On the other hand, when the offer is made directly to the shareholders without the endorsement of the company, the offer is unfriendly.

In the US, tender offers are regulated by the Williams Act. The Securities Exchange Commission's SEC regulations 14E also govern tender offers (Weston et al. 2003). The regulations focus on the following:

- The minimum length of time for which a tender offer must remain open
- A procedure for modifying tender offers after the same has been issued
- Governing insider trading in the context of tender offers
- Whether one class of shareholders can receive preferential treatment over another

The buyer should disclose certain facts pertaining to the tender offer (SEC regulations) (Weston 2003):

- Material terms of the tender offer
- The bidder's identity and background
- The bidder's history with the target company

1.11 BUYBACK OF SHARES IN INDIA

Buyback of shares in India is regulated through Section 77A, 77AA, and 77B of the Companies Act, 1956. These sections were inserted by the Companies (Amendment) Act, 1999. The Securities and Exchange Board of India (SEBI) has also stipulated relevant norms under SEBI (Buyback of Securities) Regulations, 1999. Another set of statutes have been evolved by the Department of Company Affairs, which framed the Private Limited Company and Unlisted Public Company (Buyback of Securities) Rules, 1999, pursuant to Section 77A(2)(f) and (g) respectively.

These regulations give the following reasons for buyback of shares by companies:

- To increase promoters holding
- To increase the earning per share
- To rationalize the capital structure by writing off capital not represented by available assets
- To support share value
- To thwart takeover bids
- To utilize surplus cash not required by the business

Financial experts say that buyback from the open market at a premium over the prevailing market price is the best strategy to maintain the share price in a bear run. This offers incentives to shareholders and helps maintain interest in the scrip. It also helps the company to utilize the available surplus cash effectively.

A company can buy back shares through the following routes:

- From existing shareholders on a proportionate basis. In such a case, the company is required to make a tender offer for buyback to shareholders. The shareholders who respond to the buyback offer are required to fill the requisite form transferring the shares to a special account created for the purpose, known as escrow account.
- Through open market using the book building process or stock exchanges
- Through odd lots. In case of a listed company, if the lot of the shares proposed to be bought back is smaller than the marketable lot as specified by the stock exchange, the company can go ahead with the buyback by purchasing the odd lots.
- Employees who have been issued shares pursuant to a scheme of stock option or sweat equity.

1.12 WHERE DO THE RESOURCES FOR BUYBACK COME FROM?

A company proposing to go in for buyback of shares can seek funds from any of the following sources:

- Free reserves
- Share premium account
- Proceeds from any shares or other specified securities

Here, an amount equal to the nominal value of the share intended to be bought back has to be transferred from these heads to the capital redemption reserve. The company is required to provide the details of transfer of free reserves to the redemption reserve in the balance sheet. What is important to remember is that a company cannot buyback its shares or other specified securities out of the proceeds of an earlier issue of the same kind of shares or specified securities.

1.13 CONDITIONS TO BE FULFILLED FOR BUYBACK

A company should ensure that the following conditions are fulfilled before it initiates the procedure of buyback:

- Buyback should be authorized by the Articles of Association.
- A special resolution should be passed in the general body meeting of the company. The notice of the meeting at which special resolution is proposed to be passed should be accompanied by an explanatory statement stating all the material facts about the buyback offer, reasons for opting for a buyback, the class of security intended to be purchased, the amount to be invested under the buyback offer, and the timeframe for the completion of the buyback.
- A listed company has to take the approval to the special resolution through a postal ballot.

- If the amount of shares to be bought back is 10% or less of the paid-up capital and free reserves, a board resolution is adequate to go ahead with the buyback.
- The shares that are being bought back should be free from lock-in period/ non transferability clause.
- The buyback of equity shares in any financial year should not exceed 25% of the total paid-up equity capital in that financial year.
- The debt–equity ratio—the ratio of debt owed to share capital and free reserves—should not exceed the ratio 2:1 after the buyback.
- A company going for buyback should not have defaulted in the following:
  - Repayment of deposit or interest payable thereon
  - Redemption of debentures
  - Redemption of preference shares
  - Payment of dividend, if declared, to all shareholders within the stipulated time of 30 days from the date of declaration of dividend
  - Repayment of any term loan or interest payable thereon to any financial institution or bank
- The company should not have violated the provisions of the Income Tax Act and the Companies Act with regard to the form and contents of annual accounts.
- The shares or other specified securities intended to be bought back should be fully paid up.
- If the company is listed on any recognized stock exchange, adherence to the regulations made by SEBI for buyback by listed companies is mandatory.
- A private and closely held company also needs to adhere to the regulations prescribed for buyback of shares.
- After passing of resolution but before going ahead with the buyback, a listed company is required to file a declaration of solvency in Form 4A with the Registrar of Companies and SEBI. The declaration must be accompanied by an affidavit by the board certifying that the company is capable of meeting its liabilities and will not be rendered insolvent within a period of one year of the date of declaration adopted by the board. This affidavit has to be signed by at least two directors of the company, one of whom has to be the managing director.

A company whose shares are not listed on any recognized stock exchange is not required to file the declaration of solvency with SEBI.

- Once the buyback is completed, the company is required to maintain a register of the securities/shares bought and enter the following details in the register:
  - The consideration paid for the shares/securities bought back
  - The date of cancellation of securities

- The date of extinguishing and physical destruction of securities. The provisions say a company has to extinguish and physically destroy the securities bought back within seven days of the last date of completion of buyback.
- Any other details such prescribed
- Every buyback has to be completed within 12 months from the date of passing the special resolution or board resolution, as the case may be.
- A company which has bought back shares/securities cannot make any public or rights issue of the same kind of security up to six months from the date of completion of buyback.
- A company should not directly or indirectly purchase its own shares or securities through any subsidiary company including its own subsidiary companies or investment company or group of investment companies.

If a company defaults in complying with the provisions pertaining to buyback of shares, then the company or any officer of the company who is responsible is punishable with imprisonment for a term up to two years, a fine of ₹50,000, or both.

1.14 LEVERAGED BUYOUTS

When a company acquires another company using a significant amount of borrowed funds such as bonds or loans to pay the cost of acquisition, the transaction is termed a leveraged buyout. It is worth noting that the assets of the target are offered as collateral security for the purpose of raising loans in addition to the assets of the acquirer. A leveraged buyout or high leveraged transaction or bootstrap occurs when a financial sponsor gains control over the target company's equity through the use of borrowed funds.

Since LBO involves use of debt, the assets of the company being acquired, in addition to the assets of the acquiring company, are used as collateral for securing loans. Leveraged buyouts are popular for they allow companies to make large acquisitions without having to commit a lot of capital. For example, HCA Inc. was acquired in 2006 by Kohlberg Kravis Roberts & Co. (KKR), Bain & Co., and Merrill Lynch, which paid around $33 billion for the acquisition.

An LBO most often involves a ratio of 70% debt and 30% equity, although the ratio of debt can reach as high as 90% to 95% of the target company's total capitalization. Because of this high debt/equity ratio, LBOs pose a very high risk of bankruptcy. For example, the LBOs of 1980s resulted in the bankruptcy of several prominent acquirers such as Federated Department Stores, Revco drug stores, Walter Industries, FEB Trucking and Eaton Leonard, etc.

The reason was that in some cases, the leverage ratio was nearly 100% and the interest payments were so large that the company's operating cash flows were unable to meet the obligation. For example, the bondholders of US newspaper company *Tribune* sued large Wall Street banks, including JPMorgan Chase and

Citibank, on the grounds that the 2007 leveraged buyout of the publisher that the banks arranged and financed caused its bankruptcy less than a year later. The company proposes to repay the bondholders after paying the banks that lent money for the LBO. The bondholders have filed a lawsuit seeking that they be moved up the list of priorities in which various parties are being repaid (Bullock et al. 2010).

The borrowings include a combination of pre-payable bank facilities and/or public or privately placed bonds, which are classified as high yield debt, also called junk bonds. This debt appears in the balance sheet of the acquired company, whose free cash flows are used to repay the debt. The use of significant amount of debt brings in an obvious risk of financial distress. An unforeseen event such as recession, litigation, and changes in regulatory environment can create problems and the company may struggle to meet its scheduled interest obligations or outright liquidation.

It may be interesting to understand how an LBO secures the debt capital. An LBO is financed with multiple tranches of debt that include the following (Jonathan 2002):

Revolving credit facility   Also known as revolver, it is a source that the bought-out firm relies on to secure its working capital requirements. It serves as a line of credit that allows the firm to make certain capital investments, deal with unforeseen costs, or cover the increases in working capital without having to raise additional debt or equity financing.

Bank debt   This represents finance secured by mortgaging the assets of the bought-out firm. This source carries the first claim over the cash flows of the business.

Mezzanine debt   This is termed as mezzanine debt, for it exists in the middle of the capital structure and is next to bank debt with regard to priority in repayment. Since it is lower on the list of priority in repayment, it is compensated with a higher interest rate.

Subordinated or high yield notes   These notes carry a very high rate of interest and low security. They are also referred to as junk bonds due the high risk involved. Each tranche of debt financing has different maturities and repayment terms. For example, some sources of financing require mandatory amortization of principal and scheduled interest payments.

In addition to debt financing, there is also an equity component in financing an LBO. The amount of equity is typically provided by a pool of private equity capital, thus reducing the amount of capital exposed to any one investment. Private equity is an asset class consisting of equity investment in companies that are not traded on a public stock exchange. This investment typically involves a transformational, value-added, and active management strategy.

Why do private equity firms invest in LBOs? The answer is that private equity firms receive a return on their investments through an IPO, a sale or merger of the company they control or a recapitalization. The unlisted securities are often sold to investors through private offerings or to a private equity fund—a capital pool of contributions from smaller investors. The private equity firms own 70–90% of the common equity of the bought-out firm. The remainder is generally held by the management and former shareholders.

Another source of financing an LBO is preferred equity. This source is popular as it offers attractive dividend payments on the preferred equity component and also allows holders to participate in any equity upside.

Leveraged buyouts are often termed ruthless as the huge assets of the target can be used against it as collateral in a hostile takeover. Yet LBOs are very popular due to the wealth they create for all the parties involved. Shareholders receive large take-out premiums, participating managements earn enviable returns, and investment funds receive over 30% compounded annual returns (Mohan 1990).

Leveraged buyouts have certain benefits:

- Heavy interest and principal repayments force managements to improve performance and operating efficiency.
- Debt may encourage managements to focus on initiatives such as divesting non-core businesses, downsizing, cost cutting, and investing in technological upgrades. These are very often postponed or rejected outright.
- LBOs are able to generate healthy returns for they focus on reducing unnecessary overheads and selling unrelated business units, thus cutting the company down to a productive core. For example, Beatrice Foods Inc., soon after an LBO, was split up and repackaged as several distinct companies. The same break-up strategy was applied to Uniroyal, Dr. Pepper, and Metromedia (Mohan 1990). LBO companies are repackaged as individual units for these are more valuable and are run more efficiently.

A question very often asked is, why do companies prefer debt financing for LBOs? There are two reasons:

- The use of debt increases the financial return to the private equity sponsor. This view has been expressed in the postulates of Modigliani Miller. The second postulate states, all other things being equal and within strict restrictive assumptions, the total return of an asset to its owners remains unaffected by the structure of financing. As the debt in LBO is relatively fixed, any returns in excess of the cost of capital flow through the equity holders.
- The Modigliani Miller theorem also states that the tax shield available on debt increases the value of the firm. This enables the private equity sponsor to pay a higher price than would otherwise be possible. Since income flowing through equity is taxed but interest payments on debt are not, the capitalized value of cash flowing to debt is greater than the same cash stream flowing to equity.

In a recent report, Standard and Poor's (S&P) looked at a selection of past leveraged buyouts and divided them into three categories: the good, the bad, and the ugly (www.businessweek.com). A good LBO is one that restores credit quality and returning the rating on the company to investment grade after the buyout. A bad LBO is one that faces significant financial stress after the deal, often ending in bankruptcy over a period of time. The ugly LBOs are companies whose financial performance deteriorated very quickly after the LBO, typically ending up in bankruptcy in three years or less.

The summary of the S&P analysis is given in the Table 1.1.

Table 1.1   S&P's list of the best and worst leveraged buyouts over the past few decades

Acquirer	Target	Value	Status at the time of LBO	Post-LBO status
The good				
Kohlberg Kravis Roberts (KKR)	Amphenol (APH)	$1.4 billion	It increased the company's leverage and the corporate credit rating declined to B+ from BBB−.	In December 1999, APH filed for a public offering of 2.75 million common shares and used the proceeds to pay down debt and reduce leverage leading to upgrade of the corporate credit rating to BBB−
ARAMARK	First LBO in December 1984	$900 million	Rating dropped to B from A−.	In August 1994, company returned to investment grade of BBB−
	Second LBO in May 2006	$8.3 billion	Rating was lowered to B+ from BBB−.	
KKR	Kraft (Duracell)	$1.8 billion	Duracell actually got a positive rating as market for batteries was expected to grow rapidly.	• Less than three years after its LBO, Duracell was assigned investment grade (BBB). • In 1997, Gillette acquired it in a deal valued at more than $7 billion. • Subsequently, Gillette was acquired by Procter & Gamble. • Debt reduced through IPO
Castle Harlan	Ethan Allen	$385 million	B+ rating was assigned due to an aggressive financial structure.	• Planned IPO led to a BB+ rating in February 1993. • Two years later, rating was upgraded to BBB− due to debt reduction and continued strengthening of operating result. • Rating raised to BBB in 1997, to BBB+ in 1998, and to A− in 2002.
Harley-Davidson			• B+ corporate credit rating was assigned in 1986. • Over the next 20 years, rating was upgraded six times, and the company reached investment grade in 1992.	In 1996, Harley was upgraded to A− from BBB+ and then to A+ in October 2004.

(Continued)

Table 1.1   *(Continued)*

Acquirer	Target	Value	Status at the time of LBO	Post-LBO status
The good				
KKR	Safeway (SWY)	$4.2 billion	Credit rating fell from A to B+.	• Safeway unloaded assets valued at about $2.3 billion over two years to reduce debt. • It achieved success in terms of both credit quality improvement and return on investment. • It reentered the investment-grade category, with a current rating of BBB−.
Viacom	MTV and Showtime National Amusements		Rating was downgraded to below investment grade i.e. BB+. Rating was lowered to B+ in May, 1987.	• It maintained its energetic style, with a CBS merger, and picked up two more upgrades, rising to A− in February 2001. • In 2005, it decided to split into two separate entities, i.e. an entertainment and a broadcasting company, to enhance shareholder value. • Rating moved up to BBB in January 2006.
The bad				
KKR	Amstar	$450 million	• Amstar agreed for takeover to avoid potential hostile takeover by dress pattern maker Simplicity Pattern; lowered the rating to BB−. • Rating was cut to B+ in February 1987, because total debt rose to $630 million from $235 million.	• Amstar Sugar business best known for its Domino brand was sold for about $310 million at the end of 1988. • Credit rating was lowered to CCC+ in July 1991, as financial flexibility reduced.
KKR	Evenflo & Spalding Holdings		• The group was assigned a B+ rating that was cut further to B− due to poor operating performance and negative discretionary cash flow.	• Evenflo & Spalding split into two standalone companies. • Evenflo and Spalding rated D. • Operations were renamed TopFlite Golf Co. and filed for Chapter 11 in mid-2003. • Evenflo was sold to Western Presidio in February 2007. • Evenflo now has a B− rating.
R.H. Macy	I. Magnin and Bullocks	$1.1 billion	Macy's was already sitting on a mountain of debt, and adding a little more, in retrospect, was financially imprudent.	• The company started to struggle, and Santa was a no-show in the 1991 Christmas season. • Rating was never upgraded after the LBO.

(Continued)

Table 1.1 (*Continued*)

Acquirer	Target	Value	Status at the time of LBO	Post-LBO status
The bad				
				• It put the company on the ropes early in 1992. • By January 1992, the rating was down to CCC+, and by the end of the month, bankruptcy filed.
Northwest Industries	Farley Industries	$1.5 billion	Debt rating was down- graded to B from BBB in June 1985.	• CEO Farley made a run on textile and apparel giant West Point-Pepperell. • He was forced to give up some of his stake in Fruit of the Loom. • Fruit of the Loom filed for bankruptcy in late 1999.
Private investment firm Gibbons, Green, van Amerongen	Ohio Mattress	$1 billion	• Investment bank First Boston provided $457 million bridge loan. • Company was unable to sell its proposed $475 million in junk bonds. • It needed outside assistance in the form of a capital injection from Credit Suisse, which ultimately cost it its independence.	• Company was a victim of an overpriced buyout and poor timing, but it managed to hang on. • Renamed Sealy, it went through a few ownership changes before being acquired by KKR in 2004 for $1.5 billion. • It is rated BB− today, but has never made it close to its former investment-grade rating
The ugly				
Federated Department Stores	Campeau	$6.6 billion	• Rating was downgraded to B from AA− at the time of its LBO in 1988. • Rating on the company fell further to CCC in 1989.	• It filed for Chapter 11 bankruptcy after 21 months of LBO • Emerged from bankruptcy, and in 1994 it bought Macy's. • Performance improved, and reached investment grade and further to BBB+. • $17 billion acquisition of May Department Stores in 2005 brought the rating back to BBB.
Grand Union			• Any company that can make three trips to the bankruptcy courts deserves a special place in the LBO Hall of Shame. • It was taken private in 1989 by an investor group headed by Miller Tabak Hirsch and Salomon Brothers.	• Grand Union filed for bankruptcy for the first time. • It emerged in June 1995 with a $600 million reduction in debt, a new CEO, and a rating of B. • Operating problems continued and in February 1998; it defaulted on a loan payment and once again filed for bankruptcy.

(*Continued*)

Table 1.1   (*Continued*)

Acquirer	Target	Value	Status at the time of LBO	Post-LBO status
			The ugly	
				• It was assigned a B rating after it emerged from the second bankruptcy.
				• It filed for bankruptcy for the third and last time in October 2000.
KKR, Hicks, Muse, and Tate & Furst	Regal Cinemas	$2 billion	• The company merged with KKR-owned Act III Theatres to create the largest U.S. exhibitor.	• The company couldn't fully exploit its size advantage, and the industry faced a tough operating environment.
			• Debt increased by almost $500 million, resulting in a downgrade to BB− from BB.	• The highly leveraged capital structure only magnified the decline in profitability and eventually led to multiple downgrades in 1999 and 2000.
				• After a bankruptcy restructuring, it currently operates as Regal Entertainment Group with a BB− rating.
Revco Discount Drug Centers		$1 billion	Rated BBB+	• The plan for closing stores and reducing costs sounded reasonable but timing wasn't very good.
				• Rating on the company was down to CCC− by April 1988.
				• In July 1988, it filed for Chapter 11 bankruptcy.
Thompson Family	Southland	$4.9 billion	BBB rating fell to B.	• The company sought to avoid bankruptcy by selling a controlling interest to Ito-Yokado of Japan
				• It planned restructuring of debt and preferred stock failed, and the rating fell to D.
				• It filed for bankruptcy in October 1990
				• It exited Chapter 11, and ultimately returned to investment grade in 1993 based on improving profitability and debt ratios and on strengthened financial support after it was made a wholly owned subsidiary of AA-rated Seven-Eleven, Japan.

Source: LBOs: The Good, the Bad, and the Ugly, www.businessweek.com, last accessed on 12 December 2009

1.14.1 Types of LBOs

In countries such as the US, private equity firms have yielded huge returns for investors through LBOs using the tools of financial engineering. LBOs can be classified into two, namely sponsored and non-sponsored.

Sponsored LBOs

Under sponsored LBOs, the private equity firms offer to buy a controlling stake in a company using leverage obtained from banks based on the financials of the company. The strategy is simple—commit very little of own money to purchase the business. This is the secret behind the spectacular returns, for there is very little cash invested.

The process of buyout is very interesting. The buyout firms collect large fees up front and additional advisory fees for operating a company acquired. The returns do not end here. They take away a big share of the investment profits as well. The buyout firms give management ownership that is usually less than 20% of the company. This type of buyout is called sponsored leveraged buyout, where the equity player is the sponsor.

Non-sponsored LBOs

This strategy is adopted in case of financially healthy businesses, where the financing techniques are similar, but the management gains operating control with around 85% to 100% ownership depending on the situation. These buyouts are called non-sponsored leveraged buyouts. Such buyouts are preferred over sponsored buyout even if the buyers have to overpay, for the buyers will be the ultimate owners.

The process of a non-sponsored leveraged buyout is similar to any other kind of business financing. The key requirements for a successful non-sponsored leveraged buyout include the following:

- Quality company and management team that helps gain would-be lenders or investor's confidence.
- Proactive management that is not reluctant to venture into unfamiliar territory.
- Agreement on purchase price could be based on a multiple of 4–7 times cash flow/EBITDA for small to mid-sized companies. For example, a company that makes $2 million a year EBTIDA would be worth $12 million at a 6 multiple. Once this is known, one can ask the owner the price they expect from the deal. Any price within a 4–7 range is thus acceptable.
- Identifying and evaluating financing options such as debt, equity from buyout funds, subordinated debt, insurance companies, corporate development companies, hedge funds and other lenders.

1.15 WHY ARE LBOs NO LONGER POPULAR?

Leveraged buyouts are today a subject of severe scrutiny. This is quite unlike a few years ago when they were the darling of the financial markets. The general feeling is that LBOs have been ingenious and questionable, with no great results achieved, which is forcing the financial world to do a re-think. Some experts are also of the view that all LBOs should not be treated the same way. There are obvious differences in the credit risks involved. The criticism broadly originates from the number and size of the current day LBOs. While a $2 billion LBO would raise eyebrows five years ago, a deal of $30 billion is today readily accepted. Obviously one cannot ignore the risk involved in such a deal. For example, the RJR/Nabisco deal of $24.9 billion (Asher 2009).

Critics have been crying foul because LBOs pile huge amounts of new debt on corporate balance sheets, drive down bond ratings, and consequently the market value of bonds held in the company's portfolio. Since LBOs are funded through debt, any rise in interest would drive the company to financial crisis, creating a deep recessionary impact on the economy. With fall in company revenue, servicing the huge debts becomes near impossible and bankruptcy appears to be the only way out as shown in Table 1.1. It may also spell doom for banks, insurance companies, investment houses, and pension funds that have started staying away from LBOs.

The pro-LBO group, however, feels that the risk is not as high as is being made out, as LBOs are seen across sectors, thus diversifying the risk. Given the financial tools one can run sensitized cash flow analyses to establish different interest rate scenarios, and estimate the tolerance of a borrower for higher interest rates.

1.16 MANAGEMENT BUYOUTS

Management buyout (MBO) is a process where managers and/or executives of a company purchase the controlling interest in a company from existing shareholders. The management usually buys the target business from the parent company. Of course, it is very important to establish whether the parent company is willing to sell the company. To facilitate a management buyout, a new company is incorporated to buy the business or shares of the target company.

A management buyout requires personal financial commitment of the managers in addition to a loan or equity. Funds are also arranged through the Venture Capitalists since the process is complicated and requires significant financial resources.

The success of a management buyout depends on establishing a coherent business plan that will help in obtaining the funding required for the MBO. It is necessary to convince the parent company that the managers are the best buyers for the business as they understand the business. Even the investors need to feel assured that the business shall continue successfully and provide them with a satisfactory return on investment.

Management buyouts have become popular for the following reasons:

- They provide a chance to management to run the business.
- The management team of the new company will be highly motivated, a group that has deep knowledge of the business, and is eager to make profits.

- Since the management of the new company has expert knowledge of the business of the new company, the process of commercial due diligence would be comparatively easier and less time-consuming.

Management buyouts are also capable of creating problems for the company:

- An MBO involves serious financial commitment and acceptance of risk by the management.
- The management team comprises employees who have become owners of the business. As employees, they are not affected much by the success or failure of the venture, but as owners, they feel the heat directly.
- While commercial due diligence may take less time, all other elements of the due diligence process would require time and expenditure.
- The new company is highly leveraged, i.e., has a high proportion of debt relative to equity. The heavy interest burden makes the company less competitive in terms of price.

1.17 IMPLICATIONS OF CORPORATE RESTRUCTURING

With the business world becoming very competitive and dynamic, organizations have to go through restructuring to survive and thrive. While companies initiate the process of restructuring, it is important to note that the success or failure of the measures initiated depend on the type and degree of restructuring. While strategic and operational changes address the fundamentals of the company, financial restructuring addresses the financial issues. A company looking for a major shift in business focus should pursue extensive restructuring.

However, the crux of the matter is that although restructuring is carried out for creating customer value, it affects every stakeholder and every aspect of the business.

Let us analyse the implications of restructuring on different groups.

1.17.1 Investors

Investors represent individuals, institutions, and companies that have a financial stake in the company. Investors are concerned about the immediate future and long-term returns that the company is capable of generating. Restructuring has serious financial implications, and this creates insecurity and uncertainty in the minds of the investors. It is therefore imperative for the management to share the corporate vision so that investors feel confident and remain invested in the company.

1.17.2 Customers

Restructuring often results in change of focus of the business, leading to reallocation of resources, introduction of new products or withdrawal of the existing products, changes in the after-sales policy of the company, etc. Such proposed changes can result in erosion of customer base and confidence and have severe adverse effects on future business prospects. To dispel the fears of the existing and prospective customers, the company should communicate its future plans. Post restructuring, the management should focus on the needs and expectations of the customer by providing quality products and reducing the lead time.

1.17.3 Management

Corporate restructuring results in changes in business processes, introduction of changes that suit change in processes, changes in systems, and in ensuring effective communication with all the stakeholders. The changed environment has the following implications on the management:

- Release of financial resources blocked in unproductive assets and low return assets and businesses.
- Diversion of core competencies to core areas reducing the risk of failure.
- Provision of an opportunity to the management to prove its ability to 'manage the change'.

1.17.4 Employees

Employees represent the most affected stakeholders in the process of restructuring, for it impacts them psychologically, culturally, and financially. Since they share common values, culture, assumptions and fears, restructuring poses several challenges to them. Employees have a 'patterned mindset'; hence it becomes difficult for them to adapt to the new set of challenges posed by the changed environment. This creates fear in their minds, leading to psychological turmoil. The biggest challenge they face is the need to unlearn old skills and acquire new skills.

If the employees are left to live with this fear, one can expect disastrous consequences. The management has to therefore involve the employees in the process. This is the only assured way of changing their mindset with ease and communicating to them that the organization is willing to empower them.

1.17.5 Others

Restructuring can also impact other stakeholders in the following manner:

- Reduction in competition as weak and inefficient players exit the market.
- Possibilities of seizing new opportunities to create new businesses.
- Contribution to the growth of the national economy.
- Need for the government to provide resources and subsidies to companies, which imposes a burden on the national exchequer.
- Subsidies leading to social discontent, with great potential for political instability.

Thus, one finds that restructuring provides the company with the much-required competitive edge. However, implications need to be understood and properly handled so that the benefits are not lost.

The modern business environment reflects a radical shift in the manner the business is being conducted. The changes are capable of generating both positive and negative impact on the business. In the light of this fact, managers need to critically appreciate the causes and consequences of corporate restructuring. While restructuring can prove beneficial, companies should avoid unnecessarily experimenting with new ideas and tools in the name of restructuring.

SUMMARY

Corporate restructuring deals with elements that can change the effectiveness and performance of an entity. The basic objective is to introduce path-breaking changes in the structural and performance parameters of the company so that the entity returns to the list of profit-making entities. While corporate restructuring need not necessarily yield positive results, it certainly provides the company with an opportunity to revitalize its activities and progress on the recovery path.

KEY DEFINITIONS

Acquisitions Acquisitions represent purchase of new entities to utilize the existing strength and capabilities or to exploit the untapped or under-utilized markets. They are also carried out to grow in size and prevent possibilities of future takeover attempts.

Buyback of shares/tender offers A tender offer is a public offer made by a potential acquirer to purchase some or all of the shareholder's shares in a company. The offer price is higher than the current market value of the shares. It is assumed that the premium would induce the shareholders to sell their holdings.

Capacity expansions This strategy involves expansion in the production capacity, resulting in higher trading volumes and hefty margins. This strategy works when the market is starved for goods.

Cash disgorgement Cash Disgorgement is the principle where accumulated cash resources of a business are spent or reinvested effectively.

Core business processes Core business process is about deciding what the company is good at and focusing on the strengths for attaining the goals.

Corporate restructuring Restructuring is the act of partially dismantling or otherwise reorganizing a company for the purpose of making it more efficient and therefore more profitable. It involves the reorganization of a company to attain greater efficiency and to adapt to new markets. It also implies liquidating projects in some areas and redirecting assets to other existing or new areas.

Customer delight The concept of customer delight states that only those companies that can understand and fulfil the needs and expectations of the customer shall survive.

Customer focus Customer focus is about understanding the needs of the customers and offering better and improved customer service.

Diversification Diversification is a strategy where a company enters different product or market segments to increase market penetration. The main objective of diversification is to exploit the new avenues available and add to the group profits.

Dual class stock recapitalization Under this head, the entity creates a second class of common stock that carries limited voting rights and usually preferential claim to the entity's cash flows. This is done by distributing limited voting shares on pro-rata basis to the existing shareholders. Such stocks usually carry higher rate of dividends.

Equity carve-outs Equity carve-out is the process where an IPO of a portion of the common stock of a wholly owned subsidiary is offered to raise resources. Equity carve-outs are also known as 'split-off IPOs'. This process initiates trading in a new and distinct set of equity claims on the assets of the subsidiary.

ESOPs   Employee stock option plans are contracts between a company and its employees that give employees the right to buy a specific number of the company's shares at a fixed price within a specified period of time.

Exchange offers   An exchange offer provides one or more classes of security the right or option to exchange part or all of their holdings for a different class of securities of the entity.

Financial distress   Financial distress is a condition in which the liquidation value of the firm's assets is less than the total face value of the creditor's claims.

Financial restructuring   Financial restructuring involves change in the capital structure and capital mix of the company to minimize its cost of capital. It is about infusion of financial resources to facilitate mergers, acquisitions, joint venture, strategic alliances, LBOs and stock buyback.

Forced sales   The capital structure of a company includes both equity and debt. When debt exceeds equity, the entity becomes high leveraged and often finds the debt load intolerable. To manage the situation, the company often decides to sell unrelated and underperforming assets and businesses. This is called forced sales.

Hardware restructuring   When the structure of the organization is redefined, dismantled, or modified, the restructuring is termed as hardware restructuring.

Hiving off   Hiving off is a process wherein an existing company sells a particular division to reduce unproductive expenditure and slim the organization. It also helps an entity to reap the benefits of core competencies, competitive advantage, and emergence of high capacity.

Joint ventures   A joint venture is generally understood as technical and financial collaboration either in the form of greenfield projects, takeovers, or alliances with existing companies.

Leveraged buyouts   When a company acquires another company using a significant amount of borrowed funds like bonds or loans to pay the cost of acquisition, the transaction is termed a leveraged buyout (LBO).

Leveraged recapitalization   Leverage decisions represent potential for value enhancement or defence against takeovers. Leverage recapitalization often results in operating improvements. The large overhang of debt stimulates the management to improve operations to generate sufficient cash flows to pay the debt.

Liquidation   Liquidation is initiation of bankruptcy proceedings. Here all the assets are discarded and the liabilities repaid, after which the entity ceases to exist.

Management buyouts   Management buyout (MBO) is the process where managers and/or executives of a company purchase controlling interest in a company from existing shareholders. The management usually buys the target business from the parent company.

Mergers   Mergers involve the coming together of two or more companies and pooling of resources for the purpose of achieving certain common objectives.

Non-sponsored leveraged buyouts   This strategy is adopted in case of financially healthy businesses, where the financing techniques are similar, but the management gains operating control with around 85% to 100% ownership depending on the situation. These types of buyouts are called non-sponsored leveraged buyouts.

Organizational restructuring   Organizational restructuring is a restructuring strategy designed to increase the efficiency and effectiveness of personnel through significant changes in the organizational structure.

Portfolio management   Portfolio management involves determining how each business division fits into the overall business strategy of the company, evolving strategies to position the company in the competitive environment, ascertaining the impact of the strategic decisions on the contribution of the company and the potential of the redefined strategy on achieving synergy in goals and objectives.

Portfolio restructuring   Portfolio restructuring involves divesting or acquiring a line of business perceived peripheral to the long-term business strategy of the company.

Sell-offs or divestitures Sell-offs or divestitures are attempts to come out of a product segment or sector to adjust the operations to the changing economic and political environments. They involve voluntary decisions implemented to attain the objective of shareholder wealth maximization.

Software restructuring Software restructuring involves cultural and process changes to establish a collaborative environment that facilitates growth and restructuring.

Spin-offs In a spin-off, a company creates a subsidiary whose shares are distributed on a pro-rata basis to the shareholders of the parent company. This strategy is adopted when the company feels that it would generate positive returns.

Splits Splits involve breaking up the business into independent entities to exploit opportunities of growth, raise capital, achieve efficiency, and derive taxation benefits. Splits also provide benefits of synergy, competence, and revival.

Split-ups Split-ups represent a restructuring process where companies split themselves into two or more parts.

Sponsored leveraged buyouts Under sponsored LBOs, the private equity firms offer to buy a controlling stake in a company using leverage obtained from banks based on the financials of the company.

Strategic alliances and collaborations Strategic alliances represent a long-term agreement between two or more entities to co-operate with each other in specific areas of interest. Such areas of common interest include access to new technology and product range, access to market, etc.

Targeted stock Under targeted stock, an entity's operations are split into two or more common equity claims, but the businesses remain wholly owned segments of a single parent. Here the targeted stock is regarded as common stock of the consolidated company and not of a subsidiary.

CONCEPT REVIEW QUESTIONS

1.1. Explain the concept of corporate restructuring. Discuss in brief the conceptual framework of corporate restructuring.

1.2. State the reasons that force a company to opt for restructuring. What are the barriers encountered while restructuring the business?

1.3. Why do companies restructure?

1.4. Explain the different types of corporate restructuring

1.5. Explain the strategic options that companies pursue while restructuring the business.

1.6. What is buyback of shares? Where do the resources for buyback come from? State the mandatory conditions that companies have to fulfil before going for a buyback.

1.7. What are leveraged buyouts (LBOs)? Explain the different types of LBOs.

1.8. What are the reasons for the declining popularity of LBOs?

1.9. Discuss the implications of corporate restructuring.

1.10. Write notes on the following:
   (a) McKinsey 7S model
   (b) Evolving added value structure
   (c) Cost leadership options for restructuring
   (d) Product excellence options for restructuring
   (e) SWOT options for restructuring
   (f) Asset reorganization options of restructuring
   (g) New ownership relationship options of restructuring
   (h) Reorganizing financial claims
   (i) Financial reorganization
   (j) Cash disgorgement
   (k) ESOPs
   (l) Forced sales
   (m) Organizational imperatives
   (n) Buyback of shares
   (o) Norms for buyback of shares in India
   (p) Management buyouts

PROJECT ASSIGNMENT

Analyse the corporate restructuring process initiated at Daewoo India. In addition, examine why the restructuring efforts did not yield the desired results.

REFERENCES

Bethel, J. and Liebeskind, J., 'The Effects of Ownership Structure on Corporate Restructuring', *Strategic Management Journal*, Volume 14, Issue S1, February 2007, pp. 15–31

Blatz, M., Kraus, K.J., and Haghani, S., *Corporate Restructuring, Finance in Times of Crisis*, Springer, London, 2008, pp. 13

Bowman, E.H. and Singh, H., 'Corporate Restructuring: A Symptom of Poor Governance or a Solution to Past Managerial Mistakes?', *European Management Journal*, Volume 15, Issue 3, June 1997, pp. 213–219

Bullock, N. and Li, K., 'Tribune Bondholders Sue Over Buy-out', *The Financial Times*, 6 March 2010

Chandra, P., *Financial Management—Theory and Practice*, Tata McGraw-Hill, New Delhi, 2007, pp. 917

Childers, J.J., *Real Wealth Without Risk: Escape the Artificial Wealth Trap in 48 Hours or Less*, Morgan James Publishing, New York, 2009, pp. 232

Copeland, T., Lembruber, E., and Mayers, D., *Modern Finance and Industrial Economics*, Basil Blackwell, New York, 1987

Finegan, P.T., *A Closer Look at the Value Of Split-ups*, http://www.shareholdervalue.com/shareholder_value_research/split-ups.pdf, last accessed on 12 March 2010

Gibbs, P.A., 'Determinants of Corporate Restructuring—The Relative Importance of Corporate Governance, Takeover Threat and Free Cash Flows', *Strategic Management Journal*, Volume 14, Issue S1, March 1993, pp. 51–68

Gordon, D., *Corporate Restructuring: Managing the Change Process from Within*, Harvard Business School Press, Boston, July 1994, pp. 11–14

Hite, G.L., Owers, J.E., and Rogers, R.C., 'The market for interfirm asset sales: Partial sell-offs and total liquidations', *Journal of Financial Economics*, Volume 18, Issue 2, June 1987. pp. 229–252

http://www.holcim.com/annualreport, last accessed on 21 December 2009

http://www.sethassociates.com/setting_up_a_joint_venture_in_india, Sheth Associates, New Delhi, last accessed on 23 August 2009

http://www.thefreedictionary.com/restructuring, last accessed on 3 January 2010

Joseph, A., 'Warning Signals for LBOs', *ABA Banking Journal*, Volume 81, 1989

Kuriakose, B., 'Customer the Centre of our Universe', *Inflow Outflow (L&T Valves Marketing Newsletter)*, Chennai, Volume 1, January 1997, pp. 2

LBOs: The Good, the Bad, and the Ugly, http://images.businessweek.com/ss/07/12/1203_lbo/index_01.htm, last accessed on 12 December 2009

Marshall, J.F. and Bansal, V.K., *Financial Engineering—A complete guide to Financial Innovations*, Prentice Hall of India, New Delhi, 2004, pp. 549

Membrillera, F., Necas, Z., and Ghosh, S., 'Strategic Alliances in Emerging Markets', *Delta Partners*, December 2009

Mohan, N., 'Do LBOs sustain efficiency gains?', *Akron Business and Economic Review*, Cengage Learning, Michigan, 22 September 1990

Muller, R.K., 'The Care and Feeding of Advisory board', *Journal of Business Strategy*, Volume 9, Issue 5, June 1988, pp. 21–24

NABHI's Manual for Foreign Collaboration and Investment in India, NABHI, New Delhi, April 1997, pp. 72

Olsen, J., *Note on Leveraged Buyout*, Tuck School of Business at Dartmouth College, Centre for Private Equity and Entrepreneurship, Hanover, 2002, pp. 3

Schipper, K. and Smith, A., 'Effects of recontracting on Shareholder wealth', *Journal of Financial Economics*, Volume 12, Issue 4, December 1983, pp. 437–467

Weston, F.J., Kwang, S.C., and Hoag, S.E., *Mergers, Restructuring and Corporate Control*, Prentice Hall of India, New Delhi, 2005, pp. 53

Weston, F.J., Mitchell, M.L., and Mulherin, J.H., *Takeovers, Restructuring, and Corporate Governance*, Prentice Hall, New Jersey, August 2003, pp 124–127

CASE STUDY

India Yamaha Motor

Abstract

India Yamaha Motor (Yamaha) entered the Indian market in 1980s with its 100 cc motorbikes. While other players kept growing, Yamaha has been struggling to stay afloat, and has incurred huge accumulated losses. The company planned a major restructuring exercise to turnaround. This case tries to look at issues that ailed the company and the measures the company initiated for a turnaround.

Pedagogical Objectives
- To understand and identify the reasons that forced Yamaha to opt for restructuring of its Indian operations
- To identify the measures initiated by the company to turnaround its operations in India

Introduction

The Indian two-wheeler industry has been bristling with brands, colours, and engine sizes. New models keep hitting the roads practically every month. The market has kept pace with the economic development and has been growing at a healthy rate of 18% to 28% annually. Initially scooters and mopeds enjoyed great popularity in the Indian two-wheeler market. The 1980s saw a change in this trend with the launch of 100 cc motorcycles. This was when the Indian companies started entering into JVs and technical collaborations and entities such as IndSuzuki, Hero Honda, Kawasaki Bajaj, and Escorts-Yamaha were born. Suddenly the trend shifted and motorcycles started replacing scooters. The shift in customer preferences was promoted by attractive finance options offered by banks and financial institutions. Other factors that fuelled the shift in preferences were goodies and freebies available, promotion through brand ambassadors the target buyers identified with, such as Dharmendra, Sunny Deol, Akshay Kumar, Jackie Shroff, Sachin Tendulkar, John Abraham, etc. who successfully helped the companies to connect with the youth. Companies even changed their strategy and started projecting motorcycles as a symbol of freedom, exuberance, and convenience (Kapoor 2003).

Changing Face of Yamaha

The Indian motorcycle market saw severe competition with all the players eying the ever expanding market. Yamaha has had a presence in the Indian motorcycle market since 1985 ever since it entered into technical collaboration with Escorts Motors. The partnership was built on the principle of cooperative relationship for manufacturing and selling the Yamaha brand of motorcycles in a market where demand for motorcycles had been on an upward spiral.

Initially Escorts held a 74% share in the partnership. However, with time the composition of the partnership kept changing with the investment ratio gradually going in favour of Yamaha Motor Company (YMC) by 2000. The major reason behind the change in ownership was the fact that Escorts-Yamaha's market share had been sliding while other players were consolidating their position. Yamaha Motor Company even assumed managerial control of the company and the company was renamed Yamaha

Motors Escorts Limited (YMEL). Yamaha operated in India through two entities that managed manufacturing and marketing operations and these entities had a total capital of ₹1.6 billion. When the slide continued further, Yamaha decided to restructure its Indian operations by merging the two entities. The first thing that was done was to rename the company as Yamaha Motors India Limited (YMI). The company decided to restructure its sales operations, undertook numerous measures to build a separate brand name by launching new products, overhauled the marketing strategy and realigned the HR policies to those prevailing in the industry.

Need for Restructuring

Though Yamaha did have an early success in India with its power-packed RX-100 model in the late 1980s, the company was unable to keep pace with the vehicles launched by Bajaj, TVS, and Hero Honda, which grabbed the market share. From being an almost cult product, the RX-100 lost its die-hard patrons when it failed to catch up with the two-stroke to four-stroke transition forced by the government in the early 1990s. Yamaha tried many times to launch new products and rebuild its reputation, but it always failed (Ramanathan 2010).

While Yamaha started its Indian operations long ago, it has been incurring losses since 2001 forcing the company to explore the option of acquiring managerial control in the JV. All the efforts initiated by the management to prevent losses failed to generate results and the company continued to bleed. The market share of the company, which had been sliding year after year, touched an all time low of 4% in the 7.5 million Indian two-wheeler market (www.mint.com).

During this phase of sliding market share, the company borrowed huge amounts to stay afloat. Declining sales revenue and continuous losses made it difficult to repay the loans. The deteriorating financial health of the company forced the management to plan restructuring of its Indian operations.

When the restructuring plan was announced in 2007, the company had accumulated losses of ₹3.36 billion. However, the head of the Indian operations Yukimine Tsuji, who was subsequently appointed CEO, expressed confidence that the revenue generated after restructuring would help the company repay the huge debt and the company would turn profitable in 2009–10. Contrary to the projections of the company, Morgan Stanley analysts projected that Yamaha India would be unable to achieve its target of lapping up 10 per cent market share of total motorcycle sales by 2010. Analysts projected that Yamaha India would sell 400,000 units by 2010, but will end up with an operating loss of ₹2.90 billion.

Restructuring Plan

As a first step towards restructuring the Indian entity, YMC decided to dissolve the old units and merge them into a new entity Yamaha Motors India (YMI) from April 2008. To carry out its plans, the company offered Mitsui Corporation a stake in YMI. Mitsui Corporation agreed to pick up a 30% stake (www.mint.com).

The restructuring required pumping in financial resources as the financial health of the entity was far from satisfactory. It was decided that ₹4 billion would be infused into the capital of the company, raising it from the current ₹1.6 billion to ₹5.6 billion. Of the additional capital, ₹2.32 billion was to be contributed by the parent company and ₹1.68 billion by Mitsui Investment, a subsidiary of Mitsui Corporation.

The additional financial resources were proposed to be used for launching new products in the domestic market using contemporary technology. The company believed that the use of contemporary technology along with a new marketing campaign would help it arrest the continuous slide in the market share of the company's motorcycles.

The Indian operations had an accumulated loss of ₹10 billion. As a part of the restructuring strategy, the parent company agreed to absorb the losses of YMI to ensure that the new company started its operations without any burden of the past in its balance sheet. The belief was that with no ghosts of the past in its balance sheet, the company would be able to restructure its operations and its bottom line would turn black by 2009–10. The confidence originated from the fact that while the company was restructuring its operations, the focus and direction would remain intact.

Another important element of the restructuring plan was a two-fold strategy that focussed on changes in the production facilities of the company. The plan of action proposed was to replace the 40-year-old facility at Surajpur in Uttar Pradesh, with a brand new facility and a simultaneous upgradation of the factory at Faridabad that produced engines and carried out machining and casting of components. The existing facility, it was proposed, would be used for paint jobs and manufacturing of engines and other components while the new facility was proposed to be used for bike assembly.

The company proposed to manufacture 50% of the components in-house and procure the balance through vendors (www.mint.com). This strategy was driven by the belief that it would help the company create quality benchmark for the vendors, although the company had no plans to rationalize its vendor base. On the marketing front, the company proposed to increase the number of dealers from the current level of 350 to 500 by the end of 2009, said Koji Arai, Director and Chief Sales Officer (www.mint.com).

The company committed ₹8 million for the restructuring process from 2008–10. Of this, 30% was to be utilized for developing new products and the balance was earmarked for restructuring other elements of the business.

The parent company has been providing adequate support to its subsidiaries across the globe by focusing on developing more fuel-efficient for motor cycles to improve competitiveness of its products. The company planned to spend 202 billion yen on research and development up to 2010 to help achieve in emerging and ASEAN countries and to accelerate development of environment-friendly engines (www.mint.com).

The company also decided to introduce 'India-only models'. The models were to be locally built and exported to Europe with some modifications.

Ishikawa, the CEO and anathema for most Japanese managers, went on record to say that he wants to turn around Yamaha's waning fortunes in India by transforming it into a niche, high-value player that eschews the low-margin, big-volume commuter segment, presently dominated by Hero Honda, Bajaj Auto, and TVS Motors (Ramanathan 2010).

Post-restructuring Outcomes

It was expected that the restructuring programme would speed up product development, improve quality, and cost reduction. The company was keen on reorienting the sales channel to infuse consumer-oriented policies (Kapoor 2003).

Ishikawa admitted that a big problem would be employees' attitude, which would be very difficult to change. 'The challenge is the Escorts heritage we carry,' he says, referring to the JV Yamaha had formed with Escorts in the 1980s. Though it was successful for nearly a decade, the ties soured due to differences in the style of management. It came to an end in 2000, when Escorts divested its 24% stake in the JV, letting Yamaha walk forward alone. However, the Escorts heritage remains, says Ishikawa. Work culture is 'not aggressive, not transparent. There is a need to change the mindset to make it like Yamaha's. That is why Yamaha is more active (with the Indian operations)'.

However, Ishikawa and his bosses in Japan know they cannot hide behind legacy problems. Workforce problems or challenges due to changing market dynamics have been faced by Hero Honda and other competitors as well. In the early 1980s, TVS Motors had to fight a bitter battle with its workforce only to emerge as a fine example of turnaround. The mid-to-late 1990s were tough for Bajaj Auto, which saw its domineering scooter market vanishing into thin air. However, the company bounced back under the leadership of Rajiv Bajaj with a whole new range of motorcycles, even creating new segments with Bajaj Pulsar. Of late, this has hit Hero Honda's leadership too, but the company is fighting back with new products and aggressive pricing (Kapoor 2003).

The company therefore started focussing on broad cultural change by bringing in the Japanese work ethos of single-minded devotion and discipline. To get rid of 'dead wood', the company decided to spend about ₹500 million towards a voluntary retirement scheme, which reduced the workforce from 2,400 to 2,000.

While the company was ready to sort out its internal problems, it realized that positioning its products with a new generation of consumers will be expensive and difficult. It is here that Yamaha's biggest strength would help, that is, being the world's no. 2 motorcycle company with a wide product range and technological competency. This was expected to give Yamaha India a strategic depth and range of products to fall back on, which domestic competitors such as Bajaj Auto lacked, although at present Yamaha meant very little to Indian consumers. However, the company was convinced that these bikes planned would place Yamaha in a niche market. (Exhibit 1.1)

Ishikawa's decision to go after niche markets was driven by the argument that it would not require Yamaha to compete neck-to-neck with Hero Honda and Bajaj Auto. Yamaha undertook extensive market research and concluded that there was great potential for sports bikes and release high performance 150 cc bikes. Research showed that this segment accounted for a little over 10 per cent of the market, but was gradually eating into the commuter segment. Yamaha planned to come out with these bikes as they would put the company in the niche market and also help it counter and outshine rival products such as Bajaj Pulsar and TVS Apache.

Yamaha realized that there was a strong need to win back the lost trust of the customers for which understanding the local flavour of the market was the key. The company started exploring the possibility of replicating its out-of-the-box strategy that it pursued successfully in Thailand, where it began hosting rock concerts, built Yamaha bike clubs and started sponsoring day and night events to engage youth—its key customers—riders that Hero Honda and Bajaj Auto cannot replicate. The company also started contemplating selling accessories and apparel. However, the key part of the plan was to identify new segments quickly, which would allow Yamaha to identify and address new customer segments with specific products, and think beyond replacement sales for existing customers.

One major problem the company had faced was an unimpressive and non-performing dealer network. Part of the reason was that some key dealers were Escorts dealers who had been hanging around from the days they sold tractors and farm equipment. Many of them did not feel the need to update their selling skills and approach. The company also realized that there was a strong need to improve the dealer network and focusing on key markets in B-class cities would help. Yamaha tried doing this but failed. The company launched 'Yamaha One' programme with the objective of boosting dealer effectiveness by creating one or two swanky outlets in Delhi, but overall the plan went nowhere. This failure was perceived as a big letdown for it would delay the turnaround of the company.

Post-restructuring, YMI planned to manufacture 400,000 bikes annually at the Surajpur plant. The company introduced new models such as FZ-15 and R15, which helped the company attain a 16% growth in sales during April-November 2008. During this period, the industry clocked a growth of a meagre 2.5%. While the results look impressive, Yamaha continues to incur losses and a turnaround seems miles away.

Conclusion

In spite of six tough, loss-ridden years, Yamaha refuses to exit India. It continues to concentrate on the niche market in the 200 to 250 cc category and hitting the market with high-end performance bikes. The company still feels it can turn things around and can realign its India strategy just like it did in Thailand where it tried to sell the lifestyle, and not just the product. The company plans to ramp up the capacity from 300,000 units to one million units by 2010. Yamaha also plans to bring in *R1* and *R6* by the end of the year, although its plans to launch a scooter have been shelved for now.

Discussion Question

Analyse the case and discuss the pros and cons of the restructuring strategy of Yamaha Motor India. Suggest measures that you feel the company could have taken to speed up the process of restructuring.

Exhibit 1.1   The Competitive Scenario

Company	Units sold April–Mar 2005–06	Units sold April–Mar 2006–07	Change (%)	Market share 2005–06 (%)	Market share 2006–07 (%)
Hero Honda	2,893,070	3,157,429	9.14	49.79	48.18
Bajaj	1,747,806	2,078,860	18.94	30.08	31.72
TVS	752,576	844,174	12.17	12.95	12.88
Yamaha	205,480	210,315	2.35	3.54	3.21
Honda	98,072	163,977	67.22	1.69	2.50
Others	113,555	98,889	−12.92	1.95	1.51
TOTAL	5,810,559	6,565,664	12.79	100	100

Source: Report by IMaCS for IBEF, 2008

References

Kapoor, N., *How organizations handle change—Yamaha Motors India*, http://www.scribd.com/doc/2165100/Yamaha, last accessed on 10 April 2010

Mitsui agrees to pick 30% stake in Yamaha Motors, www.mint.com, last accessed on 10 April 2010

Ramanathan, S.K., *Yamaha's New Spark Plug*, www.businessworld.com, last accessed on 13 April 2010

Seth, S., *Yamaha India will be profitable by 2010, says CEO*, www.mint.com, last accessed on 10 April 2010

2 | Takeovers

LEARNING OBJECTIVES

After studying the chapter, you will be able to understand

- the concept of takeover
- different forms of takeover
- various defences to takeover
- the benefits and disadvantages of takeover
- the takeover code
- the procedure for takeover

2.1 INTRODUCTION

Corporate takeovers play an important role in the economy. However, unlike standard market transactions, they could lead to hostility as the target company often resists the attempt of takeover by the acquirer. While the target company adopts strategies to escape the takeover, the acquirer does everything possible to counter the prevention strategies of the target. The target adopts strategies that potentially increase the cost of acquisition far above the prevailing market price of the firm and sometimes deter efficient transfer of control. While the anti-takeover tactics may be justified as being carried out in the interest of the shareholders, regulators and practitioners feel that these devices are merely rent-seeking tactics employed by insiders who profit at the expense of shareholder value and social efficiency. The shareholders generally go by the opinion of the managers as they believe that managers are in a better position to evaluate the desirability of accepting a takeover offer. This chapter discusses the takeover and anti-takeover strategies in detail.

2.2 CONCEPT OF TAKEOVER

A takeover is a process wherein an acquirer takes over control of the target company. The acquirer may do so with or without the consent of the shareholders. An acquirer may also acquire a substantial quantity of shares or voting rights of the target company. This is termed as substantial acquisition of interest.

A takeover takes place usually by acquisition through the purchase of shares held by shareholders at a specified price. The number of shares purchased enables the acquirer to gain control over the target company. The acquirer may be an individual, a company, any other legal entity, or persons acting in concert (PAC) with the acquirer.

Persons acting in concert are individuals or companies who act on behalf of, or in coordination with the acquirer to acquire a substantial number of shares in a target company. They include holding companies or subsidiary companies, mutual funds or their sponsor/trustee/asset management company, etc. The acquirer and persons acting in concert may have a formal or informal agreement in this regard.

Although it is often difficult to identify the PACs, doing so is crucial from the legal perspective. This is because legal provisions prohibit a person from acquiring shares beyond a certain number. To escape from the boundaries imposed by the regulatory framework, an acquirer may enter into an understanding with others, thus forming a PAC, for acquiring shares of the target. Although the number of shares the buyer individually purchases may be below the threshold limit, shares acquired together with the PAC, added to the buyer's own holdings may collectively exceed the threshold limit. For example, in the Arun Bajoria–Bombay Dyeing tussle, Bajoria appointed the following to act as PAC to help him acquire a stake in Bombay Dyeing: Mega Resources, Mega Stock, Hooghly Mills, Pooja Bajoria, Mohini Devi Bajoria, Lata Devi Bajoria, and Meenakshi Jati.

The acquirer generally acquires shares through a public announcement known as an open offer. An open offer is made to ensure that shareholders of the target company become aware of an exit opportunity available to them.

It is also important to understand the manner in which the price for an open offer is arrived at. It is generally based on the following parameters:

- The negotiated price under the agreement that triggered the open offer
- The highest price paid by the acquirer or the PAC with him for any acquisitions. This includes shares allotted through public issues or rights issues during the 26-week period, statutorily prescribed, prior to the date of the open offer
- The average weekly high and low of the closing prices of shares as quoted on the stock exchanges where shares of the target company are traded during the 26-week period or the average of the daily high and low prices of shares during the two-week period prior to the date of the open offer
- In cases where the shares of the target company are not traded frequently, determining the highs and lows becomes difficult. Under such circumstances, the company may use parameters such as return on net worth of the company, book value per share, earnings per share (EPS), etc.

Corporate takeovers are very common in the US and the UK, but rare in Germany, Japan, and China. The reason is that Germany practises a dual-board structure, Japanese companies have interlocking sets of ownerships known as *keiretsu*, and in China, most public listed companies are state owned.

2.3 FORMS OF TAKEOVER

A takeover can be of different types. It can be classified from the legal perspective or the business perspective. The different forms of takeover are shown in Fig. 2.1 and discussed in Sections 2.3.1–2.3.3.

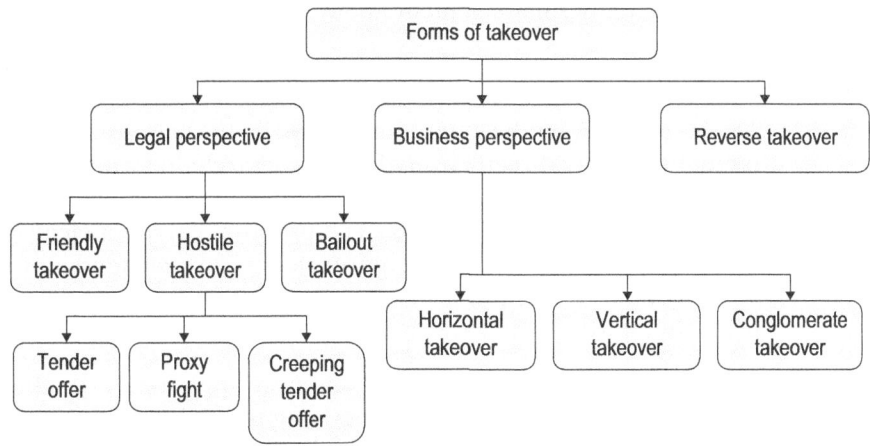

Figure 2.1   Forms of takeover

2.3.1 Legal Perspective

Corporate takeovers are governed by specific laws, which protect the target company and the shareholders. From the legal perspective, takeovers fall into three categories.

Friendly Takeover

In a friendly takeover, the acquirer acquires the shares of the target by informing the board of directors about his intention to purchase the shares of the target company. When the board feels that the offer is worth accepting, it recommends to the shareholders that the offer be accepted. Here, the acquirer may either acquire the assets or purchase the stock of the target. When a friendly takeover involves the purchase of assets, the acquirer enjoys the following advantages:

- The acquirer can purchase only those assets that it desires to purchase.
- The acquirer is not required to take over any contingent liabilities of the target company.
- The acquirer can negotiate the price with the board of directors as the approval of the shareholders is not required.

When a friendly takeover involves the purchase of the stock of the target, the following points must be considered by the acquirer:

- The acquirer has to assume the liabilities of the target firm.
- The target firm may continue to operate as an autonomous subsidiary or it may be merged with the acquiring firm.
- The approval of the shareholders of the target firm is necessary.

Hostile Takeover

A hostile takeover is one where the board of directors of the target firm refuses the offer of the acquirer to purchase the shares, but the acquirer continues to pursue the target or makes an offer bypassing the target company's management. Such a deal also includes an offer made by the acquirer without informing the target company's management about their intention of acquiring a stake in the company.

The acquirer has three options if he chooses to proceed with a hostile takeover:

Tender offer   A tender offer is one made by the acquirer to buy the stock of the target firm either directly from the firm's shareholders or through the secondary market. First, the acquirer makes an offer to buy the company's stock to the target firm's board of directors. The proposal carries a clear indication that if the offer is turned down, the acquirer shall resort to a tender offer. This strategy is expensive as the acquirer has to pay a price higher than the prevailing market price. In addition, the stock price tends to rise in anticipation of a takeover.

Proxy fight   In a proxy fight, the acquirer approaches the shareholders of the target firm with an objective of obtaining the right to vote for their shares. The acquirer hopes to secure enough proxies that would help them gain control over the board of directors and replace the incumbent management. Proxy fights are a very expensive and difficult mode of takeover, for the incumbent management team can use the target firm's funds to pay the cost of presenting its case and obtaining votes.

Creeping tender offer   This method involves purchasing enough stock from the open market to bring about a change in management.

Most countries have norms that an acquirer has to fulfil while resorting to a hostile takeover. For example, in the US, the Williams Act (1968) provides that the acquiring firm give 30 days notice to both the management of the target firm and the Securities and Exchange Commission pertaining to its desire to acquire shares of the target and the subsequent tender offer. The objective behind this regulation is to enable the target firm to formulate a defensive strategy to maintain its independence.

Bailout Takeover

This involves the takeover of a financially sick company by a financially rich company as per the provisions of the Sick Industrial Companies (Special Provisions) Act (1985). The objective of this takeover is to bail out the sick unit from losses.

2.3.2 Business Perspective

Takeovers under this category include the following types: horizontal takeover, vertical takeover, conglomerate takeover, and reverse takeover.

Horizontal Takeover

When a company takes over another from the same industry, the takeover is referred to as a horizontal takeover. The basic objective behind this type of takeover is to attain economies of scale and increase market share by entering into the segments of the company taken over.

Vertical Takeover

When a company is taken over by any of its vendors or customers, it is referred to as a vertical takeover. When the business of the vendor is taken over, it is called a backward takeover, whereas a takeover of the business of the customer is termed a forward takeover. The main purpose of the former is to attain a reduction in costs, whereas the latter aims at direct access to the market.

Conglomerate Takeover

When a company takes over another from a totally different industry, it is termed a conglomerate takeover. This type of takeover is pursued with the objective of attaining diversification.

2.3.3 Reverse Takeover

This is a takeover strategy where a private company acquires a public company. This takeover is planned to enable the private company to effectively float itself and at the same time bypass the lengthy and complex process of going public by coming out with an initial public offering (IPO). This makes the company less susceptible to market conditions. Here the public company is called a shell because all that exists of the original company is its organizational structure.

The biggest problem with reverse takeovers is that the company comes with its own history, which may be a troubled one, with sloppy record-keeping, pending lawsuits and contingent liabilities, and some shareholders. The resulting company has to live with the bad history of the target company.

2.4 TAKEOVER DEFENCES

A company that is a takeover target may resort to any one of the following takeover defences.

2.4.1 Bank Mail

A bank mail defence strategy is one where the bank of the target firm refuses financing options to the firm that is keen on taking it over. This is done with the objective of preventing an acquisition and by doing the following:
- Depriving the merger through non-availability of finance
- Increasing the transaction costs of the acquirer
- Delaying the takeover and permitting the target firm to develop other anti-takeover strategies

The acquiring firm may also try to keep other companies out of the fray. For example, Company A wanting to buy Company B may seek a guarantee from a bank that it will either finance Company A's bid or no bid at all. Such a strategy can also be used to block other companies from the takeover fray.

2.4.2 Greenmail

It is a practice where the target company purchases enough shares of another publicly traded company that poses a threat of takeover. The threat forces the target firm to buy those shares at a premium to avoid/suspend the takeover. This buyback is referred to as the bon voyage bonus, as it enables the target company to be left alone by the greenmailer. The St. Regis Paper Company provides an example of greenmail. When an investor group led by Sir James Goldsmith acquired 8.6% stake in St. Regis and expressed interest in taking over the paper concern, the company agreed to repurchase the shares at a premium. Goldsmith's group acquired the shares for an average price of $35.50 per share, a total of $109 million. It sold its stake at $52 per share, netting a profit of $51 million. Shortly after the payoff in March 1984, St. Regis became the target of publisher Rupert Murdoch. St. Regis turned to Champion International and agreed to a $1.84 billion takeover. Murdoch tendered his 5.6% stake in St. Regis to the Champion offer for a profit (Weston et al. 2003).

2.4.3 Crown Jewel Defence

Crown jewels represent the most valuable unit or department of a company. These units are categorized as crown jewels based on their profitability, value of assets owned, and future growth prospects. As these are the most valuable parts of the company, they are often used as a takeover defence. Here the company creates anti-takeover clauses whereby it gets the right to sell off the crown jewels in the event of a hostile takeover. Such a clause obviously deters the acquirer from attempting the takeover of the firm.

In extreme cases, the company facing a threat of takeover may even sell off its most attractive assets to a friendly third party or spins off its valuable assets into a separate entity. As a result of such off-loading or spin off of valuable assets, the target company appears less attractive for the company planning a takeover, which then loses interest and defers its takeover bid.

2.4.4 Poison Pill/Super Poison Put

Poison pill/super poison put is a strategy adopted to increase the likelihood of negative results over positive ones for the company attempting a takeover. This term has been derived from warfare terminology. Poison pills were pills laced with poison that spies used to carry and would consume when captured, to avoid the possibility of being interrogated for the enemy's gain. In a takeover bid, it represents an anti-takeover defence wherein the current management team of the target company threatens to quit en masse in the event of a successful hostile takeover.

The effectiveness of this strategy depends on the circumstances of the takeover. If the management team is efficient and quits en masse, the acquirer would be left without experienced leadership following the takeover. On the other hand, if the current leadership is inefficient, they may get fired after the takeover anyway. In such a case, the poison pill becomes ineffective.

2.4.5 Flip-over

It is a type of poison pill where the current shareholders of the target company are given the option to purchase discounted shares/stock after the potential takeover. The strategy involves giving a dividend in the form of rights, so that the existing shareholder can purchase equity or preference shares at a value lower than the prevailing market price. Once the takeover is complete, the current shareholders can 'flip over' the rights, allowing them to purchase the acquirer shares at a discount. This strategy results in dilution and price devaluation of the shares held by the acquirer, and defeats the very purpose of the takeover.

2.4.6 Grey Knight

A grey knight is an informal and ambiguous intervener in the takeover battle that makes a counter bid for the shares of the target company. His bid causes confusion between the original acquirer and the target company, as the intentions behind the counter bid are not clear.

2.4.7 Jonestown Defence/Suicide Pill

The Jonestown defence is another defence mechanism against hostile takeovers. Here the target firm employs tactics that might threaten its own existence, so as to thwart an imposing acquirer's bid. Since the strategy threatens the very existence of the target, it is also known as a 'suicide pill' and represents an extreme version of the poison pill.

2.4.8 Killer Bees

Under this strategy, the target company employs firms or individuals to fend off a takeover bid. The target company wants to avert the takeover attempt and either is unable to do this on its own or does not want to be seen doing so. Hence it employs other firms or individuals to do the job for it.

2.4.9 Leveraged Recapitalization

This is another strategy used to fend off a hostile acquisition. Here the target company either borrows significant additional debt that facilitates repurchase of stocks through a buyback program, or distributes a liberal dividend among the current shareholders. This leads to a sharp increase in the share price and makes the company a less attractive takeover target, for the acquirer has to pay more for the target company, thus minimizing the gains.

This strategy is also a form of poison pill that serves two purposes—increasing the debt of the target making the acquisition costly and maintaining the shareholders interest in averting the takeover attempts.

2.4.10 Lock-up Provision

It represents a strategy wherein an option is granted by the seller to the buyer to purchase a target company's stock as a prelude to a takeover. The acquirer requires a lock-up agreement before making a bid as it facilitates the negotiation progress. As a result of this arrangement, the major or controlling shareholder gets effectively 'locked up' and is not free to sell the stocks to a party other than the potential buyer.

Lock-ups can be of several types:

- Soft—one that permits the shareholder to terminate the agreement if a better offer comes along
- Hard—one that is unconditional and cannot be terminated
- Stock lock-up—where the bidder is either allowed to purchase the authorized but unissued share capital of the controlling stockholder or the shares of one or more large stockholders
- Asset lock-up—where the target firm grants an option for the acquisition of an asset. This lock-up is also known as a crown jewel lock-up.

A lock-up arrangement may take any one of the following forms:

- Break-up involving payment of termination fees
- Giving an option to the target shareholders to buy target stock
- Giving rights to target shareholders to purchase target assets
- Forcing the vote provisions in merger agreements
- Enforcing agreements with major shareholders such as voting agreements and agreements to sell shares or agreements to tender

2.4.11 Nancy Reagan Defence

This strategy is one where the board of directors of the target company say 'no' to the formal bid made by the acquirer to the shareholders to buy their shares. The board of directors has the authority to resist a takeover attempt and the matter ends there. The constitution of the company gives them this authority. The term refers to a catch-phrase coined by former US First Lady Nancy Reagan advocating 'abstinence from recreational drug use'. The attempt by Comcast to take over the Walt Disney Company in 2004 is a good example.

2.4.12 Non-voting Stock

Non-voting stock comprises shares that provide the shareholder with very little or no voting rights on issues such as election of the board or mergers. Such shares are usually issued to individuals who want to invest in the company's profitability and success, but are not interested in voting rights. Preference shares are typically non-voting shares. Such shares help in making the company a closely held company and act as a takeover defence.

For example, Warren Buffet's Berkshire Hathway Corporation has two classes of shares—Class A shares that are voting shares and Class B that are non-voting shares. The Class B shares carry $1/200^{th}$ of the voting rights of the Class A, but $1/30^{th}$ of the dividends.

2.4.13 Pac-Man Defence

This strategy is commonly used to prevent a hostile takeover. Here the target company counters the takeover bid by trying to acquire the bidder's company by making a counter offer to purchase the business of the acquiring company. This diverts the attention of the acquirer, who becomes busy in preventing the takeover of his own company. The hostile takeover attempt of Martin Marietta by Bendix Corporation in 1982 is a good example. In response to the takeover bid, Martin Marietta started buying Bendix stock with the aim of assuming control over the company. Bendix persuaded Allied Corporation to act as a 'white knight', and the company was sold to Allied Corporation the same year.

2.4.14 Pension Parachute

Companies often carry surplus cash in their pension fund, which is put to use as and when companies require resources. A pension parachute is a type of poison pill strategy that prevents the acquirer from going ahead with a hostile takeover by utilizing the surplus cash in the pension fund for financing the acquisition. Pension parachute, through corporate governance practices, ensures that the resources in the pension fund account are not put to use for financing the hostile takeover. The surplus funds remain the property of the plan's participants in the target company.

The concept of pension parachute was evolved by the law firm Kelley Dyer and Warren, and was implemented in Union Carbide. The design was upheld in Union Carbide's litigation with GAF Corporation. The hostile takeover bid was eventually withdrawn by GAF Corporation, which gained $81 million from the sales of Union Carbide stock.

2.4.15 People Pill

This is another defensive strategy adopted to ward off a hostile takeover. Under this strategy, the management of the target company threatens the acquirer that in the event of a takeover, the entire management team will resign. This strategy is a variation of poison pill defence strategy.

2.4.16 Lollipop Defence

This is a strategy wherein the target creates barriers outside its periphery to protect the company from a takeover. It is called lollipop defence as the company is compared to a lollipop, which has a hard, crunchy exterior but a soft, chewy centre. That is, the takeover is made difficult due to the initial barriers, but the company in general is an attractive takeover target (soft, chewy centre). The target company presumes that creating a lollipop-type defence provides adequate security from the takeover attempt. However, once the acquirer is able to overcome these barriers, the target stands exposed and takeover is only a matter of time.

2.4.17 Macaroni Defence

This is another takeover defence strategy wherein the company issues a large number of bonds in the market. These bonds carry a peculiar condition—if the company is taken over, the bonds will have to be redeemed at a very high price. The high redemption price of the bonds acts as a deterrent and the acquirer may be forced to give up its takeover bid.

The strategy is called macaroni defence as the redemption price of the bonds starts increasing (expanding) if the target is facing any danger of takeover, the same way macaroni being cooked in a pot does.

2.4.18 Lobster Trap

A lobster trap is an anti-takeover strategy whereby the target firm issues a charter preventing individuals with more than 10% ownership of convertible securities such as convertible bonds, convertible preference shares, and warrants from transferring these securities to voting stock. This charter becomes a barrier and hostile takeover becomes difficult. If the acquirer enters this trap, it becomes difficult to exit as the acquirer can neither acquire controlling stake in the business of the target, nor can it exit from the limited stake acquired. As a result of this decision, all that the acquirer can do is to repent its decision of making a takeover attempt. Exhibit 2.1 describes the derivation of the concept.

Exhibit 2.1   Lobster trap

To understand the relevance and utility of a lobster trap, one needs to understand what it actually is. It is a portable trap with a frame, traditionally made out of wood (nowadays of plastic), that is surrounded by a rope mesh. The traps have an opening that permit the lobster to enter a tunnel of netting—a rope mesh. The traps have two parts—the chamber and the parlour. The chamber is the area containing the bait, and it ultimately leads the victim to the parlour, the area where the lobster finally gets trapped. The traps are so designed that they have one-way entrances only and once the lobster enters the parlour, it cannot come out. Similarly, in this form of takeover defence, once the acquirer enters such a lobster trap, he cannot get out of it.

2.4.19 Shark Repellent/Porcupine Defence or Provision

Shark repellent is another measure in the series of measures taken by a target company to fend off a hostile takeover attempt. In this case, the target company makes special amendments to its bylaws that become active only when a takeover attempt is announced. The objective of these special amendments is to make the takeover less attractive to the acquirer. Shark repellent is a repellent applied by deep sea divers to prevent sharks from attacking them. In a takeover situation, the acquirer is the shark and the proposed amendments repel the shark and prevent the attack. It is important to remember that such measures are not always in the best interest of the shareholders, as they may adversely affect the financial health of the company and result in deviating the attention of management from critical business objectives.

Some of the strategies that also fall under the umbrella of shark repellent defence are poison pills, scorched earth policy, golden parachutes, and safe harbour strategies.

2.4.20 Poison Put

Poison put, also called event risk covenant, is a strategy where the bondholders and stockholders are assigned a right whereby they can demand redemption of stock before maturity, at a value in excess of the par value or purchase the company's shares at a very attractive fixed price in case of restructuring of the company, excess distribution of dividend, a leveraged buyout (LBO), or a hostile takeover attempt. Such a condition helps the management of the company to deter the takeover attempt by making the target very costly for the acquirer.

It is important to remember that this strategy can work against the company too. In times of low liquidity, the bondholders often pressurize the company to go into reorganization or to increase borrowing costs.

2.4.21 Safe Harbour

Safe harbour is a type of shark repellent that works as explained in Section 2.4.19. Here again, the target company creates barriers making it difficult for the acquirer to succeed in its takeover attempt. The barriers work to keep the target safe in the harbour and beyond the reach of the acquirer, the shark.

2.4.22 Scorched-earth Defence

The concept of scorched earth originated as a military strategy, wherein a retreating army would burn crops and trees, so that the advancing enemy would be starved of fresh supplies. As an anti-defence strategy, the scorched earth policy involves liquidating valuable and desired assets and assuming fresh liabilities, so that the proposed takeover becomes unattractive to the acquiring firm.

2.4.23 Showstopper

The concept of a showstopper implies inserting a clause that imposes an additional financial burden on the acquirer in the event of a takeover. Here, the acquirer is required to pay for the offer within a stipulated period. If the acquirer fails to pay the dues, the shareholders of the target may grant extension, subject to the acquirer agreeing to pay interest to the shareholders for the delayed payment. If the acquirer refuses to pay the additional amount, the agreement falls through. In both the events, the acquirer is the loser. If the deals fall through, the acquirer has to compensate the target; if the acquirer agrees to pay the interest, it imposes financial burden on the acquirer. Since this clause has the potential of creating financial burden on the acquirer, it deters the acquirer from going ahead with the takeover.

2.4.24 Staggered Board of Directors

A staggered board of directors is a defence wherein a certain percentage of the company's directors is replaced every year, instead of the entire board being replaced annually. This strategy makes it difficult for the acquirer to seize control over the target, as the hostile bidder has to win more than one proxy fight at successive shareholder meetings to exercise control over the target.

To facilitate staggering, the directors are classified into Class I, Class II, etc. Each class is required to vacate its post by rotation. It is for this reason that such a board is also identified as a 'classified' board.

Institutional shareholders in the US have been increasingly asking for an end to staggering boards of directors so that the practice of retiring by rotation comes to an end. This practice often results in all desirable names dropping from the list of the directors, which can affect the investor's confidence.

2.4.25 Standstill Agreement

In this form of hostile takeover defence, an unfriendly bidder agrees to limit his holdings of a target firm. This is made possible by the target firm's willingness to purchase the potential acquirer's (raider's) shares at a premium price. This offer goes a long way in enacting a standstill or eliminating the chances of a takeover attempt by the potential raider. This strategy also gives the target company some time to build up other takeover defences. While the strategy may be beneficial to the target company, equity shareholders dislike the same, for it limits the potential return on investment available through takeover.

Standstill agreements can also take another form, where two or more parties agree not to deal with other parties on a particular matter for a specified period of time. Here the target and the purchaser may enter into an agreement that they would not go ahead with an acquisition of other parties. Such an agreement allows the concerned parties to devote more time for negotiation, due diligence, and the details of a potential acquisition/defence they are currently working on.

2.4.26 Targeted Repurchase

In this strategy, the target firm purchases back its own shares from an unfriendly bidder at a price well above market value. The number of shares purchased help the target firm to regain controlling interest in the company by having adequate shareholder votes to prevent the hostile acquisition from taking place. If the strategy results in abandonment of the takeover attempt, targeted repurchase can be considered a success.

While the target company offers the best possible price, it is not necessary that the raider company accepts the same. In such a situation, the raider would continue with its attempt of hostile takeover and the target generally combines the targeted repurchase offer with another strategy, such as setting up a holding company that receives all acquired shares and begins the process of converting the same into the employee stock ownership plan (ESOPs). This obviously defeats the very objective of pursuing a hostile takeover attempt. The raider is left with no other option but to accept the market price for the shares under their control. If they do not accept it, they have to face the risk of the shares they have acquired becoming worthless once the ESOP is approved by the regulatory authorities.

2.4.27 Top-up

A top-up is a type of stock repurchase program wherein shares are repurchased from the existing shareholders of the company. The buyback results in immediate reduction of the voting power of the shareholders. However, the shareholders may subsequently increase their holdings through additional purchase which is called a top-up. For example, if Company X holds 10% shares in a company, it has 10% voting power too. Company Y offers to purchase 5% of the shares from Company X with the latter's consent. This purchase also reduces the voting power of Company X to 5%. If at a later date, Company X wants to increase its voting rights to say 8%, it can purchase 3% shares from the open market. This 3% purchase is called top-up.

The only advantage of top-up strategy is that it provides the target company with time for enhancing and strengthening its takeover defence mechanism.

2.4.28 Treasury Stock

Treasury stocks, also known as reacquired stocks, are shares/stock bought back by the issuing company with the objective of reducing the amount of outstanding stock in the open market. This strategy is a tax-efficient tool of giving cash to shareholders instead of dividends, which is perceived to be the routine obligation of the company. This strategy is adopted by companies to protect themselves against a takeover threat. It is also resorted to when the company feels that its shares are undervalued in the open market. The shares repurchased are either cancelled or held for reissue. If such shares are not cancelled, they are known as treasury shares/stock.

Treasury stocks have the following characteristics:

- They do not involve payment of any dividend.
- They have no voting rights.
- The total treasury stock should not exceed the maximum proportion of total capitalization specified by relevant legal provisions of a country.
- The possession of treasury shares does not give the company the right to vote, exercise the rights of a shareholder, receive cash dividends, or receive any part of the assets of the company on liquidation.

2.4.29 White Knight

This is a situation where a target faces a hostile takeover attempt from a company and is struggling to avoid the same. At this moment, another company makes a friendly takeover offer to the target company to help the target successfully avoid the hostile takeover bid. Since the friendly takeover offer is to save the target from the hostile attempt, the company making the friendly offer is called a white knight.

2.4.30 White Squire

A white squire is similar to a white knight. The only difference is that a white squire exercises a significant minority stake, as opposed to a majority stake. A white squire does not have any intention of getting involved in the takeover battle, but serves as a figurehead in defending the target in a hostile takeover. The white squire enjoys special voting rights for the equity stake that it holds in the company.

2.4.31 Voting Plan or Voting Rights Plan

This is a type of poison pill that the target company issues against hostile takeover attempts. This plan is implemented when the company's constitution provides for shares that carry superior voting rights compared to ordinary shares. When an unfriendly bidder acquires a substantial voting stock, it may still not be able to exercise control because the stock carrying superior voting rights will help the company fight the hostile takeover bid. For example, Asarco had a voting pattern wherein holding 99% of the company's common stock would give the holders only 16.5% of the voting power. Poison pill is a term that refers to any strategy, generally in business or politics, to increase the likelihood of negative results over positive ones for a party that attempts any kind of takeover.

2.4.32 Whitemail

Whitemail is another takeover defence strategy wherein the target company issues a large number of shares at a price quite below the market price to a friendly party. This forces the acquiring company to purchase these shares from the third party to complete the takeover. This strategy discourages the takeover as it becomes more difficult and expensive and the corporate raider must purchase shares from a party which is friendly to the target company. Once the takeover attempt is averted, the target company may either buy back the issued shares or leave them floating in the market.

2.5 BENEFITS OF TAKEOVERS

A takeover is expected to generate the following benefits:
- It helps the acquirer to attain increase in sales/revenues.
- The acquirer is able to venture into new business segments and markets with ease.
- The overall profitability of the entities improves.
- It helps the acquirer in increasing its market share.
- It reduces competition from the perspective of the acquiring company.
- The industry can reduce over-capacity by cutting down the scale of operations in the new entity.

- It helps the acquirer to expand its brand portfolio.
- The new entity is able to attain the benefits of economies of scale.
- It helps attain increased efficiency as a result of corporate synergies.
- It helps in eliminating jobs that overlap in responsibilities, thus helping in reduction of the operating costs.

2.6 DISADVANTAGES OF TAKEOVERS

A takeover results in the following disadvantages:

- It results in reduced competition and thus reduced choice for consumers.
- It results in job cuts, as the acquirer tries to reduce operating costs.
- The firms that merge may suffer from cultural differences that may lead to conflict with the new management.
- The acquirer is often burdened with the hidden liabilities of the target entity.
- The employees of the target company work in an environment of fear and uncertainty, which affects their motivational levels.

2.7 TAKEOVER CODE

The year 1992 marked the beginning of a new chapter in Indian capital markets. The year saw the enactment of the Securities and Exchange Board of India (SEBI) Act, 1992, under which SEBI was established as a regulatory body to regulate and promote the development of the securities market, and protect the interest of investors. One area of concern was that of corporate takeovers, which was viewed as an unhealthy corporate practice.

To curb the negative impact of takeovers, SEBI issued the Substantial Acquisition of Shares and Takeover Regulations in 1994. These regulations covered both friendly and hostile takeovers. In a friendly takeover, SEBI was keen to ensure that the minority shareholders got fair treatment. This should be achieved without any major hurdles, for the shareholders favour friendly takeovers and are willing to accept the offer that comes their way if it is the best option under the given circumstances. The concern was deeper in case of hostile takeovers where the company intending a takeover made the move unknown to the target's management.

The Board incorporated provisions to promote transparency in the takeover process. These regulations, however, excluded the 'bailout' form of takeover—including cases where financial institutions have invested either by way of equity or have granted term loans, and companies that were under the purview of the Board for Industrial and Financial Reconstruction (BIFR). The SEBI provisions were found inadequate due to in-built ambiguity and loop holes, and the Board's efforts to promote transparency in takeovers did not succeed.

In view of repeated failures, SEBI appointed a committee under the chairmanship of Justice P.N. Bhagwati to review the guidelines issued in 1994 and to study the effect of takeovers and mergers on securities market and to evolve appropriate provisions for regulating takeovers and mergers.

The Bhagwati committee stated the necessity for a takeover code on the grounds that the confidence of retail investors in capital markets is a crucial factor for their development. Therefore, their interest needs to be protected and an exit opportunity should be given to investors if they do not want to continue with the new management. Full and truthful disclosure should be made of all material information relating to an open offer to enable them to take an informed decision. The committee also recommended that the acquirer ensure adequate financial resources for the payment of acquisition price to the investors so that the process of acquisition and mergers will be completed in a time-bound manner. Disclosures will be made of all material transactions at the earliest opportunity.

As a major step towards protecting the interest of the minority shareholders, Clause 40 A and B of the Listing Agreements were introduced. These clauses prescribe a basic framework pertaining to initial disclosure before going ahead with acquisition of shares from the public.

Although the regulations are being made more stringent, due to the manner in which the Indian corporate sector is evolving, there is a strong need to keep reviewing them so that they remain contemporary. India's takeover code does not permit a 'poison pill' defence, but it empowers Indian companies to block hostile takeovers by foreign companies through Press Note 18 (see Exhibit 2.2). This is the 18th in a series of press releases issued by the Ministry of Industry in 1998 and reads as follows:

- The automatic route for foreign direct investment (FDI) and/or technology collaboration would not be available to those who have or had any previous joint venture (JV) or technology transfer/trademark agreement in the same or allied field in India. The Reserve Bank of India, therefore, has to stipulate a necessary declaration before applications for the automatic route are taken on record.
- Investors of technology to the suppliers of the automatic route category, therefore, will have to necessarily seek the Foreign Investment Promotion Board/Project Approval Board (FIPB/PAB) route for JVs or technology transfer agreements (including trademarks) giving detailed circumstances in which they find it necessary to set up a new JV/enter into new technology transfer (including trademark).
- The onus is clearly on such investors/technology suppliers to provide the requisite justification and also proof to the satisfaction of FIPB/PAB that the new proposal would not in any way jeopardize the interests of the existing JV or technology/trademark partner or other stakeholders. It will be at the sole discretion of FIPB/PAB to either approve the application with or without conditions or to reject it in toto, duly recording the reasons for doing so.

This essentially means that foreign companies wanting to set up new operations in India must furnish a no objection certificate from their Indian JV partners, past or present. This certificate has to be submitted to the FIPB, which is the Indian foreign investment clearing authority under the Ministry of Industry. The Board would use its discretionary powers to clear the new JV or permit the enhancement of foreign equity in an existing JV.

While takeovers may not be the best way of corporate restructuring, they appear to be a necessary evil. It is, therefore, necessary to have proper regulatory framework in place to exploit their benefits and mitigate or avoid their shortcomings. Given the fact that takeover attempts lead to the creation of monopolies and thus build anti-consumer fervour, it would be difficult to for companies formed by takeovers to get acceptance, given that the consumer movement is getting stronger globally. Another cause for concern is that there are many anti-takeover strategies, but their utility is case-specific. A company facing a takeover attempt cannot resort to all the strategies. It needs to understand the situation and adopt a suitable defence strategy accordingly. However, one cannot also deny the fact that takeovers are here to stay, for they have their roots in the universal human desire to grow and get powerful.

SUMMARY

Takeovers are a direct outcome of the corporate desire to grow big and powerful. When one evaluates the benefits and disadvantages, the former outweigh the latter. Given the fact that even closed economies are opening up their boundaries to companies from across the globe, expansion beyond national boundaries is becoming a reality. As a result, companies today have greater opportunities to spread their business across the globe. As it may not be possible for all companies to enter new markets on their own, takeover appears to be a simpler option. In spite of numerous takeover defence and legal provisions, takeovers may be difficult to eradicate from the corporate world. One needs to learn to live with this necessary evil.

KEY DEFINITIONS

Bailout takeover This takeover involves takeover of a financially sick company by a financially rich company as per the provisions of the Sick Industrial Companies (Special Provisions) Act, 1985.

Conglomerate takeover When a company takes over another company from a totally different industry, it is termed as conglomerate takeover. This is pursued with the objective of attaining diversification.

Friendly takeover This is a takeover where the acquirer acquires the shares of the target by informing the board of directors of its intention to purchase the shares of the target company. When the board feels that the offer is worth accepting, it recommends to the shareholders that the offer be accepted. Here the acquirer may either acquire the assets or the purchase of the stock of the target.

Horizontal takeover When a company takes over another company from the same industry, the takeover is referred to as horizontal takeover.

Hostile takeover In such takeovers, the board of directors of the target firm disagrees with the offer of the acquirer to purchase the shares, but the acquirer continues to pursue it or makes the offer by-passing the target company's management. The acquirer may also make an offer without informing the target company's management about its intention of acquiring a stake in the company.

Par value Par value represents the face value of a share or stock. It is the value that is specified in the constitution of the company that is registered with different statutory bodies.

Reverse takeover It is a takeover strategy where a private company acquires a public company.

Substantial acquisition of interest It is a process of takeover where an acquirer acquires a substantial quantity of shares or voting rights of the target company.

Takeover Takeover is a process wherein an acquirer takes over control of the target company.

Takeover code Takeover code is a set of statutory provisions that helps provide the target company and its shareholders with necessary protection from takeover attempts.

Takeover defences Takeover defences are strategies adopted by the target company to prevent its takeover by another company.

Vertical takeover When a company is taken over by any of its vendors or customers, it is referred to as vertical takeover. When the business of the vendor is taken over, it is called backward takeover while when the business of the customer is taken over it is termed as forward takeover.

CONCEPT REVIEW QUESTIONS

2.1 Explain the concept of takeovers. State and explain the different types of takeover strategies.
2.2 Do takeovers always succeed? What strategies do target companies employ to thwart takeover attempts?
2.3 Enumerate the benefits and disadvantages of takeovers.
2.4 Write notes on the following:
   (a) Takeover code
   (b) Forms of takeovers
   (c) Reverse takeover
   (d) Takeover defences
   (e) Poison pill/Super poison put
   (f) Leveraged recapitalization
   (g) Lock-up provision
   (h) Lollipop defence
   (i) Lobster trap
   (j) Staggered board of directors
   (k) Targeted repurchase
   (l) Treasury stock
   (m) Benefits of takeovers

PROJECT ASSIGNMENT

Study one example of each of the following:
   (a) Hostile takeover
   (b) Friendly takeover

Provide an in-depth analysis on the issues involved and results attained. What could have been done to generate better results?

REFERENCE

Weston, F.J., Mitchell, M.L., and Mulherin, J.H., *Takeovers, Restructuring, and Corporate Governance*, Prentice Hall, New Jersey, 2003

CASE STUDY

Imperial Chemical Industries' Failed Attempt to Takeover Asian Paints

Abstract
Imperial Chemical Industries (ICI) was looking at an opportunity to enter the Indian market. Instead of entering on its own, ICI wanted to make an entry by taking over a major player

in the Indian market. The company shortlisted Asian Paints as the right target to fulfil its aspirations. While the target was appropriate, the legal framework was not very conducive. This is something ICI realized a little too late. This case analyses ICI's attempt to take over Asian paints in 1997. It goes into the history of the British giant and highlights why the takeover failed. The case also peeps into Asian Paints' strategy of acquiring Government of India's stake in ICI.

Pedagogical Objectives
- To understand and identify the strategy adopted by ICI to enter the Indian market
- To identify the legal hurdles faced by ICI
- To identify the defence mechanism adopted by Asian Paints to prevent the takeover

Introduction
Imperial Chemical Industries (now taken over by AkzoNobel) was not just a premier chemical-manufacturing company of Great Britain, but also one of the most innovative companies in the world. Since its inception in 1926, ICI sought patents on more than 33,000 inventions for products ranging from chemotherapy drugs to insulating materials and polymers.

In 1993, the company reinvented itself as a new industrial giant in paint and explosives, further consolidating its reputation and tradition of developing heavy chemicals. The new ICI offered a group of world businesses with leading positions in explosives, paints, titanium dioxide, and other versatile materials such as polyurethane, polyester film, and acrylics.

The Beginning
Imperial Chemical Industries was formed in 1926 by the merger of four of Great Britain's major chemical companies—Nobel Explosives Limited (NEL), Brunner, Mond and Company Limited (BMCL), United Alkali Company (UAC), and British Dyestuffs Corporation (BDC). The birth of ICI also coincided with the rise of two other great chemical cartels: DuPont and I.G. Farben.

Of these, the most famous company was NEL, the dynamite business founded by Swede Alfred Nobel, which was largely shaped by Nobel's inventions. The founder of BMCL was Ludwig Mond, who with his partner John Brunner successfully built a strong alkali business. They produced alkalis using the Solvay, rather than the Leblanc process. The third partner of ICI was UAC, which since its conception was the largest chemical business in the world with a capitalization of more than £8 million. The fourth entity in the merger, BDC, was the youngest among the four.

World War I
At the beginning of World War I, NEL was a major ammunition supplier. But as the war progressed, there was less open warfare than predicted. It developed into an extended siege and thus came to rely more on high explosives than bullets. These high explosives were very different in composition from NEL's gunpowder. The TNT and luddite used by the English troops included coal-tar derivatives. Suddenly, BDC became a strategic player and found itself manufacturing armaments. Since TNT could be used more economically when mixed with ammonium nitrate, BMCL was also pressed into service, along with UAC.

By 1926, NEL and BMCL had emerged as the two largest companies in the otherwise shaky British chemical industry. The merger of several German chemical firms into I.G. Farben, the largest cartel in the world and the direct competitor of British companies for exports caused tremors in the industry. In light of this, NEL and BMCL considered joining I.G. Farben, but were unable to reach a satisfactory agreement with the Germans. So after months of negotiations, they decided to form a British cartel, led by Sir Harry McGowen of NEL and Sir Alfred Mond of BMCL. During this period, BDC and UAC, already weakened by a worldwide depression, were in no position to withstand pressure from their more powerful competitors, and therefore agreed to merge. The merged entities decided on the name 'Imperial,' for it intended to represent the company's ongoing importance to the British Empire and beyond.

The Birth of ICI

Imperial Chemical Industries began doing business on 1 January 1927, with 33,000 employees. The newly-formed company was divided into main product areas for alkalis, dyestuffs, explosives, general chemicals that included chlorine, acids, synthetic ammonia and metals. It also concentrated on producing cellulose products, fertilizers, lime, and a rubberized fabric known as 'leathercloth'. In 1928, the company moved into its new headquarters on Milbank, facing the Houses of Parliament in London.

In the initial years, ICI focussed on growth through fertilizers and 10% of its capital was invested in a £20 million fertilizer plant in Bellingham, England. However, the depression of 1929 in the US resulted in a fall in the demand for fertilizers, and the native demand was inadequate to support the Bellingham plant. With the intention of partially protecting its investment, ICI entered into an agreement with I.G. Farben, which established production quotas for nitrogen, the main ingredient in fertilizer. Subsequently, in 1935, the companies agreed that I.G. Farben would sell nitrogen all over Europe except in Spain, Portugal, and South and Central America, whereas ICI would control the markets in the UK, Spain, Portugal, Indonesia, and the Canary Islands. The Asian market was to be shared by both the companies.

The agreement with I.G. Farben did not help the nitrogen sales of ICI and the Bellingham plant was eventually closed, resulting in ICI's return on equity dropping to 4%. The company then tried to produce oil from coal, but could not make much headway in its fortunes despite government subsidies. These two failures forced ICI to finally give more attention to its neglected dyestuffs division.

Plastics: The New Mantra for Success

The world started producing a wide variety of synthetic substitutes used for materials such as wood, leather, and metal, and called it 'plastic'. British dye makers never used their knowledge of chemistry to diversify into plastics, specialty chemicals, or pharmaceuticals. But in 1929, ICI's alkali division discovered polyethylene, which revolutionized ICI's product range. ICI patented polyethylene and started selling it as an insulating material. In 1937, the company formed the plastics division and was assigned the task of developing its use as a moulding material. The dyestuffs division started focussing on its textile uses and the alkali division began focussing on the use of polyethylene for electrical and other unspecified uses. This was where the use of polyethylene ended. With the breaking out of World War II, scientists started using polyethylene to provide electrical insulation to radar masts. Every industry producing light metals and guns, mustard gas, detonators, and alloys started demanding ICI's chemicals. However, ICI was reluctant to expand its operations, for it realized that its capacity would remain idle once the war got over. Fortunately for ICI, they reached an agreement with the British government, whereby the government paid for the construction of new plants and ICI managed them for a reasonable fee.

After the war, ICI had to fight an antitrust suit brought by the US against the 800 agreements ICI had signed with DuPont to regulate competition, and most of ICI's productive capacity became obsolete. The 1950s did not see much growth for ICI as it had lost its monopoly over the chemical markets of Britain and its colonies, and was still dependent on its outmoded productive capacity and old-fashioned managerial style. As a result, ICI failed to defend its old territory and also failed to take advantage of the opportunities that 'decartelization' offered. Things did not change until the mid-1960s and ICI continued its tryst with destiny, manufacturing hundreds of products inefficiently. This made *Forbes* magazine comment: 'Nothing short of a full-scale industrial revolution could have saved ICI.' But increased exports and larger and more efficient plants saved the company from bankruptcy.

The 1960s saw ICI initiating ambitious expansion plans including setting up an ethylene cracker plant in Britain, fibre spinning operations in Germany, and a huge PVC plant in Bayonne, New Jersey. This course was full of inherent risks, including overcapacity. But nonetheless, this expansion permitted ICI to produce chemicals at a more competitive price. ICI also brought about drastic internal changes and shop employees began to be paid weekly rather than hourly wages, along with substantial raises. As a result, these workers began assuming duties and responsibilities that had previously been the concern of supervisors. By the early 1970s, productivity had climbed to 11%, although ICI lagged behind its competitors. The 1970s saw an erratic swing in the profits of ICI. During this decade, ICI continued to focus its attention on the US and not on Europe. When ICI purchased Atlas Chemical Industries, it was issued a restraint of trade judgment. As a result, ICI had to sell the Atlas Explosives division. These steps showed the inexperience of the management, which continued to concentrate more on American investments than on further acquisitions. The company remained a large and often inefficient company committed to many unprofitable products.

Change of Guard—Change in Fortunes

In 1982, Sir John Harvey-Jones took over the reins of ICI. This charismatic leader cut costs ruthlessly, laying off thousands of workers and closing dozens of plants in an effort to improve the company's finances. He ended ICI's dependence on bulk chemicals, which had accounted for 40% of profits in 1979, but had dropped to just 16% after three years under his stewardship. He also de-emphasized polyethylene and concentrated on higher margin products such as drugs and specialty chemicals instead. The results were impressive and by 1983, profits had climbed to $939 million—more than twice that of the previous year. Harvey-Jones also started exploring the possibilities of making additions to the company's product line. One of the most interesting products was polyester produced by genetically engineered bacteria fed on starch and water. This bacteria-produced polyester had some initial success as surgical stitching.

The Takeover Era

The 1980s saw ICI launch a major acquisition campaign, expanding investments in its North American division. ICI purchased Beatrice's Chemical division for $750 million and followed it by many smaller purchases including that of Glidden Paint. This acquisition increased ICI's paint shipments by 7%, twice the industry average. While acquisitions continued, ICI continued to face problems with bulk chemicals and decreased fertilizer sales. Additionally, the plastics market was plagued by overcapacity, and ICI had to adapt to become less dependent on its former staples. The company also found itself laden with slow-moving products and this made competition internationally difficult.

The Demerger Strategy

In 1993, ICI embarked on what its officials called 'a journey of change and transformation.' The company decided to separate its bioscience businesses—including agricultural chemicals, pharmaceuticals, seeds, and biological products—into a publicly listed company, known as Zeneca Group, which later merged to become AstraZeneca. This 'demerger' brought cheer to the company and resulted in a substantial increase in company profitability. Most notably, four years later, when ICI made its biggest acquisition to date with a $8 billion purchase of four businesses from Unilever: National Starch, Quest, Unichema, and Crosfield. This marked the company's first move into the modern age by focusing on specialty products and paints on a global scale.

The company completed that restructuring, enabling it to concentrate on growing the business and improving its performance and margins worldwide. Charles Miller Smith, the COO of the company, stated, 'In just over three years, ICI has transformed itself into one of the world's leading providers of specialty products, including food, flavour, and fragrance ingredients, as well as remaining a world leader in paints.'

Since that acquisition, ICI sold off other entities to improve its focus on paint-related products. Between 1997 and 2001, ICI claimed to make more than £6.1 billion from divestments, selling its polyester businesses primarily to DuPont, acrylics to Ineos Acrylics, and other product lines and holdings to PPG and Hunstman. It also spent more than £5.7 billion in acquisitions, investing in entities such as the catalyst science company Systenix and the specialty chemical company Uniqema.

In 1997, ICI attempted a hostile takeover attempt of Asian Paints. It purchased 3.66 million Asian Paints shares, representing a 9.1% stake, from Atul Choksey, one of the three promoters of the company and its former managing director. The two other promoters were the Dani and the Vakil families. The company's acquisition was at ₹350 a share.

However, the Asian Paints board refused to transfer the shares in ICI's name. The reason cited for this refusal was that it would result in compromising shareholders' interests and breach of the provisions of Press Note 18. Imperial Chemical Industries maintained that the stake was not acquired through a hostile bid or any backdoor methods, and had in fact made a global offer to acquire the Choksey stake. The company also argued that they had not forced any promoter to sell their stocks to them. They had made their intentions clear on the very day of purchase of the shares to the three principal promoters.

The company management also went on record to state that it was not interested in bringing in a change in management, but only wanted to forge a business alliance, which would mean a value addition to Asian Paints, its promoters, and shareholders, including ICI.

Being a conservative company, ICI had in fact taken the approval of the Reserve Bank of India for the purchase of the shares, along with legal opinion from leading lawyers in India on the deal.

The company had also taken all precautions such as acquiring less than 10% stake that would not require approval from the Foreign Investment Promotion Board (FIPB) so that the investment did not get classified as foreign direct investment (FDI). A stake of less than 10% would be insignificant in terms of effecting any change in management control, but it still faced many hurdles (Exhibit 2.2).

Imperial Chemical Industries paid the entire dues for the shares acquired, but the shares continued to be in the names of Atul Choksey and associates in the books of the company and continued to be in the custody by investment bankers, Kotak Mahindra. Then ICI approached the FIPB for permission to transfer the shares in its name, but failed to get approval since ICI did not have a 'no objection certificate' from the Asian Paints board, where the Danis and Vakils had a healthy presence through their holdings. When all the efforts of ICI to get the shares transferred failed, the custodian was forced to sell 1.88 million shares—or half of ICI's total acquisition—to the Indian government-owned mutual fund, Unit Trust of India (UTI), at around ₹281 per share in May 1998. The remaining half of ICI's block of holdings was finally sold to the Danis and Vakils in November 1999.

Many experts argue that the provisions of Press Note 18 apply to JVs and that wholly owned subsidiaries are outside its purview. But this is only partially the case. Though India permits 100% FDI in most sectors, one needs to understand that India opened up gradually, permitting FDI in various sectors in stages. The FDI caps were initially fixed at 26% or 49%, depending on the sector. These caps were gradually raised to 100% after FDI gained larger acceptance. While many Fortune 500 companies were keen on making investments in India in the first phase of liberalization, they had to enter through the JV route since only JVs were permitted. It is important to note that the provisions of Press Note 18 apply to all JVs. Besides, they are also applicable to applications moved by a company before the FIPB prior to the issue of Press Note 18, but which were still under consideration when the note was issued.

At present, the opinion within the bureaucracy is that since the domestic industry has gone through the consolidation phase and is ready to take on competition, Press Note 18 should be removed, and all hostile takeovers, irrespective of whether they are of Indian or foreign origin, should be regulated under India's takeover code. Exhibit 2.2 provides details on Press Note 18.

Discussion Questions

1. Analyse the case with reference to the growth and diversification strategies adopted by ICI.
2. Do you think ICI lacked direction? What more could ICI have done to ensure the success of its takeover attempt of Asian Paints?

Exhibit 2.2   Press Note 18

In January 2005, the Indian Prime Minister announced the scrapping of the contentious Press Note 18 pertaining to foreign financial or technical collaboration under the automatic approval route with effect from January 2005. The scrapping of restrictive Press Note 18 was hailed as, and has proved to be, a positive step towards further liberalizing foreign direct investment regulations in India.

Press Note 18

Under Press Note 18, the automatic route (which requires no prior regulatory approval) for foreign investment was not available to foreign investors having an existing or previous venture or technology transfer/trademark agreement in the same or allied field in India. Investors having a previous or existing venture or technology transfer/trademark agreement in the same or allied field in India required prior FIPB approval for such investment.

To obtain FIPB approval, the foreign investor had to give detailed circumstances in which they found it necessary to set up a new JV/enter into new technology transfer (including trademark). The onus was on such investors/technology suppliers to provide the requisite justification as also proof to the satisfaction of the FIPB that the new proposal would not in any way jeopardize the interests of the existing JV or technology/trade-mark partner or other stakeholders.

In implementing Press Note 18, the Indian government, in practice, required a letter/ certificate from the existing Indian JV partner that it had no objection to the foreign partner's new investment proposal in the same or allied field.

Press Note 18 was issued in the wake of the liberalization policy of the Government of India, which allowed 100% foreign direct investment in almost all sectors of the economy without prior regulatory approval. Prior to the 'opening up' of these sectors to 100% foreign direct investment, JV was the popular mode of foreign investment in India in view of ceilings on foreign investment in several sectors. The objective of Press Note 18, it appears, was to protect the Indian JV partner against the prospect of the foreign JV partner walking out of the existing JV and joining hands with another Indian party or establishing its wholly-owned Indian subsidiary.

Scrapping of Press Note 18

According to the terms of Press Note 1 of 2005, new JVs and technical collaborations will no longer be governed by the provisions of Press Note 18.

Pursuant to the scrapping of Press Note 18, the concerned restrictive provisions of Press Note 18 have been done away with for all future JV in India between an Indian company and its foreign partners. In the new dispensation, new JV and collaborations are being based on the free will of partners without any government interference.

An interesting development of Press Note 1 of 2005 is the acknowledgement that Indian companies as well as their foreign partners may contractually safeguard their interests in JVs through provisions in JVs/collaboration agreements that tackle 'conflict of interest' situations. For example, when a JV partner decides to invest in another JV or a fully-owned subsidiary in the same field of activity.

Non-applicability to Existing JVs

The JV existing at the time of scrapping of Press Note 18, however, continues to be protected by a few provisions of Press Note 18. Venture capital funds have, however, been exempted from the requirement of having to obtain a no objection certificate from local partners for new investments. Similar freedom has been extended to sick companies and JVs where either the domestic or foreign venture partner holds less than 3% shareholding. International financial institutions and FDI proposals in the information technology sector had been exempted from the applicability of Press Note 18 in the years 2001 and 2000, respectively.

The need for consent from both domestic and foreign venture partners will apply in the case of existing JVs only if the proposed sector of investment is the 'same' as the existing JV. Earlier, the need for consent also applied to proposed investments in an 'allied' sector as the existing JV. For purposes of Press Note 18, 'same' field means those activities that are covered under the same four-digit National Industrial Classification (NIC) 1987 code, while 'allied' field refers to those activities covered under the same three-digit NIC code.

3 Mergers and Acquisitions

LEARNING OBJECTIVES

After studying the chapter, you will be able to understand

- the concepts and genesis of mergers and acquisitions (M&As)
- the different types of M&As
- the difference between mergers and acquisitions, and the motives behind them
- the value drivers and difficulties encountered in M&As, and the reasons behind their failure
- the process of M&As, and the means of financing them
- the concepts of reverse merger and earn-outs
- M&As on the domestic front

3.1 INTRODUCTION

The corporate world is undergoing a paradigm shift, from expansion and diversification to ever-increasing mergers and acquisitions (M&As). Merger waves began in 1883 following the depression that ended that year. The first merger wave came about due to the economic expansion that occurred at the time (www.learnmergers.com). The initial trend was dominated by a few 'mega' deals involving corporate giants. However, today the whole picture is undergoing a sea change. Companies have started realizing that in the increasingly competitive, changing, and challenging environment, M&As can boost the value of their businesses.

Mergers and acquisitions have become a strategic tool that is being effectively used to acquire established brands and to expand to emerging and often low cost markets, particularly markets that provide an enormous number of skilled workers. They help counter competition, acquire new consumers, get a technological edge, improve bottom lines, etc. It is no wonder then that the corporate world is fast realizing that M&As are here to stay.

3.2 CONCEPT OF MERGER

A merger is a tool used by companies to increase their long-term profitability by expanding their operations. Mergers are carried out with mutual consent between the two companies merging with each other. The company buying the other company is called the merged or surviving entity, and the one merging with it is called the merging entity.

A merger is thus a strategy where two or more companies agree to combine their operations. Once the merger happens, one company survives and the other loses its corporate identity. The surviving company acquires all the assets and liabilities of the merging company. It either retains its identity or is re-christened.

The simplest definition of merger is, ' a combination of two or more businesses into one business'. Laws in India use the term 'amalgamation' for merger. The Income Tax Act, 1961 [Section 2(1A)] defines an amalgamation as the merger of one or more companies with another, or the merger of two or more companies to form a new company, in such a way that all assets and liabilities of the amalgamating companies become the assets and liabilities of the amalgamated company. Shareholders holding not less than nine-tenths in value of the shares in the amalgamating company or companies become shareholders of the amalgamated company (Income Tax Act, 1961—Bare Act).

Thus, as described in the act, mergers or amalgamations may take two forms (www.business.gov.in), as described in Sections 3.2.1 and 3.2.1.

3.2.1 Merger through Absorption

Absorption is a combination of two or more companies into an 'existing company'. All companies except one lose their identity in such a merger. For example, in the absorption of Tata Fertilizers Ltd (TFL) by Tata Chemicals Ltd (TCL), TCL, an acquiring company/buyer, survived after the merger whereas TFL, an acquired company/seller, ceased to exist. Tata Fertilizers Ltd transferred its assets, liabilities, and shares to TCL.

3.2.2 Merger through Consolidation

Consolidation is a combination of two or more companies into a 'new company'. In this form of merger, all companies are legally dissolved and a new entity is created. Here, the acquired company transfers its assets, liabilities, and shares to the acquiring company for cash or exchange of shares. For example, Hindustan Computers Ltd, Hindustan Instruments Ltd, Indian Software Company Ltd, and Indian Reprographics Ltd merged into an entirely new company called HCL Ltd.

A fundamental characteristic of mergers, either through absorption or consolidation, is that the acquiring company, existing or new, takes over the ownership of other companies and combines their operations with its own.

As per Accounting Standard 14 issued by ICAI in 1994 (Compendium of Accounting Standards, Accounting Standard 14), 'amalgamation' means an amalgamation pursuant to the provisions of the Companies Act, 1956 or any other statute that may be applicable to companies.

An amalgamation satisfies all the following conditions:

- After amalgamation, all the assets and liabilities of the transferor company become the assets and liabilities of the transferee company.
- Shareholders holding not less than 90% of the face value of the equity shares of the transferor company (other than the equity shares already held

therein, immediately before the amalgamation, by the transferee company, its subsidiaries, or their nominees) become equity shareholders of the transferee company by virtue of the amalgamation.

- The consideration for the amalgamation receivable by those equity shareholders of the transferor company who agree to become equity shareholders of the transferee company is discharged by the transferee company wholly by the issue of equity shares in the transferee company, except that cash may be paid in respect of any fractional shares.
- The business of the transferor company is intended to be carried on, after the amalgamation, by the transferee company.
- No adjustment is intended to be made to the book values of the assets and liabilities of the transferor company when they are incorporated in the financial statements of the transferee company, except to ensure uniformity of accounting policies.

The principal idea behind M&As is to create shareholder value that is over and above the sum of the two merging companies. This is achieved by creating a more competitive and cost-efficient company by gaining greater market share.

3.3 GENESIS OF MERGERS AND ACQUISITIONS

A detailed analysis of the history of M&As indicates that many merger movements occurred in the US, and every such movement was dominated by mergers of a particular type.

Some key observations of the merger movements of the so-called merger waves indicate:

- Merger movements often occur when the economy experiences sustained high rates of growth, as this reflects favourable business prospects.
- These movements coincide with developments in the business environment.
- The waves occur when firms respond to new investment and profit opportunities arising out of changes in economic conditions and technological innovations.
- They often result in efficient resource allocation, reallocation processes, and efficient resource utilization.
- In each of the waves, mistakes have been repeated and failures have been common.
- Mergers and acquisitions have become a global phenomenon and are no longer restricted to the US.
- A new trend that is being observed is the rise of acquirers from emerging markets.
- Research shows that merger waves result from a combination of economic, regulatory, and technological shocks (Mitchell and Mulherin 1996). Economic shocks deal with economic expansion that motivates companies to expand to meet the ever-growing demand. Regulatory shocks occur

when regulatory barriers are eliminated, paving the way for corporate communication. Technological shocks represent changes in technology that not only change the existing industries but also create new ones.

In the light of these factors, understanding the history of M&As becomes important. Let us now study the merger waves in brief.

3.3.1 First Wave (1897–1904)

The first wave of mergers occurred after the Great Depression of 1883. The wave peaked between 1898 and 1902, and ended in 1904. This wave affected all major mining and manufacturing industries. However, certain industries clearly demonstrated a higher incidence of merger activity (Nelson 1959). Professor Ralph Nelson's study showed that eight industries—primary metals, food products, petroleum products, chemicals, transportation equipment, fabricated metal products, machinery, and bituminous coal—saw nearly two-thirds of the merger activity.

The first wave saw predominantly horizontal mergers and industry consolidations resulting in near monopolistic market structures. Some of the giants born during this wave include JP Morgan, Standard Oil, General Electric, Eastman Kodak, American Tobacco Inc., Navistar International, and U.S. Steel (which merged 785 separate steel operations including DuPont Inc.)

This wave left political circles worried as a large number of monopolies came into existence, further aggravating the situation. Hence, the Sherman Act was enforced to check rising monopoly, but mergers continued unabated. Due to lack of sufficient manpower, the Justice Department could not aggressively pursue antitrust enforcements (Gaughan 2007).

The reasons for the growing number of M&As were as follows:

Interpretation of provisions of Sherman Act The US Supreme Court was initially unwilling to literally interpret the anti-monopoly provisions of the Act. In the case of American Sugar Refining Company, the court ruled that it was not a monopoly and hence did not restrain trade. This ruling was driven by the interpretation of the Sherman Act, which the court interpreted as an act focused on regulating stockholder trusts, through which investors would invest funds in a firm and entrust their stock certificates with directors who would ensure that they received dividends for their 'trust certificates' (Gaughan 2007). However, due to a misguided focus, the law was not applied to prevent the formation of monopolies in several industries.

Relaxation of corporation laws by some states As a result of this relaxation, companies got a chance to expand their operations without any legal hindrance. They were able to secure capital and acquire stock in other companies. However, M&As registered a decline in the states where the corporation laws were enforced (Gaughan 2007). This trend was not universal, as some states that did not relax the corporation laws also succeeded in curbing M&As.

Development of US transportation system This resulted in the growth of markets. Companies merged with other local companies to retain their market shares and to compete with their distant rivals (Gaughan 2007).

Expansion of firms This resulted in economies of scale in production and distribution, and greater efficiency. This encouraged companies to go for mass production and M&As were seen as a convenient way of achieving this (Federal Trade Commission Publication 1981).

The US economy also saw a few takeover battles wherein judges and elected officials were bribed to ignore legal provisions. During 1867–1868 in one such takeover involving the Erie Railroad, Cornelius Vanderbilt was pitted against Daniel Drew, Jim Fisk, and Jay Gould. This takeover attempt turned violent, leading to increased public awareness and concern about unethical business practices.

These events subsequently paved the way for tougher securities laws and antitrust legislations and the legal system got the teeth to discourage unethical takeover tactics.

3.3.2 Second Wave (1916–1929)

The second wave of mergers witnessed the consolidation of several industries. Unlike the earlier monopolies trend, the second wave was characterized by the rise of oligopolistic industry structure. This period is also referred to as the *period of oligopoly*. The events of the previous wave forced the US Congress to enact stricter laws that would prevent exploitation of the market and reduce the power wielded by monopolies (Gaughan 2007).

Several vertical mergers and oligopolies but fewer monopolies were produced in this wave. It was also a period of first large-scale conglomerates as many diverse and unrelated firms merged together. The wave also saw disproportionate numbers of mergers in primary metals, petroleum products, food products, chemicals, and transportation equipment (Gaughan 2007). Some of the prominent corporations of today such as General Motors, IBM, John Deere, and Union Carbide were born during this wave.

The US government had realized the threat posed by unfair business practices such as cartels or pools. It used the Clayton Act and the Sherman Act to crack down on unfair business practices (Gaughan 2007).

During this period, radio became popular as a medium of entertainment and companies started using it for advertising. The era of merchandizing and product differentiation thus began.

A number of legislations such as the Public Utility Holding Company Act, 1935, that empowered the SEC to regulate corporate structure and voting rights were enacted.

The worst fears were realized when the stock market crashed on 28 and 29 October 1929, by nearly 13% and 12%, respectively. The crash continued and led to severe economic and social turmoil. As the free fall in the market continued and people lost their life's savings, demand in the market declined drastically. Solvency and not expansion became the agenda of the crash-affected companies (Gaughan 2007). This event marked the end of the second wave of M&As.

3.3.3 The 1940s

The trend in the market had changed from 'Getting big soon' to 'Small is beautiful'. Even the governments across the globe started encouraging small enterprises, and various incentives were extended to small firms. As a result, the decade saw large companies taking over smaller firms with the motive of getting tax relief. Firms were encouraged to sell businesses to outsiders since the estate taxes were very high and selling businesses within the family was very expensive. While mergers continued, they did not result in concentration of economic power, since most of them held very insignificant portions of the industrial assets.

3.3.4 Third Wave (1965–1969)

This period, also known as conglomerate merger period, saw intensive merger activity backed by booming economies. The most unusual element of this period was that smaller firms targeted larger companies for acquisition. Most of the mergers resulted in diversified conglomerates, i.e., companies that conduct a large percentage of their activities in different industries.

Some prominent conglomerates that came into existence during this period were Long-Temco-Vought (LTV), Litton Industries, and ITT. In addition to these, there were many small firms moving into areas outside their core business activities.

The US continued to amend/replace old laws by enacting new legislations that made expansion tougher. The Celler-Kefauver Act was passed to cover the loopholes of the Layton Act that did not prevent or prohibit the anti-competitive acquisition of a firm's assets. As the legal environment made horizontal and vertical mergers tougher, companies saw that the only route of expansion left was forming conglomerates.

The third wave ended when Litton Industries in 1968 announced a decline in its quarterly earnings for the first time in 14 years. Conglomerates found the market hostile as it registered an increased selling pressure on the stock prices (Gaughan 2007). The antitrust lobby was resolute about preventing mergers for they believed that they are anti-competitive and result in abuse of power. To further increase pressure on conglomerates, the Tax Reform Act was passed in 1969 with the motive of curbing manipulative accounting practices that created paper earnings to temporarily support stock prices. It restrained financing acquisitions through debt financing by stating that bonds would be treated as common stock for the purpose of earnings per share (EPS) computations. This obviously nullified increase in earnings on paper.

Conglomerates started becoming unpopular because of the following reasons:

- It was observed that buyers often overpaid for the diverse companies they purchased.
- Companies would move away from specialization resulting in deteriorating performances. For example, Revlon's core cosmetics business suffered when they ventured into health care.

3.3.5 The 1970s

The decade of the 1970s, also known as the era of hostile takeovers, saw a dramatic decline in the number of mergers. Yet the decade saw some trendsetting events:

- A change in the 'acceptable takeover behaviour'
- The beginning of aggressive takeover of prominent firms, such as INCO's (International Nickel Company's) attempt to takeover ESB, the largest battery maker; a bid for Otis Elevator by United Technologies; attempt at hostile takeover of Garlock Industries by Colt Industries (Gaughan 2007)
- Sanctioning of aggressive advances by investment banks
- Starting of consultancy services by investment bankers in anti-takeover defences

3.3.6 Fourth Wave (1984–1989)

This wave, also known as the wave of mega mergers, saw the relative percentage of hostile takeovers in the total volume of takeovers increasing dramatically. In addition, some of the largest firms became targets of acquisition. The period saw a lot of merger activity in the oil and gas, drugs, medical equipment, banking, and petroleum industries.

The leading mega mergers of this period include Chevron and Gulf Oil, Philip Morris and Kraft, Texaco and Getty Oil, DuPont and Conoco, British Petroleum and Standard Oil of Ohio, U.S. Steel and Marathon Oil, and Kohlberg Kravis and Beatrice.

The fourth wave was characterized by the following:

- The concept of the 'corporate raider' made its appearance. Corporate raiders, sometimes called 'company breakers,' are investors who engage in the act of directed or orchestrated hostile takeover of a company. A corporate raider often goes after a corporation, with an eye on selling off the assets of the company to generate huge profits for himself.
- Investment bankers started playing a very aggressive role in pursuing M&As, as advisory fees were a great source of risk-free income.
- Offensive and defensive strategies became common.
- Mega deals were often financed with large amounts of debt, such as leveraged buyouts.
- Conflicts arose between the federal and state governments. Many state governments started passing anti-takeover legislations at the behest of local companies. The federal government saw this as an infringement on interstate commerce, leading to conflict.
- Many deals were motivated by the non-US companies who had a desire to expand into the larger and more stable US market.
- Different sectors responded to deregulation differently. For example, the response of the broadcasting sector was quicker than that of air transport.

3.3.7 Fifth Wave (1992 onwards)

This period saw a major economic transition in many economies, paving the way for increased aggregate demand, longest post-war expansion of companies, and rise in stock market values. This phase saw large mega-mergers happening; few hostile deals and more strategic mergers occurred. The fad of financing merger deals through debt also got eroded and increased use of equity financing was noticed. Roll-ups became popular, and fragmented industries were consolidated through large-scale acquisition of companies. The trend was very common in industries such as funeral printing, office products, and floral products.

Some of the prominent companies that underwent consolidation during this wave include Office Products USA, Floral USA, the Fortress Group, US Delivery Systems, Coach USA, and Comforts Systems USA.

Privatization of state-owned enterprises took place in this period. The concept of emerging market bidders also evolved during this time. These companies came into being as a result of acquisition of private businesses and consolidation of relatively smaller competitors in emerging markets. The takeover of Arcelor by Mittal, acquisition of Peninsular and Oriental Navigation Company by Dubai-based Ports World, and takeover of Corus Group by Tata Steel are some important examples (Gaughan 2007).

However, the European countries did not find the prevailing takeover trends suitable, as a large number of national enterprises were getting targeted. Hence, they were compelled to make the takeover of major national enterprises difficult. For example, the French government merged Suez SA and Gaz De France SA to fend off Italian utility Enel SpA; Spain brought in a new law to prevent German E. on AG's takeover bid of Spanish utility Endesa SA (Gaughan 2007).

While the global economies are battling out one of the worst recessions, M&As continue, though at a slower pace.

3.4 TRADITIONAL AND MODERN VIEWS

If one tries to analyse the turn of events in the area of M&As, one can notice a drastic shift in the way they are looked at, over a period of time. Thus, M&As can be analysed on the basis of the traditional and modern points of view.

The traditional view focused on competition (Machiraju 2008) and often resulted in horizontal mergers, creating a condition of monopolistic competition. The basic motivation was survival in the market through growth generally achieved through M&As. The entity would thus protect itself from takeover attempts. The motto was 'make them like us' and the selection of the target was based on its size and quality.

One major weakness of the traditional practices was that there was very little done on the front of due diligence. In addition, the post-merger integration was commonly applied after the deal got consummated. The end result would be delays and frictions that diminished the benefits of the transaction (Walters 2004).

The general perception created as result of these frictions was that M&As destroyed, rather than created shareholder value.

The modern view looks at M&As as a vehicle to change the control of the firms' assets (Walters 2004). Mergers and acquisitions are favoured because they initiate a process of allocation and reallocation of resources by firms in response to changes in economic conditions and technological innovations. From being looked upon as a vehicle to combat competition, M&As are today being looked upon as a tool for gaining competitive advantage and strategic growth.

It is argued that to become a global organization, organic growth alone is not enough. The entities should be effectively integrated so that they create shareholder value and improve the competitive strength of the business. This is where M&As are becoming indispensable.

The success rate of M&As is increasing due to better deal governance, better deal selection, effective due diligence, and better focus on integration. The main reason behind this increased success rate has been identified as the early application of the integration process and the same being carried out in a disciplined way.

The motivation for M&As in modern times is to expand geographically into markets in which the entity is traditionally absent or weak. The other motives that drive this process include benefits of economies of scale, improvements in operating efficiency, impact on the market structure and power pricing, improved financial stability, and increased possibility of attracting and retaining human capital. In short, the modern approach talks of achieving strategic interdependence through resource sharing, functional and management skill transfer, and combination benefits.

3.5 CLASSIFICATION OF MERGERS

Mergers may take different forms. The most commonly evolved relationships between the merging companies can be classified as follows:

3.5.1 Horizontal Merger

Under this strategy, two companies that are in direct competition and sharing the same product lines and markets merge. The merger is based on the assumption that it will provide synergy and allow enhanced cost efficiencies to the new business. It is presumed that the merger would give benefits such as staff reduction and decrease in related costs, economies of scale, opportunity to acquire technologies unique to the target company, and increased market reach and industry visibility.

Some popular horizontal mergers include Daimler–Benz and Chrysler, Glaxo Wellcome Plc., SmithKline Beecham Plc., Exxon and Mobil, Volkswagen and Rolls Royce and Lamborghini, and Ford and Volvo.

Though popular, horizontal merges have a flip side too. They result in the creation of large entities that cause ripple effects in the sector and sometimes throughout the economy. Large horizontal mergers are perceived as anti-competitive, for they give the new entity an unfair competitive advantage over its competitors. Hence, most countries regulate large horizontal mergers by enacting competition acts. This does not mean that horizontal mergers are always bad. They are encouraged when the resulting benefits outweigh the ill effects of reduction in competition (Fenton Kathryn 2008).

To evaluate the proposals of horizontal mergers in a fair way, some regulatory authorities grant permission, but impose *ex ante* obligations on the merged entity where the merger would otherwise be perceived as anti-competitive. For example, in both the US and Europe, national regulatory authorities impose conditions on a merger perceived as anti-competitive (US Department of Justice and Federal Trade Commission 1992).

3.5.2 Vertical Merger

Vertical mergers are usually mergers of non-competing companies where one's product is a necessary component or complement of the other's. Such a merger is typified by one firm engaged in different aspects of production say, growing raw materials, manufacturing, transporting, marketing, and/or retailing.

Such mergers can achieve pro-competitive efficiency benefits. Vertical integration can lower transaction costs, lead to synergistic improvements in design, production, and distribution of the final output/product and thus enhance competition. Consequently, most vertical arrangements raise few competitive concerns (Varney 1995).

Vertical mergers involve two firms in different stages of production/operation merger. Such mergers can take the following forms.

Market extension merger   As the name suggests, this is a merger between two companies that sell the same products, but in different markets.

Product extension merger   A product extension merger is designed to increase the type/range of products that a company sells in a particular market. Such a merger occurs when two companies selling different but related products in the same market merge.

Vertical mergers may also take the form of forward, backward, and balanced integration.

Forward integration   Here the target firm is involved in the next stage(s) of production/operation. For example, the supplier of raw materials merges his firm with a regular procurer of the raw material from him. This can help him create opportunities to monitor the upstream supplier's competition.

Backward integration   Here the target company is involved in the previous stages of production/operation. For example, a manufacturer of a product merges his firm with the provider of the raw materials. By eliminating the provider of raw materials, the manufacturer can achieve collusion in the upstream market.

Balanced integration   This is a situation where the company sets up subsidiaries that both supply them with inputs and distribute their outputs.

The basic objective of a vertical merger is to eliminate costs of searching for vendors, contracting prices, payment collection, advertising and communication, and coordinating production. Such a merger can have a very positive impact on production and inventory since information flows efficiently within the organization.

It is to be noted that vertical mergers need to be timed appropriately. History shows that vertical mergers occur when two firms decide to integrate their businesses to capitalize on the rising demand for their products.

Some examples of vertical mergers are Usha Martin and Usha Beltron, Time Warner Inc. and Turner Corporation, Silicon Graphics Inc.'s merger with Alias Research Inc. and Wavefront Technologies Inc., Apple and Intel, Reliance Industries Limited and Reliance Petrochemicals Limited, Tata Industrial Finance Ltd and Tata Finance, Hindustan Unilever Limited (formerly Hindustan Lever Limited) and Tata Oil Mills Co. (TOMCO), Torrent group and Ahmedabad Electric Company, Surat Electric Company, and so on.

Vertical mergers are also viewed as anti-competitive as they can rob the supply business of its competition. For example, if a firm has been receiving material from two separate firms and the receiving firm decides to acquire both the firms, the merger would put an end to the competition between the supplying entities. Such mergers tend to create monopolies.

In addition, vertical mergers are designed to evade pricing regulations. For example, when regulation seeks to constrain the market power of a natural monopoly, the monopolist may have incentives to integrate vertically into unregulated markets to extract the monopoly gains denied to it in the regulated market (www.business.gov.in).

Due to the flip side of vertical mergers, regulatory authorities do not always favour them. In many cases, such mergers are granted approvals subject to certain conditions, such as the merged entity being directed to stay away from activities that are anti-competitive to the extent that they could harm public interest. This is because all antitrust laws work on the maxim 'the protection of competition, not competitors'.

An anti-competitive theory states that vertical mergers create barriers in the market by foreclosing rivals from access to needed inputs in the market and/or raise the prices in the market or reduce the quality of the product (www.learnmergers.com). Such strategies make it difficult for new firms to enter the market.

3.5.3 Conglomerate Merger

The US Supreme Court describes a conglomerate merger as 'one in which there is no economic relationship between the acquiring and the acquired firm' (FTC and Procter & Gamble Company 1967), i.e., companies which have no relation with their products. Conglomerate mergers are mergers involving firms in different or unrelated business activity. Such mergers are preferred by firms that plan to increase their product lines.

Firms opting for conglomerate mergers control a range of activities in various industries that require different skills in specific managerial functions, such as research, applied engineering, production, and marketing. A competitive edge in these functions can be attained by external acquisition and mergers; it is generally not possible through internal development. These types of mergers are also called concentric mergers. Firms operating in different geographic locations prefer conglomerate mergers.

Conglomerate mergers can be classified as follows:

- Pure conglomerate mergers involve firms that have nothing in common.
- Mixed conglomerate mergers involve firms that are looking for product extensions or market extensions.

These mergers are further classified as follows:

Financial conglomerates   These are active in providing funds to every segment of operation and in exercising control. They are the ultimate financial risk takers. They not only assume financial responsibility and control, but also play a major role in all the operating decisions.

They focus mainly on improving risk–return ratio, reducing business-related risks, improving the quality of general and functional managerial performance, and providing an effective competitive process. They can distinguish between performance based on underlying potentials in the product market area and results related to managerial performance.

Managerial conglomerates   They focus on providing managerial counseling and interacting on decisions with the motive of increasing the potential for improving performance. Such conglomerates come into play when two firms of unequal managerial competence combine.

Concentric companies   A merger is termed concentric when there is a carry-over of specific management functions or any complementarities in relative strengths between management functions. This distinction between general and specific management functions is the primary difference between managerial conglomerate and concentric company.

There are many reasons for firms deciding to merge into a conglomerate, including increasing market share, synergy, and cross-selling. Firms also merge to diversify and reduce their risk exposure. However, if a conglomerate becomes too large as a result of acquisitions, the performance of the entire conglomerate can suffer. This was seen during the conglomerate merger phase of the 1960s.

Conglomerates are guided by two philosophies. One, by participating in a number of unrelated businesses, the parent corporation is able to reduce costs by using fewer resources. Two, by diversifying business interests, the risks inherent in operating in a single market are mitigated.

The most common examples of conglomerate mergers are News Corporation, Sony, Time Warner, Walt Disney Company, Aditya Birla Group, Berkshire Hathaway, General Motors, Mahindra Group, Motorola, Tata Group, Hyundai, and Mitsubishi.

The flip side of conglomerate mergers is that contributing to aggregate increase in economic power often results in possible non-economic effects due to an increase in the general economic concentration (Staff of Federal Trade Commission 1969). Critics also fear that economic concentration would lead to corresponding aggression in political power by fewer but more powerful conglomerate firms, placing major decisions—both political and economic—in the hands of a few individuals or firms that have direct accountability to the general public (Hearings on Acquisitions and Mergers by Conglomerates of Unrelated Businesses 1978).

3.5.4 Accretive Merger

Accretion is natural growth in size or extent by gradual external addition. Accretion implies 'value creation'. Accretive mergers occur when a company with a high price-to-earnings ratio (P/E) purchases a company with a low P/E. As a result, the EPS of the acquiring company increases.

In an all-stock deal, if a company acquires a target with a lower P/E ratio, it must be accretive to earnings. Here the target company's earnings are lower and the acquirer can add these to its own earnings and still achieve a higher earnings rate. This is because the merger results in operational and financial synergies and boosts the earnings of the acquiring company. For example, Hewlett-Packard announced a merger with services company EDS in 2008. The belief of the company was that in view of the Generally Accepted Accounting Principles (GAAP), the deal would be non-GAAP accretive in 2009 and GAAP accretive in fiscal year 2010. Similarly, when RIL approved the merger with IPCL, the swap was decided to be one share of RIL for every five shares of IPCL. This was believed to be EPS accretive for the shareholders of RIL.

3.5.5 Dilutive Merger

The word dilutive implies 'destruction' or 'dilution'. A dilutive merger is one where the EPS of the acquiring company falls after merger. Since the EPS declines, the acquiring company's share price also declines, as the market expects a decrease in the company's future earnings. The expected decline could be because the market forces feel the merger would destroy value and would not result in synergies post merger.

As a matter of principle, a dilutive merger or acquisition occurs when the P/E ratio of the acquiring firm is less than that of the target firm.

In cases where there is lack of a reliable and standard measure of post-merger performance, EPS earnings are used as a proxy for value creation. They get represented through accretion or dilution. For example, copper mining company Phelps Dodge International Corp. entered a dilutive merger with Canadian nickel miners Inco and Falconbridge in 2006.

3.6 CONCEPT OF ACQUISITION

Acquisition is an attempt made by one firm to gain a majority interest in another firm. The firm attempting to gain a majority interest is called the acquiring firm and the other firm is called the target firm. Once the acquisition is completed, the acquiring firm becomes the legal owner and controller of the business of the target firm. The acquiring firm pays for the net assets, goodwill, and brand name of the company bought.

Acquisitions are actions through which companies seek to achieve economies of scale, increased efficiency, and enhanced market visibility. In an acquisition, unlike in a merger, there is no exchange of stock or consolidation as a new company even though it involves one company purchasing another.

Some prominent acquisitions include the following:

- Google's largest acquisition in March 2008 when it acquired DoubleClik, an advertising company
- Mahindra & Mahindra's acquisition of 90% stake in German company Schoneweiss
- Acquisition of Mumbai-based Ambit RSM by PricewaterhouseCoopers' (PwC)

It is important to note that acquisitions may lead to the following:

- A subsequent merger
- Establishment of a parent–subsidiary relationship
- A strategy of breaking up the target firm and disposing off part or all its assets
- Conversion of the target firm into a private firm

3.7 STRATEGIES FOR ACQUISITION

Acquisition involves a process of identifying the right target. However, research shows that most companies identify the wrong acquisition targets. A research conducted by PwC, HBS, and Acquisitions International indicates that 60% of the companies that go for acquisition in the UK in any given year achieve nothing. Of the remaining 40% of the companies, 63% regret the purchase they made.

This happens because the structure of the marketplace lends itself to failure due to four reasons (Sweeting 2007):

- Too few targets
- Inappropriate targets
- Lack of creativity
- Lack of forward planning

The most surprising element is that corporate buyers make all the four mistakes concurrently.

To make acquisitions more effective and meaningful, companies need to adhere to the following:

- Increase the number of targets
- Always explore alternatives available and not chase the one everyone else is bidding for
- Compare the targets concurrently in an attempt to choose the right and the best target

- Buy firms with assets that meet the current needs to build competitiveness
- Provide adequate financial resources so that profitable projects would not be lost
- Identify targets that are more likely to lead to easy integration and building synergies
- Continue to invest in research and development as a part of the firm's overall strategy

3.8 TYPES OF ACQUISITIONS

Acquisitions, as discussed, involve acquiring a majority stake in another company so that control changes hands. It is imperative that the right target is identified or else the process itself can escalate into a major problem for all the parties involved. In order to ensure that the right target is found, a company may choose between various forms and options.

These forms are discussed in Sections 3.8.1 and 3.8.2.

3.8.1 Assets Purchase

Under this method, the acquiring firm purchases specific identifiable assets for the business. These assets are perceived as having potential to add value to the acquiring company. In some cases, it may also assume specified liabilities. This helps the acquiring company to reduce the risk of taking on unknown liabilities such as seller's contracts, employees, etc.

The acquiring company is keen on the purchase mode as it can acquire the assets at a comparatively lower price. This potentially reduces future capital gains tax upon a sale of the assets. In addition, it increases the future depreciation cost, thereby reducing income tax.

If one evaluates this method from the point of view of the target company, it typically does not prefer asset sales method, for the target company has to pay capital gains tax on the difference between the assets sold and purchase price allocated to such assets. This could be substantial if assets are heavily depreciated. In addition, if the target company desires to use the proceeds of the asset sale for paying dividend to the stockholders, dividend would be subject to an additional tax, thus increasing the burden on the target company. Instead, the target company prefers selling the entire business, with employees in place and without the need to wind down the company.

This method suffers from the following limitations:

- It requires purchase agreement to allocate purchase price among specific list of assets.
- The acquiring company must be assured that all necessary assets are listed.
- Closing the deal is comparatively difficult for the following reasons:
  - For titled assets such as vehicles and property transferring, the ownership title of each asset becomes a tedious task.

- The consent of the shareholders is required for each transfer.
- If the entire business is being sold, each employee must be terminated and re-hired by the acquirer. This can create a lot of employee benefit issues.

3.8.2 Stock Purchase

Under this method, the acquirer purchases the entire outstanding equity of the target company. It is a method whereby the acquirer purchases the entire company and all assets and liabilities of the business that come with it. Stock purchase does not cause any disruption in the operations which can continue as usual.

This method is popular because of the following reasons:

- Closings are simplified.
- Fewer contract consents and very little paper work is required to transfer specific assets.
- All employees and employee benefits are transferred with the stock sale.

One needs to take care that if the shares are widely held, a transmittal letter needs to be distributed to shareholders to facilitate the exchange of their shares for the consideration by delivery of their stock certificates.

This method is preferred by the target company as the target only incurs capital gain on the difference between basis in stock sold, which is not subject to depreciation, and purchase price for stock. In addition, no dividend has to be paid to distribute the proceeds of sale to stockholders and double taxation can be avoided. Finally, the target is not required to tackle any issues relating to winding up of the company after closing.

However, the acquiring company quite obviously does not prefer this method for it cannot pick and choose assets and liabilities. In addition, it has to inherit everything, including unknown liabilities such as seller's contracts and employees. The tax basis in the assets purchased does not step up. There is potential of a heavier capital gains tax on a future sale of heavily depreciated assets although lower depreciation provision reduces the tax liability.

3.9 TOOLS FOR ANALYSIS

Mergers, acquisitions, and restructuring require adoption of appropriate strategies to succeed. Various strategic models have been evolved to help companies plan their activities and operations. Let us now discuss some of these strategies.

3.9.1 SWOT Analysis

Mergers, acquisitions, and corporate restructuring facilitate expansion and diversification of corporate entities. When an entity goes ahead with any of these strategies, the perception is that it would generate competitive advantage and help the entity grow unabated. However, the fact is that no strategy generates only benefits; it is only one element of a series of outcomes that are generated. In the light of this, understanding the SWOT of these strategies is essential. Once the factors contributing to SWOT are understood, the entity can evolve appropriate strategies and act accordingly.

Let us analyse the four elements of SWOT—strengths, weaknesses, opportunities, and threats as shown in Fig. 3.1.

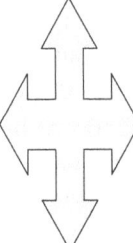

Strengths

- Increased market share
- Access to better technology
- Increased profits
- Acquisition of stock at minimal price
- Reduction in debt
- Opportunity to acquire end-to-end solutions
- Competitive advantage

Threats

- Unfriendly legal framework
- Takeover threats
- Changes in technology
- Changes in customer tastes and preferences

Weaknesses

- Style of management
- Aggressive trade unionism
- Creation of monopoly
- Integration difficulties
- Absence of skilled manpower
- Increasing costs

Opportunities

- Expansion opportunities
- Better ability to raise capital
- Self-reliance
- Tax concessions
- Demographic shifts

Figure 3.1   SWOT framework

Strengths

Strength represents elements that are capable of creating a positive impact on the entity by creating competitive advantage. These elements add to the earning and growth potential of the entity. Strength can vary from product strength to strategic strength. The sub-elements include increased market share, access to better technology, increased profits, acquiring stock at minimal price, reduction in debt, opportunity to acquire end-to-end solutions and competitive advantage.

Let us analyse these elements in brief:

Increased market share   Mergers, acquisitions, and corporate restructuring enable a company to enter new markets where it was never present before. This provides an opportunity to expand its market base and spread its wings geographically. For example, Bharti Airtel's entry into the African market after taking over Zain.

Access to better technology   The target gets access to better technology. Once the entities merge, it can bring better and improved technology and the acquirer can accrue benefits from the same. For example, The combination of Sony and Ericsson bought technological benefits to both the entities as both possessed technological expertise.

Increased profits   Entry into new markets and expansion of product range results in expansion of the customer base and market share of the acquirer. This adds to the existing revenue of the entity and brings benefits of economy of scale, resulting in increase in profits. For example, the merger of Reliance Petroleum with Reliance Industries resulted in cost savings due to economies of scale, thus adding to the revenue of the merged entity.

Acquisition of stock at minimal price   It is believed that mergers happen when the market value of the target company's stock does not reflect its true or potential value. This could also happen when the management is not running the operations of the company to its full potential. This brings opportunities of acquiring the stock at a minimal price since the market may not be able to anticipate and identify the positives. Once the target changes hands, competitive advantage starts materializing over a period of time, changing the fortunes of the company and the stock prices start rising. This is obviously in favour of the entity that has acquired shares at a comparatively lower price.

Reduction in debt   The decision to restructure/merger helps the entity to write off the accumulated losses and eliminate intangible assets from its balance sheet and makes it look healthier. Similarly, it could bring cash into the business either through the new entity or through issue of shares, or through sale of assets. The resources so generated can be used for repaying the debt appearing in the balance sheet. This would further make the balance sheet look healthier and favourably change the debt-equity ratio.

Opportunity to acquire end-to-end solutions   Firms decide to merge with each other because they see synergistic benefits in the combination. These synergistic benefits increase productivity, reduce costs, improve efficiency levels, and above all provide end-to-end solutions in terms of technology, financial reengineering, and HR through their core competencies.

Competitive advantage   Mergers are pursued as they have the potential to help the entities multiply their strength using their core competencies. For example, an entity could be very strong technologically and the other could have a very effective distribution network. After merger, if the technological advantage is used effectively to develop new products, the distribution network can be exploited to ensure that the products reach out to the customers quickly and the market is captured.

Weaknesses

Weaknesses are the elements that give a company its competitive disadvantage. These elements can include components such as the style of management, aggressive trade unions, and creation of monopoly.

Let us analyse these elements:

Style of management   Successful mergers and restructuring require a very different mindset. It works when the management is open to new ideas and willing to encourage open communication, freedom of expression and functional autonomy. While these are critical elements to help carry out the merger and restructuring, the autocratic and highly centralized style of management proves a major hurdle and adds to the problems of the merged entity.

Aggressive trade unionism   Organizations have trade unions that work towards protecting the interest of the employees. An entity that is in the midst of restructuring its operations finds the trade union to be a major hurdle in its way. The trade union always perceives the plans and actions of the management as anti-labour, and hence objects to all their actions. The negative and non-cooperative approach of the trade union does not allow the management to go ahead with its plans, howsoever genuine they may be, or howsoever serious the management may be about reviving the activities so that all the stakeholders benefit. The trade union not only looks at the acts of the management with suspicion, but also intervenes in the implementation process.

Creation of monopoly   The most common complaint against the merger and restructuring process is that it facilitates combination to two entities and leads to the creation of monopolies. Consumers always feel exploited by monopolies, for they can otherwise dictate the market and manipulate market conditions, supply, pricing, quality, etc. to their advantage. In the light of these manipulations, even the state enacts laws that could prevent or control the formation of such monopolies.

Integration difficulties   A merger brings together entities that are different from each other culturally, size-wise, technology-wise, process-wise, etc. When the entities merge, they have to integrate their systems, process and culture. The process of integration is very difficult and tedious. If the two entities do not integrate effectively, it can create conflicts and vitiate the work environment. It may also contribute towards the failure of the merger.

Absence of skilled manpower   As stated earlier, the process of merger calls for an effective merger of two entities. This not only requires re-aligning the work culture and other cultural aspects, but also needs skilled manpower to carry out the plans effectively. In the absence of skilled manpower, the process of merger and restructuring becomes difficult and often fails.

Increasing costs   When entities merge, the new entity could have a catch-22 like situation with two persons from the merging entities responsible for the same job. While the two persons need not contribute positively to the productivity and revenue, they certainly generate additional cost for the company. The situation gets worse when the persons starting creating hurdles for each other, instead of cooperating and coordinating. This affects productivity and increases the overheads further.

Opportunities

Opportunities represent external conditions that are favourable and help a company attain its planned objectives. If the merging entities identify and exploit opportunities to their advantage, it would help the entity attain its planned objectives with ease. The possible opportunities that come the company's way include expansion opportunities, better ability to raise capital, self-reliance, tax benefits, and demographic shifts in its customer base.

Let us briefly analyse these elements:

Expansion opportunities   Mergers enable entities to enter markets previously under the control of their partner entity. As such, the company is not required to put in tedious and time-consuming efforts to create a market for its products. The market already exists, and all that the company is required to do is to spread awareness about the merger and continue selling the product. In case the brand name is changed, the company needs to launch a campaign to spread awareness on this account too. Expansion of the market helps the company to improve its bottom line. For example, when L&T Cement with sold and re-christened Ultra Tech Cement, the company undertook a massive drive that stated that L&T Cement would be known as Ultra Tech Cement.

Better ability to raise capital   Mergers and restructuring enable the companies to restructure their balance sheets and make the same look healthy. This is done by eliminating intangible and fictitious assets and selling off assets that are lying idle. The funds so generated can thus be used to repay debt so that the high leveraged capital structure becomes balanced. Once restructured, the balance sheet starts looking healthy. If the company then enters the capital market or approaches a bank for finance, the same can be raised with ease.

Self-reliance   The synergistic benefits that accrue to a company through M&As make the company self-reliant. As a result of this, the company's dependence on outside vendors gets reduced and this helps the company to execute its plans effectively. This can, in the course of time, be used by the company as an opportunity to expand its business and become innovative.

Tax concessions   The companies that merge or restructure often absorb each other's accumulated losses and set off the same against the accumulated profits of their partner entity. Again if the merger is in the interest of the country the entities can seek tax concessions/tax holidays from the state. This enables the company to improve its bottom line and thus, financial position.

Demographic shifts   When companies enter new markets, they get the advantage of getting control over a new market that could have a very different demographic structure. This can be exploited by the company to introduce new products and expand its product portfolio. The new markets could also provide opportunities for introducing technologically-advanced products and entering new market segments hitherto not tested by the company.

Threats

Threats represent external conditions that could cause damage to the company and create hurdles in the way of pursuing and attaining its planned objectives. These factors could have an adverse impact on the entities merging since the structure, product portfolio, culture, and market size of the entity change. If the company wants to successfully attain its planned objectives, threats need to be managed effectively. The common threats faced by an entity include unfriendly legal framework, takeover threats, changes in technology and changes in customer taste and preferences.

Let us analyse these elements:

Unfriendly legal framework   The legal framework prevalent in different countries is not always favourable to M&As. While countries such as the US, UK, and India are open to M&As, countries such as Germany, China, and Japan have a very different framework. Germany has a dual board structure, Japan has interlocking of interests, and China has state ownership of companies.

Countries such as India allow M&As, but subject to fulfilment of stringent legal norms. The legal norms create hurdles for the entities and also cause unprecedented delays that may deprive the company of the opportunity to exploit prevailing favourable conditions.

Takeover threats   Companies that merge and restructure their operations may make good profits. Once they become successful, they can become takeover targets and other entities might see the synergies in taking over such entities. Given the trend in the market today, companies are always on the lookout for targets, especially companies that are doing well and have growth potential.

Changes in technology   Technology is an area that changes practically every day. A company that merges with other entities or restructures itself and acquires the latest technology also faces a threat in terms of changing technology. As the technology becomes outdated and obsolete, the entity is required to invest more in new technology. Given the fact that the technology life cycle is getting shorter by the day, the risk of obsolescence is high, which could increase the costs of the company. In addition, the employees might show a great deal of resistance adopting new technology at regular intervals.

Changes in customer tastes and preferences Like technology, changing customer tastes and preferences is another threat that companies have to face regularly. An entity might invest heavily in the latest technology, but a change in the tastes and preferences of the customers may render the available technology redundant, causing huge losses to the company. For example, companies that rely heavily on IT have to regularly upgrade the same since technology changes are very fast. If they hesitate to change the technology, they will lose customers.

In short, a SWOT analysis provides a clear insight into the challenges and issues that face a merged or restructured entity. A company needs to be aware of the issues and factors that affect the company's operations in the market, so that the strategies and policies are attuned to the market trends.

Critics however feel that SWOT analysis is not suitable to diverse and dynamic markets of modern day, because of the following reasons:

- It generates a long generic list of sub-elements.
- The toll is more descriptive and less analytical.
- The sub-elements are just listed and not prioritized.
- The tool is used only as an instrument of planning and not implementation.

3.9.2 BCG Matrix

In the early 1970s, Bruce Henderson of the Boston Consulting Group developed a portfolio planning model and named it the BCG matrix. The model was based on the observation that a company's business units can be classified into four categories based on combinations of market growth and market share relative to the largest competitor. It was for this reason that the matrix was also known as the 'growth-share matrix'.

In the model, market growth serves as a proxy for industry attractiveness, and relative market share serves as a proxy for competitive advantage. The matrix, thus, aims to map the business unit's position within these two important profitability determinants. The profitability of the divisions thus helps the company to finalize the preferred distribution of cash and other resources among different divisions. The analysis indicates that it is more attractive for an entity to have a high share in a high growth market than have markets that are slow-growing, where the entity has a small share. When the market growth and market share are divided into two parts, one gets the 2×2 matrix.

The cells of the matrix are used to classify the businesses of the diversified entity into categories such as stars, cash cows, question marks, and dogs as shown in Fig. 3.2.

Stars

Stars are high-growth companies, where the company holds a high market share. Such a division/entity is likely to generate adequate cash and always be self-sustaining. Such divisions need to put in a lot of effort in protecting their enviable positions and profit margins and increase turnover to derive cost-related economies.

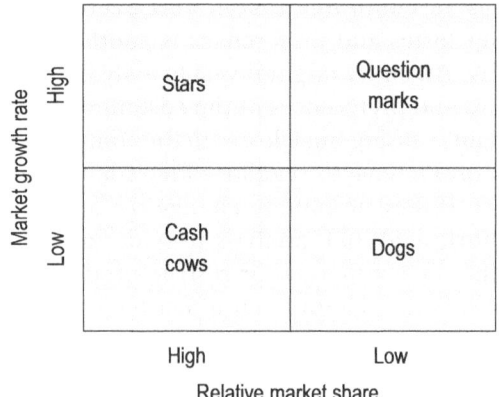

Figure 3.2   BCG matrix

An acquirer should try to identify such divisions in the market, and if possible, acquire them at all costs. In case it already owns such a division, the strategy to be adopted to attain further growth is to be aggressive—the entity should invest aggressively in research and development and expand its product portfolio. For example, when BMW bought Rover, experts thought its products would help the German automaker reach new customers. However, the company was not able to capitalize on this opportunity, and it sold the Rover to a British firm and the Land Rover to Ford.

Cash Cows

Cash cows are divisions that hold a high share in mature markets, but do not have much growth potential left. On account of the high market share, such divisions are able to generate adequate profits which can be used to fund divisions classified as stars or question marks. One should remember that companies often use the returns of one division to support other high potential business units.

If an entity owns such a division, its strategy should be to defend and maintain their position in the market so that the division can be 'milked'.

Question Marks

Such divisions represent one with a low share, but a very high potential for growth as it is operating in fast-growing markets. Such divisions need a lot of cash to exploit the growth opportunities available in the market. As such the generic strategy for such a division is that of high-risk. If the entity is able to generate cash through the cash cows divisions, the same should be invested aggressively in question marks. If the entity is unable to generate cash, then this division should be divested, as sustaining the division with its present low share is difficult.

Dogs

These are businesses that have a very small share in the market and have a very low growth potential. They do not hold much future promise and are on the verge of dying. Investing in such divisions reflects a narrow view of the business, having no future except high risk. One needs to remember that such divisions are cash traps and can only eat into the profits of the company.

While looking for targets, the acquirer should avoid acquiring such companies as they would not add any value but would result in increased losses and turn out to be a bad 'buy' decision.

Similarly, if the company owns any such unit or division, it is better to divest it as soon as possible, or else it would keep churning out losses and affect the overall profitability of the group. In simple words, these divisions are like dogs that one should shoot—by liquidating and leaving the markets.

3.9.3 GE Matrix

Critics have criticised the BCG matrix on the grounds that it is relatively narrow in its approach and is exceedingly simple. To address this criticism, General Electric (GE) developed the GE matrix, also known as the GE Business Screen. This is a portfolio management technique that focuses on industry attractiveness and competitive position. These two factors are further divided into 3 categories, making it a 3×3 matrix. The cells are then used to classify the business units into winners, losers, question marks, average businesses, and profit producers.

If one looks at Fig. 3.3, both market growth and market share appear in the broad list of factors that determine the overall attractiveness of the industry and the quality of the firm's competitive position.

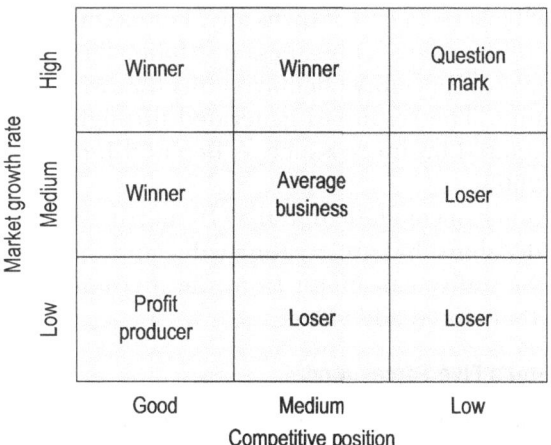

Figure 3.3 GE matrix

The factors that determine the overall attractiveness of the industry are as follows:

- Market growth
- Market size
- Competitive intensity
- Capital requirements

When these factors are assessed collectively it simply implies that the greater the market growth and the larger the market, the lesser is the capital requirement and the lesser is the competitive intensity, making the industry more attractive.

The other determinants of an organization's competitive position in an industry are as follows:

- Market share
- Technological know-how
- Product quality
- Service network
- Price competitiveness
- Operating costs

A business with a larger market share, better technological know-how, high product quality, a quality service network, competitive prices, and low operating costs is in a favourable competitive position in the market.

The GE matrix is a very reliable tool of implementing and managing a firm's diversification strategy. The acquirer can analyse the growth prospects of the firm's business and plan the resource deployment strategy of the entity with the objective of maximizing performance.

The matrix suggests that an entity should invest in winners and question where the industry attractiveness and competitive position are both favourable; It should maintain the market position of average businesses and profit producers where industry attractiveness and competitive position is average, and should sell losers, in case it owns any. For example, Unilever undertook a major exercise of assessing its business portfolio. Based on the results, it decided to sell off several speciality chemical units that were not contributing to the firm's profitability. The resources generated through such divestitures were used to acquire related businesses such as Ben and Jerry's, Homemade, and Slim-Fast (Griffin 2008).

Thus one can conclude that the GE matrix can also be used as a tool to ascertain the divisions that are creating value and the ones that are destroying value, so that the entity can divest from the divisions destroying value and acquire division that would add value.

3.9.4 Porter's Five Forces Model

The business strategy of an entity is determined to a great extent by the nature of competition prevailing in the industry. The degree and intensity of the competition in the industry determines the profit potential of an entity. If the intensity of competition is high, companies tend to spend heavily on activities that deal with competition, such as advertisement and price wars. etc. The performance of an entity depends to a great extent on the external factors. Figure 3.4 summarizes Porter's five forces model.

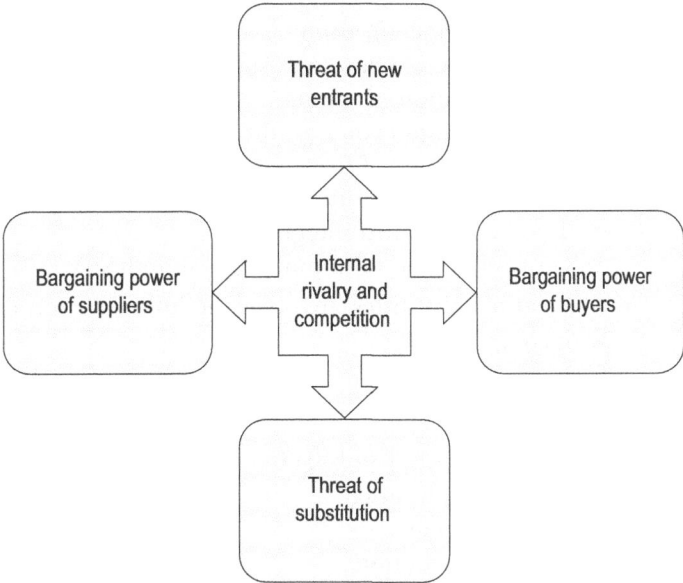

Figure 3.4   Porter's five forces model

Porter's model is based on the logic that a corporate strategy should be able to counter the opportunities and threats prevailing in the organization's external environment. This is especially true in case of the competitive strategy, which the argument states should be based on the understanding of industry structures and the way they change.

Porter has identified five competitive forces that according to him shape every industry and every market. These forces not only determine the intensity of competition but also influence the profitability and attractiveness of an industry.

- Bargaining power of suppliers
- Threat of substitution
- Bargaining power of buyers
- Barriers to entry/threat of new entrants
- Internal rivalry and competition

Of these, three forces constitute 'horizontal' competition, namely threat of substitute products, the threat of established rivals, and the threat of new entrants; the other two forces constitute 'vertical' competition, namely the bargaining power of suppliers and the bargaining power of customers. The model can be used by the manager to understand the industry in which the firm operates better.

When the corporate strategy is evolved, one needs to ensure that these elements are suitably modified so that the position of the organization improves. Porter's model supports analysis of the driving forces in an industry. Based on the information derived from the five forces analysis, the management can decide how to influence or exploit particular characteristics of their industry.

Let us now try and understand each of these elements:

- 'Bargaining power of suppliers' involves the following sub-elements:
  - Supplier concentration
  - Importance of volume to supplier
  - Differentiation of inputs
  - Impact of inputs on cost differentiation
  - Switching costs of firms in the industry
  - Presence of substitute inputs
  - Threat of forward integration
  - Cost relative to total purchases in industry
- 'Threat of substitutes' involves the following sub-elements:
  - Switching costs
  - Buyer inclination to substitute
  - Price performance trade-off of substitutes
- 'Bargaining power of buyers' involves the following sub-elements:
  - Bargaining leverage
  - Buyer volume
  - Buyer information
  - Brand identity
  - Price sensitivity
  - Threat of backward integration
  - Product differentiation
  - Buyer concentration vs industry
  - Substitutes available
  - Buyers incentives
- 'Barriers to entry' involves the following sub-elements:
  - Absolute cost advantage
  - Proprietary learning curve
  - Access to inputs
  - Switching costs
  - Government policy
  - Economies of scale
  - Capital requirements
  - Brand identity
  - Access to distribution
  - Expected retaliation
  - Proprietary products
- 'Degree of rivalry and competition' involves the following sub-elements:
  - Exit barriers
  - Industry concentration
  - Fixed costs/value added

- Industry growth
- Intermittent overcapacity
- Product differences
- Switching costs
- Brand identity
- Diversity of rivals
- Corporate stakes

According to Porter, the model should be used at the industry level, and is not designed to be used at the industry group or industry sector level. An industry represents a market where similar or closely related products and/or services are manufactured and sold to buyers. Firms that compete in a single industry should at least try and develop one of the five forces for themselves. Porter states that the fundamental issue for a diversified company is selection of industries in which the company should compete. This becomes a critical issue while targeting companies for mergers, acquisitions and diversification. A thorough analysis of these elements is required to be done and only thereafter should the company proceed with its plans of M&As.

3.10 DISTINCTION BETWEEN MERGERS AND ACQUISITIONS

People very often talk of mergers and acquisitions in the same breath and treat them as synonyms. However, the two terms are slightly different. The differences between a merger and an acquisition are important to value, negotiate, and structure a client's transaction. Both mergers and acquisitions involve one or multiple companies purchasing all or part of another company. The main distinction between a merger and an acquisition is how they are financed.

When a company takes over another company and establishes itself as a new entity, the process is called acquisition. Here the target company ceases to exist while the buyer company continues.

A merger, on the other hand, is a process where two entities agree to move forward as a single entity as against remaining separately owned and operated entities. Mergers are typically more expensive than acquisitions, with the parties incurring higher legal costs.

The stock of the acquiring company continues to be traded in an acquisition, whereas in case of a merger, the stocks of both the entities are surrendered and the stocks of the new company are issued in its place.

In reality, one entity buys another and allows the acquired firm to proclaim that the action is merger and not acquisition. This is done to ward off the negativity often associated with acquisitions.

Very often, it is noticed that companies prefer mergers over acquisitions though it may sound unusual. Some of the more frequently encountered reasons are as follows (Mastracchio and Zunitch 2002):

- A merger does not require cash.
- A merger may be accomplished tax-free for both parties.

- A merger lets the target company realize the appreciation potential of the merged entity, instead of being limited to sales proceeds.
- A merger allows the shareholders of smaller entities to own a smaller piece of a larger pie, increasing their overall net worth.
- A merger of a privately held company into a publicly held company allows the target company shareholders to receive a public company's stock.
- A merger allows the acquirer to avoid many of the costly and time-consuming aspects of asset purchases, such as the assignment of leases and bulk-sales notifications.
- Merger is of considerable importance when there are minority stockholders. The transaction becomes effective and dissenting shareholders are obliged to go along once the buyer obtains the required number of votes in support of the merger.

One very often finds that sometimes the deal is very unfriendly—the acquiring company manipulates events and forcefully takes over the target. Such a deal is called a hostile takeover. It would therefore not be wrong to say that a purchase is considered a merger or an acquisition on the basis of whether the purchase is friendly or hostile, and how it is announced. However, the fact remains that M&As are strategies targeted at synergy.

3.11 MOTIVES BEHIND MERGERS AND ACQUISITIONS

While one often hears CEOs saying that M&As are inspired by a desire to diversify or achieve higher growth rate, the reasons could be varied. Some of the commonly identified reasons are as follows:

3.11.1 Synergy

Synergy is the most essential component of mergers. In mergers, synergy between the participating firms determines the increase in value of the combined entity. In other words, it refers to the difference between the value of the combined firm and the value of the sum of the participants (Damodaran Aswath 1997). Synergy accrues in the form of revenue enhancement and cost savings. For example, if firms A and B merge and the value of the combined entity—V(AB)—is expected to be greater than (VA + VB), the sum of the independent values of A and B, the combined entity is said to be benefitting through synergy.

Synergy can take the following forms:

Operating synergy   This refers to the cost savings that come through economies of scale or increased sales and profits. It leads to the overall growth of the firm (Damodaran 1997).

Financial synergy   This is the direct result of financial factors such as lower taxes, higher debt capacity or better use of idle cash (Damodaran 1997). When a firm with accumulated losses or unabsorbed depreciation merges with a profitable firm and the combined firm can set off such losses against its profits, a financial synergy, known as tax shield, occurs. The following are some examples:

- When HUL acquired Lakme, it helped HUL to enter the cosmetics market through an established brand.
- When Glaxo and Smithkline Beecham merged, they not only gained market share, but also eliminated competition between each other.
- Tata Tea acquired Tetley to leverage Tetley's international marketing strengths.

3.11.2 Acquiring New Technology

To remain competitive, companies need to constantly upgrade their technology and business applications. To upgrade technology, a company need not always acquire technology. By buying another company with unique technology, the buying company can maintain or develop a competitive edge. A good example is a merger of a logistics company such as a land transport entity with an airline cargo company. Another example is a merger between Blackberry and Treo which can incorporate cell phone capability and email connectivity in one device; palm pilots and tablet laptops can provide benefits to both the entities.

3.11.3 Improved Profitability

Companies explore the possibilities of a merger when they anticipate that it will improve their profitability. The results of the International Business Owners Survey, 2004, carried out by Grant Thompson, conducted across 26 countries in Europe, Africa, Asia-Pacific, and the US, showed that 34% of businesses use M&A to maintain or improve profitability. For example, European Media Group Bertelsmann, Pearson, and others have driven their growth by expanding into the US through M&As.

3.11.4 Acquiring a Competency

Companies also opt for M&As to acquire a competency or capability that they do not have, and which the other firm does. For example, the ICICI–ITC alliance made the retailer network and depositor base available to the merging entity. Similarly, IBM merged with Daksh for acquiring competencies that the latter possessed.

3.11.5 Entry into New Markets

Mergers are often looked upon as a tool for hassle-free entry into new markets. Under normal conditions, a company can enter a new market, but may have to face stiff competition from the existing companies and may have to battle out for a share in the existing market. However, if the merger route is adopted, one can enter the market with greater ease and avoid too much competition. For example, the merger of Orange, Hutch, and Vodafone took place to achieve this objective.

3.11.6 Access to Funds

Often a company finds it difficult to access funds from the capital market. This weakness deprives the company of funds to pursue its growth objectives effectively. In such cases, a company may decide to merge with another company that is viewed as fund-rich. For example, TDPL merged with Sun Pharma since TDPL did not have funds to launch new products.

3.11.7 Tax Benefits

Mergers are also adopted to reduce tax liabilities. By merging with a loss-making entity, a company with a high tax liability can set off the accumulated losses of the target against its profits, gaining tax benefits. For example, Ashok Leyland Information Technology (ALIT) was acquired by Hinduja Finance, a group company, so that it could set off the accumulated losses in ALIT's books against its profits.

3.12 IDENTIFYING VALUE DRIVERS IN MERGERS AND ACQUISITIONS

A merger is a game of drawing synergy. The acquiring firm, which wants to optimize value gains, attempts to increase synergy and minimize the premium that it has to pay to the target company (Chakravarty 1998). Thus,
Value created through M&A = Increase in synergy − Decrease in premium
   Let us analyse the statement in detail.

3.12.1 Increase in Synergy

Synergy is the result of increase in efficiency of the combined entity. However, it depends on the manner in which the acquiring entity is able to tap the efficiency gains. The efficiency gains accrue on account of the following:

- Improvements in style of management so that administratively the company becomes stronger
- Improvements in financials by restructuring the capital structure to reduce cost and increase possibilities of efficient deployment of financial resources
- Improvements in operational efficiency with the objective of increasing productivity, reducing or eliminating rejections and wastages
- Change in the ability to control risk
- Reduction in inefficiencies existing before the merger took place

The synergies can be exploited only when the value of the combined entity exceeds the sum of its parts. To attain this objective, the combined entity should be able to increase its revenue, reduce the volatility in its earnings, or even reduce its costs.

3.12.2 Decrease in Premium

Paying a comparatively lower price for the target company is another way of increasing the net gain from a deal. The acquiring company should identify market imperfections while valuing the target company. These imperfections should then be indexed against other players in the industry so that the appropriate price of the shares the target company can be determined. This is where the acquirer can ascertain the appropriate amount payable for the target and avoid paying high premium for the target.

Synergy can be attained by focussing on the following key variables:

Managerial Skills

Managerial skills are an important input for every entity, as important as capital and other forms of labour. These skills can range from industry specific skills to generic skills. When a company decides to take over another company, the decision is influenced by the fact that managerial skills and resources are transferable. The acquirer therefore, proposes to take over the target company, eliminate inefficiencies existing in the target company and transfer its own managerial skills and efficiencies to the target company and thus derive value. If this is done successfully managerial synergy is achieved. Such synergies ensure that the market share of the combined entity is more than the parts.

While achieving managerial synergies is core to the decision to merge, these often remain elusive. This is due to the following reasons:

- Identifying relative managerial abilities is difficult.
- Transfer of skills is not always easy unless the merging entities belong to the same industry.
- Rooting out the inefficient practices that are often embedded in the organizational culture is difficult.

Boosting Marginal Revenue

The revenue per unit can be improved if the acquiring entity is able to redirect the available cash resources to industries that are more attractive and remunerative, thus improving the ROI of the merged entity. The return on investment improves when revenue rises while costs and investments remain unchanged.

Companies believe that M&A generates financial synergy by reducing the cost of capital. This happens since cash rich companies keep exploring attractive business opportunities to invest surplus funds. Secondly, tax laws distinguish between internally and externally generated funds and offer tax benefits to acquiring companies.

Here again it is wrong to presume that the combined entity would be able to procure funds at a low cost. The belief that a diversified company has better profit generating ability may not always be true. It may result in more uncertainty, given the size and diversified business portfolio.

Lowering Total Costs

The general view is that revenue improves if total cost declines. To achieve this objective, the merged entity should reduce transaction costs and eliminate existing market inefficiencies.

The presumption that cost can be reduced after merger originates from the fact that integration results in better coordination and planning, reduced technical costs, assured supply, lower transaction costs, better bargaining capacity, etc. The overall impact of these elements is that the technical, transaction, and uncertainty cost goes down. Merger also improves control over production processes, resulting in economies reducing the total cost further. If the company can maintain its marginal revenue, margins are bound to improve.

Critics however say that a merger has a very limited ability to reduce transaction costs and efficiencies are quite often overestimated. Given this, the cost reduction is actually very minimal. They further argue that post merger the capital requirements increase and this imposes additional burden on the company. In addition, the flexibility and bargaining power goes down further affecting the company's cost of capital. If the company decides to pass on the benefits of reduced cost to the distributors or to subsidies the products, profitability may actually decline.

Reducing Marginal Costs through Operating Synergy

A merger is driven by the notion that it will result in economies of scale and bring down the marginal cost of operations. The belief is driven by economic theory, which says that marginal cost declines as production increases, bringing down the average cost. This results from rationalization of production and increased scale of operation.

Not everybody agrees with this argument since economic theories are assumption-driven and hence not always true. Secondly, smaller companies can be more profitable due to the inherent flexibility they possess. Thirdly, larger companies have very high administrative costs due to large and complicated structures. Finally, large entities may often possess excess capacity on account of underutilization of available capacity due to prevailing market conditions.

Reducing Beta

Another school of thought propagates that mergers can lower the 'beta' of the company.

Beta is the measure of the volatility, or systematic risk of a security or a portfolio in comparison to the market as a whole. Beta is calculated using regression analysis and reflects the tendency of a security's returns to respond to the swings in the market.

A beta of 1 indicates that the security's price will move with the market. A beta of less than 1 means that the security will be less volatile than the market. A beta of greater than 1 indicates that the security's price will be more volatile than the market. For example, if a stock's beta is 1.4, it is theoretically 40% more volatile than the market. Similarly, if a stock's beta is 0.75, it is theoretically 25% less volatile that the market. Beta is used in the capital asset pricing model (CAPM), a model that calculates the expected return of an asset based on its beta and expected market returns. It is also known as beta coefficient.

A company can increase its valuation by either increasing its earnings or reducing risk. Risks are classified as systematic risks and unsystematic risks.

Systematic risk is the risk that cannot be reduced or predicted in any manner. It is almost impossible to protect oneself against this type of risk. For example, increase in interest rates or changes in government legislation. Since one can do little about this risk, the commonly adopted approach is to simply acknowledge it and incorporate its effect on the future expected returns. Systematic risk is also known as un-diversifiable risk as it affects the entire market.

Unsystematic risk is the risk that is specific to an asset. It is company-specific. This risk can usually be eliminated through diversification. Such risks include business, financial, liquidity, exchange rate, country, and market risks. Unsystematic risk is also known as specific risk and refers to the events that affect a small number of stocks/companies.

To tackle unsystematic risks, companies opt for brand extensions, try to reduce technological and marketing risks, reinforce managerial skills, etc.

The problem faced here is that to reduce this risk, companies may diversify into unrelated product areas or product lines and dilute the original brand image. The company also suffers if it does not possess the competency for managing unrelated businesses.

3.13 REASONS FOR FAILURE OF MERGERS AND ACQUISITIONS

While there is often a great hype when a merger or acquisition is announced, the end result is not always positive. Quite often, M&As destroy rather than add value to the acquirer's business. The most common reasons for failure are as follows.

3.13.1 Unrealistic Price Paid for Target

The process of M&A involves valuation of the target company and paying a price for taking over the assets of the company. Quite often, one finds that the price paid to the target company is much more than what should have been paid. While the shareholders of the target company stand benefited, the shareholders of the acquirer end up on the losing side. This is because they have to carry the burden of the overpriced assets of the target company which dilutes the future earnings of the acquirer. Having bid over-enthusiastically, the buyer may find that the premium paid for the acquired company's shares (the so-called 'winner's curse') wipes out any gains made from the acquisition (Henry 2002).

This phenomenon is generally noticed in the later years when the acquirer has to revalue the assets and write of goodwill booked at the time of M&A.

3.13.2 Difficulties in Cultural Integration

Every merger involves combining of two or more different entities. These entities reflect different corporate cultures, styles of leadership, differing employee expectations and functional differences. If the merger is implemented in a way that does not deal sensitively with the companies' people and their different corporate cultures, the process may turn out to be a disaster. There may be acute contrasts between the attitudes and values of the two companies, especially if the new partnership crosses national boundaries. While the process is being executed, these differences are known but often ignored. As years pass by and the combined entity tries to synergize the operations, these differences surface and often lead to failure of the merger. For example, the merger of Daimler-Benz with Chrysler. While Daimler-Benz's culture stressed on a more formal and structured management style, Chrysler favoured a more relaxed, freewheeling style.

3.13.3 Overstated Synergies

Mergers and acquisitions are looked upon as an important instrument of creating synergies through increased revenue, reduced costs, reduction in net working capital and improvement in the investment intensity. Overestimation of these can lead to failure of mergers.

3.13.4 Integration Difficulties

Companies very often face integration difficulties, i.e., the combined entity has to adapt to a new set of challenges given the changed circumstances. To do this, the company prepares plans to integrate the operations of the combining entities. If the information available on related issues is inadequate or inaccurate, integration becomes difficult.

3.13.5 Inconsistent Strategy

Mergers and acquisitions that are driven by sound business strategies are the ones that succeed. Entities that fail to assess the strategic benefits of mergers face failure. It is therefore important to understand the strategic intent. This has been discussed later in the chapter.

3.13.6 Poor Business Fit

Mergers and acquisitions also fail when the products or services of the merging entities do not naturally fit into the acquirer's overall business plan. This delays efficient and effective integration and causes failure. For example, the decision of HUL to take over the business of Modern Bakery.

3.13.7 Inadequate Due Diligence

Due diligence is a crucial component of the M&A process as it helps in detecting financial and business risks that the acquirer inherits from the target company. Inaccurate estimation of the related risk can result in failure of the merger.

3.13.8 High Leverage

One of the most crucial elements of an effective acquisition strategy is planning how one intends to finance the deal through an ideal capital structure. The acquirer may decide to acquire the target through cash. To pay the price of acquisition, the acquirer may borrow heavily from the market. This creates a very high leveraged structure and increases the interest burden of the company.

This increased interest cost may consume a big portion of the earnings and defeat the very purpose of acquisition.

3.13.9 Boardroom Split

When a merger is planned, it is crucial to evaluate the composition of the boardroom and compatibility of the directors. Managers or directors who are suddenly deprived of authority can be particularly bitter. Specific personality clashes between executives in the two companies are also very common. This may prove to be a major problem, slowing down or preventing integration of the entities.

3.13.10 Regulatory Issues

The entire process of merger requires legal approvals. If any of the stakeholders are not in favour of the merger, they might create legal obstacles and slow down the entire process. This results in regulatory delays and increases the risk of deterioration of the business. While evaluating a merger proposal, care should be taken to ensure that regulatory hassles do not crop up.

3.13.11 HR Issues

A merger or acquisition is identified with job losses, restructuring, and the imposition of a new corporate culture and identity. This can create uncertainty, anxiety and resentment among the company's employees (Appelbaum et al. 2000). Again, research shows that a firm's productivity can drop by between 25–50% while undergoing such a large-scale change, mainly due to the demoralisation of the workforce (Tetenbaum 1999). Companies often pay undue attention to the short-term legal and financial considerations involved in a merger or acquisition, and neglect crucial HR issues relating to corporate identity and communication, which impact workers' morale and productivity (Balmer and Dinnie 1999). These HR issues are crucial to the success of M&As.

3.14 PROCESS OF MERGERS AND ACQUISITIONS

A merger involves fairly complex legal considerations. Sections 391 to 394 of the Companies Act, 1956, contain the provisions for amalgamation. These provisions apply while closing a merger deal. Since the process is extremely complicated, companies hire the services of investment bankers and other financial intermediaries to find suitable target companies and assist in the process of negotiations.

The process of merger and acquisition can be broadly divided into two phases, viz. the planning phase and the implementation phase. The planning phase involves development of the business and the acquisition plan. The implementation phase involves searching the target, screening the target, contacting the target, negotiation, integration and evaluation. Let us understand each step in detail.

3.14.1 Planning Phase

This phase deals with evolving an appropriate strategy for mergers and acquisitions and is extremely critical as it puts the entire process on track and ensures that it reaches the intended destination.

Develop Business Plan

The process of merger is a strategic process as it involves identifying a target that fits into the strategic goals of the company, and increases the net cash flows and reduces risk. To have a clear idea on the merger plans, it is necessary that the company develops a business plan that effectively communicates the vision and mission of the firm and the strategy proposed to achieve the mission.

A business plan deals with the following elements:

- Industry where a company desires to compete
- Determining how to compete effectively
- Undertaking an internal analysis of the company to understand its relative strength and weaknesses
- Defining the mission statement of the company
- Setting objectives intended to be attained
- Selecting the objective attainment strategy

Develop Acquisition Plan

Once the internal analysis is completed and the company feels that the time is right for a merger and acquisition strategy, it starts preparing the acquisition plan. The plan covers the following elements:

- Key objectives
- Resource constraints
- Appropriate tactics for implementing the proposed transactions
- Schedule or timetable for completing the process of acquisition

This step is crucial as it gives valuable inputs on all the later stages of the process. Figure 3.5 illustrates the process of M&A.

3.14.2 Implementation Phase

It is often observed that companies chart out a great plan, but when the time of implementation is at hand, the company is not able to carry the plan forward. This may happen because it may not be able to identify the right target. Hence implementation phase is very critical, and should ensure that the company is able to shortlist appropriate targets. Let us see in detail how this phase is carried out.

Search Companies for Acquisitions

Once the planning phase is completed, the company starts searching for potential acquisition candidates. The search process involves establishing a primary screening process based on factors such as industry, size of the transaction, and geographic location. The search strategy includes the use of databases, law firms, investment bankers, brokers, etc. for identifying prospective candidates. This is the step where the actual merger negotiation process starts between the acquirer and the target firm.

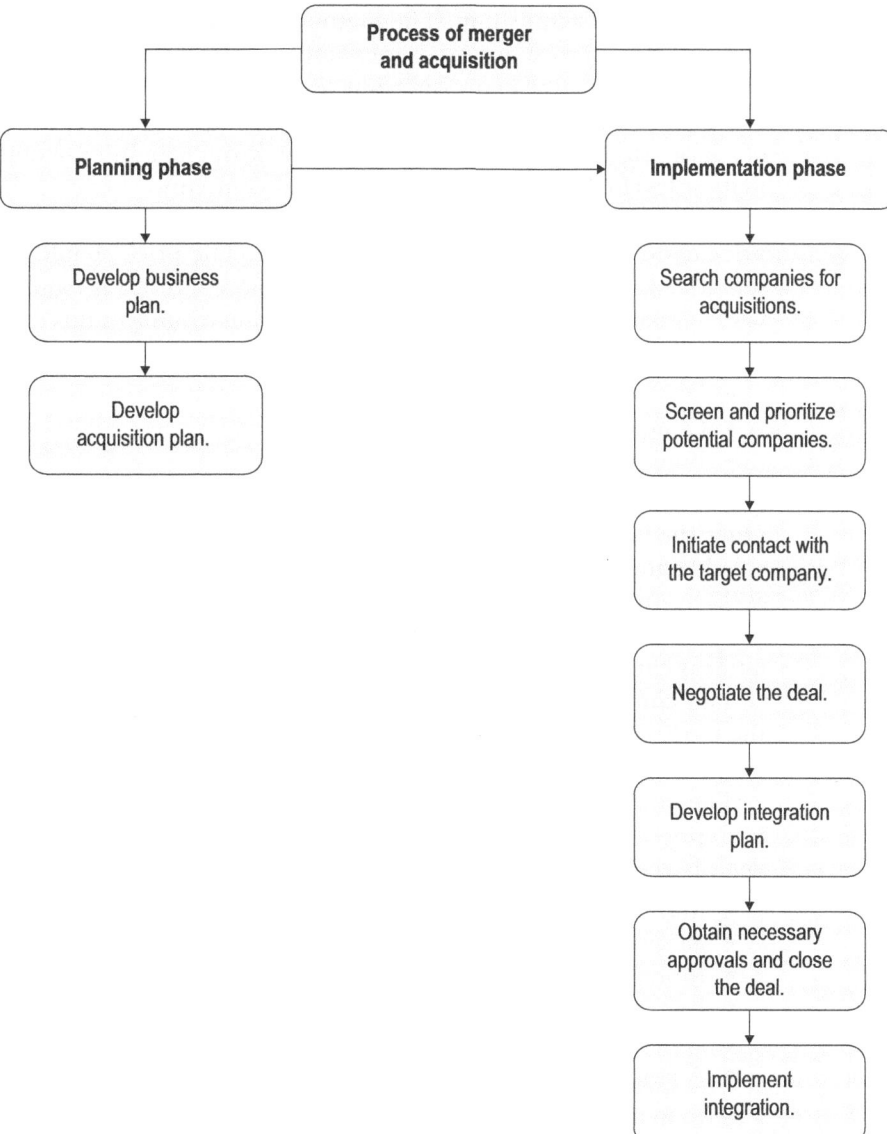

Figure 3.5   Process of merger and acquisition

Screen and Prioritize Potential Companies

The screening process starts with the reduction of the initial list of potential candidates identified earlier. The screening may be done on the basis of market segment, product line, firm's profitability, degree of leverage, market share, etc.

Initiate Contact with Target Company

This step is one where the acquirer meets the target company and puts forth the proposal of acquisition. The method of establishing contacts with the target may differ from case to case. For example, a small target where the acquirer has no contacts, a letter expressing interest is sent. In the case of a medium-sized company, the target is contacted through an intermediary; whereas in the case of a large-sized company, contact is again through an intermediary, but with the highest level of management of the target company.

The acquirer should also ensure that the target company is valued so that a price can be quoted while making an offer. The price should not be very conservative as the target company may show no interest. Likewise, it should not be very aggressive, as the acquirer may be buying trouble in this case. The acquirer may use any one of the following methods for the purpose:

- Discounted cash flow method
- Comparable companies method
- Book value method
- Market value method

Once the target company shows interest in the offer, the acquirer and the target should enter into a confidentiality agreement. As per the agreement, the acquirer seeks historical data and information and collateral information from the target. Similarly the target seeks information from the acquirer to ascertain whether the latter is capable of raising the finance needed for the transaction.

The confidentiality agreement is mutually binding and makes available to the party confidential information that is not available on public domain. The agreement generally has a reasonable expiry period.

The next sequence in the chain of events is to sign a letter of intent. This letter represents a preliminary agreement between the parties to go ahead with the deal. It generally includes the following information:

- Major terms and conditions
- Responsibilities of both the parties
- Mode of payment of fees
- Expiration date
- Non-competing clause
- Amount of the purchase consideration to be kept in the escrow account

Failure to adhere to the conditions stated in the letter of intent may create legal liabilities on the defaulting party.

Negotiate Deal

Under this step, a number of activities go on simultaneously. It is here that the purchase consideration is determined. 'Purchase consideration' implies the following:

Total purchase consideration This is the value of cash, stock, new debts issues and/or non-financial assets taken at current value that would be given to the shareholders of the target company towards settlement of the purchase price.

Total enterprise value This is the total consideration plus the market value of the target firm's debt assumed by the acquiring company. The value represents the approximate value of the investment made by the acquiring firm to purchase the target firm.

Net purchaser price This is the total purchase price plus other assumed liabilities less the proceeds from redundant assets of the target company. This amount may be more or less than the total purchase price.

The acquirer also undertakes the due diligence process in this step. This process facilitates verification of assets and liabilities, identification and quantification of risks, protection needed against prevailing risks, identifying synergy benefits, and post acquisition planning.

If the due diligence process reveals some information that influences the purchase price, then the same is taken as the starting point of negotiating the deal. Once this is done, the acquirer and the target structure the deal; they construct an appropriate set of compensation, legal, tax and accounting structure to deal with the issues of risk and reward. The structuring process influences issues such as determining ownership, mode of transferring the assets, protecting the interests of the owners, methods of sharing the risk of the transaction, etc.

Develop Integration Plan

After the due diligence is carried out, the acquirer develops a plan for integration, focussing primarily on the financial angle. This helps the acquirer ascertain the maximum price he can offer to the target company for the deal. The purchase price represents the present value of the target company plus the synergy created by the combination discounted at the acquirer's cost of capital. The acquirer should go ahead with the deal as long as the net present value (NPV) is greater than or equal to zero.

Obtain Approvals and Close Deal

Once the deal is finalized, the acquirer and the target need to secure the consent of the shareholders, regulatory authorities, and third party consents. All filing required by law should be done on time to avoid legal hurdles.

The parties to the agreement need to ensure that all provisions of the Companies Act, 1956, SEBI Takeover Regulations, provisions of the Competition Act, 2002, and implications of the Income Tax Act, 1961, are strictly fulfilled.

Once these requirements are fulfilled, a definitive purchase and sale agreement needs to be prepared stating the obligations of both the parties before and after the closing the deal.

The length of the document depends on the complexity of the transaction. They are as follows:

- Purpose of the acquisition
- Purchase price

- Allocation of price
- Mode of payment of purchase price
- Details of liabilities assumed
- Representations and warranties
- Covenants
- Undertaking that the target would abide by the warranties and representations
- Agreement of indemnity for liabilities that may arise due to misrepresentations and breaches of warranties and covenants

Implement Integration

Having expectations and achieving them are two different things. Mergers and acquisitions are initiated with the hope that the combined entity would generate synergies. To attain the desired synergy, the acquirer evolves a plan for integrating the two entities. The plan is evolved with the sole objective of ensuring that the combined entity performs in line with the expectations, based on which the deal was executed.

Thus, the process of M&A is very lengthy and time-consuming; it needs to be carried out effectively and efficiently. Showing unnecessary haste can prove costly and detrimental to both the companies.

3.15 FINANCING MERGERS AND ACQUISITIONS

Financing a merger and acquisition is the most challenging task. Once the deal is finalized, the acquirer is required to settle the purchase consideration agreed between him and the target company. The amount required depends on the size of the transaction and the financial position of the acquirer.

The purchase consideration may either be initial consideration or deferred consideration. Initial consideration is the term used for consideration that is paid to the seller on completion of the transaction. Deferred consideration, on the other hand, is consideration that is to be paid to the target company at a later date. The sale agreements generally provide for a combination of these.

Deferred consideration is used in situations where the final price is not known on completion of the deal on account of post-completion adjustments, retentions as security for future claims, and earn-outs.

Adjustments come into play where the value of an asset delivered is more than the agreed amount or vice versa. Retentions represent holding back of some amount by the acquirer when the due diligence process indicates a potential liability. The amount is retained back as security for an agreed period of time. Earn-outs is an arrangement where a part of the consideration is calculated by reference to the future performance of the target company. These are often used as incentives where owner-managed companies are sold and the managers are to continue working with the firm post sale also.

Earn-outs are a useful device to link the overall purchase price to the future profitability of the target company where a greater degree of value is expected to be realized post-completion (Hoare and Jennings 2007).

The most common modes of settling the purchase consideration include cash, equity capital, and loan capital. Let us try and understand each of them.

3.15.1 Cash

This is the most common element of settling the purchase consideration. Cash is likely to come from reserves built by the acquirer over the years. The amount can also be raised through borrowings, equity offerings, debt offerings, or financial assistance.

A cash deal makes sense when interest rates are falling. This is because the deploying the available cash profitable may not be easy. In addition, a cash deal does not dilute the EPS of the acquiring company.

All said and done, it leads to a heavy cash outflow and hence places constraint on the near-future activities of the acquiring company.

3.15.2 Equity Capital

In order to make up for a part or the entire purchase price, an acquirer may choose to issue shares of his/her own enterprise. This mode is used where the acquirer's entity is a listed company as it is easier to compute its value. The acquirer may issue shares with restrictions relating to dealings in the shares for a limited period so as to maintain an orderly market for the shares (Hoare and Jennings 2007).

3.15.3 Loan Capital

The target company also opts for debt instruments such as debentures or loan notes, to settle a part of the purchase consideration for tax planning purposes. Loan notes, like debentures, are a record of the acquirer's indebtedness to the target company to whom loan notes are issued. The loan notes state the amount of indebtedness, interest payable, and terms and conditions of repayment (Hoare and Jennings 2007). The loan notes may be secured or unsecured depending on the creditworthiness of the acquirer, or the same may be offset through higher interest rate being offered on the loan notes.

If the target is acquired through debt, the deal is termed leveraged buyout. Here the debt taken for the takeover is often shown in the balance sheet of the acquired company.

3.16 REVERSE MERGER

Reverse merger is the acquisition of a public company by a private company, allowing the private company to bypass the usually lengthy and complex process of going public. The publicly traded corporation is known as a 'shell corporation' because it has little or no assets. Even though it continues to be a publicly traded corporation, its assets have evaporated through bankruptcy or liquidation and now all that remains is its internal structure and shareholders. The private company obtains the shell company by purchasing controlling interest through a new issue of stock. The reason why a private company acquires such a company is because it has a viable business. The private company 'reverse merges' into the already existing public company, and an entirely new operating entity comes into existence. Reverse mergers are also known as reverse takeovers or RTOs or back-door listing. It is a viable option available to small- to medium-sized privately held companies that are looking to raise additional capital to make acquisitions.

Reverse merger originated as an alternative to the traditional initial public offering (IPO) process for companies that want the benefits of being a public company without the expense and complexities of the traditional IPO. It is often suggested as the best option for the following purposes:

- Provides greater access to the capital markets
- Increases the company's visibility in the investment community
- Offers the opportunity to utilize its stock to make acquisitions

Reverse merger is a quicker, easier, and cheaper route to becoming a public company. Compared to a new public company's ability to raise additional capital, an RTO attracts an investment following, and utilize its public shares as a cheap currency for acquisitions.

3.16.1 Process of Reverse Merger

Let us now understand how the process of reverse merger is carried out. In a reverse merger, a private company merges with a publicly listed company that has no assets or liabilities. This publicly traded corporation is called a 'shell' since all that remains of the original company is the corporate shell structure. By merging with such an entity, the private company becomes public. After the private company obtains a majority of the public company's stock and completes the merger, it appoints new management and elects a new board of directors. The new public corporation thus establishes a base of shareholders sufficient to meet the listing requirements.

The concept of reverse merger is not new. It has been around for almost as long as regulated capital markets have existed, in one incarnation or another. The concept was very popular in the 1980s. The 1990s saw the concept flourishing again with the advent of the internet gold rush, when every sort of company was looking to cash in on the internet phenomenon.

Reverse merger as a tool has been used by shell companies in two forms:

- Under the first form, a failed public company is sold to recoup some of the cost of the failed business. Such shells deals are risky as they have the potential for unknown liabilities, lawsuits, dissatisfied shareholders, and other potential 'skeletons in the closet'.
- Under the second form, companies are created for the specific purpose of being sold as a shell in a reverse merger transaction. Such deals typically carry less risk of having unknown liabilities.

Statutory bodies across the globe have initiated various measures to discourage the practice of keeping a shell company publicly listed for sale in a reverse merger. The main aim behind the regulation has been to decrease penny stock fraud by increasing the minimum capital requirements and the minimum price requirements for the purpose of listing.

While the regulatory measures might have discouraged companies from getting listed in the major stock exchanges, most of them moved to the over-the-counter (OTC) exchanges and quite a few also disappeared entirely. What is more disheartening to note is that most of the companies that choose the reverse merger process become substantially worse off after the process.

What needs to be remembered is that such companies generally bring a great deal of indiscipline in the market and affect the investor's confidence. It is worth mentioning that the process of traditional IPO is adopted because not all companies desirous of entering the capital markets are 'not ready for prime time'. They are effectively a 'publicly traded private company.' Such entities have an illiquid, low priced stock, a low valuation, and little to no institutional following (Molloy and Fung 2006). Again such companies are not attuned to the culture of stringent disclosure norms and often end up violating the statutory provisions.

Entities that opt for a reverse merger often face a number of challenges such as low stock price, poor or low liquidity, no institutional following to raise the stock price, inability to make acquisition, failure to adopt stock incentive plans due to low stock price, difficultly in private placements due to low public valuation, etc. Critics opine that small companies should explore other alternatives for raising additional capital such as remaining private and raising capital through private placement or going through the merger and acquisition route.

3.16.2 Myths about Reverse Mergers

Companies are often attracted towards reverse merger because of the following myths (Molloy and Fung 2006):

- The costs are significantly lower than the cost of an IPO.
- Time required is considerably less than for an IPO.
- The IPO may have to be withdrawn due to unstable market conditions.
- Initial public offerings require greater attention from top management.
- Having underwriters does not help.
- Reverse mergers increase the liquidity of the shares.
- The share price improves, thus improving the company's valuation.
- By getting listed on the stock exchanges, the access to the capital markets for future stock offerings improves.
- They improve the ability to make acquisitions using the company's public stock.
- The process improves the company's ability to use stock incentive plans to attract and retain key employees.

3.16.3 Examples of Reverse Mergers

Here are some popular examples of reverse mergers:

- Trans-India Acquisition Corporation (TIL) reverse merged with Hyderabad-based photovoltaic (PV) modules maker Solar Semiconductors Ltd in 2008.
- Lloyds Steel reverse merged with Lloyds Metal, a group company in 1998.
- Henkel Spic India Ltd proposed to merge with Henkel India Ltd, formerly known as The Calcutta Chemical Company Ltd in 2004. The merger put all the manufacturing activities under the merged entity.
- Jindal Iron and Steel Company reverse merged into Jindal Vijayanagar Steel in 2003.
- TVS Electronics Limited (TVS-E) reverse merged with TVS eTechnology in 2003.
- ICICI Limited reverse merged with ICICI Bank in 2002.
- REO Motor Car Company staged a reverse 'hostile' takeover of a small publicly traded company, Nuclear Consultants. Eventually, this company became the modern-day Nucor in 1999.
- ValuJet Airlines was acquired by AirWays Corp. to form AirTran Holdings, in 1997.
- Aérospatiale was acquired by Matra to form Aérospatiale-Matra in 1999.
- The game company Atari was acquired by JT Storage in 1996.
- US Airways was acquired by America West Airlines in 2005.
- The New York Stock Exchange was acquired by Archipelago Holdings to form NYSE Group in 2005.
- ABC Radio was acquired by Citadel Broadcasting Corporation, with the goal of spinning the former off from its parent, Disney in 2007.
- Frederick's of Hollywood parent FOH Holdings was acquired by apparel maker Movie Star in 2006.

3.17 CONCEPT OF EARN-OUTS

Companies opting for M&As need to be innovative as market pressures can create a lot of hurdles in successfully negotiating a deal, especially gaps in the price expectations of the acquirer and the target company. Earn-outs have become popular as a tool to help bridge this gap especially in the emerging technology businesses.

Earn-outs are designed to satisfy the target company's demand to receive compensation for the anticipated future value of the transferred assets and the acquirer's desire to avoid over-paying for potential, but as yet unrealized, value. This method is used when small companies in high-growth, high-tech, or service industries are sold. In practice, an earn-out splits the purchase price into two parts. The first is payment at closing of the deal and the second is one or more contingent payments dependent upon the satisfaction of future sales targets, product developments or other milestones. A survey done by the *CFO* magazine shows that earn-out terms were found in 4% of all reported US deals and nearly 10% of reported deals valued at or below $250 million in the first four months of 2002 (Harris 2002).

Earn-outs are thus an arrangement whereby a part of the purchase price is calculated by reference to the future performance of the target company. The deal describes a payment to shareholders selling their shares in the target company and the payment made by the acquirer is based on the company's profits in a specified period, usually after the closing of the sale. The acquirer typically pays 60–80% of the purchase price up front with the remaining 20–40% structured as an earn-out and paid out over time as the acquired company achieves certain levels of sales or profitability. For example, a target company may offer to sell its business for ₹2 billion based on projected earnings, but the acquiring company is willing to pay only ₹1 billion based on historical performance. The target then insists on making an earn-out whereby the acquirer should pay some more amount if the business achieves a certain level of earnings, say ₹1 billion plus 5% of gross sales over the next three years. This deal will help the target to get more than what the acquirer proposed under the original deal, and at the same time, the acquirer will pay less than what the target company proposed originally under the deal.

Of course, there is a catch in the deal brokered. If the acquired business fails to raise earnings to pre-decided benchmarks after the acquisition, the acquirer pays nothing more to the target for the business than the initial sum.

3.17.1 Criteria for Determining Earn-outs

Earn-outs can be based on criteria that can range from growth in sales or EBIT to customer retention, product integration, and technology development. Whatever forms the basis of working the earn-out, both parties negotiate hard as the deal imposes a contingent liability on the acquirer and raises hopes of getting more than the original deal price for the target company. In spite of this challenge, company's adopt earn-outs to help close complex deals. For example, Google's acquisition of dMarc Broadcasting Inc., which ran an online system enabling advertisers to buy radio airtime, was based on the earn-out principle. The up-front purchase price was fixed at $102 million. Google agreed to pay dMarc up to $1.14 billion in contingent payments over the next three years if certain product integration, net revenue, and advertising inventory performance targets are met.

Similarly, when eBay Inc. purchased the voice-over-Internet-protocol company Skype Technologies SA for about $2.6 billion, the deal involved a performance-based earn-out worth an additional $1.5 billion. The earn-out payments were based on Skype achieving a net revenue and gross margin-based target based on the number of active users.

3.17.2 Advantages of Earn-outs

If one scrutinizes an earn-out deal, its advantages can be readily appreciated:

- Instead of a potential deal collapsing due to a price gap, an earn-out can be designed to create a win–win situation for both buyer and seller.
- Technology companies that can secure exit without engaging in the downsizing could devastate and perhaps even destroy the business. The stakeholders can earn a substantially greater payout than would otherwise be available without an earn-out.
- The acquirer can avoid the risks associated with overpaying for an immature technology and/or an unproven team.
- It provides a strong incentive for the key personnel to work hard to increase the value of the acquisition, by developing the technology, training the buyer's personnel and otherwise working to foster the integration of the businesses.

3.17.3 Weaknesses of Earn-outs

While there is no argument that earn-outs are here to stay, they have some weaknesses:

- It is very difficult to ascertain the degree to which the operation of the acquirer's business will be constrained by the earn-out rules.
- In a reasonably fair earn-out structure, both the target and the acquirer are required to accept some unexpected risks when the expected results are adversely affected due to unforeseen factors.
- In a less than equally negotiated deal, one of the parties may find it has little control over the end results of the earn-out. For example, the acquirer may typically only pay more when the business has been successful, while the target may end up receiving much less than what was anticipated in unforeseen situations.

In the light of these weaknesses, the parties to the deal should work towards minimizing the possibility of unforeseen consequences arising after the closing. If one analyses the earn-outs being worked out in the business world, one finds that both the acquirer and the target pay little attention on how earn-outs actually work, resulting in last-minute negotiations and structures that give rise to unnecessary conflict after closing of the deal. To avoid post-deal conflicts, the target must secure as much control as possible over the use of the assets, budgets, and hiring of marketing and sales teams. It should also incorporate penalties to compel the acquirer to abide by contractual restrictions. Such penalties are best designed as liquidated damages provisions, requiring the acceleration of an earn-out payment or other cash payments. It is done to avoid the need for a seller to commence litigation to try to compel the buyer's performance. Sellers should consider an acceleration or modification of the earn-out upon the sale of the buyer's business, disposition of assets, or change in the buyer's business that would adversely affect the seller's chances for obtaining the earn-out. Sellers might also demand a guaranteed minimum payment for an earn-out.

In addition to concentrating on the operation of the business after the closing, the seller should ensure that there are retention incentives for the key people needed to execute the business plan. These incentives can come from both the buyer in the nature of stock options, performance bonuses and the like and from the seller. A seller should consider rewarding and penalizing key members of the seller's personnel working for the buyer after the closing, to allocate a portion of the earn-out and to restrict payouts unless performance objectives are satisfied. Buyers will frequently consent to special provisions with respect to seller personnel due to their incentive to keep the personnel properly motivated.

It is in the interest of both the parties to ensure that the metrics for the earn-out are as clear and comprehensive as possible so that disputes can be avoided after the closing. Objective, easily identifiable, and measurable targets are very important. For example, basing an earn-out on gross revenues rather than net revenues avoids substantial negotiation and potential uncertainty relating to appropriate costs that can reduce gross earnings and the earn-out results. Of course, the buyer might prefer to calculate the earn-out based on net earnings, with flexibility to reflect true earnings performance since it more accurately reflects the economic value of the business.

3.18 MERGERS AND ACQUISITIONS IN INDIA

Indian companies have also started opting for M&As on a large scale. A study done by the global consulting firm Grant Thornton indicated that the acquisition value by India Inc. had touched $16 billion in 2005. According to them, this trend is getting accelerated with every passing quarter. All major entities across sectors, such as Dr Reddy's, Suzlon Energy, Ranbaxy Labs, Videocon, VSNL, Tata Chemicals, Tata Steel, and Wipro have been on an acquisition spree (Thiagarajan 2006). The sectors that have been seeing hectic activity include telecom, pharma, software, steel, automotive, FMCG, and chemicals.

There are some concerns relating to these acquisitions, which India Inc. needs to address urgently. Disclosure in most of the deals remains sketchy as no standardized format has been set for disclosure requirements for M&As. Companies have managed to get away revealing the minimum. There are extreme cases. For example, when Suzlon acquired Hansen Transmissions, the European wind turbine gearbox manufacturer, they disclosed only the deal value and revenues and no information pertaining to margins, growth potential or fair value was made available. Whereas, when Tata Chemicals acquired Brunner Mond Group, UK, they provided exhaustive details of the deal, valuation and synergies/growth prospects in the existing line of business. Furthermore, it also held a conference call with analysts to provide additional information. Such a transparent approach needs to be adopted, which helps the company get the backing of all the stakeholders.

Most of the deals involving Indian companies are cross-border deals. The deals have been both inbound (foreign companies buying out Indian companies) and outbound (Indian companies buying out overseas companies). This argument is substantiated by a CII–Boston Consulting Group study of 2005 that showed a three-fold rise in overseas buyouts by Indian companies. This trend noticed that M&A deals are unique and progressive, and are the direct outcome of the following factors:

- Increasing competitive pressures and changing market dynamics are forcing companies to align their strategies to market realities. In the pharma sector, they have forced companies such as Ranbaxy Labs and Dr Reddy's to launch a flurry of acquisitions.
- Changing scale and size is forcing companies to pursue sector consolidation. In the IT sector, for example, all major players such as IBM, EDS, Accenture, TCS, Infosys, and Wipro are jostling with each other to pursue consolidation.
- The buckling ancillary industry in the US is opening new acquisition opportunities for Indian companies such as Bharat Forge, Sundram Fasteners, and Amtek Auto.
- Rapidly consolidating sectors such as steel, metals, automobiles and auto components, chemicals, textiles, oil and gas are encouraging Indian Companies such as the Tata Group, Hindalco, Sterlite, ONGC, Videsh Sanchar Nigam Ltd., etc. to venture into the global turf with greater confidence and speed.
- Rise of private equity is also giving the much needed fillip to M&As. This trend has been noticed in Holcim's deal with ACC and Gujarat Ambuja, and Vodafone's stake in Bharti Tele-Ventures. In retailing, textiles and construction sectors may usher in a new chapter in the M&A deals of India Inc.

While India Inc. is riding a wave of growing trend of M&As, the deals present substantial upside and downside to the stakeholders. While the deals promise value for integration, not all of them deliver it. This continues to remain a big challenge. All deals are not transparent, and stakeholders are often kept in the dark on many aspects of the deal. The need is to evolve a mechanism whereby, companies are mandated to provide separate financials for the acquired entity for at least two to three quarters. This, it is felt, will help the stakeholders to draw inferences of contribution from organic and inorganic business.

3.18.1 Examples of Mergers and Acquisitions in India

While M&As have been an important component of 'India Rising,' the following have been some of the largest mergers and acquisition deals of India Inc.

Tata Steel–Corus   This deal saw Tata Steel purchasing a 100% stake in the Corus Group at 608 pence per share in an all-cash deal cumulatively valued at $12.2 billion. This deal made Tata Steel the world's fifth-largest steel group.

Vodafone–Hutchison Essar   Under this deal, Vodafone bought the controlling interest of 67% held by Li Ka Shing Holdings in Hutch-Essar for $11.1 billion. After the deal, the holdings are Vodafone 52%, Essar Group 33%, and other Indian nationals 15%.

Hindalco–Novelis   Hindalco Industries, a Kumar Mangalam Birla-led Aditya Birla Group flagship Aluminium and copper major acquired Canadian company Novelis Inc. in a $6 billion, all-cash deal. This deal made Hindalco the global leader in aluminium rolled products and one of the largest aluminium producers in Asia. The post-acquisition combined revenues in excess of $10 billion would ensure that Hindalco enters the Fortune-500 list of world's largest companies based on sales revenues.

Ranbaxy–Daiichi Sankyo   This deal has been the largest-ever deal in the Indian pharma industry, where Japanese drug firm Daiichi Sankyo acquired a majority stake of more than 50% in domestic major Ranbaxy for over $4.5 billion. The deal resulted in creating the world's 15th biggest drug maker.

ONGC–Imperial Energy   ONGC made a takeover offer to Imperial Energy Plc for $2.8 billion. The offer was accepted by an overwhelming 96.8% of the total shareholders. Obviously government support played a major role in this deal.

NTT DoCoMo–Tata Teleservices   This deal saw Japanese telecom giant NTT DoCoMo picking up a 26% equity stake in Tata Teleservices for about $2.7 billion. The deal involved DoCoMo issuing fresh equity and acquisition of shares from the existing promoters.

HDFC Bank–Centurion Bank of Punjab   The HDFC Bank acquisition of Centurion Bank of Punjab for $2.4 billion is one of the largest mergers in the financial sector in India. This takeover saw Centurion Bank shareholders getting one share of HDFC Bank for every 29 shares held by them. The acquisition also made HDFC Bank the second-largest private sector bank in India.

Tata Motors–Jaguar Land Rover   This deal has been in the news as one of India's top corporate entities, Tata Motors, acquired luxury auto brands—Jaguar and Land Rover—from Ford Motor for $2.3 billion. This deal also had another Indian company Mahindra & Mahindra in the fray for the prestigious brands. As per the deal, the Tatas chipped in $600 million towards JLR's pension plan.

Sterlite–Asarco   Sterlite Industries Ltd. acquired Asarco LLC for $1.8 billion. The deal size actually fell by almost $1 billion, from a projected estimate of $2.6 billion due to devaluation of mining assets and a sharp fall in copper prices.

Suzlon–REpower   Wind power major Suzlon Energy acquired Germany's leading manufacturers of wind turbines REpower for $1.7 billion. The deal is very strategic as REpower controls 10% share of the overall market.

RIL–RPL   Reliance Industries Ltd approved a scheme for amalgamating its subsidiary Reliance Petroleum Ltd (RPL) with the parent company. This all-share merger deal between the two Mukesh Ambani group firms was valued at about $1.68 billion. The RIL–RPL merger swap ratio was fixed at 16:1.

This merger was one where no fresh treasury stock got created and the parent's holding in the petroleum unit stood cancelled. Almost 200 million existing treasury of shares continued. The merger created a behemoth with a total refining capacity of 1.24 million barrels of crude a day, which is a quarter of the world's total complex refining capacity.

The merger, it was expected, would unlock significant operational and financial synergies that existed between RIL and RPL. Through this merger, RIL would be able to consolidate a complex refinery with minimal residual project risk, while complementing RIL's product range. There would be further gains from the reduced operating cost arising from synergies of combined operations.

This discussion clearly points out that M&As, although not always successful, are here to stay. This is because the combining entities have been relying on conventional wisdom and guess work instead of hard-nosed analysis and discipline. However, failures over the years have made companies more analytical and focused. As a result, M&As are pursued as a strategy based on a detailed study of the environment, sound analysis, and regulatory adherence. Companies can certainly do better if synergies are clearly identified and expectations are not hyped. This can certainly ensure that the deal does not turn sour and helps the acquirer achieve anticipated results.

SUMMARY

The dynamic business environment requires strategies that are capable of generating growth through synergies in M&As. While faulty execution leads to disaster and chaos, all one needs to ensure is that the process is carried out after proper study and analysis of the factors and anticipated goals.

KEY DEFINITIONS

Absorption   Absorption is a combination of two or more companies into an existing company. All companies except one lose their identity in such a merger.

Acquisition   Acquisition is an attempt made by one firm to gain a majority interest in another firm. The firm attempting to gain a majority interest is called the acquiring firm and the other firm is called the target firm.

Consolidation   Consolidation is a merger of two or more companies into a 'new company'. In this form of merger, all companies are legally dissolved and a new entity is created. Here, the acquired company transfers its assets, liabilities, and shares to the acquiring company for cash or exchange of shares.

Conglomerate merger   A conglomerate merger is 'one in which there is no economic relationship between the acquiring and the acquired firm'. Conglomerate mergers are mergers involving firms that are in different or unrelated business activity. Such mergers are preferred by firms that plan to increase their product lines.

Earn-outs   Earn-outs are an arrangement whereby a part of the purchase price is calculated by reference to the future performance of the target company. The deal describes a payment to shareholders selling their shares in the target company and the payment made by the acquirer is based on the company's profits in a specified period, usually after the closing of the sale.

Merger   Merger is a strategy where two or more companies agree to combine their operations to derive the benefits of synergy.

Merger waves   These are phases in which M&As occurred across the globe. Each wave had some unique features of its own.

Modern view   The modern view looked at mergers and acquisitions as a vehicle to change the control of the firms' assets. It is viewed as a process of allocation and reallocation of resources by firms in response to changes in the economic conditions and technological innovations of the market. Mergers and acquisitions are looked upon as a tool of gaining competitive advantage and a strategy for attaining growth.

Reverse merger   Reverse merger is the acquisition of a public company by a private company, allowing the private company to bypass the usually lengthy and complex process of going public. The publicly traded corporation is known as a 'shell corporation' because it has little or no assets. Even though it continues to be a publicly traded corporation, its assets have evaporated through bankruptcy or liquidation and now all that remains is its internal structure and shareholders. The private company obtains the shell company by purchasing controlling interest through a new issue of stock.

Traditional view of mergers   The traditional view focused on competition and often resulted in horizontal mergers that created conditions of monopolistic competition. The basic motivation was survival in the market through growth generally achieved through M&As. The selection of the target was based on its size and quality.

CONCEPT REVIEW QUESTIONS

3.1 Explain the concept of mergers. Give a brief account of the merger and acquisition waves that the business world has seen.

3.2 What do you mean by acquisition? Explain the different types of acquisitions.

3.3 How does a merger differ from an acquisition?

3.4 'Mergers are not always driven by a desire to diversify and grow'. Comment.

3.5 Why do companies go for M&As?

3.6 State and explain the variables that drive value in M&As.

3.7 'Mergers and acquisitions do not always generate value.' Comment.

3.8 Why do merger and acquisitions fail?

3.9 Explain the process of mergers and acquisition in detail.

3.10 Write notes on the following:
  (a) Genesis of M&As
  (b) Classification of mergers
  (c) Acquisition strategies
  (d) Financing M&As
  (e) Reverse merger
  (f) Earn-outs
  (g) M&As in India

PROJECT ASSIGNMENTS

3.1 Make a study of M&As carried out by Indian companies since liberalization.

3.2 Make a study of financing strategies undertaken by Indian companies post-2001 to finance mergers and acquisition.

3.3 Undertake a study of reasons for the failure of M&As in India.

3.4 Analyse the following M&As in detail:
  (a) Tata–Corus Steel
  (b) RIL–RPL
  (c) Vodafone–Hutchison Essar
  (d) Mittal–Arcelor

REFERENCES

1992 Horizontal Merger Guidelines, The US Department of Justice and Federal Trade Commission, Washington, 1997

Chakravarty, V., 'How to Add Value to M&A', *Business Today* 7(5), 1998, pp. 7–21

Chandler, A.D., 'The Coming of Oligopoly and its Meaning for Antitrust, National Competition Policy, Historian Perspective on Antitrust and Government Business Relationships in United States,' *Federal Trade Commission Publication,* Washington, August 1981, pp. 72

Compendium of Accounting Standards, Accounting Standards 14, ICAI, New Delhi, pp. 2

Damodaran, A., *Damodaran on Valuation—Security Analysis for Investment and Corporate Finance,* 2nd edition, John Wiley and Sons, Boston, 2002, pp. 52–54

Edward, E.H. and Jennings, N., 'Consideration', *Mergers and Acquisitions,* Ed. Jonathan, R., Kogan Page, London, 2007, pp. 75–78

Fenton, K., *Mergers and Acquisitions: Understanding the Antitrust Issues,* 3rd edition, American Bar Association, Section of Antitrust Law, Chicago, February 2008

FTC and Procter and Gamble Company Case, U.S. Supreme Court, Case No. 386 US 568, 577, Washington, April 1967

Gaughan, P.A. and Patrick, A., *Mergers, Acquisitions and Corporate Restructuring,* 4th edition, John Wiley and Sons, New Jersey, 2007, pp. 32

Griffin, R.W., *Management,* Cengage Learning Inc., Florence, 2008, pp. 219

Harris, R., 'Caution: Earnouts Ahead—Tying Price to Performance can be a Good Way to Acquire Hard-to-value Companies—If You're Careful', *CFO Magazine,* June 2002

http://www.learnmergers.com/mergers, last accessed on 9 January 2009

http://business.gov.in/growing_business/mergers_acq.php, last accessed on 9 January 2009

Income Tax Bare Act, http://law.incometaxindia.gov.in/Dit/Income-tax-acts, last accessed on 9 January 2010

James, M. and Fung, M., *The Reverse Merger: Backing into Wall Street's Worst Idea,* Mirus Technology Group Research, Boston, 2006

Krishnan, T., 'India Inc. on M&A Overdrive', *Business Line,* 16 April 2006

MacAvoy, P., Staff of Federal Trade Commission, *Economic Report on Corporate Mergers, Working Paper,* Alfred P. Sloan School of Management, Cambridge, 1969

Machiraju, H.R., *Mergers, Acquisitions and Takeovers,* New Age International, New Delhi, 2003, pp. 1

Mark, M. and Mulherin, J. H., 'Impact of Industry shocks on Takeover and Restructuring Activity,' *Journal of Financial Economics,* Volume 41, Issue 2, June 1996, pp. 193–229

Mastracchio, N.J., Jr and Zunitch, V.M., Difference between Mergers and Acquisitions, *Journal of Accountancy,* November 2002, New York, pp. 675

Nelson, R., 'Movements in American Industry 1895–1956', *The National Bureau of Economic Research,* Cambridge, 1959, pp. 71–105

Sweeting, M., 'Acquisition target Strategies', *Mergers and Acquisitions,* Ed. Jonathan, R., Kogan Page, London, 2007, pp. 31

Varney, A.C., *Vertical Merger Enforcement Challenges at the FTC,* PLI 36th Annual Antitrust Institute, San Francisco, 17 July 1995

Walters, I., *Mergers and Acquisitions in Banking and Finance – What works, What fails and Why,* Oxford University Press, New York, 2004, pp. 99

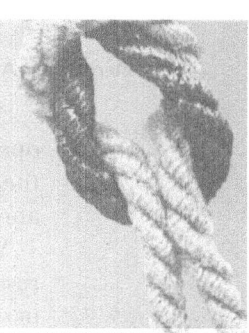

4

Due Diligence

LEARNING OBJECTIVES

After studying the chapter, you will be able to understand

- the concept of due diligence
- the need for due diligence
- the types and the process of due diligence
- the parties involved in the due diligence process
- due diligence reporting
- why due diligence fails and how to avoid it
- what it requires to make an effective due diligence team

4.1 INTRODUCTION

Mergers and acquisitions (M&As) involve a huge investment of financial resources. No buyer would like to lose money through a bad deal. To evaluate the commercial viability of a deal, the buying company undertakes a process known as due diligence. While due diligence is not an insurance against a bad deal, it certainly provides enough assurance that the deal is per se not bad.

4.2 CONCEPT OF DUE DILIGENCE

The term 'due diligence' is used by different people in different contexts. In general, it implies an activity involving either the performance of an investigation of a business or person, or the performance of an act with a certain standard of care (Adukia 2009). In some other cases, it is used to mean a required legal obligation, although the term more commonly applies to a voluntary investigation. Some common examples of due diligence in various organizations are the evaluative steps carried out by venture capitalists before and during each investment phase of a start-up company. It can also include the precautionary steps taken by one company in deciding whether to acquire another, by evaluating whether the buy is good or bad (www.eyesonchina.com).

Due diligence is also described as the process of investigation performed by investors into the details of a potential investment, such as an examination of operations and management and the verification of material facts. In short, it is the process of evaluating a prospective business decision by getting information about the financial, legal, and other material state of the other party.

When the concept is analysed from the financial angle, it implies a process of research and analysis that takes place before an acquisition, investment, or business partnership to determine the value of the firm in question (Adukia 2009).

Similarly, for the banking industry it means the responsibility of bank directors and officers to act in a prudent manner in evaluating credit applications.

In the securities market, it refers to the responsibility of underwriters to explain the details of new securities to interested purchasers (Adukia 2009).

Due diligence is legally defined as 'a measure of prudence, activity, or assiduity, as is properly to be expected from, and ordinarily exercised by, a reasonable and prudent person under the particular circumstances; not measured by any absolute standard but dependent on the relative facts of the special case' (www. charlesmillsconsulting.com).

The basic function of due diligence in any merger or acquisition is to assess the potential risks of a proposed transaction by inquiring into all relevant aspects of the past, present, and predictable future of the business to be purchased. The term is also used in securities law to describe the duty of care and review to be exercised by officers, directors, underwriters, and others in connection with public offerings of securities.

The due diligence effort in a merger transaction should include basic activities to meet diligence standards of common law and best practices. These activities include the following:

Financial statements review   It confirms the existence of assets, liabilities, and equity in the balance sheet, and determines the financial health of the company based on the income statement.

Management and operations review   It determines the quality and reliability of financial statements, and helps to gain a sense of contingencies beyond the financial statements.

Legal compliance review   It checks for potential future legal problems stemming from the target's past.

Document and transaction review   It ensures that the paperwork of the deal is in order and that the structure of the transaction is appropriate (Lajoux 2003).

In short, due diligence involves investigation and evaluation of a management team's characteristics, investment philosophy, and terms and conditions prior to committing capital. It is undertaken to determine the value of its subject and unearth any current or potential issues. The process helps in getting a realistic picture of how the business is performing now and how it is likely to perform in the future (Lajoux 2003).

Due diligence can also be transactional in nature. This process involves an investigation by an investor or advisors of the accurate and complete character of the target company's business. The target may be an acquisition candidate, a joint venture or strategic alliance partner, a prospective public offering registrant, or a company the investor is considering for minority interest private placements (Rosenbloom 2002).

Due diligence, as a process, makes sense when it is linked to the investor's corporate strategy. It includes investigating the target's legal status from its proper legal authorization to do business to its actual or contingent liabilities and all points in between. It also includes analysing the target's historical, current, and projected financial statements. When the investor and the target are in the same industry, transactional due diligence explores financial, operational, or managerial synergies between them.

The potential investor generally uses in-house resources or outsources the job to experts who specialize in due diligence and corporate investigations. The purpose, however, remains the same—to investigate the background and principals of the target company. A potential investor may also seek legal counsel and professional accountants to get an expert advice in all areas (Adukia 2002).

The process is crucial, as on completion of the exercise, one knows the following:

- What one is getting into
- What are the needs to be fixed
- What it will cost to fix them
- Whether the prospect is the right target to take on

4.3 NEED FOR DUE DILIGENCE

We now have a fair idea about due diligence and its increasing importance in today's complex business environment. Organizations today operate in a very uncertain environment that is full of risks, some of which can be controlled, but most of which cannot. Organizations have always been functioning with scarce resources, but given the huge size of today's business entities, the element of risk has increased drastically. Organizations are obviously concerned about committing resources, for not all investments generate profits. To understand the past and the future earning capabilities of the entity, one needs to thoroughly analyse the industry and the environment in which one is expected to operate.

Due diligence becomes crucial due to the following reasons:

- Due diligence enables the investor to know the strengths and weaknesses of the business one is buying. There is no second view on the fact that buying a business with unexpected difficulties and risks can be disastrous. Due diligence is necessary to allow the investor to find out everything that he needs to know about the subject in question.
- Due diligence gives a fair value of the investment to the potential investor, thereby increasing his bargaining power. In the absence of due diligence, the investor often relies on facts and figures provided by the vendor, which need not necessarily be correct. Once the process of due diligence is completed

and the investor gets a fair idea of what he is getting involved in, he has the following options:

- Withdrawing the deal
- Adjusting the valuation of the investment
- Going ahead with the deal as quoted by the vendor

If the buyer/investor fails to undertake due diligence, he is left with no choice but to agree to the price stated by the vendor.

- Due diligence helps in identifying the hidden irregularities existing in the business. Very often, on the face of it things seem fine since events are very cleverly window dressed. It is only when one decides to undertake a microscopic analysis of facts and events that the irregularities come to light. Sitting back and doing nothing is unlikely to protect one from being cheated. If a reasonable step or precaution is not taken, any defence is likely to fail. The question that often arises is 'What is a reasonable step?' It is all about verifying the facts that are communicated by one person to another. For example, if a seller of wristwatches claims that a watch he has produced is waterproof and that it is a diver's watch, all that one needs to do is to place the watch in a bowl of water. This simple test can reveal whether the watch is waterproof, and can avoid future problems and related costs. Thus, due diligence is a reliable tool for identifying inherent irregularities that are otherwise hidden.
- Due diligence is an effective tool for ensuring that the prevailing system of checks works. For example, if an organization has in place a programme of checks, it must work. Having a system in place that nobody follows is as bad not having a system at all. A system is something that demands periodic or even constant monitoring. In creating a system, one must consider all aspects of the business, from the design stage to after-sales, identify the risks, adopt appropriate controls and safeguards, record the actions, and keep the systems under review. All this is best done through due diligence.

4.4 WHAT DOES DUE DILIGENCE INVOLVE?

Due diligence is a very lengthy process of reviewing information. The information that is reviewed includes the following:

- Historical financial data
- Current financial data
- Forecasted financial information
- Business plans
- Minutes of directors' meetings and management meetings
- Audit paperwork files
- Contracts with suppliers, customers, and staff
- Confirmation/representations from financiers, debtors, etc.

There is a caveat involved. Due diligence should not be restricted to reviewing documentation alone. Discussions with staff, both formal and informal talks, visiting the target's premises, and observing the ongoing activities also give an idea about the state of the target.

4.5 TRANSACTIONS REQUIRING DUE DILIGENCE

As we have already discussed, due diligence provides a deep insight into the activities of the business alongside the prevailing business environment and the future prospects of the business. These are the areas where due diligence proves indispensable.

4.5.1 Mergers and Acquisitions

An M&A is a transaction where one entity combines with another for deriving perceived benefits. As the focus is on perceived benefits, one needs to analyse the past, present, and future business prospects of the related industry and firm. The analysis covers all the areas highlighted, and the entire process is carried out through due diligence.

The potential buyer carries out extensive due diligence to know more about the target company. The expectation of the purchaser or acquirer from the transaction is to get better value from whatever the target is presently doing. During the process of due diligence, the buyer tries to identify and accordingly take steps to reduce uncertainties. The cost of due diligence is much less than the cost of a bad acquisition.

As part of the due diligence process, the prospective buyer sends a question-naire to the target company requesting full details of the business including financials, patents, licenses and collaboration agreements, and employment contracts. The due diligence team also reviews regulatory and press clippings, media reports, etc., to find out whether there are any legal and regulatory issues, existing and pending lawsuits, and other litigation involving the entity. The team also undertakes a detailed study to look for conflict of interest and other problems. The entire due diligence process includes analysis of the following aspects:

Personnel

People constitute the most important element of any organization. However, it is also true that not all employees are invaluable and indispensible. During the M&A, the buyer has to absorb the human resources of the target company. Hence it is imperative for the buyer to review employees' skills, experience, wages, payroll procedures, and other relevant human resources issues. Based on this analysis, they determine whether there is any deadwood in the target company. Accordingly the buyer would negotiate and, if possible, get rid of the deadwood.

Financial Operations

The end objective of any M&A deal is to improve the company's bottom line. A buy that would lower or destroy value makes no sense. The buying entity tries to figure out the financial implications of the buy. The following details of the target company are examined:

- The company's books and records
- All accounting and book-keeping methods
- Analysis of the cash flows, both present and projected
- Accounts receivable
- Debts and bank/lender relations
- Service/product pricing and its consistency with industry standards

Financial records are the heart and soul of the company's performance and hence need to be carefully analysed.

Marketing

If one analyses the company, one understands that marketing activities generate revenue and thus bring profits to the business. The future earning potential to a great extent depends upon the marketing activities and related strategies of the target company. It is therefore crucial to examine the following:

- The company's advertising campaigns
- Public relations programmes, if any
- Marketing and sales strategies
- Marketing and advertising strategies of the competitors

Once the buying company gets a feel of these elements, it can easily conclude on the relevance and importance of striking a deal.

Property and Equipment

Another important element of an M&A deal is the property and equipment of the target company that the acquiring company takes over. Here again, the acquirer would like to take over only the assets that will prove beneficial to them. They need to take the following steps:

- Review all the related leases and/or deeds.
- Conduct appraisals for all equipment and assets.
- Consider depreciation in property and equipment values.

This also helps the buyer to estimate the purchase consideration for the deal, which is the value it finally pays for taking over the business of the target company.

Business Operations

Understanding the business operations of the target company is crucial for an acquiring company, for this is the real key to success. The analysis herein includes the following:

- Location of the organization
- Adherence to inventory management techniques
- Vendor management
- Overall administrative policies

- Receivables and customer relationship management
- Safety management and insurance cover taken
- Any other aspects specifically related to the business one proposes to buy (www.allbusiness.com)

A popular myth about due diligence is that it is the buyer alone who is keen in carrying out this exercise. Due diligence is as important to a seller as it is to a buyer. This is because sale of a business invariably includes warranties given by the seller in relation to certain aspects of the business. For example, the seller is usually asked to warrant that the activities of the business do not infringe on any third-party intellectual rights, and that no third parties are infringing on any of the company's licenses, IT systems, etc. To ensure that such issues are properly addressed, it is preferred that the seller too carries out a due diligence exercise on his own.

Similarly, sellers also need to conduct due diligence to determine the ability of the buyer to complete the sale transaction, analyse the past record of previous acquisitions by the buyer, etc. This gives a fair idea to the seller about the ability and willingness of the buyer to complete the transaction initiated. Once the seller is sure about the seriousness with which the buyer is pursuing the deal, he can be rest assured that the deal would reach its logical conclusion.

4.5.2 Partnerships

A partnership is a relationship between persons who come together for carrying on a business activity and decide to share the profits or bear the losses arising from it. Since it represents a legal relationship, it is important that the concerned parties conduct negotiations and investigate the affairs of the interested individuals before entering into such a relationship, to avoid future problems and disputes.

Due diligence is carried out in the following forms of partnerships:

- Strategic alliances and partnerships
- Business partners and alliances, partnering agreements, and business coalitions
- Just-in-time suppliers and relationships, sole suppliers, and outsourcing arrangements
- Technology and product licensing, joint development agreements, technology sharing, and cross licensing agreements
- Franchisees and franchisers
- Value added resellers, value added dealers, and distribution relationships

4.5.3 Joint Ventures and Collaborations

Before entering into a major commercial agreement such as a joint venture or collaboration with a company, a collaboration partner may want to carry out due diligence. This is particularly true in cases where a large company decides to join hands with a smaller company or a start-up company. What needs to be remembered is that the due diligence in such cases may not be an extensive one as in the case of an acquisition, but the larger company will conduct due diligence to ensure that its investment in the smaller company is capable of yielding returns. It also helps the larger company to confirm that the start-up has the requisite systems, personnel, expertise, and resources to meet its obligations.

To conclude, one could say that due diligence is all about understanding the viability of the project one is getting involved in. Due diligence obviously is not what the critics think it to be:

- A slow torture in the form of a lengthy checklist
- A stress test for the executive team
- A chance to prove that one team is smarter than the other
- A justification to drive home a valuation
- A delay tactic until another fund takes interest (www.entrepreneurs.about.com)

4.6 PEOPLE INVOLVED IN DUE DILIGENCE PROCESS

The due diligence process includes the company's professional advisors such as people dealing with legal, tax, accounting, and operational issues. Let us try and understand the role of each of these professionals in the entire process.

4.6.1 Legal Professionals

The modern business environment is so complex that even mid-sized deals involve experts in corporate, tax, real estate, employee benefits, insurance, and other kinds of legal specialists. Companies do not like to take any chances on the legal front. Hence the involvement of legal experts is always preferred in the process of due diligence. Most of the legal work related to due diligence is done in-house if the companies have adequate legal staff. Outside counsel is also likely to be involved in larger and complex transactions.

4.6.2 Financial Professionals

Today's organizations require huge financial resources for their operations. Whether it is a case of due diligence for the purpose of M&A or private placement, both the investor and the target typically rely on in-house personnel such as CFOs and finance controllers to guide them through the process. Quite often, companies hire the services of outside auditors for the purpose. Apart from these, companies even hire the services of underwriters, registrars, investment bankers, and commercial banks to manage national and cross-border public offerings. These agencies use their expertise and perform due diligence before raising funds for the transaction.

4.6.3 Operational Professionals

No buyer just buys another business. Buyers must evaluate every material aspect of the target's business so that it does not result in value destruction instead of value creation post merger. For this purpose, key in-house operating personnel as well as outside consultants are instructed to scrutinize the target's business and report their findings to the decision makers. Operational due diligence includes investigating the target's intellectual property (IP), its production, sales and marketing efforts, human resources, and other operational issues. For financial investors, the problem of valuing these operations is magnified if the investor is from a different industry. Therefore, it is essential that the operational professionals selected to conduct due diligence have domain knowledge of that particular industry.

4.7 PARTIES INTERESTED IN DUE DILIGENCE

Apart from individuals who are actively involved in carrying out the process of due diligence, there are individuals who are interested in the outcome of the process. They include employees, trade unions, shareholders and creditors, vendors, customers, the government, and the society. Let us examine why they are interested in the outcome of the process.

4.7.1 Employees

We have already discussed that due diligence is not carried out by the buyer alone. The seller is also as keen to participate in the process. Due diligence is undertaken to address the fears of the employees that post merger they might be laid off or their salaries may be reduced. Due diligence gives a fair idea about the motives of the buyer and what he proposes to do once the merger is complete. While carrying out due diligence for the prospective buyer, employees may perceive the threat of large-scale layoffs. The same can be addressed through the process of negotiation, and the buyer can give them the assurance that the interests of the employees would be taken care of.

4.7.2 Trade Unions

Trade unions are associations that fight for the rights of the employees and ensure that they are not unnecessarily exploited or harassed. Unions are interested in due diligence for they want to ensure that no employee faces the axe or cut in pay post merger. They ensure that the agreement addresses the concerns of the employees and assures them continuity in employment.

One also needs to understand that unions are often common across industries. If the interests of employees in one industry are not taken care of, employees from other industries may also distance themselves from the union. This may invariably endanger the very continuance and existence of the union.

4.7.3 Shareholders and Creditors

Shareholders and creditors have a financial stake in the business. They are not only concerned about the principal amount invested by them, but also expect regular returns from the project. Their interest in due diligence originates from this desire. Due diligence gives them a fair idea about the risk involved in the project, which in turn determines future returns from the business. Their investment decisions are purely driven by the future earning possibilities of the business.

If due diligence indicates that the project is highly risky and returns are uncertain, they may decide against making an investment in the business and vice versa.

4.7.4 Vendors

Vendors are entities who supply various inputs such as raw materials, tools, and equipment to the business. Their fortune is related to the company to which they supply the inputs and other requirements. The due diligence exercise gives them a very clear idea on the direction in which the merger is moving. The decision of continuing the relationship or distancing one's business from the entity is based on the results of due diligence.

4.7.5 Customers

Customers desire that their needs and requirements should be fulfilled by the company. When a merger happens, there can be drastic changes in the business model. This may affect the product range of the company and thus the capacity to fulfil customer needs. Due diligence provides details about the future operational strategy of the business and helps them decide on their consumption patterns.

4.7.6 Government

The state is responsible for ensuring that the rights and privileges of all the stakeholders are protected. Post merger, the entire business model of the company might undergo drastic changes, affecting the stakeholders adversely. Based on the projections and findings of the due diligence process, the government can decide on the course of action it needs to pursue to protect the interests of the stakeholders. If the government finds that the merger will have an adverse impact on the stakeholder's rights, it may enact laws to prevent or reduce the adverse impact of the merger.

4.7.7 Society

Every society provides resources for all types of activities. While resources are scarce and resource requirement unlimited, the society performs the role of a watchdog so that wastage of resources can be curtailed. It is important for the society to understand the course that events are taking and ready itself for appropriate action. This is where the due diligence process provides it with the much-needed feedback and basis for action.

4.8 STEPS IN DUE DILIGENCE

The essence of any due diligence exercise is its ability to reduce uncertainties, confirm assumptions, define scope, and prioritize issues. The entire exercise combines an understanding of the organization, the operations of the company, technologies, logistics, corporate strategy, finance, and summary of the complex issues into concise, easily understandable terms.

The process of due diligence comprises the phases shown in Fig. 4.1.

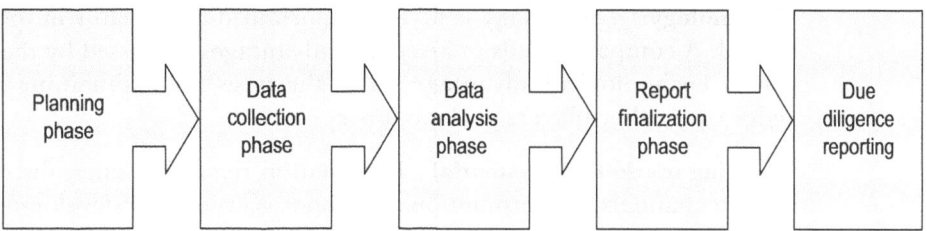

Figure 4.1   Steps in due diligence process

4.8.1 Planning Phase

This is a stage where all the initial planning relating to the conduct of due diligence is done. It includes the processes described in this section.

Defining Scope

The entity desirous of undertaking due diligence constitutes a committee or team for carrying out the entire exercise. The due diligence team discusses the proposed transaction and defines the objectives intended to be attained through the exercise. Once the objectives have been established, the availability of resources is studied and determined and the areas on which the team has to focus are defined.

Deciding Focus Area

After deciding the scope of due diligence, the next step is to decide on the focus area. The focus areas generally include the following:

Sustainability of business   The sustainability of the business can be understood by considering the target company's business plan, vision, strategic alliances, synergies, new products, new customers, customer base, etc.

Financials   Here key financial variables are reviewed. They normally include assets, liabilities, cash flow, inventory turnover, revenues, accounting procedures, and policies.

Competition   The focus here is on understanding the competition in the market for it influences the business plans and strategy to a great extent.

Management team and organizational culture   Understanding the prevailing culture, outlook, and capability of the management team is of prime importance while conducting due diligence. These variables provide direction and drive the activities of the organization.

Potential liabilities   It is important to identify the potential risks and liabilities that an organization would face if it enters the industry or merges with another entity. The issues to be considered would include IP rights, pending regulatory issues, liens, lawsuits, etc.

Technology   Technology is a very important differentiator in today's business world. A company needs to assess the advantages possessed by the target in this area. Technological advantage forms the basis for maintaining a competitive edge over other players in the industry.

Existing market and potential   Information regarding sales, distribution, marketing channels, and promotional methods is crucial for developing the business plan. Appropriate information on these key variables must be collected and kept ready for reference.

Business-to-business fit   It is not necessary that the two merging entities are the right fit for each other. Instead of merging and then realizing that the merger is destroying value, it makes sense to determine in the very beginning whether the two businesses fit well in the scheme of things planned. If there is a good fit between the two businesses, it would create corporate synergy. The synergy might arise due to complementary strategy, personnel, financial situation, etc.

Finalizing Team Structure

The entire exercise of due diligence requires varied skills and expertise. While forming the due diligence team, one should ensure that the members possess specific skills and background so that the due diligence process is successfully completed. The team members should be capable of collecting and analysing information about the target company, the transactions, industry, and due diligence objectives. The members should know the information to be collected, the number of site visits necessary to collect relevant information, the analyses to be performed and the type of report to be delivered at the end of the due diligence process.

Defining Responsibilities

Every due diligence effort requires integration of efforts and communication with multiple parties. Planning should be done in such a manner that responsibilities and expected outputs are clearly defined, and the team can work collectively towards a common goal.

Defining Time Schedules

Before starting the due diligence process, it is better to define the time schedule for each step. Scheduling the time of each key step helps in achieving results in the desired timeframe and helps the parties attain the desired goal without loss of time and energy.

Communicating Information Requirements

The success of any due diligence program depends on the team's ability to collect complete, accurate, and timely information. Each member needs to collect information as early and specifically as possible so that delays can be avoided. This can be done by informing team members of the expectations from them and timelines.

Finalizing Templates and Tools Required

Based on scope, needs, and objective, the due diligence team should decide on tools to be used such as internet database search, regulatory database search, questionnaires, worksheets, and other communication methods such as interviews and emails. If the tools are not identified, the entire process becomes haphazard and delays would be inevitable.

4.8.2 Data Collection Phase

This stage involves collecting existing business process data. The approach used for data collection depends on a number of factors including the desired precision, the nature of questions that need to be answered, and the availability of time, money, and access to information providers. The sources of information that can be tapped include the Internet, regulatory organizations and their databases, competitors, vendors, customers, industry associations, etc.

The research can be qualitative or quantitative. While qualitative research involves conducting in-depth interviews and asking two or three relevant questions from information providers, quantitative research is done via surveys that are conducted among a sample of customers. The information is then extrapolated to the entire population.

The data collection phase usually starts with a meeting with the company management. Here, the investors meet with the target company management to clarify the due diligence process, the issues that should be addressed, and the meetings and site visits that need to take place. Next, the due diligence team makes an initial request for information needed, such as business plans, forecast, financial statements, sales figures, market data, customer lists, technology specifications, and supplier contacts. After the initial meeting, the team initiates the rest of the process. This includes interviews and questionnaires with the suppliers, customers, employees, etc., to know their perceptions of the company's products and services and its position alongside competitors. The relevant information is then collected and examined.

4.8.3 Data Analysis Phase

This stage involves analysing the collected data and drawing conclusions from the same. During the due diligence process, the team may not have consistent findings, i.e., the team may uncover some issues that lead to a favourable impression of the organization and others that cause concern. The right approach to the process would be to focus on the organization's financial health, its capacity to deliver in future, its reputation and approach to working. The team should also get a perspective on the leadership of the organization.

The analysis of due diligence findings depends on a variety of factors. All factors need to be considered and evaluated and the organization should balance them to arrive at a decision. Once the team is sure that all factors have been considered and have been given due weightage, it can give a positive recommendation.

4.8.4 Report Finalization Phase

After the completion of data collection and analysis, the due diligence team prepares the final report and submits the same to the investors. The conclusions so presented in the report become an integral part of the decision-making and negotiation process.

4.8.5 Due Diligence Reporting

The due diligence report contains the key findings of the process. It is submitted to the management for consideration and adoption (Refer to Appendix A—due diligence checklist).

The key features of due diligence reports are as follows:

- It should reflect a fair and independent analysis and evaluation of financial and commercial information.
- It should ensure collection, analysis, and interpretation of financial, commercial, and tax information in detail.
- The report should provide properly reviewed and analysed financial information to bidders and various stakeholders.
- It should provide feedback on auditing of the special purpose accounts.

The reports are prepared by analysing and compiling the data collected during the due diligence process. It helps to clearly point out the potential risks and a company's current financial situation. If the reports are meticulously prepared and presented, they help save a lot of money, time, and effort for the management.

Professional consultants take up the task of preparing a due diligence report on behalf of clients. They not only prepare a report, but also assist in making sound decisions. This also helps the client save lot of money, and time spent on collecting and analysing financial and commercial information.

4.9 TYPES OF DUE DILIGENCE

Due diligence provides valuable information to the buying company and helps in identifying the right target. While there are many elements to a due diligence study, not all are needed for every decision. Based on individual needs and requirements, companies undertake specific due diligence studies. The different types of due diligence include the following:

- Financial due diligence
- Legal due diligence
- Operational due diligence
- IP due diligence
- IT due diligence
- Human resource due diligence

4.9.1 Financial Due Diligence

Financial due diligence analyses the financially performance of an entity, both qualitatively and quantitatively. It helps in getting a sense of earnings on a normalized basis. Financial due diligence is crucial, for it provides reliable information on the anticipated performance of a business as represented by the seller. Besides, it looks into the underlying assumptions that have been used in preparing the projections, and ensures that the conclusions are reasonable and objective (www.plantemoran.com).

Financial due diligence involves evaluating a company's historical, current, and prospective operating results as disclosed in its historical, current, and projected financial statements, tax returns, and other information (Adukia 2009).

From these data, an income statement review can establish trends in revenue and profits, investor returns, and compound growth rates. Examination of cost of sales, selling, general and administrative expenses, interest, and other fixed charges can lead to a thoughtful profit margin analysis.

Financial due diligence involves in-depth analysis of the balance sheet, cash, marketable securities, receivables, inventory, prepaid expenses and other current assets, as well as the value of fixed assets. On the liability side, the analysis covers accounts payable, taxes, and debt obligations are closely examined. Financial due diligence also analyses contingent liabilities.

Financial due diligence also analyses the assets and liabilities to be acquired in the future. For example, is the pricing for raw materials on par with the market value? Are there finished goods in stock that are unlikely to be sold within the next three to six months? Regarding liabilities, it is important to acquire only the liabilities that have been incurred by the seller for purchases of inventory or services that occurred prior to the closing date (www.entrepreneurs.about.com).

Finally, financial due diligence will look at whether federal and state taxes have been filed appropriately by the seller. Does the seller have a nexus in other states? Do they file in those states? It is important to ensure that the seller has complied with all tax requirements.

4.9.2 Legal Due Diligence

Legal due diligence consists of a scrutiny of all, or specific parts, of the legal affairs of the target company with a view of uncovering any legal risks and provide the buyer with an extensive insight into the company's legal matters (www.bvhd.dk). Additionally, legal due diligence often improves the buyer's bargaining position and ensures that necessary precautions in relation to the transaction are taken.

Legal due diligence is crucial for venture capitalists. These firms have a team of lawyers who conduct legal due diligence prior to investing in a company. These lawyers check whether the company has any significant legal problems, and whether it is being properly operated. The venture capitalists' lawyers demand a bulk of documents and information about the company (www.allbusiness.com). The objectives of a legal due diligence exercise may vary from case to case. Some of the basic objectives may be summarized as follows:

- Gathering information from the target company
- Uncovering the target company's strong and weak sides, relevant risks, and advantages in connection with the transaction

- Minimizing the risk of unexpected situations
- Improving the seller's bargaining position
- Identifying areas where representations and warranties from the seller should be obtained in the acquisition agreement

The precise extent of legal due diligence depends on the activities of the target company and the nature of the transaction. The documents that legal due diligence aims at verifying include the following:

- IT law and IT contracts
- IP rights
- Patents, copyrights, and other IP-related documents
- Company law
- Finance
- Employment law
- Data protection law
- Consumer protection law
- General contract law
- Minutes and consents of the board of directors and shareholders
- Confidentiality and invention assignment agreements with employees
- Tax and financial documents
- Legal disputes and other kinds of conflicts
- Marketing practices regulation
- National and EU competition laws
- Public procurement law

The findings of the legal due diligence process are summarized in a due diligence report, offering a complete picture of the target company's legal situation. In addition to conveying a general overview, the report clearly identifies areas that require particular attention, thereby making it easier to evaluate the impact of the legal findings on the acquisition as a whole. Further, the report often pinpoints those areas where specific representations and warranties are needed (www. entrepreneurs.about.com).

4.9.3 Operational Due Diligence

Operational due diligence is integral to a buyer's ability to properly evaluate a business for a potential acquisition. Operational due diligence involves an on-site analysis of the daily processes of the target business and how the business operates. The analysis includes an evaluation of the key employees, managers, independent contractors, suppliers, and other factors that are necessary for the business to conduct normal operations.

Operational due diligence may also extend to conducting investigation outside of the actual business. When researching market and industry trends, the communities in the area surrounding the business location may be potential new market competition (www.lgloomarlaw.com).

Comprehensive operational due diligence enables a buyer who purchases a business to get a detailed understanding of how to manage the daily business operations, which will, in turn, lead to a trouble-free transition after the consummation of the acquisition.

In operational due diligence, the buyer understands exactly how the business works, and what is happening within the business from an operational point of view. The team spends a great deal of time observing the business operations. The process also includes interviewing customers, authors, and current employees. Sometimes even ex-employees and former business associates are interviewed. It is imperative that the buyer spends considerable time getting to know everyone on the management team who will be remaining with the business after the transaction.

Operational due diligence looks at a transaction with the aim of helping the buyer decide on the steps he needs to take to realize improvements in productivity and profitability. This includes examining work centres, material flow, scrap generation, and inventory levels—in short, employing lean manufacturing principles to achieve maximum profitability (www.entrepreneurs.about.com).

A purchase price based on multiple of earnings may include certain operational inefficiencies. Operational due diligence will define these along with the cost of implementing the efficiency improvements measures for the buyer. The seller can benefit from operational due diligence by identifying and implementing the changes necessary to increase earnings before interest, taxes, depreciation, and amortization (EBITDA) and increasing the multiples due to lower risk.

Operational due diligence varies dramatically from target to target. It involves gathering information on the following (Lajoux 2003):

New product or service creation   Due diligence requires an understanding of how the target firm creates new products and services. Operational due diligence tries to understand the process of new product development, whether it is organized or random, whether the target uses research and development (R&D) to inflate earnings, the target's IP, defensible know-how possessed by the target, etc.

Markets   In addition to understanding the target's products/services, operational due diligence also gathers information regarding the target's market. It collects information regarding the target's customers, whether the market is growing or has matured, the target's market share, factors affecting demand in the target's market, segmentation of the market, seasonality, etc.

Competition   Due diligence enables the investor to know the target's competitors. It provides a sound basis for understanding the market share of the competitors, the basis on which the competition is waged, such as price, service, quality, and the target's expertise in these fields.

Sales   Operational due diligence also gains information on the sales force of the target. It provides information on the sales forces' salary, compensation pattern, etc.

People/Organizational matters   Operational due diligence also gathers information on the number of employees, their functions, whether the company's workforce is trained or untrained, etc.

4.9.4 Intellectual Property Due Diligence

Conducting proper due diligence involves examining not only the financial information of a company, but also assessing the company's key assets. This is required because the earning potential of a company depends on the type and quality of assets it possesses. While evaluating assets, one needs to carefully review IP assets of the target company. It is imperative to conduct a thorough IP assets due diligence before engaging in investments because economies are becoming increasingly technology-driven.

Intellectual property due diligence is essential for investment in virtually every type of target company. It is especially significant when the target involved is in the technology sector as in this industry, most products and services involve IP assets. Given the modern day business environment, IP due diligence is unavoidable since companies invest a substantial amount in technology. However, IP due diligence should not be limited to transactions involving the technology sector. Even traditional bricks and mortar enterprises own and rely upon IP assets as an integral component of their business. Examples range from the ingredients and manufacturing process for Coca-Cola, a closely guarded trade secret, to the many domestic and international trademarks owned by multinational conglomerates such as Tata, HUL, Reliance, etc. The process of identifying all IP assets, verifying ownership and ensuring that they are free of encumbrances for the intended business use is fundamental to any merger, acquisition, or investment.

The focus is gradually shifting to IP due diligence for it provides a prospective investor with detailed information about the IP assets of a target. These assets often affect pricing or other key elements of the proposed transaction and, in certain circumstances, even recommend termination of the proposed investment. One needs to remember that the consequences of mismanaging or ignoring IP due diligence can be severe. It may so happen that after the deal is concluded, the investor may realize that the target does not have ownership of the sought-after IP assets or that the IP assets have been transferred or encumbered by third-party interests or litigation. Such events can ruin the proposed business plans of the investor and render his investment worthless (Hildebrand and Klosek 2009).

Goals of IP Due Diligence

Given the seriousness of the issue, one needs to understand the need and relevance of IP due diligence. The key point here is that IP due diligence is affected by the target company's policies and practices relating to document retention and organization, registration procedures and the location of the IP assets, as well as the length of time in business, maturity of the management team, and the target company's industry environment. From an IP due diligence perspective, a start-up in business for one year would present a very different challenge from a well-established firm with stable legal relationships, form documents and a records library. While it would not be wrong to say that reality usually lies between these two extremes, the goal of IP due diligence is always the same: protecting the investors. This can be best accomplished by focusing on the following steps:

Identify and locate IP assets The basic goal of IP due diligence is to identify and locate the IP assets of the target. This list may be extremely varied depending on the nature of the business. It could include patents and/or patentable subject matter, copyrights, trademarks, domain names, trade secrets, mask works, inventions, works of authorship, hardware and devices. In addition, some IP assets require closer evaluation and analysis than others due to various factors including complexity, competition, and foreign registration of IP assets.

Ascertain nature and scope of target's claimed rights in IP assets The target may not have uniform rights on all the IP assets. The target's rights could range from outright ownership to a license in the IP assets. Hence before deciding on the investment, ascertaining the target's rights in IP assets becomes important.

Evaluate validity of target's rights on IP assets Evaluating the validity of the target's rights on the IP assets involves making a judgment about the relative strength of rights claimed by the target. Special care should be taken to ensure that the target's actual rights conform with the facts disclosed to the potential investor. It should also be ensured that the rights should be sufficient to permit continued operation of the business without interruption.

Evaluate any potential IP infringement claims IP assets due diligence mostly involves infringement issues. This step includes analysis of situations where the target's IP assets may infringe a third party's rights, or the target may have a valid claim of infringement against a third party. Either of these situations have the potential to seriously disrupt the operation of the business.

Analyse any grant of IP rights made by target This step involves analysis of licenses, distribution agreements, reseller arrangements and any other transaction by the target involving a transfer of rights in the IP assets that may impact their value. For example, if the target has granted an exclusive license to its primary invention for a period of five years, a business plan that contemplates issue of additional licenses for the same technology would not work.

Conducting IP Due Diligence Effectively

The task of carrying out IP assets due diligence is very complex and calls for a thorough analysis of different variables and factors. For effective IP assets due diligence, the following elements need to be remembered:

Ensure right team composition The success of this exercise depends on having the right persons on the due diligence team. Failure to do so would mean a wrong beginning to a very complex task. To begin with, the team appointed to conduct

IP due diligence must have a basic understanding of the primary product lines, business environment, and future plans of the target to remain focused primarily on the IP assets that are relevant to the business. The team should also understand the relative importance of the proposed investment to the client since the members would also be required to participate in the investor's evaluation of a proposed transaction.

Ensure that IP due diligence plan reflects importance of deal   Once the right team has been constituted, the team should be instructed to develop a well-drafted IP due diligence request. The request involves use of questions that would help in identifying areas that merit further inquiry as evidenced by a positive response. Likewise, a negative response to certain questions permits the legal team to move on to areas of genuine concern that are relevant to the business and/or the specific transaction at issue.

Take nothing on faith   When the target is requested to disclose all the facts on the matter in the IP due diligence request, the target is expected to be transparent and disclose all the details correctly. However, believing this to be true every time can prove disastrous. It may so happen that the target may not disclose all the details in spite of being requested to do so. To avoid future problems, the team should do an independent research on every related aspect.

Investigation is needed in the following areas:

- Conducting searches in appropriate databases in all relevant jurisdictions to identify patent rights including pending and/or provisional patent applications, registered patents, registered copyrights, and registered trademarks,
- Examining, analysing, and verifying the results of such searches
- Verifying claimed but unregistered IP rights
- Reviewing and analysing relevant provisions of executed agreements that could include licenses, consulting and confidentiality agreements, assignments, and other documents
- Conducting interviews with key business and technology development staff at the target and, where the situation warrants, with previous employees and consultants
- Examining and analysing the potentially of infringing registrations and third-party IP rights and
- Any other efforts thought appropriate to the situation

Verify all information   Seeking information from the target on the related rights pertaining to the IP assets marks the beginning of the process. It should be followed by computerized search of the relevant patents. Such searches can often reveal that the ownership interests were not what was expected or communicated by the target. This should be followed by a manual search. One should not be surprised if the manual search ultimately reveals that the computerized search was erroneous. Such errors can creep in due to errors in preparing computerized documents. Even the reverse can happen—the computerized search might appear to be accurate and no further manual search would be performed. Subsequently it would be known that the computerized search had given the wrong result. This highlights the importance of verifying information that is presented through more than one source.

Understand relationship between documents and core business   While it is extremely important to examine all agreements, registrations, filings, and other documents to ensure that they are valid, the team must establish a clear relationship between such documentation and the relevant IP assets. For example, the buyer might be interested in acquiring a division of the target holding a large collection of patents. Prior to investment, the target might provide the team with voluminous documentation ostensibly pertaining to the patents. However, an inspection of the documentation might reveal that the information provided might actually be related to patents that have nothing to do with the target's core business.

Ascertain impact of foreign laws on deal   In recent years, the numbers of cross-border M&As have increased dramatically. As a result, many individuals developing IP assets might be from outside the country. This situation increases the likelihood that IP due diligence will involve review and analysis of not only domestic IP assets, but the IP assets abroad. The complexity increases since quite a few countries treat IP on the basis of complex treaties and conventions executed by and among many different nations. Hence, it is important to avoid making assumptions about foreign IP assets based on an understanding of the domestic laws and procedures.

Understanding Issues with Reference to Specific IP Assets

The nature and extent of the due diligence depends on the type of IP rights involved. Intellectual property rights can be broken down into four main categories:

- Patents
- Trademarks
- Copyrights
- Trade secrets

The problem involved while carrying out IP due diligence is that each class of IP rights calls for use of different methods of review. This section presents recommendations for steps to be taken while reviewing IP assets in each of these classes of rights. While these guidelines are not universally applicable, they provide a fair idea of how the system works in general.

Patents   The following steps need to be taken while carrying out the due diligence of patents:

- Review all issued, pending, and abandoned patent applications—both domestic and foreign. Such a review should include not only those patents owned by the target, but also those previously owned or licensed by the target.

- Examine all patent searches conducted by or on behalf of the target in relation to the inventions of the target.
- Confirm whether all issued patents are being properly maintained and that the target has paid all the related dues and fees.
- Review and evaluate all threatened or pending interferences.
- Evaluate the scope and nature of any transfer of rights by evaluating the relevant agreements including licensing and manufacturing agreements.
- Investigate the underlying technology of the target.

Trademarks   The following steps need to be taken while carrying out the due diligence of trademarks:

- Examine all trademarks and service marks used by the target.
- Examine all trademarks and service marks registered by the target within the country and abroad.
- Examine both the geographic area of use and the date of the first use of the trademark in the given territory.
- Examine the prosecution files for any registrations of pending applications and examine all trademark searches performed in connection with such pending applications.
- Review all quality control manuals, files, or guidelines relating to goods or services sold under the marks.
- Review all trademark licenses, not only through trademark license agreements, but also through all other types of agreements that include trademark licenses, including, for example, co-branding agreements and marketing and distribution agreements.

Copyrights   The following steps need to be taken while carrying out the due diligence of copyrights:

- Review all copyrighted works that the target has created, commissioned or to which it has acquired rights.
- Evaluate all work-for-hire agreements and contracts relating to consulting services and development work.
- Review all documents concerning copyright registrations, including applications, correspondence, transfers, and security interests.
- Review all licenses related to copyrighted works used by target.
- Review and evaluate the target's policy for identifying and protecting its copyrights in the works it develops or has developed.
- Review and evaluate the efforts undertaken by the company to avoid claims of copyright infringement and obtain proper copyright clearances.
- Identify and evaluate all actual or pending claims of copyright infringement asserted against the target.

Trade secrets The following steps need to be taken while carrying out the due diligence of trade secrets:

- Obtain an inventory of all material trade secrets utilized by the target.
- Determine whether non-disclosure agreements have been executed with key employees, consultants, and other individuals or entities having access to the target's confidential information.
- Determine whether non-compete agreements have been executed between the target and its key personnel.
- Review the employment records of key personnel.
- Consider the impact of recent arrivals and/or departures of key personnel.
- Evaluate the adequacy of exit interviews.
- Evaluate security policies including physical, technical, and administrative security procedures employed by the target.
- Review and evaluate all relevant agreements including know-how licenses and technical assistance agreements.

4.9.5 Information Technology Due Diligence

Information technology has become a top priority area in all M&A deals, given the heavy reliance on information technology for business operations, management information and financial reporting in today's business environment. On the one hand, IT represents one of the largest capital and operational expenditure items. Owners of a business are constantly working on finding better ways of deriving value and leverage from IT assets (www.pwc.com).

The processes of IT due diligence pose different issues before the team involved in the task. It is important that the team prepares well for the process and the following four steps need to be taken towards due diligence preparation in case of M&A (Sisco 2002):

- Sending an IT request list to the target company
- Compiling an onsite discovery process outline
- Conducting a review of the requested materials
- Scheduling and coordinating the onsite visit

Let us briefly analyse each of the steps:

Sending IT request list to target company The process starts with the preparation for the onsite visit by learning as much as one can beforehand. As soon as the letter of intent to acquire the other company is agreed upon and signed, the buyer/investor company should send due diligence discovery lists to the target company. One of those request lists should be for technology information.

The technology leaders generally seek information on the following:

- Technology in place
- Stability
- Growth capacity
- Support methods

- IT organization
- Contracts
- Software ownership and licensure
- Costs
- Ongoing support costs
- Key investments planned
- Capital investments needed
- Planned initiatives
- Risks
- Client satisfaction and needs related to technology

The IT due diligence request list provides plenty of insights prior to an onsite visit by tech experts.

Compiling onsite discovery process outline   The tech team touches base with the chief information/technology officer (CIO/CTO) of the target company before the actual onsite visit. The primary goal of this interaction is to understand the discovery process and information one is trying to seek. This is a certain way of ensuring that the visit becomes more productive, for it allows the target company to prepare fully and to make efforts to 'clean up' a little, which does not necessarily amount to hiding information. In addition, one's observation skills generally help in determining whether things have been 'cleaned up' before the planned visit. One can make use of an IT business assessment checklist to ensure that all relevant information is provided to the team during the visit. One can even request that the details be forwarded to the team well in advance so that no item is missed out during the course of the visit.

The primary objective of the IT due diligence effort is to maximize the opportunity to discover relevant issues surrounding the company's technology and accordingly initiate corrective measures.

Conducting review of requested materials   If the IT business assessment checklist is received in advance, one gets enough time to review the materials before going onsite. One can accordingly prepare a questionnaire to gain more insight during the visit. This exercise provides the following benefits:

- It helps the team to get familiar with the IT aspects of the target company.
- It increases both parties' productivity during the onsite discovery process.
- It gives credibility to the team visiting the target company. Remember, there is a good chance that the new company's IT organization might report to or might work closely with the same team that visited the target company after the acquisition.

Coordinating the onsite review   To make the entire process effective, one can also undertake a coordination exercise involving the following:

- Introduce oneself and explain the role one is expected to play during the due diligence visit.

- Know something about the CIO/CTO of the target company.
- Discuss the IT due diligence process.
- Share basic information on the IT business assessment checklist.
- Remind the CIO/CTO to explain the team's presence onsite, so that the company's acquisition plans are kept confidential.
- Set up the initial interviews with senior management first, as it is helpful to learn their goals and objectives and the IT department's client perspectives before talking to IT managers.
- Exchange contact information, including cell phone numbers.
- Provide the CIO/CTO an opportunity to ask questions.

4.9.6 Human Resource Due Diligence

Human resource (HR) due diligence is a process that aims at assessing the contribution of the HR function to the success of the business in a purchasing, outsourcing, or market testing environment. By using a comprehensive model of the HR function experience in day-to-day delivery of HR services, and extensive industry knowledge, one is able to provide organizations with a fresh approach to HR due diligence, function reviews and HR audits.

While HR due diligence involves valuing the contribution of HR, HR reviews involve an in-depth approach to meeting specific objectives and terms of reference to increase the strategic alignment, effectiveness, and efficiency of the HR function. Human resource audit, on the other hand, is a 'snapshot' review that uses a systematic approach to identify any major areas of improvement in the HR function. This is often used as input into the HR planning process.

Human resource due diligence helps in the following ways:

- Establishing a link between organizational objectives and the HR function
- Determining HR's influence on the skills and motivation of the workforce
- Determining the managers' views of the HR function
- Ascertaining the outcomes produced by the HR deliverables
- Measuring the adequacy of HR measures, metrics and benchmarks
- Ascertaining the total cost of the HR function and industry comparisons
- Ascertaining the HR team structure, skills and motivation

Human resource due diligence forms the basis of providing strategic business support on the following areas:

- Organizational culture
- Executive compensation and 'golden parachute' contracts
- Collective bargaining agreements and potential change of ownership liabilities
- Defined benefit and contribution pension plans
- Post-retirement benefits
- Retention and severance plans
- Health and welfare insurance structure and reserves
- HR functional structure and service delivery

- HR information system (HRIS)
- Employment Litigation

Human resource due diligence aims at seeking answers to the following issues:

- Analysing HR structure and policies in the target company
- Ascertaining whether the target company possess human resources to support the products, technology, markets or goodwill
- Evolving an action plan to retain key individuals after the merger
- Evolving a strategy action plan to integrate the target company's HR processes and culture with the buyer company quickly and smoothly to minimize uncertainties among employees and demonstrate value to customers
- Evolving the right approach information to make staffing and organizational decisions quickly to avoid unnecessary anxiety, destructive rumours, and unwanted departures
- Visualize the skills, experience, knowledge, specific industry experience, and contacts that may be lost post merger, determine the impact of these potential losses and designing coaching, employee development or recruiting plans to replace key competencies.

4.10 LITIGATION ANALYSIS

When one company sells or otherwise transfers all its assets to another company, the successor is not liable for the debts and tort liabilities of the predecessor. The successor may be liable, however, under the following circumstances:

- If the successor has expressly or implicitly agreed to assume liability
- If the transaction is a merger or consolidation
- If the successor is a 'mere continuation' of the predecessor
- If the transaction was fraudulently designed to escape liability (Lajoux 2003)

The original edition of *The Art of M&A*, largely written by attorneys, deals with litigation analysis. The analysis of the target requires a special procedure, usually conducted by trained litigation analysts. The primary reviewer obtains a list of all litigation, pending and threatened, and then gets copies of all relevant pleadings.

Before reviewing specific cases, the primary reviewer examines what cases the seller believes are covered by liability insurance, and determines what cases, if any, are covered. As the two do not always coincide, it is critical to review all insurance policies.

The individual responsible for litigation analysis must have a working knowledge of both the structure of the transaction—such as whether it is to be a stock or asset purchase—and the corporate and tort law rules concerning successor liability for debts and torts, especially with regard to compensatory and punitive damages. These are then applied case by case.

When acquiring a company, a buyer wants to make sure it will not inherit a legal problem it did not know about. The buyer must be alert to threats of possible litigation from various stakeholders. True to the theme 'future shock', the following areas have been undergoing some change in the recent years.

- Customers as well as competitors, suppliers, and other contractors might sue over the following:
  - Contract disputes
  - Cost/quality/safety of product or service
  - Debt collection, including foreclosure
  - Deceptive trade practices
  - Dishonesty/fraud
  - Extension/refusal of credit
  - Lender liability
  - Other customer/client issues
  - Restraint of trade
- Employees including current, past, and prospective employees or unions might sue over the following:
  - Breach of employment contract
  - Defamation
  - Discrimination
  - Employment conditions
  - Harassment/humiliation
  - Pension, welfare, or other employee benefits
  - Wrongful termination
- Regulators might sue over the following:
  - Antitrust (in suits brought by government)
  - Environmental law
  - Health and safety law
- Shareholders might sue over the following:
  - Contract disputes (with shareholders)
  - Divestitures or spin-offs
  - Dividend declaration or change
  - Duties to minority shareholders
  - Executive compensation (such as golden parachutes)
  - Financial performance/bankruptcy
  - Financial transactions (such as derivatives)
  - Fraudulent conveyance
  - General breach of fiduciary duty
  - Inadequate disclosure
  - Insider trading
  - Investment or loan decisions
  - M&A scenarios (target, bidder)
  - Proxy contents
  - Recapitalization

- Share repurchase
- Stock offerings
- Suppliers might sue over the following:
  - Antitrust (in suits brought by suppliers)
  - Business interference
  - Contract disputes
  - Copyright/patent infringement
  - Deceptive trade practices

4.11 DOES DUE DILIGENCE INSURE AGAINST M&A FAILURE?

Many M&As fail due to inadequacy of the traditional due diligence process as well as the limited extent and duration of the process. Consequently, there are three important phases of due diligence—prior to, during, and after acquisition. While companies are very careful about the first two stages, the third stage gets neglected, and that is when problems start. The buyer needs to, therefore, ensure that the due diligence process continues even after the deal is completed. In addition, the team for all three phases should include the same individuals so that there is continuity in the analysis and the team members can correlate the happenings.

The first two steps ensure that there are no major problems faced before the deal gets completed and that those identified have been adequately addressed in the transaction documents. Many problems are avoided there. Since companies ignore the third step, due diligence after acquisition, it is then that matters get aggravated.

Therefore, one needs to remember that due diligence is an ongoing process that should continue even after the deal is concluded. It also ensures the following:

- The organization avoids unnecessary losses and expenses.
- The organization's governing body is able to demonstrate that it has engaged in effective oversight.
- Senior officers of the company avoid job- and bonus-threatening adverse events.

A number of factors can contribute to post-M&A disappointments; lack of ongoing due diligence is often one of the leading factors.

To avoid disappointments, the following points need attention through post-acquisition due diligence.

4.11.1 Due Diligence Involving Financial Issues

The company initiates the process of due diligence on financial issues as these are critical to the success of the company. The process focuses on the following:

- Lack of attention to ongoing due diligence can lead to significant unbudgeted liabilities and the diversion of time and energy of key executives.

- With the ever-increasing ability to scan and manipulate documents, it is well within the ability of the creative yet malevolent employee to alter documents and create fictitious originals, such as the signature-authority list.
- Dormant bank accounts should be closed as soon as possible for they are a breeding ground for manipulative practices.
- Unexpected voiding of invoices from the organization's accounts receivable system should be investigated, particularly if the organization is structured in such a way that people who are authorized to void an invoice are also authorized to receive or issue checks.

Critics often argue that these issues can be addressed through the process of financial audit. One should remember that such manipulations need not get traced when a large number of transactions are being checked. Even if they are checked, the costs of investigation and attempted recovery, coupled with the diversion of management time can be significant. Furthermore, if the loss is huge and the organization is a listed entity, it may affect the reputation of the company and sentiments of all stakeholders.

4.11.2 Due Diligence Involving Organizational Records

A company is required to maintain various records including legal, financial, human resources, marketing, and strategic plans. The company should ensure that it maintains all the records systematically so that they can be referred to in future. A list of records that companies maintain includes the following:

- Periodic review of the minutes of board meetings needs to be done.
- Record retention policies are often advocated across countries as a reliable tool of reference. Regardless of the type of record retention policy the organization has in place, it is vital that periodic due diligence be undertaken to ensure compliance with the policy.

4.11.3 Due Diligence Involving Legal Compliance

Every company is a legal entity and is required to adhere to various laws and procedures. While adherence to laws is a statutory requirement, maintaining proper records constitutes the collection of very important proof that no provisions of the law are being violated. Legal requirements often have future implications and as such maintaining proper records is of utmost importance. The issues addressed here include the following:

- Records help ensure that the organization is in compliance with applicable law.
- Depending on the nature and size of an organization', professional advisors should be engaged to evaluate the laws and regulations as applicable, and to help management design a due diligence plan. This not only helps monitor compliance with existing laws and regulations, but also aids in keeping abreast of trends toward new legislation, and to be proactive in recommending actions so that compliance can be achieved in an orderly, cost-effective, and timely manner.

4.11.4 Due Diligence Involving Interaction of Contracts

Practising due diligence is key to the success of the business. A company enters into various contracts and agreements in the course of its operations. Ensuring that the related records are systematically maintained is critical. One may require these records at any point of time in future. Therefore, due diligence before entering into key contracts and agreements, and summarizing and cross-referencing critical terms for future reference, is important for avoiding inadvertent conflicts.

4.11.5 Due Diligence Involving Information Systems

Companies today have moved from manual-centric processes to ones that are technology driven. A great deal of investment has been made in technology. While part of the investment in technology is with the objective of bringing efficiency, it is also driven by legal requirements. A company uses information technology to handle issues such as the following:

- It helps to get tuned to the rapid shift from manual system infrastructure to technology driven infrastructure.
- It ensures adherence to regulatory compliance that are coming into force.

4.11.6 Due Diligence Involving Key Customers and Suppliers

The success of any business depends on the manner in which operations are planned and executed. Customers and suppliers have a very important role to play in the entire process. It is very important that proper due diligence processes are in place so that operations can be made effective and efficient. In order to attain this end, companies must ensure to consider the following issues:

- There is a strong need to initiate ongoing monitoring of the operations and plans of key customers and suppliers, for it can reveal important information on its current financial and operational status, as well as near-term future events.
- The exercise can also reveal a deteriorating financial condition in advance.

Thus if due diligence is carried out in the first two stages only and not thereafter it cannot guard against the failure of M&A.

4.12 DUE DILIGENCE TEAM

One of the key requirements in evaluating a possible M&A is a strong due diligence team capable of carrying out a quick and effective review of the assets after the confidentiality agreement has been attained. The composition of an effective due diligence team will vary greatly depending on the asset to be reviewed. If the team lacks the right persons, the very purpose of due diligence stands defeated.

The organization should ensure that the members of an effective due diligence team have the following attributes:

- The team members must have first-hand experience in the industry to which the target belongs.
- The team should have experts from different areas, such as HR specialists, functional area managers, individuals with knowledge of the national and organizational culture, etc. Such expertise is valuable, and helps the team attain the buy-in from line management, which can be hard to get if a key functional area is shut out of the integration process.
- The team should be capable of quickly identifying both the positive and negative aspects of the property to be acquired.
- The members should be willing to carry out a site visit to evaluate the current condition of the assets to be acquired—both the physical assets as well as the personnel.
- The members should possess excellent negotiation skills.
- The team members should have time to lead the project and serve as team members. Time constraints and confidentiality will make it difficult to replace these people later in the process.
- The team should be co-located within a secure environment, such as a corporate headquarters. Sometimes it makes more sense to locate the team near the target.
- The team should be familiar with the strategic and financial rationale behind the acquisition. The members should understand enough detail to be able to identify critical diligence issues.
- The team should be trained to identify and zero in on specific issues, including the analysis and data required. It thus helps to avoid the 'analysis paralysis' that can result from an undirected data search.
- Care should be taken to develop and communicate rules of engagement between the diligence team and the target company. This avoids cultural conflicts and ensures that the team acts in a manner that reflects the acquirer's intentions.
- The team should get analytical tools and techniques so that it can rapidly get its arms around potential synergies and integration challenges. This helps the team complete its task within the allotted time and budget.
- There must be a healthy flow of information from the due diligence team to the integration team. Therefore, include diligence team members in the integration planning team to ensure that diligence rationale and data analysis are properly leveraged (Adolph et al. 2009).

4.13 WHY DOES DUE DILIGENCE FAIL?

Due diligence is a challenging task, and quite often the team handling the task goes off track, giving disastrous results. There are three 'themes of failure' that most often derail the due diligence exercise (Adolph et al. 2009). These are described in Sections 4.13.1–4.13.3.

4.13.1 Failure to Focus on Key Issues

The due diligence team may fail to focus on key issues because of the following reasons:

- The due diligence team spends a lot of time on collecting irrelevant data and then rushes through the necessary step of clarifying the rationale for the deal and sources of expected value.
- Teams often focus on finding new methods of analysis. It is similar to reinventing the wheel. Instead of spending time on these things, they should use tested diligence methodology, standardized formats and simple software. This will save time, keep the process focused, and thus permit a higher level of analysis.
- Teams are also found guilty of being reluctant to share information among the team members. Sharing resources helps in quickly identifying 'deal killers'.

4.13.2 Failure to Identify New Opportunities and Risks

The team can identify new opportunities and risks by doing the following:

- The team should test the key assumption of the management before proceeding with the task. This may help them to remain focussed on areas that may create significant value.
- The team should probe deeply into the merits of the deal to identify the value drivers and key risks. Instead of relying solely on the information provided by the target company, they should also collect information from other sources customers, vendors, employees, etc.

Remember, due diligence is more than an audit. It does not aim at verifying the facts alone but also aims at validating the assumptions that underpin the business plan and detecting risks or inconsistencies.

4.13.3 Failure to Allocate Adequate/Right Resources

The team can allocate adequate/right resources by doing the following:

- Put the best people on the team. Make sure that the members chosen possess the right expertise and are from those functional areas of the firm that will be affected by the deal.
- The due diligence process is a time-crunch affair, but don't make the problem worse by setting arbitrary deadlines. The team needs to be given adequate time to research, review, and report.
- Provide the due diligence team with adequate resources such as space to work, equipment, software, staff, and access to the right data and people. Relieve them of their daily responsibilities so they can focus on the task at hand.

The due diligence process is critical in every M&A exercise. It is the only way of ensuring that the buyer is getting the best value for the money he proposes to invest in the purchase. Due diligence helps to avoid surprises after the documents have been signed. A thorough review of what you are buying before it is yours is the best way to ensure that the company acquiring the target is protected against unwanted surprises down the road.

SUMMARY

The process of due diligence is very crucial in M&A, for it provides a deep insight into the viability of the proposals. The stakeholders also gain confidence in the proposal and provide the requisite support for executing the deal successfully. While due diligence facilitates evaluation of all the aspects of the proposal, it does not guarantee success. It is just a tool for evaluation and not an insurance against failure.

KEY DEFINITIONS

Due diligence Due diligence is the process of investigation, performed by investors, into the details of a potential investment, such as an examination of operations and management and verification of material facts. It is the process of evaluating a prospective business decision by getting information about the financial, legal, and other material states of the other party.

Due diligence reporting Due diligence reporting is all about preparing a report on the key findings of the process and submitting the same to the management for consideration and adoption.

Financial due diligence Financial due diligence analyses the financial performance of an entity, both qualitatively and quantitatively.

HR due diligence HR due diligence is a process that aims at evaluating the contribution of the HR function to the success of the business in a purchasing, outsourcing, or market testing environment.

Intellectual property due diligence Intellectual property due diligence is a process that provides a prospective investor with detailed information about the intellectual property assets of a target. These assets often affect pricing or other key elements of the proposed transaction or, in certain circumstances, even recommend termination of proposed investment. Intellectual property rights can be broken down into four main categories:

- Patents
- Trademarks
- Copyrights
- Trade secrets

IT due diligence IT due diligence involves analysing the use and relevance of IT services for business operations, management information and financial reporting in business. It also involves finding better ways of deriving value and leverage from IT assets.

Legal due diligence Legal due diligence consists of a scrutiny of all, or specific parts, of the legal affairs of the target company with a view of uncovering any legal risks and providing the buyer with an extensive insight into the company's legal matters.

Litigation analysis Litigation analysis involves ascertaining whether the acquirer shall become liable for the debts and tort liabilities of the predecessor.

Operational due diligence Operational due diligence involves the on-site analysis of the daily proceedings of the target business and how the business operates. The analysis includes an evaluation of the key employees, managers, independent contractors, suppliers, and other factors that are necessary for the business to conduct normal operations.

Partnership A partnership is a relationship between persons who come together for carrying on business activity and decide to share the profits or bear the losses so arising.

CONCEPT REVIEW QUESTIONS

4.1 Explain the concept of due diligence. Why do companies feel the need for due diligence?

4.2 What does due diligence involve?

4.3 Explain the transactions where due diligence is crucial.

4.4 Discuss the choice of people who are to be involved in the due diligence process. How are they different from the people interested in due diligence?

4.5 Explain the process of due diligence in detail.

4.6 Does due diligence insure against M&A failure?

4.7 Why does due diligence fail?

4.8 Write notes on the following:
   (a) Due diligence reporting
   (b) Types of due diligence
   (c) Financial due diligence
   (d) Legal due diligence
   (e) Operational due diligence
   (f) Intellectual property due diligence
   (g) IT due diligence
   (h) Human resource due diligence
   (i) Conducting intellectual property due diligence effectively
   (j) Understanding issues with reference to specific IP assets
   (k) Litigation analysis
   (l) Due diligence team

PROJECT ASSIGNMENT

Analyse the due diligence process adopted by Tata Steel and Corus.

REFERENCES

Gerald, A., Gillies, S., and Krings, J., *Strategic Due Diligence: A Foundation for M&A Success*, Booz & Co., UK, 2009

Hildebrand, M.J and Klosek, K., *Intellectual Property Due Diligence: A Critical Pre-requisite to Capital Investment*, www.library.findlaw.com, last accessed on 29 June 2009

http://www.eyesonchina.com/process_of_due_diligence.pdf, last accessed on 26 June 2009

http://charlesmillsconsulting.com/what_is_due_diligence?, last accessed on 26 June 2009

http://www.allbusiness.com/company-activities-management/company-structures-ownership/ 15183687-1.html, last accessed on 1 September 2010

http://entrepreneurs.about.com/od/financing/a/duediligence.htm, last accessed on 29 June 2009

http://www.plantemoran.com/services/business-advisory-services/due-diligence, last accessed on 29 June 2009

http://www.bvhd.dk/english/areas-of-expertise/legal-due-diligence, last accessed on 29 June 2009

http://www.allbusiness.com/business-finance/equity-funding-private-equity/2976486-1, last accessed on 29 June 2009

http://www.pwc.com/gx/en/IT-due-diligence-services, last accessed on 29 June 2009

http://articles.techrepublic.com.com/5100-10878_11-1038700.html, last accessed on 12 August 2009

Lajoux, A.R., 'M&A Due Diligence in the New Age of Corporate Governance', *Ivy Business Journal*, January–February 2003, pp. 3

Rajkumar, A., *Handbook on Due Diligence*, http://www.carajkumarradukia.com/handbook_new.asp, last accessed on 4 October 2009, pp. 2

Rosenbloom, A.H., *Due Diligence for Global Deal Making*, Bloomberg Press, San Francisco, 2002, pp. 3

www.lgloomarlaw.com, last accessed on 29 June 2009

CASE STUDY

Advent Limited and Pourshins Limited

Abstract

Advent Limited (Advent) was keen on taking over Pourshins Limited (Pourshins) so that it could conveniently expand its operations in the UK and Europe. To be very sure that the buy was not a wrong decision, Advent initiated the process of due diligence. The case tries to analyse the due diligence process adopted by Advent.

Pedagogical Objectives

- To understand and identify the strengths of Pourshins
- To analyse the key variables studied by Advent under the process of due diligence
- To identify the weaknesses in the process adopted by Advent

Introduction

Advent is an Indian BPO (business process outsourcing) company with excellent business in the UK and Europe. Pourshins, a UK-based company with an American management, was to be acquired by the Indian company. To take over and acquire the UK company, due diligence is being undertaken by the acquirer (Advent Limited).

Background of Pourshins

Pourshins was established in 1985 and made sound progress in the BPO business. It has been known as 'caterer' to various airlines in the world.

The company's business has been in the following areas, as shown in Fig. 4.2:

- Financial services: 66%
- Healthcare: 25%
- Insurance: 9%

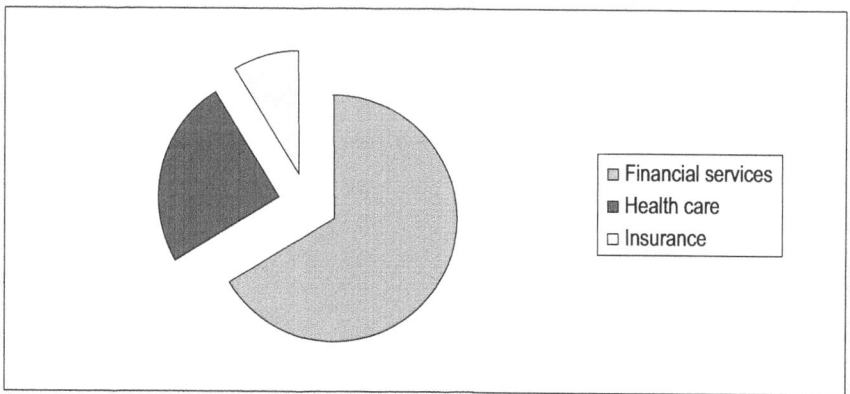

Figure 4.2   Business areas of Pourshins

Their key clients in Europe and the UK comprise five clients in financial services, two clients in healthcare, and two clients in insurance.

The target BPO company initially had 150 employees to take care of clients in Europe and the UK. The facility is shared between the target and other group companies. The BPO division has seen an unprecedented growth in the last few years and the employee strength currently stands at 175. The BPO business has grown at the rate of 9% over last year, and growth in the business has ranged at 25%–30% per annum.

Sectors of Growth

The BPO sector has the potential to facilitate growth of the insurance business, and performs the following key activities for the clients:

- New business
  - Pre-screen and capture
  - Underwriting and underwriting support
  - Delivery requirements and follow-ups
  - Policy issuance
  - Fund application
  - Refund

- Customer service
  - Queries complaints
  - Quotes
  - Administrative process in force
  - Premium management
  - Error reporting
  - Balancing
  - Loans
  - Withdrawals
  - Dividends

- Title
  - Address change
  - Certificate reissue
  - Quotes and reinvestments
  - Assignments
  - Correspondence

- Termination
  - Claims examination and adjudication
  - Maturities, surrender, and exchange

- Financial services
  - Equity research
  - Commercial and residential mortgages processing
  - Cost management
  - Internal audit
  - Accounting services
  - Expenses tracking and accounts payable management
  - Imaging data entry adjudication

- Healthcare
  - All activities specified under insurance
  - Claims submission
  - Claims adjudication
  - Claims validation

The company charges professional fees of $20 per transaction, based on the number of trans-actions the company executes.

Financial Data

The revenue earned during the last two years based on monthly transactions, which were not uniform, was as follows:

- 2007–2008: $250 million
- 2008–2009: $325 million

Other data is as given in Table 4.1.

Table 4.1   Revenue and volume growth of the target company's clients

Client	Revenue growth	Volume growth
1	29%	25%
2	10%	−8%
3	−1%	−4%
4	45%	−
5	−26%	−
6	14%	16%
7	19%	−
8	60%	2%
9	−	−

The headcount by process is as given in Table 4.2.

Table 4.2   Number of clients of target company based on process

Client	Processes						
	P1	P2	P3	P4	P5	P6	P7
1	−	1	2	2	3	5	3
2	1	1	2	3	2	2	1
3	30	35	35	50	60	25	50
4	20	25	20	25	20	20	25
5	40	20	10	5	15	10	5

(Continued)

Table 4.2   (*Continued*)

Client	Processes						
	P1	P2	P3	P4	P5	P6	P7
6	5	2	1	1	1	1	5
7	15	10	5	8	10	10	5
8	20	22	25	30	20	20	20
9	60	65	65	62	60	62	65

The client is looking for a detailed analysis of the target, its key clients, capabilities, and analysis of support functions, if any. Due diligence involves coordinated activities and discussions with the acquirer and the target company, including site visits.

Discussion Questions
1. Prepare a due diligence report.
2. What steps will you take to prepare the report?
3. What information will you gather from the target company for submission to the acquirer?

5 | Legal Issues in Mergers and Acquisitions

LEARNING OBJECTIVES

After studying the chapter, you will be able to understand the following legal provisions for merging entities:

- Provisions of the Companies Act, 1956
- SEBI Buyback of Securities Regulations, 1998
- SEBI Substantial Acquisition of Shares and Takeovers, 1997
- Listing Agreement norms
- SEBI delisting of shares norms
- Corporate governance issues
- Provision of Income Tax Act, 1961
- Foreign Exchange Management Act (FEMA), 1999
- Competition Act, 2002

5.1 INTRODUCTION

Mergers and acquisitions (M&As) are very complicated and lengthy affairs. Since the stakes are high, the merging entities are required to adhere to a number of provisions to ensure that the interest of all the stakeholders is protected. While M&As successfully elevate the functional performance of the entity, they have the potential to create monopolistic power, often resulting in exploitation of customers. Countries across the globe understand the flip side of M&As and therefore enforce laws to control their anti-competitive nature. Keeping in line with these global trends, the Indian economy has also evolved a very comprehensive set of laws that govern all aspects of M&As. The basic objective is to ensure that the process is carried out meticulously and the interest of all the stakeholders is protected. In this chapter, we shall discuss the following legal provisions that are prevalent in the country:

- Companies Act, 1956
- SEBI (Buyback of Securities) Regulations, 1998
- SEBI (Substantial Acquisition of Shares and Takeovers) Regulations, 1997
- Listing Agreement norms

- SEBI delisting of shares norms
- Corporate governance issues
- Provision of Income Tax Act, 1961
- Foreign Exchange Management Act (FEMA), 1999
- Competition Act, 2002

5.1.1 Concepts of Appointed Date and Effective Date

Before we discuss the legal provisions, let us understand the meaning of two very crucial terms: appointed date and effective date.

- The *appointed date* connotes the date of amalgamation—the date from which the undertaking including assets and liabilities of the transferor company vests in the transferee company.
- The *effective date* signifies the completion of all the formalities of merger.

5.2 COMPANIES ACT, 1956

The Companies Act, 1956 is one of the most important legislations in India that empowers the central government to regulate the formation, financing, functioning, and winding up of companies.

It provides an elaborate mechanism for regulating organizational, financial, managerial, and all other relevant aspects of a company. The Act empowers the central government with the right to do the following:

- Inspect the books of accounts of a company
- Direct special audits and order investigations into the affairs of a company
- Launch a prosecution in case of violation of the Act

The provisions of the Act have been designed to ensure that companies conduct their affairs in accordance with them, and that no unfair practices, prejudicial to the public interest, are being resorted to by any company or a group of companies. The Act also empowers the company to examine whether there is any mismanagement which may adversely affect any interest of its stakeholders.

The Companies Act is administered by the central government through the Ministry of Corporate Affairs and the Registrar of Companies (ROC), official liquidators, public trustee, Company Law Board, Director of Inspection, etc. The ROC controls the task of incorporation of new companies and administration of running companies. Let us now look at the Act in detail for our purposes.

5.2.1 Introduction

The terms 'merger' and 'amalgamation' have not been defined in the Companies Act, 1956. The two terms are treated as synonyms and used interchangeably. According to the *Concise Oxford Dictionary* (10th edition) amalgamation means 'to combine or unite to form one organization or structure'.

The provisions related to mergers and amalgamations are contained in Sections 390–396A in Chapter V, Part VI of the Companies Act. Let us see the provisions of each of these sections, which deal with matters pertaining to 'arrangement' and 'compromise'.

5.2.2 Section 390

This sections deals with the 'arrangement' that includes reorganization of the share capital of the company. This is done either by consolidation of shares of different classes or by the division of shares into different classes, or both.

This section also provides that unsecured creditors who may have filed suits be treated at par with other unsecured creditors.

5.2.3 Section 391(1)

This section deals with 'compromise'. It is an arrangement carried out at the behest of the court on an application made by the company, or any creditor, member, or the liquidator where a company is being wound-up. Compromise is generally carried out between the company and its creditors or between a company and its members.

5.2.4 Section 391(2)–(7)

These sections state that every scheme of arrangement and compromise should be approved by three-fourth of the creditors or members present and voting either in person or by proxy.

5.2.5 Section 393(1)

This section deals with disclosure of the terms of arrangement and compromise. It clearly states that the notice calling the meeting of creditors or members should clearly state the terms of arrangement and compromise and their effects. It should also state any material interest of any of the top officials of the company. If the notice is given through an advertisement, the same should give details of the place from where the copies of the statement on the terms of the arrangement and compromise can be obtained. The copies are to be provided by the company free of cost.

5.2.6 Section 393(2)

This section states that if the arrangement and compromise are likely to affect the rights of the debenture holders, a statement giving information and explanation relating to the trustees of the deed for securing debenture capital needs to be given.

These sections provide that if these provisions are violated, the company and every officer of the company shall be punishable with a fine that may extend up to ₹50,000. In addition, any officer who is required to give information on self but fails to do so shall be punishable with a fine that may extend up to ₹5,000.

5.2.7 Section 394

This section provides that the court has powers to sanction a compromise or arrangement scheme proposed in connection with a scheme for reconstruction of the company or amalgamation of two or more companies.

The court may provide for the following sanctions:

- Transfer of whole or part of the property or liabilities of the transferee (target) to the transferor (acquirer)
- Allotment or apportioning the shares, debentures, or other like interests among the transferor or transferee
- Continuing the suit by or against the target by or against the acquirer
- Dissolution, without winding up, by any transferor
- Dissent by any person to the scheme of compromise or arrangement within stipulated time and in a stipulated manner
- Matters that are necessary to carry out the scheme in a complete and effective manner

The approval of the court is subject to the condition that the scheme is not prejudicial to the interests of the members or to the public.

Once the scheme is approved, the following changes shall take place:

- All the property and liabilities shall stand transferred to the transferee company.
- All the property that was under any 'charge' should be deemed to be free from the said charge once an order to that effect is passed. The order should accordingly be incorporated in the records of the company.

Once the order is passed, the company should file a certified copy of the order with the ROC, failing which every officer who is at default shall be punishable with a fine up to ₹500.

5.2.8 Section 394A

This section states that the court should communicate the details of all the notices of compromise and arrangement to the central government. It should then seek and consider the representations made by the central government before passing any order. The court, in this case, should ensure that all material facts pertaining to the company and its functioning have been duly disclosed in the application before making any order.

Once the order is passed, copies of the same should be filed with the ROC and annexed with every copy of memorandum of association issued after the copy has been filed.

Any default in this regard is punishable with a fine of up to ₹100 for each copy where default occurs. Once the court admits the application, a stay is imposed on all suits or proceedings against the company. In addition, before sanctioning the scheme, the court has to classify creditors or members, so that the company offers identical compromise to investors belonging to one class. This procedure is followed in the case of a company that is a going concern.

Finally, the scheme needs to be approved by the requisite majorities and it becomes binding on all the members of the company whether consented to by all or not. For ascertaining three-fourths majority, the members present at the meeting are counted and not the total number of members. The court may reject the scheme if it feels that the scheme is fraudulent or is intended to cover the misdeeds of the directors.

5.2.9 Section 376

This section states that reconstruction or amalgamation shall be void when it is prohibited under the following provisions:

- The memorandum or articles of association
- Resolution passed in the general body meeting or by the board of directors
- An agreement between the company and any other person

5.2.10 Section 395

This section deals with the acquisition of shares of shareholders expressing dissent over the scheme or contract approved by the majority involving the transfer of shares.

Refer to Appendices B–E for a better understanding of the provisions of the Companies Act.

5.3 POWERS OF COURT

The court enjoys immense powers with regard to sanctioning amalgamation schemes proposed by companies. The court can use these powers and make provisions in the order on the following matters:

- Transfer of the whole or any part of the undertaking, property, or liabilities of any target to the acquirer
- Allotment or appropriation of any shares, debentures, or other like interests in that company by the acquirer under the compromise or arrangement
- Any legal proceedings pending by or against each other
- Dissolution of the acquirer's company without winding up
- Making provisions for any person who shows dissent to the compromise or arrangement, provided such dissent has been filed within the stipulated time and in the manner prescribed
- Any other issue necessary to ensure the reconstruction or amalgamation is carried out fully and effectively

Before passing any order, the court should consider the report of the ROC and the official liquidator prior to sanctioning the scheme of amalgamation or reconstruction, which should state that the affairs of the company are being conducted in a manner that is not prejudicial to the interest of members or the public in general.

The court can also sanction the scheme with retrospective effect. However, if the effective date is too far in the past, it can have adverse implications for the new entity, such as non-compliance with various laws.

In cases where the entire undertaking of the transferor company is transferred to the transferee company without affecting the rights of the creditor or members and also without any reorganization of capital of the transferee company, the transferee company need not file a separate petition.

The approval of shareholders and creditors—secured and unsecured—needs to be obtained in meetings convened under the directions of the court, which shall appoint a chairperson and an alternate chairperson for such meetings. Once the court receives a request that the meeting needs to be convened, it issues directions on the following:

- Date, time, and place of meetings
- Appointment of chairperson for the meetings
- Contents of notice and the manner of service of notice
- Determination of the class/classes of members and creditors whose meetings are to be held
- Determination of quorum
- Any other matter as the court may deem fit

If the transferee proves before the court that the creditors and members have given their consent to the scheme of amalgamation with their interest not adversely affected, the court shall exercise its discretion and grant approval to the proposed scheme. Voting of members or creditors at court-convened meetings is to be done through poll only.

Under Section 391(2), the resolution approving the scheme of amalgamation should be passed by the majority in number representing three-fourths in value of the creditors or members. The three-fourth strength includes members or creditors present in person or through proxies at the time of meeting.

The chairperson of the meeting is required to submit to the court a report of the proceedings of the meeting, which should include the following:

- The number of persons present in the meeting
- The number of persons voting in person and through proxy
- The value of shares/indebted amount
- The votes cast in favour of the resolution
- The votes cast against the resolution

5.4 SEBI (BUYBACK OF SECURITIES) REGULATIONS, 1998

The SEBI (Buyback of Securities) Regulations, 1998 are applicable to companies wanting to buy back shares or other specified securities listed at the stock exchange. The Act states that a buyback cannot be done for delisting shares from the stock exchanges. Let us now look at this topic in detail.

5.4.1 Introduction

Before we make an attempt to understand the provisions of SEBI (Buyback of Securities) Regulations, 1998, we should understand the concept of buyback.

5.4.2 Concept of Buyback

Buyback is a mechanism of financial restructuring through which a company purchases its own shares or other specified securities. Here, a company offers to take back its shares owned by the investors at a specified price generally determined or arrived at on the basis of the average market price of the shares in the past few months. The value is determined by adding a certain amount as premium so that more shareholders are attracted to offer their holding under the proposed buyback scheme. The amount of premium depends on the financial strength of the company opting for the buyback.

5.4.3 Provisions of Section 77 (of Companies Act, 1956)

Section 77 of the Companies Act, 1956, prohibits a limited company from buying back its own shares. The basic reason for such a prohibition was a feeling that allowing companies to buy back their shares could give rise to companies 'trafficking' in their own shares, leading to undesirable practices in the stock market, such as insider trading or other unhealthy influences on stock prices (www.primeacademy.com). The only way a company could attempt a buyback was through compliance with the provisions of and adherence to the procedure for reduction of share capital as specified under Sections 100–104 of the Companies Act, 1956, which involved confirmation by the court.

5.4.4 Amendments to Section 77

After several discussions and deliberations at various forums, a working group on the Companies Act, 1956, was constituted by the central government. Based on the recommendations of this working group, Sections 77A and 77B were inserted into the Companies Act. The proposed amendment was suggested to bring Indian law in parity with its British counterpart (report of working group on the Companies Act). Once the amendment was incorporated into the Companies Act, the concept of buyback of securities got incorporated in the Companies Act by the Companies (Amendment) Ordinance 1998.

Section 77A of the Act expanded the scope of the company and bestowed the power to a company to purchase its own securities subject to the provisions of Section 77A(2) and Section 77B of the Act. Post this amendment, SEBI issued the SEBI (Buyback of Securities) Regulations 1998, which is applicable to listed companies. All other companies were regulated by Private Limited Company and Unlisted Public Limited Company (Buyback of Securities) Rules, 1999.

5.4.5 Why do Companies Opt for a Buyback?

Companies go for a buyback of shares on account of one or more of the following reasons (www.jurisonline.in):

- To increase the promoters' holding
- To increase the earnings per share (EPS)
- To improve return on capital, return on net worth, and shareholder value
- To provide an additional exit route to shareholders in conditions where the shares are undervalued or are thinly traded
- To enhance consolidation of stake in the company
- To utilize the surplus cash to the shareholders through buyback
- To have an optimum capital structure
- To rationalize the capital structure by writing off capital not represented by assets
- To support the share value in the capital market by reducing the floating capital
- To thwart a hostile takeover attempt
- To pay surplus cash not required by business

5.4.6 Sources for Buyback

Section 77(1) of the Companies Act, 1956 clearly stipulates the sources of funds the company can use for buyback of shares. These include the following:

Free reserves   A company can utilize its free reserves to fund its buyback plans. This is done by transferring a sum equal to the nominal value of the share planned to be bought back to the capital redemption reserve and subsequently utilizing the same for executing the buyback of shares. The company, however, should provide the details of such transfers in the balance sheet. A transfer to capital redemption reserve account is not permitted when the securities are not shares. The central government is authorized to notify other securities as specified securities from time to time and such notified securities may not be shares.

Share premium account   The balance appearing in the share premium account can also be utilized for carrying out the buyback of shares. Here again, the amount to be utilized for the purpose of buyback is transferred to the capital redemption reserves and then channelized for the purpose of buyback.

Proceeds of any shares or other specified securities   The company can also utilize the proceeds of any shares or other securities issued to facilitate the buyback. However, no buyback of any kind of shares or other specified securities can be made out of the proceeds of the same kind of shares or same kind of other securities. For example, proceeds from the issue of preference shares cannot be used for financing buyback of preference shares.

5.4.7 Prerequisites of Valid Buyback

Any company desirous of going ahead with a buyback plan should do so strictly in accordance with the conditions prescribed under Section 77A(2).

The norms prescribed include the following:

- A company can go ahead with buyback of shares provided it is authorized under the articles of association. If the articles are silent on this aspect, the company should amend the articles as per the procedure laid down in Section 31. Once it is amended, the proposal to buyback shares can be pursued.
- The company should pass a special resolution in the general meeting of the company authorizing the buyback.
- A buyback proposal should be approved by the board of directors by means of a board resolution passed at its meeting. The amount intended to be bought back should not exceed 10% of the total paid-up equity capital and free reserves of the company. Again, the board can exercise this power, provided it has not made an offer for the buyback of the share under its authority during the preceding 365 days.
- In addition to this, the company is also required to pass a special resolution in its general meeting as per the procedure laid down.
- The overall limit for any buyback of securities that may be resorted to by a company should not exceed 25% of the company's paid-up capital and free reserves.
- The buyback debt–equity ratio should be within the permissible 2:1 range. However, the central government is empowered to relax the debt–equity ratio in respect of a class of companies, but not in respect of any particular company.
- The shares intended to be bought back must be fully paid-up.
- If the shares or other specified securities intended to be bought back are listed on any recognized stock exchange, then the buyback should be done strictly in accordance with the SEBI (Buyback of Securities) Regulations, 1998.
- Where the buyback involves shares or other specified securities that are not listed on any recognized stock exchange, the company should comply with the provisions of the Private Limited Company and Unlisted Public Company (Buyback of Securities) Rules, 1999.
- Every buyback is required to be completed within 12 months from
  - the date of passing the special resolution,
  - the date of passing the board resolution, or
  - the date of declaration of the result of the postal ballot where the resolution is passed through postal ballot (Section 77A(4) of the Companies Act, 1956).
- The notice of the meeting containing the special resolution relating to buyback of shares should be accompanied by an explanatory statement that

should clearly address the following issues and should state all material facts related to the proposal:

- The necessity for buyback
- The class of security intended to be purchased by the buyback
- The amount to be invested under buyback
- The time limit for completion of buyback

- The company must file a declaration of solvency with the ROC and SEBI in the prescribed form before the buyback is carried out. This is done to guarantee the company's solvency for at least a year after the completion of the buyback. A company whose shares are not listed on any stock exchange need not file this declaration with SEBI.

- Once the process of buyback is completed, the company is required to physically extinguish and destroy the securities within seven days from the last day on which the buyback process is completed. In case the shares are in dematerialized form, the same should be deleted from the records of the company.

- A company should maintain a register containing the particulars of the bought-back securities, including the consideration paid for them, the date of cancellation, the date of physically extinguishing and physically destroying securities and other such particulars as may be prescribed. The register is required to be completed within seven days of the date of completion of buyback.

- A company that has completed a buyback of shares cannot make a further issue of securities within a period of six months from the date of completion of the buyback process. The company can, however, issue bonus shares and discharge its existing obligations such as conversion of warrants, stock option schemes, sweat equity, or conversion of preference shares or debentures into equity shares.

- Once the buyback process is completed, the company should file a return with SEBI and the ROC in the prescribed format within a period of 30 days. A private company and a public company whose shares are not listed on a recognized stock exchange should file the return of buyback with the ROC only.

Non-compliance with the aforesaid provisions is a punishable offence under Section 77A(11) of the Companies Act.

5.4.8 Modes of Buyback

As per the provisions of Section 77A(5) read with Regulation 4 of SEBI (Buyback of Securities) Regulations, 1998, securities can be bought back from the following sources:

- Existing security holders on a proportionate basis
- The open market through the following:
  - Book building process in accordance with Regulation 17
  - Stock exchanges in accordance with Regulation 15

- In odd lots where the shares of a listed company are smaller than the marketable lot. A *marketable lot* is the minimum number of shares that one needs to purchase every time one decides to purchase the shares of a company from the stock market.
- Securities issued to employees of the company under stock option or sweat equity

5.4.9 Prohibited Modes of Buyback

As per the provisions of Section 77B of the Companies Act, a company is restricted to buyback its shares

- through a subsidiary company including its own subsidiary company,
- through any investment company or group of investment companies,
- if the company has defaulted in respect of
  - repayment of deposit or interest payable thereon,
  - redemption of debentures or preference shares,
  - payment of dividend to any share holder, or
  - repayment of any term loan or interest payable thereon to any financial institution or bank, and
- through negotiated deals, spot transactions, private arrangements, and insider dealings.

The other provisions that need to be monitored by the company planning a buyback of shares are as follows:

- The offer price should have a floor price. The floor price is determined on the basis of the average traded price of 26 weeks, as quoted on the stock exchange where the shares of the company are most frequently traded, preceding the date of public announcement. The floor price so determined is without any ceiling of maximum price.
- If the related securities are infrequently traded, the offer price shall be determined as per regulation 20(5) of the SEBI (Substantial Acquisition and Takeover) Regulations.
- The entire process needs to be carried out transparently. The stock exchange(s) is (are) required to provide the infrastructure facility for display of the price at the terminals of the trading members, so that the investors can access the price on the screen.
- When the securities are being delisted, the acquirer is required to allow a further period of six months for any of the remaining shareholders, who have not utilized the earlier opportunity of surrendering the securities, to tender securities at the same price.
- The stock exchanges are required to monitor the possibility of price manipulation and keep a special watch on the securities that are in the process of getting delisted.
- The ROC and transfer agent should cooperate with the Clearing Corporation to determine the genuineness of physical securities upfront.

- In case the quantity eligible for acquiring securities at the final price offered does bring the public shareholding below the required level of public holding for continuous listing, the company will continue to remain listed.
- Delisting of securities does not result in extinguishing of the paid-up share capital as in the case of buyback of securities.
- In case of partly paid-up securities, the price determined by the book building process shall be applicable to the extent the call has been made and paid.
- The amount of consideration for the tendered and accepted securities shall be settled in cash.

5.4.10 Advantages of Buyback of Shares

A company decides to go ahead with a buyback proposal due to the following benefits:

Low market price   A company goes for buyback its shares to take advantage of low market price of the shares prevailing in the stock market.

Boost to share price   A company also considers buyback to give a boost to the share price, which according to the company has been unfairly low. It is also expected that once the buyback process comes to an end, the value of the shares generally starts rising. The reason behind this is decline in the floating stock of the shares in the market.

Utilizing excess cash   Buyback is also beneficial to companies that have excess cash. It is a better option than paying dividend, because once dividend is paid, investors expect the same amount or higher dividend regularly. A company cannot be sure about its cash reserves. In case the company's cash dwindles in the future years, it might not be able to sustain the rate of dividend paid in the past and this might invite the wrath of the shareholders.

Infuse ESOP   A company might like to take advantage of the lower price to infuse its employee stock option program (ESOP). Before going ahead with the same, the company may decide to buy back shares, so that the floating stock does not increase substantially.

Safeguard from hostile takeover bid   A company may buy back its shares to safeguard itself from hostile takeover bids. Buyback reduces the number of shares in the market, resulting in an increase in the market price. This makes the takeover costly for the acquirer and may deter his plans of attempting a takeover.

5.4.11 Disadvantages of Buyback of Shares

Buyback of shares suffers from a number of disadvantages, which may be due to the following factors:

Flaw in legal provisions   Section 77A(2) states that a company whose shares are listed on a recognized stock exchange should carry out buyback of shares in accordance with the regulations made by SEBI. There is a serious lapse in this provision. As per the definition of 'recognized stock exchange' under Section 2(39) of the Act, a stock exchange which is notified by the central government in the official gazette is a recognized stock exchange for the purpose of that provision. The fact is that till date the central government has not recognized a stock exchange for the purpose of Section 77A. The absence of such a notification is a fatal omission, for if a company decides to buy back its own securities, it is technically invalid and cannot be acted upon (www.jurisonline.com).

Flaw in Income Tax Act   Section 115-O of the Income Tax Act, 1961, states that dividend tax at the rate of 10% has to be paid on any amount declared, distributed, or paid by way of dividend by any domestic company. However, buyback of shares made under Section 77A of the Act is not treated as dividend by virtue of Section 2(22)(iv) of the Income Tax Act. In addition, it is not mandatory for a company to declare dividend under the Act.

Taking advantage of this legal provision, a company/subsidiary may refrain from declaring dividend and transfer the entire or substantial profits to reserve every year. Once a healthy amount is accumulated under reserves, a company can buyback 25% of the shares at book value, which in any case will be more than the face value.

Subsequently, six months later, the company can issue further shares to the extent of shares brought back. This process can be repeated any number of times (refer to Annexure 5.1). This lacuna in the act allows the company to go ahead with buyback to repatriate profits without paying dividend taxes by subsidiaries of foreign companies. Similarly, subsidiaries of Indian companies can also distribute profits without paying any dividend tax (www.jurisonline.com).

Enhancing promoter's holdings   Buyback is resorted to by companies to enhance the promoters' holdings in the company rather than shareholders' wealth. Retail investors may decide to offer their shares under the buyback option, while the promoters may not. As a result, the promoters' holding in the company increases, thus making them more powerful.

Delisting of companies   In the case of multinational companies, buyback is often motivated by a desire to get the company delisted from the Indian bourses. Under the present guidelines, if the promoters are able to get more than 90% shares, the law permits delisting (www.jurisonline.com).

No restriction on number of buybacks   A company can resort to repeated buybacks year after year as there is no restriction on the number of times a company can buy back shares. In addition, the company is only required to allow a cooling off period of six months between a buyback and re-issue of the same kind of shares. Every time a company goes for a buyback and then a re-issue, the promoter's equity holding in the company increases, making them more powerful and the retail investors weaker.

Insider trading   It is observed that buyback announcements are often preceded by insider trading by the promoters. It benefits the promoters as they are the ones behind insider trading.

Therefore, if the legal provisions are suitably amended, stringent provisions are added to the laws, and people using buyback for their benefit are penalized, the aforesaid weaknesses can be taken care of.

5.5 SEBI (SUBSTANTIAL ACQUISITION OF SHARES AND TAKEOVER) REGULATIONS, 1997

The SEBI (Substantial Acquisition of Shares and Takeover) Regulations, 1994 is a landmark regulation enacted by SEBI. It lays down procedures to be followed by an acquirer for acquiring the majority of shares or controlling in another company, so that the process of takeover is carried out in a fair and transparent manner.

Keeping in mind the changing circumstances, the regulations have been amended a number of times. Under one such amendment, the SEBI Takeover Code was rechristened by enacting SEBI (Substantial Acquisition of Shares and Takeover) Regulations, 1997 substituting SEBI (Substantial Acquisition of Shares and Takeover) Regulations, 1994. Let us look at this topic after studying the relevant background.

5.5.1 Introduction

There has been a phenomenal increase in takeover activity across the globe. While takeovers may add value and generate competitive advantage, they are not always favoured, as discussed in Chapter 2. To ensure that takeovers are carried out with the intention of benefiting all the stakeholders, various laws have been enacted. One of them is SEBI (Substantial Acquisition of Shares and Takeover), 1997.

Before we make an attempt to understand the provisions of the act, we need to understand the concept of substantial acquisition of shares and the procedure through which the acquirer can acquire shares of the target company.

5.5.2 Concept of Substantial Acquisition of Shares

Takeover is a process whereby an acquirer takes control of the target company. However, when an acquirer acquires substantial quantity of shares or voting rights of the target company, it is termed as substantial acquisition of shares.

Before we make an attempt to understand the term 'substantial', we need to understand the term 'persons in concert'. This term is used repeatedly in the related act.

Acting in concert implies working in cooperation/coordination to acquire voting rights or control of the target company, either directly or indirectly. In this context, persons acting in concert (PACs) are individuals/companies/any other legal entities who act together with the objective of acquiring substantial shares or voting rights in the target company and gaining control over the target company. The PAC may enter into a formal or informal agreement in this regard.

Acting in concert is a takeover strategy whereby individuals and companies acquire a substantial number of shares in the target company in a disguised manner, and avert legal complications. Each member acquires enough number of shares, so that individually each one remains below the threshold limit, but collectively they exceed the threshold limit.

Unless the contrary is established, certain entities are deemed to be PAC—such as a company with its holding company or subsidiary company, a mutual fund with its sponsor/trustee/asset management company, etc.

With this background, we can now elaborate on the concept of 'substantial' in the right perspective. The SEBI (Substantial Acquisition of Shares and Takeover) Regulations, 1997 defines substantial quantity of shares or voting rights distinctly for two different purposes, as described here:

Threshold of Disclosure to be Made by Acquirer(s)

This is further divided into two categories as follows:

5% or more but less than 15% shares or voting rights Any person/acquirer who in his individual capacity or along with PAC, if any, acquires shares or voting rights that when taken together with his existing holding entitle him to hold 5%, 10%, or 14% shares or voting rights of target company, should disclose the aggregate of his shareholding to the target company within two days of acquisition or within two days of receipt of intimation of allotment of shares.

More than 15% shares or voting rights Any person falling under this category and holds more than 15% shares but less than 75% or voting rights of target company, is required to disclose his purchase/sale, along with the aggregate of his shareholding to the target company and stock exchanges within two working days, as and when he purchases or sells shares aggregating to 2% or more.

Similarly, any person who holds more than 15% shares or voting rights of the target company or every person having control over the target is required to disclose his aggregate shareholding in the target company within 21 days from the financial year ending March 31 as well as the record date fixed for the purpose of dividend declaration.

This responsibility is not restricted to a person holding 15% shares or voting rights alone. Even the target company is required to inform all the stock exchanges where the shares of target are listed every year within 30 days from the financial year ending March 31 as well as the record date fixed for the purpose of dividend declaration.

Trigger Point for Making Open Offer by Acquirer

This is further divided into three categories as follows:

15% shares or voting rights This provision states that an acquirer who intends to acquire shares in the target company, that along with his existing shareholding would entitle him to exercise 15% or more voting rights, then the acquirer can acquire additional shares only after making a public announcement to that effect and acquire at least additional 20% of the voting capital of target company from the shareholders through an open offer.

Creeping acquisition limit An acquirer having 15% or more, but less than 75% of shares or voting rights of a target company, can acquire such additional shares as would entitle him to exercise more than 5% of the voting rights in any financial year is also required to make a public announcement with the objective of acquiring at least 20% shares of target company from the shareholders through an open offer.

Consolidation of holding Under this provision, an acquirer having 75% shares or voting rights of a target company can acquire further shares or voting rights only through an open offer from the shareholders of the target company.

5.5.3 Procedure for Substantial Acquisition of Shares

A company/individual interested in acquiring shares of another company should adhrere to the following five-step procedure:

Making Public Announcement

The acquirer should make a public announcement in the newspapers disclosing the intention to acquire shares of the target company from the existing shareholders by means of an open offer. The announcement should carry the following specific disclosures:

- Offer price
- Number of shares to be acquired from the public
- Identity of the acquirer
- Purpose of acquisition
- Future plans of the acquirer, if any, regarding the target company
- Change in control over the target company, if any
- Procedure to be followed by the acquirer in accepting the shares tendered by the shareholders
- The period within which all the formalities pertaining to the offer should be completed

The acquirer should ensure that the shareholders of the target company are aware of an exit opportunity available to them through the ensuing open offer. Once the acquisition is made, the acquirer should, through a merchant banker, make an announcement making one of the following decisions within four working days of entering into an agreement:

- To acquire shares
- To acquire shares/voting rights of target company
- After any such change or changes as would result in change in control over the target company

Where the acquisition or change in control is indirect, the acquirer should make an announcement giving necessary information within three months of consummation of the acquisition or change in control or restructuring of the parent or the company holding shares of or control over the target company.

Issuing Letter of Offer

A letter of offer is a document addressed to the shareholders of the target company containing the following information:

- Disclosures of the acquirer/persons acting in concert
- Target company
- Financials of the acquirer
- The offer price
- Justification of the offer price
- Number of shares to be acquired from the public
- Purpose of acquisition
- Future plans of acquirer, if any, regarding the target company
- Change in control of the target company, if any
- The procedure to be followed by the acquirer in accepting shares tendered by the shareholders
- The period within which all the formalities to the offer would be completed

A letter of offer is not vetted by SEBI, but the acquirer can seek the services of a merchant banker to carry out due diligence and ensure that the acquirer duly discharges its responsibility.

The merchant banker is required to send the letter of offer within 45 days from the date of public announcement, along with blank acceptance forms, to all the shareholders whose names appear in the register of the company on the specified date.

Determining Offer Price

The acquirer may seek the help of the merchant banker for determining the offer price. A merchant banker ascertains the offer price based on the following parameters:

- Negotiated price under the agreement which triggered the open offer
- The highest price paid by the acquirer or persons acting in concert with him for any acquisition, including those who acquired it by way of allotment in public or rights or preferential issue during the 26 week period prior to the date of the public announcement.
- Average of weekly high and low of the closing prices of shares as quoted on the stock exchanges, where shares of the target company are most frequently traded during 26 weeks or the average of the daily high and low prices of shares during the two weeks prior to the date of the public announcement. The shares of a company are said to be frequently traded when the annualized trading in the shares of the company during the preceding six months is more than 5% of the listed number of shares.

In case the shares of the target company are not frequently traded, then the offer price is determined on the basis of the fundamentals of the company such as return on net worth of the company, book value per share, EPS, etc. The information used for determining the offer price in such a case should also be disclosed.

It is important to note that any amount paid in excess of 25% of the offer price towards non-compete agreement should also be added to the offer price.

Determining Duration of Offer

The offer made by the acquirer to acquire shares in a target company remains open for 30 days. Shareholders willing to sell their stake in the target company should send their share certificate(s)/related documents to the Registrar or the merchant banker as specified in the public announcement and letter of offer, so that the shares are delivered/credited in the account of the acquirer before the expiry of the period of offer.

Discharging Dues of Shareholders

The acquirer is required to pay consideration to all those shareholders who have accepted the offer and accordingly surrendered their holdings to the registrar or merchant banker, as required, within 30 days from the closure of the offer.

5.5.4 Other Provisions of the Act

The Act deals with the provisions that the acquirer needs to fulfil as and when he intends to acquire controlling interest or voting rights in the target company. The Act was first introduced in 1997 and its amended versions were introduced in 2007 and 2009.

Section 18(3) states that as and when the acquirer decides to acquire controlling shares of the target, he should fulfil the following while filing the draft letter of offer with SEBI:

- Pay a fee by bankers' cheque or demand draft drawn in favour of the 'Securities and Exchange Board of India' and payable at Mumbai.
- A promoter or every person forming part of the promoter group is required to disclose the details of shares that are pledged to him/them. The details have to be disclosed within seven working days from the introduction of the amendment introduced under Section 8A of the Act.
- A promoter or every person forming part of the promoter group of a company shall, within seven working days from the date of creation of pledge on shares of that company held by him, inform the details of such pledge of shares to that company.
- A promoter or every person forming part of the promoter group of any company shall, within seven working days from the date of invocation of pledge on shares of that company pledged by him, inform the details of invocation of such pledge to that company.
- The company is also required to disclose the aforesaid information to all the stock exchanges within seven working days of the receipt of the information. The details provided should include the following:
    - Aggregate number of pledged shares of a promoter or every person forming part of the promoter group taken together with shares already pledged during that quarter by such promoter or persons exceeding 25,000; or

- Aggregate of total pledged shares of the promoter or every person forming part of the promoter group along with the shares already pledged during that quarter by such promoter or persons exceeds 1% of total shareholding or voting rights of the company, whichever is lower.

The fee slabs for acquiring controlling shares are shown in Table 5.1.

Table 5.1   Fees to be paid while filing the draft letter for acquiring shares

Offer size	Fee (₹)
Less than or equal to ₹10 million	₹100,000
In excess of ₹10 million but less than or equal to ₹50 million	₹200,000
In excess of ₹5 million but less than or equal to ₹100 million	₹300,000
In excess of ₹10 million but less than or equal to ₹10 billion	0.5% of the offer size
In excess of ₹10 billion but less than or equal to ₹50 billion	₹50 million plus 0.125% of the portion of the offer size in excess of ₹10 billion
In excess of ₹50 billion	₹100 million

5.6 LISTING AGREEMENT NORMS

Listing is a process whereby securities are admitted to the trading privileges of a recognised stock exchange. The securities may be of any public limited company, central or state government, quasi-governmental, and other financial institutions/corporations, municipalities, etc.

The listing is done in accordance with the provisions of the Securities Contracts (Regulation) Act, 1956, Securities Contracts (Regulation) Rules, 1957, Companies Act, 1956, guidelines issued by SEBI, and the rules, by-laws, and regulations of the concerned exchange.

5.6.1 Introduction

Companies that raise capital from the market are expected to provide the investors with liquidity in their investment—entry and exit routes to the investors. To this end, the conomies of the world have a well-regulated capital market, and stock exchanges. An investor can buy and sell securities on the exchanges based on certain prescribed norms.

5.6.2 Concept of Listing

Listing means admission of securities to trading privileges/dealings on recognized stock exchanges through a formal agreement.

Listing is done in accordance with the provisions of the Securities Contracts (Regulation) Act, 1956; Securities Contracts (Regulation) Rules, 1957; Companies Act, 1956; guidelines issued by SEBI and the rules, by-laws, and regulations of the respective stock exchanges in India.

The listing guidelines require companies to fulfil various formalities and adhere to disclosure requirements as and when a company plans the following:

- A public issue that may be an Initial Public Offering (IPO) or Further Public Offering (FPO)
- Preferential issues
- Issue of Indian Depository Receipts (IDRs)
- Amalgamation that implies mergers, acquisitions and reconstruction of companies
- Going ahead with qualified institutions placements (QIPs)

5.6.3 Objectives of Listing

The objectives of listing are as follows (www.bseindia.com):

- To provide liquidity to securities
- To mobilize savings for economic development
- To protect the interest of investors by ensuring full disclosures by listed entities
- To provide a mechanism for effective management of trading in securities
- To provide cost-effective access to capital

5.6.4 Guidelines for Listing in India

India has two very active stock exchanges. These are the Bombay Stock Exchange (BSE) and National Stock Exchange of India (NSE). The two exchanges allow companies to get listed on their respective bourses to enjoy trading privileges, subject to fulfilment of their prescribed norms.

Let us make an attempt to understand the norms prescribed in this regard.

BSE Norms

The norms prescribed by the BSE are as follows:

Listing requirements for companies through IPO and FPO   The BSE categorizes companies into two for the purpose of listing—large cap companies and small cap companies.

Large cap companies are those that enter the market with a minimum issue size of ₹100 million and market capitalization of not less than ₹250 million. All other companies are treated as *small cap companies* according to listing norms.

A large cap company has to fulfil the following requirements:

- The minimum post-issue paid-up capital of the company shall be ₹30 million
- The minimum issue size shall be ₹100 million
- The minimum market capitalization of the company shall be ₹250 million. (Market capitalization is the total value of the post-issue paid-up number of equity shares multiplied with the issue price.)

A small cap company has to fulfil the following requirements:

- The minimum post-issue paid-up capital of the company shall be ₹30 million.
- The minimum issue size shall be ₹30 million.
- The minimum market capitalization of the company shall be ₹50 million
- The minimum income/turnover of the company shall be ₹30 million in each of the preceding three 12-month periods.
- The minimum number of public shareholders after the issue shall be 1000.
- A due diligence study needs to be conducted by an independent team of chartered accountants or merchant bankers appointed by BSE, the cost of which will be borne by the company. BSE may waive the requirement of a due diligence study if a financial institution or a scheduled commercial bank has appraised the project in the preceding 12 months.

In addition to these requirements, all companies shall also be required to fulfil the following additional requirements:

- The issuer is required to include a disclaimer clause as part of the offer document stating that in the event of the company failing to meet the market capitalization requirement of BSE, the securities of the issuer would not be listed on the BSE.
- The applicant, promoters, and/or group companies should be at default in compliance to the Listing Agreement.
- The aforesaid eligibility criteria shall be in addition to the conditions prescribed under SEBI (Disclosure and Investor Protection) Guidelines, 2000.

Listing requirements for companies already listed on other stock exchanges Companies that are already listed on other stock exchanges and seeking listing at BSE are required to fulfil the following requirements:

- The company shall have a minimum issued and paid-up equity capital of ₹30 million.
- The company shall have a profit-making track record for the preceding three years. The revenues/profits arising out of extraordinary items or income from any source of non-recurring nature should be excluded while calculating the profit-making track record.
- The minimum net worth of the company, that is equity capital and free reserves should be ₹200 million.
- The minimum market capitalization of the listed capital shall be at least twice the amount of the paid-up capital.
- The company should have a track record of paying dividend for at least the last three consecutive years and the rate should be at least 10% each year.
- A minimum 25% of the company's issued capital shall be with non-promoter shareholders as per Clause 35 of the Listing Agreement. Out of this

non-promoter holding, no single shareholder shall hold more than 0.5% of the paid-up capital of the company individually or jointly with others except in the case of banks/financial institutions/foreign institutional investors/ overseas corporate bodies and non-resident Indians.

- The company should be listed with any of the regional stock exchanges for at least two years.
- The company should have signed an agreement for demat trading with Central Depository Securities Limited (CDSL) and National Securities Depository Limited (NSDL)

Requirements for companies delisted by BSE seeking re-listing   It is possible that a company previously delisted by BSE may be seeking re-listing at BSE. Such a company is required to make a fresh public offer and comply with the guidelines of SEBI and BSE regarding IPOs.

Permission to use name of BSE in company's prospectus   Companies that offer shares through public issue and desiring to list the same should obtain prior permission from BSE to use their name in the company's prospectus or offer for sale document before filing a copy of the same with the ROC.

The company's application seeking permission to use the name of BSE in its prospectus is placed before the listing committee of BSE, which evaluates the application based on the promoter's background, company, project, company's financials, risk factors, and other aspects and once satisfied with the findings grants permission to the company.

Submission of letter of application   Section 73 of the Companies Act, 1956, states that a company seeking to list its securities on stock exchanges should submit a letter of application to the stock exchanges where it proposes a list its securities before filing a copy of the prospectus with the ROC.

Allotment of securities   The listing norms provide that a company should complete the allotment of securities offered through public issue within 30 days of the date of closure of the issue and seek the approval of the designated stock exchange for approval of the basis of allotment.

If the company raises capital through the book building process, allotment of securities should be completed with 15 days from the date of closure of the issue, failing which the company is required to pay interest at 15% to investors.

Trading permission   SEBI guidelines clearly state that the company issuing securities should complete the requirements for trading at all the stock exchanges where the securities are to be listed. This needs to be done within seven working days of finalization of the basis of allotment.

The norms further state that the company should also dispatch the allotment letters and share certificates/credit the securities in depository accounts/issue refund orders as per the SEBI (Disclosure and Investor Protection) Guidelines,

2000 within the stipulated timeframe and obtain the listing permissions of all the exchanges whose names were included in the prospectus or offer document.

In the event of some stock exchange denying listing permission to the company, the company cannot proceed with the allotment of shares. However, the company can file an appeal before SEBI under Section 22 of the Securities Contracts (Regulation) Act, 1956.

Requirement of 1% security   The listing provisions state that companies making public/rights issues should deposit 1% of the issue amount as security deposit with the designated stock exchange before the issue opens for subscription. The amount is kept as security until the allotment process is completed. If the company fails to resolve the complaints of investors regarding delay in sending refund orders/share certificates, non-payment of commission to underwriters, brokers, etc., the amount is forfeited.

Payment of listing fees   All companies listed on BSE are required to pay to BSE the annual listing fees by April 30 of every financial year as per the schedule of listing fees prescribed from time to time. In case the company fails to pay the amount by April 30 each year, it will have to pay an interest of 12% per annum from May 1 onwards. The company is also required to pay service tax at the applicable rates.

Compliance with Listing Agreement   Companies desirous of getting their securities listed on BSE are required to enter into an agreement with BSE, called the Listing Agreement. The agreement requires that the company make certain disclosures and perform the following acts:

- Provide prompt transfer, registration, sub-division, and consolidation of securities
- Give proper notice of closure of transfer books and record dates
- Forward six copies of unabridged annual reports, balance sheets, and profit and loss accounts to BSE
- File shareholding patterns and financial results on a quarterly basis
- Intimate the happenings that are likely to materially affect the financial performance of the company and its stock prices, promptly to the stock exchange
- Comply with the conditions of corporate governance, etc.

A company failing to adhere to the terms and conditions of the Listing Agreement may face disciplinary action that includes penalty and/or delisting of securities. Penal action is initiated against the defaulting companies.

NSE Norms

The listing norms prescribed are quite similar to BSE, but there are certain areas where the guidelines differ.

Listing in case of IPOs   Companies that propose to come out with IPOs and list their shares on the NSE have to fulfil the following eligibility criteria:

Capital requirements   The paid-up equity capital of the applicant company should not be less than ₹100 million and the capitalization of the applicant's equity should not be less than ₹250 million. For the purpose of determining the paid-up equity capital, the post issue paid-up equity capital for which listing is sought is taken into account. For the purpose of determining the capitalization value, the product of the issue price and the post issue number of equity shares is considered.

The provision also states that the market capitalization, at the price at which the company issues the equity, should not be less than ₹1 billion, even though the paid-up capital of the applicant can be less than ₹100 million, but in no case should it be less than ₹50 million.

NSE further stipulates that the company should include a disclaimer clause in the offer document stating that if the company fails to fulfil the requirement of paid-up capital and market capitalization the securities would not be listed on NSE.

Adherence to legal provisions   The company should have adhered to conditions prescribed by the Securities Contracts (Regulations) Act, 1956, Companies Act, 1956, Securities and Exchange Board of India Act, 1992, any rules and/or regulations framed under the statutes, as also any circular, clarifications, and guidelines issued by the appropriate authority under relevant statutes, before NSE grants permission to the company to list its shares.

Submission of annual reports   The applicant company is also required to submit annual reports of the preceding three financial years to NSE along with a certificate in respect of the following:

- The company has not been referred to the Board for Industrial and Financial Reconstruction (BIFR)
- The net worth of the company has not been wiped out by the accumulated losses and has not resulted in a negative net worth
- The company has not received any winding up petition admitted by a court

No disciplinary action   There should have been no regulatory or disciplinary action by a stock exchange or regulatory authority in the past three years against the applicant company. The period in case of promoters/promoting company, group companies, companies promoted by the promoters/promoting company of the applicant company is restricted to one year.

Redressal mechanism for investor grievances   The company should ensure that the company/promoters/group companies/companies promoted by the promoting company

- has/have a healthy track record in redressal of investor grievances
- has/have arrangements in place for servicing its investors

- favours/favour a philosophy of investor service and protection
- has/have not defaulted in respect of payment of interest and/or principal to the debenture/bond/fixed deposit holders, and this should be certified by the auditors of the company

Distribution of shareholding   The applicant/promoting company's shareholding pattern for the previous three years has to be submitted along with the application for listing.

Details of litigation   The applicant, promoters/promoting company, group companies, companies promoted by the promoters/promoting company should also submit details of the litigation record, nature of litigation, status of litigation filed by the company or against the company during the preceding three years to the exchange.

Track record of director(s) of company   The company should also submit relevant disclosures regarding the status of criminal cases filed or nature of the investigation being undertaken against any director for any offence, which could have an effect on the business of the company. The offence could relate to serious crimes such as murder, rape, forgery, and economic offences.

Listing of securities of existing companies   Companies that are already listed have to fulfil the following eligibility criteria:

Paid-up capital   The paid-up equity capital of the applicant company should not be less than ₹100 million and the market capitalization of the applicant's equity should not be less than ₹250 million.

For determining the amount of paid-up equity capital, the existing paid-up equity capital as well as the paid-up equity capital after the proposed issue for which listing is sought is taken into account.

The requirement of ₹250 million market capitalization is not applicable to listing of securities issued by government companies, public sector undertakings, financial institutions, nationalized banks, statutory corporations, and banking companies who are otherwise bound to adhere to all the relevant statutes, guidelines, circulars, clarifications, etc. issued by various regulatory authorities from time to time.

The paid-up equity capital of the applicant shall not be less than ₹250 million. In case the market capitalization is less than ₹250 million. The securities of the company should have been traded for at least 25% of the trading days during the last 12 months preceding the date of submission of application by the company, or the market capitalization of the applicant's equity shall not be less than ₹500 million or the applicant company should have a net worth of not less than ₹500 million in each of the three preceding financial years. The company is required to submit a certificate from the statutory auditors in respect of the net worth.

The market capitalization should be calculated by using a 12-month moving average of the market capitalization over a period of six months immediately preceding the date of application.

For the purpose of calculating the market capitalization over a 12-month period, the average of the weekly high and low of the closing prices of the shares as quoted on the National Stock Exchange during the last 12 months and if the shares are not traded on the National Stock Exchange, such average price on any of the recognised stock exchanges where those shares are frequently traded shall be taken into account while determining market capitalization after making the necessary adjustments pertaining to rights/bonus issue/split.

Net worth represents the paid-up equity capital plus free reserves excluding revaluation reserves minus miscellaneous expenses not written off minus balance in profit and loss account to the extent not set off.

Adherence to legal provisions   The applicant company should have adhered to all the relevant legal provisions of Securities Contracts (Regulations) Act, 1956, Companies Act, 1956, Securities and Exchange Board of India Act, 1992, any rules and/or regulations framed under foregoing statutes, including circular, clarifications, and guidelines issued under relevant statutes.

Documents pertaining to track record   The applicant is also required to submit the following documents reflecting its track record for a period of three years:

- The company has not been referred to the Board for Industrial and Financial Reconstruction (BIFR).
- The net worth of the company has not been wiped out by the accumulated losses and has not resulted in a negative net worth.
- The company has not received any winding up petition admitted by a court.

Other provisions   The following conditions must also be satisfied:

- The shares of the applicant company should have been listed on any other recognized stock exchange for at least the last three years or listed on the exchange having nationwide trading terminals for at least one year.
- The applicant company should have paid dividend in at least two out of the three financial years immediately preceding the year in which listing application has been made, the applicant has distributable profits in at least two out of the last three financial years and the same is duly certified by the auditors of the company or the net worth of the applicant is at least ₹500 million.

No disciplinary action   No disciplinary action should have been taken by any other stock exchange and regulatory authorities in the past three years against the applicant company. In addition, no disciplinary action should have been initiated against the promoters/promoting company, group companies, and companies promoted by the promoters/promoting company of the applicant company in the past one year.

Redressal mechanism   The applicant company should have the following in place:

- A healthy track record in redressal of investor grievances
- Arrangements in place for servicing its investors

- Favours a philosophy of investor service and protection
- Has not defaulted in respect of payment of interest and/or principal to the debenture/bond/fixed deposit holders, and this should be certified by the auditors of the company

Shareholding pattern   The applicant/promoting company's shareholding pattern for the previous three years has to be submitted along with the application for listing.

Details of litigation   The applicant, promoters/promoting company, group companies, and companies promoted by the promoters/promoting company should also submit details of the litigation record, the nature of litigation, status of litigation filed by the company or against the company during the preceding three years to the exchange.

Track record of director(s) of company   The company should also submit relevant disclosures regarding the status of criminal cases filed or nature of the investigation being undertaken against any director for any offence, which could have an effect on the business of the company. The offence could relate to serious crimes such as murder, rape, forgery, and economic offences.

Change in control of company   In the event where new promoters take over a listed company resulting in change in management and/or the company utilizes the funds raised through public issue for purposes other than those mentioned in the offer document, the company needs to make an additional disclosures with regard to change in control of a company and utilization of funds raised from the public.

5.6.5 Benefits of Listing

Listing of securities generates the following benefits:

Improves ability to raise additional capital   Listing improves the credibility of the company in the eyes of the stakeholders, thereby increasing the company's ability to raise further capital to finance expansion, diversification and acquisitions. The company may use financing routes such as preferential issue, rights issue, QIPs, American depositary receipts (ADRs), global depositary receipts (GDRs), and foreign currency convertible bonds (FCCBs).

Provides liquidity   Listing provides continuing liquidity to the shareholders of the listed entity. It provides an exit route to equity investors and employees who have obtained shares through ESOPs. This also helps in broadening the shareholder's base.

Independent valuation   Listing helps generate an independent valuation of the company by the market in terms of the daily price prevailing in the exchange.

Improves company's profile   A listed company is covered in research reports, and in one or more indices of the stock exchanges. This raises a company's profile in the eyes of the customers, suppliers, investors, financial institutions, and the media.

Disclosures   A listed company is required to adhere to better and timely disclosures as prescribed in the Listing Agreement. Disclosures thus protect the interest of the investors.

Automated trading   An automated trading system ensures consistency and transparency in the trade and enhances investor's confidence and visibility in the market. It also helps in reducing the cost of trading for the investor. The use of communication technology provides instant access to investors from every location.

Regular flow of information   The trading system provides reliable and timely trade and post-trade information, corporate announcements, results, corporate actions, etc. This helps the investors to know the depth of the market and helps them in making intelligent investment decisions.

5.7 SEBI (DELISTING OF SECURITIES) GUIDELINES, 2003

The Act prescribes conditions for removal of securities from the trading privileges of the stock exchange. The company desirous of getting its shares delisted is required to adhere to the conditions prescribed in the SEBI (Delisting of Securities) Guidelines, 2003.

5.7.1 Introduction

The guidelines have been issued under Section 11(1) of SEBI Act, 1992, and are read with Sub-section (2) of Section 11A of SEBI Act. The objective of these guidelines is to protect the interest of investors in the securities market.

5.7.2 Terminology

The following terms need to be understood for a clear understanding of the guidelines:

- *Delisting of shares*, also referred to as reverse book building, represents a mechanism whereby the promoter or acquirer offers to buy back shares from the shareholders through respective book running lead managers (BRLMs). The shares so acquired through the buyback process are used by companies for delisting their shares from stock exchange(s).

The process represents an important tool for efficient price discovery through the book building process. While the reverse book building is open, offers are collected from the shareholders at various prices above or equal to the floor price. Once the offer closes, the buyback price gets determined.

- *Compulsory delisting* under the Act means delisting of the securities of a company by an exchange.
- *Delisting exchange* implies the exchange from which the securities of the company are proposed to be delisted under the SEBI guidelines.
- *Exchange* implies any stock exchange which has been granted recognition under Section 4 of the Securities Contracts (Regulation) Act, 1956.
- *Voluntary delisting* means removing the securities of a company from the trading privileges of a stock exchange. The application to delist a company is made by the promoter, an acquirer, or any person other than the stock exchange.

5.7.3 Applicability of Voluntary Delisting

The provisions of the Act apply to delisting of securities of companies under the following scenarios:

- The promoters seek voluntary delisting of the company.
- The public shareholding falls below the minimum limit specified in the listing conditions or Listing Agreement as a result of any acquisition of shares of the company or scheme or arrangement.
- Promoters of the companies voluntarily seek to delist the securities from all or some of the stock exchanges.
- A person in control of management seeks to consolidate his holdings in a company whereby the public shareholding in the company falls below the limit specified in the listing conditions or Listing Agreement.
- Companies are compulsorily delisted by the stock exchanges.

It is important to note that a company is not permitted to use the buyback provisions to delist the securities of the company.

5.7.4 Voluntary Delisting of Securities of Listed Company

A company listed on any stock exchange can apply for voluntary delisting, subject to the following conditions:

- The securities of the company have been listed on any stock exchange for a minimum period of three years.
- The investors have been given an exit opportunity before the shares are delisted from the stock exchange. The exit price in such cases needs to be determined in accordance with the book building process described in Clauses 7–10, 13, and 14 of the guidelines. Again, an exit opportunity is not required to be given in cases where securities continue to be listed in a stock exchange having nationwide trading terminals.

5.7.5 Procedure for Voluntary Delisting

The process of voluntary delisting has been made difficult for the companies listed on Indian stock exchanges through provisions such as shareholders' approval, the discretionary power given to exchanges, and the minimum number of equity shares the acquirer needs to acquire at the exit price determined by the public shareholders.

The promoter or acquirer desirous of getting the securities of the company delisted from any recognized stock exchange is required to adhere to the following provisions:

- Pass a special resolution at the general meeting to obtain approval of shareholders of the company. The resolution shall remain valid for a period of one year.
- The votes cast in favour of the delisting proposal must be at least twice the votes cast against the proposal by the public shareholders.

- The company has to seek an in-principle approval from the stock exchange from where it seeks to delist its shares by making an application in the specified format along with a copy of the special resolution passed at the general meeting.
- Once the in-principle approval from the stock exchange is obtained, the company has to come out with a public announcement in the manner provided in the guidelines.
- The company has to comply with the other additional conditions as may be specified by the concerned stock exchanges from where securities are to be delisted.
- The acquirer must buy back an adequate number of shares so that their shareholding increases to 90% or the level of promoter shareholding post offer is the aggregate percentage of pre-offer promoters holding and half of the offer size, whichever is higher. This requirement is irrespective of the level of public shareholding applicable to the company under the Listing Agreement with the stock exchanges. This means that if the promoters holding already have 90% shareholding at the time of seeking delisting, they shall propose to buy back the remaining 10% of the public shareholding and shall have to buy at least half of the equity shares offered (5%) to be acquired to delist its equity shares.
- The acquirer needs to provide the public shareholders an exit opportunity at a price determined by the book building process. This price has to be higher than the floor price for the buyback, which has to be disclosed by the company in a public announcement.

5.7.6 Public Announcement for Voluntary Delisting

The SEBI guidelines stipulate that the promoters or acquirer should make a public announcement stating its intention of getting the securities delisted from the stock exchange. The guidelines further stipulate that the public announcement should contain the information as specified in Schedule I, shown in Fig. 5.1. Before making the public announcement, the promoter should appoint a merchant banker registered with SEBI to facilitate the process of delisting.

5.7.7 Exit Price for Voluntary Delisting of Securities

The delisting guidelines stipulate that the promoter of a company, which desires to delist from the stock exchange, needs to offer an exit option to the investor. The guidelines further state that the exit price for delisting of securities should be determined in accordance with the book building process as described in Schedule II of the guidelines, as given in Fig. 5.2.

5.7.8 Public Announcement of Final Price

As stated in the discussion, the final price is determined through the book building process. Once the final price is determined, the promoter or acquirer should

---

SCHEDULE I
CONTENTS OF THE PUBLIC ANNOUNCEMENT

1. The floor price and how it was reached
2. The dates of opening and closing of the bidding
3. The name of the exchange or exchanges from which the securities are sought to be delisted
4. The names and addresses of the trading members as well as the bidding terminals and centres through which bids can be placed
5. Description of the methodology to be adopted for determination of acceptable price
6. Period for which the offer shall be valid
7. The necessity and the object of the delisting
8. Full and complete disclosure of all material facts
9. The proposed timetable from opening of the offer till the settlement of the transfers
10. Details of the escrow account and the amount deposited therein
11. Listing details and stock market data
    (a) high, low, and average market prices of the securities of the company during the preceding three years
    (b) monthly high and low prices for the six months preceding the date of the public announcement
    (c) the volume of securities traded in each month during the six months preceding the date of public announcement
12. Present capital structure and shareholding pattern
13. The likely post-delisting capital structure
14. The aggregate shareholding of the promoter group and of the directors of the promoters, where the promoter is a company and/or persons who are in control of the company
15. Name of compliance officer of the company
16. The public announcement should be signed and dated by the promoter.

Source: Securities and Exchange Board of India (Delisting of Securities) Guidelines, 2003

Figure 5.1   Contents of public announcement for delisting

ensure fulfilment of the following within two working days of the determination of the final price, by doing the following:

- Making a public announcement of the final price in leading newspapers clearly stating whether the price has been accepted or not by the promoter or acquirer
- Communicating the final price with the information whether the same is accepted or not, to all exchanges from which delisting is sought to be made

5.7.9 Delisting from Exchanges not Having Nationwide Terminals

A company listed on any stock exchange or exchanges, other than those having nationwide trading terminals, can seek delisting. While making an exit offer to the shareholders, it is not compulsory for the company to remain listed on any stock exchange just because it is a regional stock exchange.

5.7.10 Minimum Number of Shares to be Acquired

The delisting norms clearly state that delisting is permitted only when the public shareholding falls below a certain minimum limit as specified by the

SCHEDULE II
THE BOOK BUILDING PROCESS

1. The book building process shall be made through an electronically linked transparent facility.
2. The number of bidding centres shall not be less than 30, including all stock exchange centres and there shall be at least one electronically linked computer terminal at all bidding centres.
3. The promoter shall deposit in an escrow account, 100% of the estimated amount of consideration calculated on the basis of the floor price indicated and the number of securities required to be acquired. The provisions of clause 10 of the Securities and Exchange Board of India (Buyback of Securities) Regulations, 1998 shall be applicable mutatis mutandis to such escrow account.
4. The offer to buy shall remain open to the security holders for a minimum period of three days. The security holders shall have a right to revise their bids before the closing of the bidding.
5. The promoter or acquirer shall appoint 'trading members' for placing bids on the online electronic system.
6. Investors may approach trading members for placing offers on the online electronic system. The format of the offer form and the details that it must contain shall be specified.
7. The security holders desirous of availing the exit opportunity shall deposit the shares offered with the trading members prior to placement of orders. Alternately they may mark a pledge for the same to the trading member. The trading members in turn may place these securities as margin with the exchanges/clearing corporations.
8. The offers placed in the system shall have an audit trail in the form of confirmations, which give broker ID details with time stamp and unique order number.
9. The final offer price shall be determined as the price at which the maximum number of shares has been offered. The acquirer shall have the choice to accept the price. If the price is accepted, then the acquirer shall be required to accept all offers upto and including the final price but may not have to accept higher priced offers, subject to clause 15. An illustration is given below:
10. If final price is accepted the acquirer shall have to accept offers up to and including the final price, i.e., 240 shares at the final price of ₹130.
11. At the end of the book build period the merchant banker to the book building exercise shall announce in the press and to the concerned exchanges the final price and the acceptance (or not) of the price by the acquirer.
12. The acquirer shall make the requisite funds available with the exchange/clearing corporation on the final settlement day (which shall be three days from the end of the book build period). The trading members shall correspondingly make the shares available. On the settlement day, the funds and securities shall be paid out in a process akin to secondary market settlements.
13. The entire exercise shall only be available for demat shares. For holders of physical certificates the acquirer shall keep the offer open for a period of 15 days from the final settlement day for the shareholders to lodge the certificates with custodian(s) specified by the merchant banker.

Source: Securities and Exchange Board of India (Delisting of Securities) Guidelines, 2003

Figure 5.2 The bookbuilding process

listing conditions or agreement. However, when the offer is accepted by fewer shareholders and the total shares outstanding do not fall below the minimum stipulated limit, it is interpreted as 'failure of the offer'. In such a case, the promoter or acquirer is not permitted to acquire any securities pursuant to the offer.

When the offer sails through, the payment of consideration for shares acquired is to be paid in cash or by cheque.

5.7.11 Delisting of One or All Classes of Securities

A company may delist one or all classes of securities. The procedure however should be carried out subject to adherence to the following provisions:

- When equity shares of a company are delisted, the fixed income securities can continue to remain listed on the stock exchange.
- An entity that has convertible instruments outstanding cannot delist its equity shares until conversion option has been exercised.

5.7.12 Compulsory Delisting of Companies by Stock Exchanges

A stock exchange is authorized to delist companies for non-compliance with the Listing Agreement provided the company has been suspended for a minimum period of six months. Stock exchanges can also delist companies as per the norms provided in Schedule III, depicted in Fig. 5.3.

SCHEDULE III
NORMS AND PROCEDURE FOR DELISTING OF SECURITIES
BY THE STOCK EXCHANGES

A. NORMS

1. The percentage of equity capital (floating stock) in the hands of public investors
   This may be seen with reference to
   (a) Existing paid-up equity capital
   (b) Market lot
   (c) Share price—very high, medium, low
   (d) Market Capitalization
   (e) SEBIs Takeover Regulations—Regulation 21(3)
   (f) Clause 40A of the Listing Agreement
2. The minimum trading level of shares of a company on the exchanges. There should be some liquidity in every trading cycle. There should be some volume of trading for price discovery on the market. The company should appoint market makers. Criteria of no-trading may be considered.
3. Financial aspect/business aspects
   (a) The company should generate reasonable revenue/income/profits. It should be operational/working. It must demonstrate earning power through its financial results, profits, reserves, and dividend payout for the last 2/3 years.
   (b) If there is hardly any public interest in the securities of the company then it is for consideration whether its 'listed company' label needs to be retained any more.
   (c) The company should have some tangible assets. It is for consideration as to what value of assets the company should own in order to be listed continuously listed.
4. Track records of compliance of the Listing Agreement requirements for the past three years
   (a) Submission of audited/unaudited results, annual report, and other documents required to be furnished to the Exchange
   (b) Book closure record date with due notice
   (c) Payment of listing fee
   (d) Service to investors, especially with regard to timely return of shares duly transferred, timely payment of dividend, communication of price-sensitive information, etc.
   (e) Failure to observe good accounting practices in reporting earnings and financial position

Figure 5.3   SEBI norms governing delisting by stock exchanges   *(Continued)*

(f) Publishing half yearly unaudited/audited results

(g) Frequent changes in accounting year, share transfer agent, registered office, and name.

5. Promoters/Directors' track record, especially with regard to insider trading, manipulation of share prices, unfair market practices (e.g., returning of share transfer documents under objection on frivolous grounds with a view to creating scarcity of floating stock in the market, causing unjust aberrations in the share prices, auctions, close-out, etc. (what depends upon the director's trading position?).

6. If whereabouts of the company, its promoters/directors are not available and even the letters sent by the Exchange return undelivered and the company fails to remain in touch with the Exchange.

7. The company has become sick and is unable to meet current debt obligations, is unable to adequately finance operations, has not paid interest on debentures for the last 2–3 years, has become defunct, has no employees, or has a liquidator appointed, etc.

8. On the basis of these norms and other relevant information available about the company, its promoters/directors, project, litigations, etc., a profile of the company should be prepared and then a decision on delisting should be taken by the Exchange.

B. PROCEDURE

1. The decision on delisting should be taken by a panel to be constituted by the Exchange comprising the following:
   (a) Two directors/officers of the Exchange (one director to be a public representative)
   (b) One representative of the investors
   (c) One representative from the Central Government (Department of Company Affairs)/Regional Director/Registrar of Companies
   (d) Executive Director/Secretary of the Exchange

2. Due notice of delisting and intimation to be given to the company as well as other stock exchanges where the company's securities are listed

3. Notice of termination of the Listing Agreement to be given

4. An appeal against the order of compulsory delisting may be made to the SEBI.

Source: Securities and Exchange Board of India (Delisting of Securities) Guidelines, 2003

Figure 5.3 (*Continued*)   SEBI norms governing delisting by stock exchanges

The stock exchange is required to give adequate and wide public notice through newspapers, including one English national daily of wide circulation, and through display of the notice on the notice board/website/trading systems of the exchange. The stock exchange has to provide a period of 15 days within which any person who may be aggrieved by the proposed delisting can make a representation. The final decision on delisting is made only after the representation is received.

Once the stock exchange finally decides to go ahead with its decision to delist a company, it should give adequate and wide public notice to the fact of delisting. The stock exchange should also ensure that fair value of such securities is disclosed in all its public notices. In addition, the exchange is also required to display the name of such company(ies) on its website.

5.7.13 Rights of Securities Holders in Case of Compulsory Delisting

The Securities and Exchange Board of India (Delisting of Securities) Guidelines 2003 lists certain requirements that companies need to fulfil before delisting their shares. The sole objective of these guidelines is to protect the interest of the securities holders of the company proposing to delist its shares from stock exchange(s).

The following are the guidelines for delisting:

- The promoter of the company should compensate the securities holders by paying fair value of the securities held by them. The fair value of securities is determined by persons appointed by the stock exchange out of a panel of experts, which shall also be selected by the stock exchange, having regard to the factors mentioned in regulation 20 of the SEBI (Substantial Acquisition of Shares and Takeover) Regulations, 1997.
- The stock exchange should ensure that adequate public notice is given through newspapers and displayed on the notice boards/trading systems of the stock.

5.7.14 Delisting Pursuant to Rights Issue

The guidelines provide for adherence to the following in case of delisting pursuant to a rights issue:

- The promoters or the persons in control of the management shall be allotted shares under the rights issue even if they subscribe to the unsubscribed portion, which may result in public shareholding falling below the permissible minimum level.
- This is possible only after the promoters have made adequate disclosures relating to this in the offer document.
- It is imperative that the promoters agree to buy out the remaining securities at the price of the rights issue or make an offer for sale to bring the public shareholding at the level specified in the listing conditions or Listing Agreement to remain listed.
- Where the rights issue is not fully subscribed, the public shareholding would obviously fall below the permissible minimum level as specified in the listing condition or the Listing Agreement. In such a case, the promoter(s) of the company is (are) required to delist the securities by providing an exit opportunity as stated in the guidelines or may make an offer for sale of their holdings so that the public shareholding is raised to the minimum level specified in the Listing Agreement or in the listing conditions within a period of three months.
- In case the securities holders feel aggrieved by the compensation/fair value, they can enforce their claim to compensation/fair value through the arbitration mechanism of the exchange in the manner laid down in its byelaws and provided for under the SEBI guidelines.

5.7.15 Reinstatement of Delisted Securities

Reinstatement of delisted securities is a mechanism whereby the securities of a delisted company are once again admitted to the trading privileges at a stock exchange.

The guidelines specify fulfilment of the following conditions for reinstatement of delisted securities:

- Delisted securities can be reinstated by the stock exchanges with a cooling period of two years. In other words, relisting of securities is allowed only after two years of delisting of the securities.
- The company would be required to fulfil all the listing requirements like a new company getting listed at stock exchanges to get reinstated.
- The reinstatement is subject to the scrutiny of application and relevant documents and approval of the application by the Central Listing Authority.

5.7.16 Rights of Promoters

The SEBI guidelines relating to delisting of securities bestow the following rights on the promoters:

- The promoters may not accept the securities at the offer price determined by the book building process.
- In case the promoters decide not to accept the offer price determined by the book building process, they will take the following measures:
  - Not make an application to the exchange for delisting of the securities
  - Ensure that the public shareholding is brought up to the minimum limits specified under the listing conditions within a period of six months from the date of such decision, using any of the following modes:
    o By issue of new shares complying with the regulatory provisions
    o By making an offer for sale of their holdings in compliance with relevant provisions
    o By selling their holdings through the secondary market in a transparent manner

In case the promoters fail to raise the public shareholding in within six months, they have to offer for sale to the public such portion of their holdings as would bring up the public shareholding to the minimum limits specified in the Listing Agreement or the listing conditions. The holdings are to be offered to the public at a price determined by the Central Listing Authority.

5.7.17 Restrictions Imposed on Company Proposing Delisting

SEBI norms state that a company cannot apply for delisting of its equity shares if it violates one or more of the following norms:

- Buyback of equity shares is initiated by the company.
- Any preferential allotment is made by the company.
- A period of three years has elapsed since the listing of that class of equity shares on any recognized stock exchange.
- Any convertible instruments issued by the company in the same class of equity shares that are sought to be delisted are outstanding.
- It is not clear whether a company will be required to take approval from all the stock exchanges having nationwide terminals in case it is listed on more than one such stock exchange.

5.8 CORPORATE GOVERNANCE ISSUES

The concept of corporate governance came into the global business limelight after a string of collapses of high profile companies such as Enron, the Texas-based energy giant, and WorldCom, the telecom behemoth. The business world was shocked by both the scale and the duration of the unethical and illegal operations of these two companies. The failure of these two companies saw more US companies coming under attack. The problem, as noticed, was widespread with companies from Parmalat in Italy to the multinational newspaper group Hollinger Inc. which revealed significant and deep-rooted problems in its corporate governance. All these occurrences highlighted that that something was thoroughly wrong in the area of corporate governance all over the world.

Corporate governance was a central issue in all developing economies even before the recent spate of corporate scandals. The corporate world needs effective corporate governance systems to promote the development of strong financial systems that can drive economic growth globally. Let us now look at the issue in detail.

5.8.1 Introduction

The corporate world has always been faced with ethical dilemmas and accusations pertaining to lack of transparency and fairness in dealings. While the charge has turned out to be wrong in some cases, the collapse of giants such as Enron, Arthur Anderson, WorldCom, and Tyco proves all is not well in the corporate world. Stakeholders have often been let down by unethical acts of people at the helm of affairs in companies.

In the light of such stunning failures and collapses, business leaders, law makers, regulatory bodies, researchers, and academicians and other stakeholders have been debating the need for a framework that could curb the unethical and illegal tendencies in the corporate world. While the aforesaid names focus attention on US companies, the fact is that such problems are a global phenomenon, and are more widespread then is being visualized and understood. Tackle the problem effectively, economies around the globe have started working towards evolving for ethical and transparent functioning of entities. Various initiatives, in the form of enactments such as the Sarbanes–Oxley Act and the Birla Committee Report on Corporate Governance, have been put in place to deal with the menace globally. The term coined for these initiatives aimed at regulating corporate entities came to be popularly known as *corporate governance*.

5.8.2 Concept of Corporate Governance

Corporate governance is about the whole set of legal, cultural, and institutional arrangements that determine what public corporations can do, who controls them, how that control is exercised, and how the risks and returns from the activities they undertake are allocated (Blair 1995).

One needs to appreciate that corporate governance is vital to the integrity and efficiency of financial markets and thus to the economic growth of the country. It signifies a well-defined, well-structured, and well-communicated system to manage, direct, and control the conduct of business of a company, thus meeting the expectations of the stakeholders.

Corporate governance works on the basis on the following accepted principles:

- Honesty, trust, and integrity
- Openness
- Performance orientation
- Responsibility and accountability
- Mutual respect
- Commitment to the organization

The aforesaid principles aim at addressing the following issues:

- Systems relating to internal controls
- Procedure to be followed while appointing internal auditors
- Independence of the company's external auditors and the quality of their audits
- Management of risk associated with the business
- Financial statements to be prepared by the entity
- Procedure for reviewing the compensation of the chief executive officer (CEO) and other senior executives
- Resources to be made available to directors for carrying out their duties effectively
- The manner and procedure for nominating individuals for positions on the board
- Dividend policy to be adopted by the company

5.8.3 Clause 49 of Listing Agreement

Clause 49 of the Listing Agreement deals with corporate governance to be followed by a listed entity. With the objective of promoting ethical practices and transparency, the Government of India appointed the Kumar Mangalam Birla Committee to study various issues pertaining to absence of transparency. The committee submitted its report in the year 2000–01. Based on its recommendations, the concept of corporate governance was evolved.

Two years after the recommendations were in place, SEBI appointed a committee under the chairmanship of Narayana Murthy to evaluate the adequacy of the existing practices and to further improve the existing practices. The Murthy Committee submitted the draft recommendations on corporate governance norms. After deliberations, SEBI accepted the recommendations in August 2003 and asked stock exchanges to revise Clause 49 of the Listing Agreement based on Murthy Committee recommendations. However, the industry was not happy with the recommendations of the Murthy Committee, and SEBI instructed the committee to meet again to consider the objections.

The committee revised the earlier recommendations and the revised Clause 49 was adopted. The companies were instructed to adhere to these norms by the end of financial year 2004–05. The revised recommendations resulted in major changes in the following areas:

- Independence of directors
- Whistleblower policy
- Performance evaluation of non-executive directors
- Mandatory training of non-executive directors

Let us briefly analyse some proposed changes.

Independence of Directors

The basic requirement that a person needs to fulfil to qualify as an independent director is that the director can receive remuneration, but should not have any other financial interest or relationship with the company, its promoters, its management or its subsidiaries. Any financial interest is believed to have to potential to impact the independence of judgment of the director.

The revised Clause 49 states that the person identified for the post of independent director should fulfil the following conditions:

- The aforesaid relationship is extended to the management, holding company, and associates in addition to the existing list.
- The person should not be related to any of the promoters or persons occupying management positions at the board level or at one level below the board.
- The person should not have been an executive of the company in the preceding three financial years.
- The person should not be a partner or an executive, or should not have been a partner or an executive during the preceding three years, in the following:
  - The statutory audit firm or the internal audit firm associated with the company.
  - The legal and consulting firms that have a material association with the company.
- The person should not be a material supplier, service provider, customer, a lessor, or lessee of the company.
- The person should not be a substantial shareholder of the company owning two percent or more of the block of voting shares.

A listed company is required to obtain a declaration annually from all independent directors confirming compliance with all six conditions of independence.

Non-executive Directors' Compensation and Disclosures

The revised clause states that prior approval of shareholders is required for payment of fees/compensation to non-executive directors. In case the company decides to give stock options, the limit for the maximum number of stock options that can be granted in any financial year and in aggregate should be disclosed.

Other Provisions Relating to Board of Directors

As per the revised clause, the gap between two board meetings has been reduced to three months from four months. In addition, a code of conduct for board members and senior management shall be laid down by the board and needs to be uploaded on the website of the company. Finally, the board members and senior management should affirm compliance with the code on an annual basis and the annual report shall contain a declaration to this effect signed by the CEO.

Audit Committee

The norms with regards to the audit committee state the following:

- Two-thirds of the members of the audit committee shall be independent directors.
- All members of the audit committee shall be financially literate, with financial and accounting knowledge.
- The minimum numbers of audit committee meetings in a year have been increased to four from three.

The role of the audit committee now also includes the following matters:

- Matters required to be included in the directors' responsibility statement
- Reviewing the functioning of whistle blower mechanism, if in existence
- Reviewing the performance of statutory and internal auditors

Review of the following by the audit committee is mandatory:

- Management discussion and analysis of the financial condition and results of operation
- Statement of significant related party transactions
- Management letters/letters of internal control weaknesses issued by the statutory auditors
- Internal audit reports relating to internal control weaknesses
- Reviewing the appointment, removal, and terms of remuneration of the chief internal auditor.

The audit committee's authority to review the company's financial and risk management policies stands withdrawn and assigned to the board.

Subsidiary Companies

These are new requirements pertaining to subsidiary companies:

- At least one independent director on the board of the holding company shall be a director on the board of a material non-listed Indian subsidiary company—an entity whose turnover or net worth exceeds 20% of the consolidated turnover or net worth respectively of the listed company and its subsidiaries.
- The audit committee of the holding company shall review the financial statements, and in particular the investments made by the unlisted subsidiary company.

- The minutes of the board meetings of the unlisted subsidiary company shall be placed at the board meeting of the holding company.
- The management needs to periodically bring to the attention of the holding company a statement of all significant transactions and arrangements entered into by the unlisted subsidiary company—transaction or arrangement that exceed 10% of the total revenues/expenses/assets/liabilities of the subsidiary.

Disclosures

The disclosure requirements were also revised as follows:

- Statements on transactions with related parties need to be placed before the audit committee periodically.
- Details of material individual transactions with related parties, which are not in the normal course of business, shall be placed before the audit committee.
- Details of material individual transactions with related parties or others, which are not on arm's length basis should be placed before the audit committee together with the management's justification for the same. However, while stating these revisions, the word 'material' has not been defined.
- In case any accounting treatment is different from that prescribed in accounting standard, the same should be stated in the financial statements together with management's explanation.
- The company needs to lay down procedures to inform board members about the risk assessment and minimization procedures. The board needs to review their relevance at regular intervals.
- The audit committee should be informed about the use of funds raised through public/rights/preferential issues on a quarterly basis. In case the funds have been used for purposes other than those stated in offer document/prospectus, the same needs to be placed before the audit committee on an annual basis. Such statements should be certified by the statutory auditors.

CEO/CFO Certification

This requirement is based on the Sarbanes–Oxley Act of USA, which had also been recommended by the Naresh Chandra Committee set up in 2002–03.

The Clause requires the CEO and the chief financial officer (CFO) to certify to the board the annual financial statements in the prescribed format. It is expected that this certification will provide comfort to the non-executive directors and act as the basis for the board to make a directors' responsibility statement. However, the same is not to be included in the annual report of listed companies.

Compliance Report

The format of quarterly report to be submitted to the stock exchanges has been revised as per the revised requirements of Clause 49. This report can be signed by the CEO or the compliance officer. Again, the annual corporate governance report should disclose adoption or non-adoption of non-mandatory requirements.

Non-mandatory Requirements

The revised conditions include five new items under non-mandatory requirements with the existing item on postal ballot has been deleted:

- The independent directors may not have in the aggregate a tenure exceeding a period of nine years on the board of the company.
- Companies shall move towards a regime of unqualified audit reports.
- Board members need to be trained in the business model of the company as well as risk profile of the business parameters of the company and responsibilities of directors and how best to discharge it.
- The performance non-executive directors shall be evaluated by a peer group comprising the entire board.
- Companies need to set up a whistleblower policy.

There is no doubt that the revised corporate governance norms are stringent and in line with the desired regulations, but the same need to be followed in spirit and should not become another set of regulations on paper.

5.9 PROVISIONS OF INCOME TAX ACT, 1961

The Income Tax Act, 1961 is the statute on income tax in India. It provides for levy, administration, collection, and recovery of income tax. This Act is the most complex statute in India and has been often criticized on various grounds. The criticism, notwithstanding the law, has occupied a very important place in the economic structure of India. The government proposes to replace the law with a new statute called the 'Direct Taxes Code'. Let us examine the topic in detail.

5.9.1 Introduction

Certain transactions pertaining to mergers are covered under The Income Tax Act, 1961. The provisions relate to tax concessions to the Indian companies that merge/demerge. These deals, of course, need to satisfy the conditions pertaining to Section 2(19AA) and Section 2(1B) of the Indian Income Tax Act as per the applicable situation.

5.9.2 Merger as Defined under Income Tax Act, 1961

Mergers can be defined to mean unification of two players into a single entity. Under Section 2(1B) of the Income Tax Act, 1961, amalgamation is defined as mixing up or uniting together. It is a process where one company unites with another company and ensures that the following conditions are met:

- All properties are transferred to the amalgamated company.
- All liabilities are transferred to the amalgamated company.
- Shareholders holding at least three-fourths in the value of shares of the amalgamating company become shareholders of the amalgamated company.

When one looks at mergers in India, companies whose shares are transferred under the deal are entitled to exemptions from capital gains tax under the Indian Income Tax Act. The companies can either be of Indian origin or foreign origin. However, a different set of rules is applicable for foreign company mergers, a merger where an Indian company owns the new company formed out of the merger of two foreign companies. In case of foreign company mergers, the share allotted to the merged foreign company in place of shares surrendered by the amalgamating foreign company are termed as a transfer and hence taxable under the Indian tax laws (www.articlebase.com).

Section 5(1) of the Indian Income Tax Act states that global income accruing to an Indian company would also be included under the head *scope of income* for the Indian company.

5.9.3 Important Tax Provisions for Mergers and Acquisitions

The Income Tax Act, 1961 includes the following provisions pertaining to M&As:

Amortization of Expenditure in Case of Amalgamation or Demerger

Section 35DD provides that any expenditure incurred for the purpose of amalgamation or demerger, deduction of an amount equal to one-fifth of such expenditure is allowed for each of the five previous years beginning with the year in which the amalgamation or demerger takes place.

Capital Gains

Section 45 of the Income Tax Act, 1961 deals with the procedure for determination of the amount chargeable under capital gains tax. Capital gains tax is levied as and when transfer of a capital asset results in profit termed herein as capital gain. The term transfer is defined in the Income Tax Act in an inclusive manner. Under the Income Tax Act, 'transfer' does not include any transfer in a scheme of amalgamation of a capital asset by the amalgamating company to the amalgamated company, if the latter is an Indian company.

From assessment year 1993–94, any transfer of shares of an Indian company held by a foreign company to another foreign company in a scheme of amalgamation between the two foreign companies will not be regarded as 'transfer' for the purpose of levying capital gains tax.

Further, the term 'transfer' also does not include any transfer by a shareholder in a scheme of amalgamation of a capital asset being a share or the shares held by him in the amalgamating company if the transfer is made in consideration of the allotment to him of any share or shares in the amalgamated company, and the amalgamated company is an Indian company.

Special Provision for Computing Cost of Acquisition of Certain Assets

Section 43C states that when an asset which becomes the property of an amalgamated company is sold by the amalgamated company as stock-in-trade, the cost of the said asset for the purpose of computing the profits or loss on sale of asset shall be computed as:

Cost of acquisition of the asset plus cost incurred on among improvements to the said asset minus cost incurred in connection with facilitating the transfer of the asset by the amalgamating company.

Transfer under Section 47

This section states that any transfer of a capital asset, being a share or shares held in an Indian company, by the amalgamating foreign company to the amalgamated foreign company shall not be treated as capital gains if:

- At least 25% shareholders of the amalgamating foreign company continue to remain shareholders of the amalgamated foreign company
- The transfer does not attract tax on capital gains in the country in which the amalgamating company is incorporated.

Carry forward and Set-off of Accumulated Loss and Unabsorbed Depreciation

Section 72A of the Income Tax Act, 1961 contains a set of special provisions that deal with carry forward and set off of accumulated business loss and unabsorbed depreciation allowance in certain cases of amalgamation.

Unabsorbed losses of the amalgamating company are deemed to be the losses for the previous year in which the amalgamation was effected. The amalgamated company, subject to fulfilment of certain conditions, has the right to carry forward the loss for a period of eight assessment years immediately succeeding the assessment year relevant to the previous year in which the amalgamation was effected. There is no time limit specified for carry forward of unabsorbed depreciation.

These conditions include the following:

Amalgamating company

- The company should be engaged in the business in which the accumulated loss occurred or depreciation allowance remains unabsorbed for three or more years.
- The company has held three-fourths of the book value of the fixed assets on the date of amalgamation and the same have been held by it two years prior to the date of amalgamation.

Amalgamated company

- The company holds three-fourths of the book value of the fixed assets of the amalgamating company for a period of five years from the date of amalgamation.
- The company continues the business of the amalgamating company for a minimum period of five years from the date of amalgamation.
- The company fulfils any condition prescribed under Rule 9C to ensure revival of the business of the amalgamating company or to ensure that the amalgamation is for a genuine business purpose.

If the company fails to fulfil the conditions stated, the set off of loss or allowance of depreciation made in any previous year shall be treated as income of the amalgamated company and becomes chargeable to tax for the year in which the conditions are violated.

In the case of a demerger, the following conditions shall apply:

- The loss or unabsorbed depreciation is allowed to be carried forward and set off in the hands of the resulting company provided the same is directly related to the entity transferred.
- In case the assets are not directly related to the undertaking transferred, the loss or unabsorbed depreciation gets apportioned between the demerged entity and the resulting company in the same proportion in which the assets of the company have been retained.

Cost with Reference to Certain Modes of Acquisition

Section 49(2) of the Income Tax Act, 1961 deals with the cost of acquisition of shares in an amalgamated company. The cost of acquisition shall be the value at which the shares have been acquired.

In case of demerger, the cost of acquisition shall be the proportion as the net book value of the assets transferred in a demerger bears to the net worth of the demerged company immediately before the demerger.

Deduction of Certain Expenditure Incurred

Section 35 provides for continuance of deduction of certain expenditure incurred by the amalgamating company or demerged company as the case may be in the hands of the amalgamated company or resulting company, post amalgamation or demerger such as capital expenditure on scientific research, expenditure on acquisition of patents or copyrights, expenditure on know-how, and expenditure for obtaining license to operate telecommunication services.

Tax of Sale of Business/Slump Sale

Section 50 of the Income Tax Act, 1961 states that sale of business will be considered a 'slump sale', under the following conditions:

- There is a sale of an undertaking.
- The sale is for a lump sum consideration.
- No separate values being assigned to individual assets and liabilities.

If separate values are assigned to assets, the sale will be regarded as an *itemized sale*.

Indian tax laws have specifically clarified that the determination of the value of an asset or liability for the sole purpose of payment of stamp duty, registration fees, or other similar taxes or fees shall not be regarded as assignment of values to individual assets or liabilities.

In a slump sale, the profits arising from a sale of an undertaking would be treated as a capital gain arising from a single transaction. Where the undertaking being transferred was held for at least 36 months prior to the date of the slump sale, the income from such a sale would qualify as long-term capital gains. If the undertaking has been held for less than 36 months prior to the date of slump sale, then the income would be taxable as short-term capital gains.

Where an itemized sale of individual assets takes place, profit arising from the sale of each asset is taxed separately. Demerger is a special category of slump sale.

Stamp Duty Aspects of M&A

Stamp duty is payable on the value of immovable property transferred by the demerged/amalgamating/transferor company or value of shares issued/consideration paid by the resulting/amalgamated/transferee company. In certain states such as Maharashtra, Gujarat, and Rajasthan, there are specific provisions for levy of stamp duty on amalgamation/demerger order.

In addition to the stamp duty on transfer of business, additional stamp duty on issue of shares is also payable at the rates prevailing in the state where shares are issued.

5.10 FOREIGN EXCHANGE MANAGEMENT ACT, 1999

The provisions of Foreign Exchange Management Act (FEMA), 1999 are applicable to cross-border M&As. It aims at regulating cross-border M&As as the deal may involve use of foreign exchange for settling of the transaction.

The law contains provisions relating to issuance and allotment of shares to foreign entities. The Foreign Exchange Management (transfer or issue of security by a person residing outside India) Regulation, 2000 issued by the Reserve Bank of India (RBI) vide notification no. FEMA 20/2000-RB dated 3 May 2000 contains general provisions for inbound and outbound cross-border M&As in India.

The provisions state that once the scheme of merger or amalgamation of two or more Indian companies has been approved by a court in India, the transferee company or new company can issue shares to the shareholders of the transferor company resident outside India subject to the following conditions (www.lexvidhi.com):

- The percentage of shareholding of persons resident outside India in the transferee or new company does not exceed the prescribed sectoral cap.
- The transferor company or the transferee/new company is not engaged in activities that are prohibited under the FDI policy.

5.11 COMPETITION ACT, 2002

India has for a very long period adopted policies of 'control'. In the earlier days, the competition law of India was the Monopolies and Restrictive Trade Practices Act, 1969 (MRTP Act). The need for amending the Act was felt in 1991 when economic reforms were undertaken. The need for an effective competition regime has also been recognized since then.

Keeping in tune with the new economic policy, India enacted a new competition law called the Competition Act, 2002. In fact, the MRTP Act has metamorphosed into the new Competition Act, 2002 and the new law was designed to repeal the extant MRTP Act. The new law initiated the process of constituting the regulatory authority, namely, the Competition Commission of India. The provisions of the new law were brought into force in a phased manner.

The Competition Act, 2002 is essentially divided into four compartments:

- Anti-competition agreements
- Abuse of dominance
- Combinations regulation
- Competition advocacy

Let us examine the Act in detail now.

5.11.1 Introduction

Competition Act, 2002 replaced the MRTP Act, 1969. The Competition Act has been enacted with the following objectives:

- Preventing practices that have an adverse effect on competition
- Promoting and sustaining competition in markets
- Protecting the interests of consumers
- Ensuring freedom of trade carried on by other markets participants in India

The Act states that no person or enterprise shall enter into a combination, in the form of an acquisition, merger, or amalgamation that causes or is likely to adversely impact competition in the market. In case it is ascertained that the arrangement has an adverse effect, then the combination is treated as void under the Act.

The enterprises desiring to enter into a combination are required to give a notice to the Commission to that effect, although it is voluntary.

All combinations are not subject to scrutiny unless they exceed the threshold limits in terms of assets or turnover specified by the Competition Commission of India.

5.11.2 Combinations under Competition Act, 2002

Combination includes acquisition of control, shares, voting rights, or assets, or acquisition of control by a person over an enterprise. The person concerned controls another enterprise engaged in competing businesses, and mergers and amalgamations between the entities is made difficult by the thresholds specified in the Act in terms of assets or turnover. The provisions of the Competition Act state that if a combination causes or is likely to cause an appreciable adverse effect on competition within the relevant market in India, it is prohibited and can be scrutinized by the Commission. The following sections discuss these provisions.

Section 3

The section governs anti-competitive agreements and prohibits agreements that are capable of generating an adverse effect on competition such as the following:

- Production
- Supply
- Distribution
- Storage
- Acquisition or control of goods
- Provision of services

Section 4

This section prohibits the abuse of a dominant position enjoyed by an enterprise in the market. Under the Monopolies Act, a threshold of 25% constitutes a position of strength and represents a dominant position.

Section 6

A combination is a merger of two enterprises or acquisition of control, shares, voting rights, or assets of an enterprise. The section states that an enterprise that enters into combination that is likely to cause adverse effect on competition is void.

The Commission, while regulating a combination, considers the following factors existing in the market (www.lexvidhi.com):

- Actual and potential competition on account of imports
- Extent of entry barriers
- Level of combination
- Degree of countervailing power
- Possibility of a combination with the objective of significantly and substantially increasing prices or profits
- Extent of effective competition likely
- Availability of substitutes before and after the combination
- Market share of the entities to the combination, individually and as a combination
- Possibility of the combination removing the vigorous and effective competitor or competition
- Nature and extent of vertical integration
- Nature and extent of innovation
- Possibility of the benefits of the combination outweighing the adverse impact of the combination

5.11.3 Mergers and Effects

A merger represents a transaction that aims at bringing about change in the control of different business entities, enabling one business entity to control a significant part of the assets or decision-making process of another. While a merger may be perceived as a normal activity within the economy and an effective tool to expand business by the companies, it possesses elements that adversely affect competition. Companies enter into merger for they think it is a tool of achieving market power, which in affects competition negatively. Hence, mergers are covered under the Competition Act due to their anti-competitive fervour. The aspects of mergers covered under the Act include the following:

- Acquisition of shares
- Voting rights
- Assets or acquisition of control over an enterprise

Mergers are anti-competitive because of the following factors:

- Reduce the number of entities in the market
- Increase the market share of the merged entity
- Enable the merged entity to exercise market power and impact prices, restrict output, increase cost of rivals, increase entry barrier, etc.

5.11.4 Threshold Limits under Competition Act, 2002

The entities merging together are required to give notices to the Competition Commission of India (CCI) subject to the following conditions:

- Within 30 days of the approval of the proposal relating to the merger by the board of directors of the companies, or
- Execution of any agreement/document for acquisition—no combination can come into effect unless 210 days have passed from serving such notice to the CCI or grant of approval by CCI, whichever is earlier.

The threshold limit for entities merging in terms of assets or turnover under the Competition Act, 2002 is as follows:

In India The acquiring and the acquired entities jointly have

- assets of more than ₹10 billion, or
- turnover of more than ₹30 billion, or the group has
- assets of more than ₹40 billion, or
- turnover of more than ₹120 billion.

In India or outside India The acquiring and the acquired entities jointly have

- assets of more than $500 million (including > ₹5 billion in India), or
- turnover of more than $1500 million (including > ₹15 billion in India), or the group has
- assets of more than $2000 million (including > ₹5 billion in India), or
- turnover of more than $6000 million (including > ₹15 billion in India).

In short, one needs to remember that the Competition Act does not seek to eliminate combinations, and but only aims to eliminate their harmful effects.

This discussion clearly indicates that companies trying to merge have to adhere to a number of legal provisions if they decide to go ahead with their decision on merger. Failure to adhere to these norms can lead many complications and legal restrictions. While many people might argue that the legal provisions make things complicated and cause unprecedented delays, the objective behind the legal provisions is to protect the interest of the stakeholders and help the economy grow without any hiccups.

SUMMARY

The process of mergers and acquisitions involves a series of regulatory measures. There are plenty of laws that attempt to address every aspect of mergers and acquisitions. The legal provisions have been introduced with the objective of regulating the entire process and not for preventing or discouraging mergers. While the Indian economy is on a roll, one cannot be too lenient on the legal front as any laxity can have disastrous consequences for our growing economy.

KEY DEFINITIONS

Amalgamation Amalgamation means to combine or unite to form a single organization or structure.

Arrangement Arrangement is a process that includes reorganization of the share capital of the company and is done either by consolidation of shares of different classes or by the division of shares into shares of different classes or both.

Buyback of shares Buyback is a mechanism of financial restructuring through which a company purchases its own shares or other specified securities.

Compromise Compromise is an arrangement that is carried out at the behest of the court on an application made by the company or any creditor or member or the liquidator when a company is being wound-up.

Delisting of shares/reverse book building This is a mechanism whereby the promoter or acquirer offers to buy back shares from the shareholders through respective book running lead managers (BRLMs). The shares so acquired through buyback process are used by companies for delisting their shares from stock exchange(s).

Free reserves This is an amount created out of the profits of the company and not earmarked for any specific purpose.

Independent directors An independent director is a director who can receive remuneration but should not have any other financial interest or relationship with the company, its promoters, its management or its subsidiaries that can impact the independence of judgment of the director.

Letter of offer A letter of offer is a document addressed to the shareholders of the target company containing information on the company and justifying its intention to acquire the shares.

Listing of shares Listing means admission of securities to the trading privileges/dealings on recognized stock exchanges through a formal agreement.

Persons acting in concert Persons acting in concert implies working in cooperation/coordination to acquire voting rights or control of the target company, either directly or indirectly.

Public announcement This is an announcement made by the acquirer in the newspapers disclosing its intention to acquire shares of the target company from existing shareholders through an open offer.

Share premium account Share premium is an amount generated by the company when it sells its share above face value. The amount can be used by the company in any manner it deems fit.

Substantial acquisition of shares   It is a process whereby an acquirer takes control of the target company by acquiring a substantial quantity of shares or voting rights of the target company.

Voluntary delisting   Voluntary delisting means removing the securities of a company from the trading privileges of a stock exchange. The application to delist a company is made by the promoter or an acquirer or any other person other than the stock exchange.

CONCEPT REVIEW QUESTIONS

5.1 Enumerate the powers of the court with reference to sanctioning the scheme of amalgamation.

5.2 Define the concept of buyback of shares. Highlight the provisions of Section 77.

5.3 Why do companies go for a buyback? State the prerequisites of a valid buyback.

5.4 Explain the advantages and weaknesses of buyback of shares.

5.5 Explain the procedure for substantial acquisition of shares

5.6 Explain the concept of listing of shares. What are its objectives?

5.7 Explain in detail the guidelines for listing of shares in India on the BSE and NSE, respectively.

5.8 State and explain the important tax provisions relating to mergers and acquisitions.

5.9 Write notes on the following:
   (a) Provisions of Sections 391 to 396A of the Companies Act
   (b) Sources for buyback
   (c) Modes of buyback
   (d) Prohibited modes of buyback
   (e) Substantial acquisition of shares
   (f) Substantial quantity of shares or voting rights
   (g) Guidelines for listing of shares in India in BSE
   (h) Guidelines for listing of shares in India by NSE
   (i) Benefits of listing
   (j) Applicability of voluntary delisting
   (k) Voluntary delisting of securities of a listed company
   (l) Procedure for voluntary delisting
   (m) Right of the promoters for delisting of shares
   (n) Clause 49 of the Listing Agreement
   (o) Foreign Exchange Management Act, 1999 and mergers
   (p) Competition Act, 2002 and mergers

PROJECT ASSIGNMENT

Analyse the taxation issue involved in the Hutch–Vodafone merger. Why did the merger fail?

REFERENCES

Blair, M.M., *Ownership and Control: Rethinking Corporate Governance for the Twenty-First Century*, Brookings Institution Press, Washington, 1995, pp. 12

http://www.primeacademy.com/smartmails/sat_31_1_09.htm, last accessed on 23 May 2010

http://jurisonline.in/2008/09/buy-back-of-securities-a-critical-approach/, last accessed on 2 August 2010

http://www.bscindia.com/about/abintrobse/listsec.asp, last accessed on 12 August 2010

http://www.nseindia.com/content/debt/debt_listprocedure.htm, last accessed on 12 August 2010

http://www.articlesbase.com/regulatory-compliance-articles/merger-of-a-company-an-introduction-536801.html, last accessed on 23 August 2010

http://www.lexvidhi.com/article-details/mergers-and-acquisitions-a-basic-understanding-and-governing-laws-16.html, last accessed on 27 August 2010

Income Tax Act as Amended by Finance (No. 2) Act 2009, Government of India, www.simpletaxindia.org, last accessed on 9 April 2010

Para 3.9, Report of the Working Group on the Companies Act, 1956, www.jurisonline.in, last accessed on 9 April 2010

Sen, D.K., 'Clause 49 of Listing Agreement on Corporate Governance', *The Chartered Accountant*, December 2004, pp. 807–809

Annexure   Indian companies that have opted for buyback of shares through open market purchase

Name of the company	Maximum buyback price (₹)	Total aggregate amount (₹)	Start date +	End date ++	Closure date
Ace Software	10.00	250 million	13 October 2003	24 August 2004	–
Ace Software	20.00	10 million	14 May 2007	28 September 2007	28 September 2007
Aegis Logistics	143.00	170 million	14 August 2009	8 July 2010	6 February 2010
AKZOINDIA	350.00	1.31 billion	29 September 2006	13 September 2007	26 July 2007
AKZOINDIA	575.00	20 million	10 August 2007	11 July 2008	11 July 2008
AKZOINDIA	575.00	1.84 billion	17 February 2009	18 December 2009	18 December 2009
AKZOINDIA	575.00	1.84 billion	17 February 2009	18 December 2009	8 November 2009
Alembic	55.00	330 million	8 December 2008	13 November 2009	13 November 2009
Amrutanjan Health	450.00	60 million	24 December 2008	18 November 2009	13 April 2009
ANGIND	215.00	1.61 billion	28 July 2008	2 January 2009	2 January 2006
Apcotex Inds	90.00	40 million	21 December 2009	15 October 2010	7 May 2010
Apollo Tyres	25.00	1.22 billion	23 April 2009	18 March 2010	19 March 2010
ARO Granite	55.00	60 million	29 June 2009	7 June 2010	8 June 2010
Austin Engr	65.00	30 million	27 January 2009	7 January 2010	8 January 2010
Avantel	50.00	30 million	27 May 2009	25 April 2010	4 August 2009

(Continued)

Annexure   (*Continued*)

Name of the company	Maximum buyback price (₹)	Total aggregate amount (₹)	Start date +	End date ++	Closure date
Balrampur Chini	100.00	180.97 million	8 February 2002	20 January 2003	22 January 2003
Bhagyanagar India.	65.00	90.6 million	1 October 2001	1 July 2002	2 July 2002
Bhagyanagar India	40.00	200 million	4 November 2009	18 May 2010	20 May 2010
BHEL August 2002 Future	10.00	65 million	20 August 2001	28 September 2001	1 October 2001
Blue Star	75.00	260.04 million	15 February 2002	3 February 2003	5 February 2003
Bombay Dyeing	60.00	1.43 billion	7 September 2001	22 July 2002	23 July 2002
Bombay Dyeing	65.00	310.98 million	7 November 2002	27 August 2003	29 August 2003
Bosch	4,500.00	6.39 billion	15 December 2008	23 October 2009	28 October 2009
Bright Bros	50.00	50 million	29 December 2009	25 June 2010	25 June 2010
Britannia Inds	750.00	550 million	10 September 2001	27 July 2002	28 November 2001
Britannia Inds	650.00	920 million	5 September 2002	5 August 2003	3 June 2003
Daiichi Kark	36.00	210 million	25 May 2009	27 April 2010	27 April 2010
Deccan Chron	100.00	1.8 billion	12 August 2009	25 January 2010	21 October 2010
Deepak Fert	22.00	374.1million	6 May 2002	20 January 2003	24 January 2003
DIL	250.00	60 million	13 April 2005	16 March 2006	18 August 2005
DLF	600.00	11 billion	17 October 2008	9 July 2009	5 May 2009
ECE Inds	30.00	430 million	24 February 2003	19 November 2003	21 November 2003
EID Parry	160.00	470 million	15 December 2008	28 October 2009	2 March 2009

(*Continued*)

Annexure   (*Continued*)

Name of the company	Maximum buyback price (₹)	Total aggregate amount (₹)	Start date [+]	End date [++]	Closure date
ETC Networks	50.00	616.3 billion	18 May 2005	20 April 2006	21 April 2006
ETC Networks	62.00	70 million	4 September 2006	23 April 2007	23 April 2007
Exide Inds	70.00	250 million	10 January 2002	23 December 2002	26 December 2002
FDC	40.00	360 million	24 November 2008	11 August 2009	5 August 2009
Fineline Circ	10.00	1 million	11 October 2004	22 August 2005	23 August 2005
FINOLEX IND.	40.00	600 million	26 April 2001	2 April 2002	26 March 2002
Finolex Inds	40.00	350 million	19 August 2002	26 July 2003	20 August 2003
Gateway Distr	110.00	640 million	11 August 2008	24 January 2009	27 January 2009
GE Shipping	42.00	1.5 billion	26 December 2000	30 November 2001	19 April 2001
GG Dandekar	250.00	11.3 million	30 January 2002	30 June 2002	2 July 2002
Gitanjali Gems	120.00	1.44 billion	19 August 2009	18 December 2009	18 December 2009
Glaxosmithkl Phar	800.00	230.65 billion	9 May 2005	28 April 2006	22 December 2005
Godrej Cons	100.00	93 million	21 January 2002	8 January 2003	4 June 2002
Godrej Cons	175.00	46 million	12 August 2002	21 July 2003	3 October 2002
Godrej Cons	175.00	100 million	24 January 2003	7 January 2004	17 September 2003
Godrej Cons	400.00	50 million	23 May 2005	9 May 2006	4 July 2005
Godrej Cons	150.00	150 million	4 December 2008	24 September 2009	4 March 2009
Godrej Inds	275.00	990 million	25 May 2009	28 July 2009	24 July 2009
Goldiam Intl	85.00	90 million	7 May 2008	31 December 2008	23 October 2008

(*Continued*)

Annexure   (*Continued*)

Name of the company	Maximum buyback price (₹)	Total aggregate amount (₹)	Start date [+]	End date [++]	Closure date
Goldiam Intl	50.00	50 million	16 November 2009	29 October 2010	12 January 2010
Great Eastern Shipping	42.00	1 billion	23 August 2001	25 July 2002	26 July 2002
Great Offshore	750.00	550 million	7 May 2008	30 March 2009	18 September 2008
GSS America	250.00	200 million	25 February 2009	28 January 2010	5 August 2009
Gujarat Ambuja Exports	38.00	260 million	16 April 2007	15 January 2008	15 January 2008
Gujarat Fluo	300.00	610 million	21 August 2008	20 March 2009	24 March 2009
HEG	350.00	490 million	13 October 2008	18 August 2009	21 August 2009
Heritage Foods	30.00	30 million	24 January 2002	3 January 2003	29 March 2002
Hindalco Industries	825.00	4.28 billion	8 February 2002	29 January 2003	2 August 2002
Hindustan Unilever	230.00	6.30 billion	3 October 2007	13 September 2008	1 February 2008
HOV Serv	50.00	50 million	2 February 2009	12 January 2010	18 January 2010
Hydro S&S Inds	60.00	260 million	26 February 2009	15 September 2009	22 September 2009
India Infoline	43.00	990 million	18 December 2008	28 November 2009	1 December 2009
Indiabulls Fin	210.00	38 billion	9 December 2005	17 November 2006	17 February 2006
Indiabulls Sec	33.00	830 million	14 May 2009	5 March 2010	8 March 2010
IPCA Lab	600.00	600 million	3 December 2008	10 November 2009	11 November 2009
IVP	22.00	22.7 million	2 April 2002	20 September 2002	21 September 2002
Jayshree Tea	75.00	83 million	4 June 2001	31 March 2002	–

(*Continued*)

Annexure (*Continued*)

Name of the company	Maximum buyback price (₹)	Total aggregate amount (₹)	Start date +	End date ++	Closure date
Jindal Poly	350.00	1.5 billion	22 December 2008	28 August 2009	5 May 2009
Jindal Poly	400.00	730 million	12 October 2009	30 July 2010	21 December 2009
John Flower	62.50	29.5 million	5 November 2001	24 July 2002	25 July 2002
Kama Holdings	21.00	33.9 million	30 August 2002	29 October 2002	8 November 2002
Kama Holdings	275.00	6.61 billion	19 December 2005	7 December 2006	7 December 2006
Kesoram Inds	40.00	313.7 million	9 October 2001	21 June 2002	26 June 2002
Kesoram Inds	40.00	185 million	27 January 2003	8 December 2003	3 September 2003
Kilburn Engr	40.00	30 million	24 February 2009	28 January 2010	28 January 2010
LKP FIN	90.00	90 million	24 February 2009	21 January 2010	16 July 2009
Madras Cements	4,200.00	640 million	29 February 2008	30 January 2009	7 April 2008
Maestros Med	75.00	30 million	18 November 2008	26 October 2009	26 October 2009
Mangalam Cem	75.00	220 million	5 February 2009	16 January 2010	4 August 2009
Mastek	750.00	650 million	20 May 2008	26 November 2008	24 July 2008
Mazda	10.00	4.2 million	22 July 2003	28 August 2003	11 August 2003
Merck	435.00	450 million	10 June 2009	19 May 2010	21 May 2010
Monnet Ispat	300.00	750 million.	8 December 2008	22 October 2009	22 May 2009
MRO Tek	55.00	80 million	21 May 2007	29 March 2008	25 May 2007
MRO Tek	55.00	80 million	4 June 2007	29 March 2008	19 October 2007

(*Continued*)

Annexure (*Continued*)

Name of the company	Maximum buyback price (₹)	Total aggregate amount (₹)	Start date +	End date ++	Closure date
MRO Tek	25.00	50 million	19 March 2009	24 February 2010	25 February 2010
Natco Pharma	150.00	70 million	12 February 2007	30 July 2007	30 July 2007
Nava Bharat Vent	170.00	500 million	6 January 2009	11 December 2009	12 August 2009
OCL INDIA	80.00	100 million	8 October 2001	18 July 2002	15 January 2002
Patni Computer	325.00	2.37 billion	10 July 2008	6 February 2009	28 October 2008
Pennar Inds	40.00	130 million	15 September 2009	26 April 2010	29 March 2010
Poddar Pigm	42.00	100 million	10 November 2009	23 August 2010	9 February 2010
Polaris Soft	115.00	490.million	1 June 2005	26 April 2006	10 November 2005
Prime Sec	50.00	500 million	12 December 2005	27 September 2006	19 January 2006
Prime Sec	101.00	20 million	27 January 2006	5 January 2007	2 March 2006
Provogue India	100.00	500 million	2 September 2009	12 February 2010	15 February 2010
R Systems	150.00	80 million	29 October 2008	6 September 2009	1 September 2009
Rain Commodities	307.00	260 million	25 September 2008	30 April 2009	3 December 2008
Raymond Limited	160.00	1.87 billion	7 March 2001	14 February 2002	30 April 2001
Reliance Infra	525.00	3.5 billion	21 June 2004	8 June 2005	9 June 2005
Reliance Infra	1,600.00	8 billion	17 March 2008	4 March 2009	4 February 2009
Reliance Infra	700.00	7 billion	25 February 2009	16 April 2009	9 April 2009
Revathi Equip	700.00	10 billion	22 January 2007	28 June 2007	28 June 2007
RIL	303.00	11 billion	31 July 2001	4 June 2002	–

(*Continued*)

Annexure   *(Continued)*

Name of the company	Maximum buyback price (₹)	Total aggregate amount (₹)	Start date +	End date ++	Closure date
RIL	570.00	29.99.billion	10 January 2005	26 December 2005	5 August 2005
Sandesh	180.00	20 million	16 April 2009	30 November 2009	1 December 2009
Sasken Comm	260.00	400 million	15 September 2008	17 April 2009	27 October 2008
Selan Expl	25.00	20 million	10 April 2002	29 January 2003	30 January 2003
Selan Expl	25.00	10.75 million	19 May 2003	21 April 2004	–
Selan Expl	230.00	130 million	23 January 2009	4 January 2010	10 November 2009
Selan Explo	25.00	25 million	3 April 2001	22 November 2001	23 November 2001
SIEMENS Limited	250.00	805.2 million	25 June 2001	14 June 2002	17 June 2002
Sirpur Paper	40.00	70 million	9 August 2002	23 January 2003	24 January 2003
Softsol India	55.00	70 million	7 September 2009	31 March 2010	1 April 2010
Solitaire Mach	8.00	9.5 million	21 October 2002	28 June 2003	2 July 2003
SRF	250.00	350 million	4 July 2006	22 June 2007	26 September 2006
SRF	160.00	700 million	2 July 2008	24 April 2009	20 April 2009
Sun Pharma	750.00	1.2 billion	7 January 2003	19 December 2003	6 October 2003
Supreme Industries	125.00	250 million	8 December 2008	25 November 2009	9 February 2009
Supreme Petro	14.00	110 million	31 December 2008	4 December 2009	7 December 2009
Surana	50.00	60 million	30 September 2008	20 April 2009	21 January 2009
Tips Inds	75.00	200 million	11 June 2010	23 August 2010	–
TTK Healthcare	120.00	110 million	25 February 2009	18 September 2009	22 September 2009

(Continued)

Annexure   (*Continued*)

Name of the company	Maximum buyback price (₹)	Total aggregate amount (₹)	Start date [+]	End date [++]	Closure date
TV Today	115.00	290 million	16 March 2009	30 July 2009	23 July 2009
Valiant Comm	32.00	30 million	7 October 2008	7 September 2009	21 May 2009
Venkys India	65.00	72.8 million	19 September 2002	8 September 2003	12 June 2003
Winsome Yarns	10.00	60.9 million	2 May 2002	20 August 2002	21 August 2002
Zen Tech	110.00	50 million	23 March 2009	30 October 2009	5 November 2009

Source: Buyback Archives, www.bseindia.com, last accessed on 11 February 2011

Note:

[+] Start date refers to date from which the company intended to start buyback.

[++] End date refers to latest closing date.

6 | Valuation and Accounting Issues

LEARNING OBJECTIVES

After studying the chapter, you will be able to understand
- the concept of valuation
- the factors considered for valuation
- the different methods of valuation
- the difficulties in valuing companies

6.1 INTRODUCTION

The term 'value' is highly subjective. One very rarely finds unanimity among people about the value of a given commodity. What is more surprising is that value for the same person varies with changes in externalities and internalities over a period of time. To assign a value to an entity is all the more difficult because one can control corporate resources even by partially owning them. These are all paradoxes of value, and what one needs to know before making investment decisions is the real value of the asset, security, or entity.

In a merger and acquisition (M&A) or takeover, the financial aspects of the transaction are crucial. These represent the true value of the asset and are obviously based on the benefits that shall accrue in terms of financial gains, such as increase in productivity and enhanced dividend-paying capacity of the merged entity. Since the entire exercise is based on assumptions, one often ends up paying an excessive price for a target, simply because one is too optimistic in presuming synergistic benefits. The result of an enthusiastically optimistic valuation is that one may overestimate the value creation potential of the merged entity.

This reminds us of the story of Vincent Van Gogh. During his lifetime, he painted over 800 paintings, but could sell only one for $25. Later on, one of those unsold paintings sold for $40 million. It would not be wrong to say that if beauty is in the eye of the beholder, then the thing's worth is in the wallet of the holder, for cash is the only thing that has a fixed value. The value of virtually everything else depends on the following:

- Who is the owner or potential owner?
- What are the conditions?
- Who is the judge?

While people argue that value is reality, absolute value is a myth.

6.2 CONCEPT OF VALUATION

It is often argued that no rational buyer would pay more for an asset than its true worth. Though this may be true, it is seldom the case. For value is driven by not just financial considerations, but also by aesthetic and emotional considerations. While this may be true of items such as a piece of art or music, the value of a target company should be determined by a function of business logic that drives the decision of merger and acquisition and takeover. The logic one is referring to is the cash flows one expects from the business post deal, but much also depends on the bargaining power of the acquirer and the target. Since business is based on dynamic considerations, valuation also becomes a dynamic process. As a result, the same deal would be valued differently by the same player at different times or by different players at the same time.

Valuation of a business entity centres around three fundamental concepts, namely going concern value, liquidation value, and market value.

6.2.1 Going Concern Value

Going concern value assumes that a business entity has infinite life and shall continue to exist irrespective of the life of the promoter. This is because in the eyes of law, a business entity has an identity separate from its owners/promoters. Hence, its life does not depend on the life of the owner/promoter. Since it is assumed that a business entity/corporate has infinite life, it is expected to survive for an infinite period and will keep generating earnings or revenues forever. It is for this reason that one argues that the value of a business, on the basis of going concern concept, increases with time and finally becomes a perpetual annuity.

The term 'perpetual entity' implies that a company shall continue to exist irrespective of its shareholders. Consequently, the value of a business on going concern basis will be the present value of perpetual annuity, with or without growth. In short, the value of a business under this concept is based on the earning potential of the entity.

6.2.2 Liquidation Value

This is the value that the entity shall realize on liquidation after incurring all incidental costs—the value when a business entity goes out of business or ceases to exist. This value also normally increases with time assuming inflationary pressures, but it decreases with use of plant and machinery, building, and furniture. The increase in the value of real estate over time more than offsets the decrease in the value of other assets. It has been observed that liquidation value moves along with the replacement cost of the assets. Hence, the value of a business according to the liquidation concept depends more on realizable or replacement value of its underlying assets rather than the earning potential of the business.

6.2.3 Market Value

A third dimension emerges in case of valuation of listed companies, and that is the market price of the shares of the entity. It represents the price at which corporate ownership, and therefore corporate resources, are available. However, this price may not necessarily be based on the underlying fundamentals of the company. Instead, it is more or less governed by market sentiments and the forces of demand and supply. Experience indicates that in the short term, a market moves by sentiments rather than by fundamentals. If prevailing sentiments are favourable, the value of the entity increases and vice versa.

Above all, the value of an entity or a company largely depends upon non-quantitative personal and strategic considerations. At times, these considerations play a decisive role in buying or selling a firm, quite often defying all logical and quantitative considerations. Personal considerations are based on subjective considerations of buyers and sellers.

It is clear from this discussion that the valuation exercise is a complex interaction of quantitative and non-quantitative considerations. Quantitative models often set boundaries, which at times are too large to be of any use. Under such conditions, one uses the process of negotiation and deal structuring to decide the price of a company.

During the initial stages, quantitative considerations play a major role in setting a benchmark value for the company, while qualitative considerations play a vital role during the negotiation or deal structuring stage.

As one is required to consider a plethora of elements during an acquisition, the valuation exercise becomes a highly complex, time consuming, and lengthy task. It is a science in so far as it relates to valuation techniques generally adopted by M&A professionals. However, this often gives only an 'arithmetic price' which may not always give the full story. Indeed, there is a lot more to 'value' than price and one needs to understand the journey from 'price' to 'value'.

6.3 FACTORS TO BE CONSIDERED FOR VALUATION

Valuation is a very complex process. Throughout the valuation process, one needs to keep the purpose of valuation in mind. The process of valuation serves many purposes, such as the following:

- Impending sale of the entity
- Completing relevant legal proceedings
- Undertaking estate planning
- Settling shareholders' disputes
- Raising additional capital

When the aim of the valuation process is to sell the business, then the process should objectively determine a fair market value. The fair market value should, however, be suitably adjusted for the expected synergies and fit that the target may generate for the acquirer.

In addition, beyond the standard valuation methodologies, one needs to consider the following factors while valuing a business entity:

- The nature of the business and its operating history
- The stage of evolution of the target company, i.e., whether the target is a profitable company or is in the early stage of technology development, etc.

- The industry/sector dynamics
- The economic outlook and market sentiments
- The book value and financials of the entity
- The entity's earnings and dividend-paying capacity
- The value of the entity's intangible assets such as quality of management, especially in knowledge-based or intellectual property-based business
- Market value of other entities engaged in similar business
- Identifying whether the target is healthy or financially troubled
- Potential liabilities of the company such as environmental claims, tax demands, and off-balance sheet liabilities
- Sources of bias in valuation

These factors provide an insight into elements that may not necessarily feature in the balance sheet of the company, but have the potential to create/destroy the future value of the business. Hence, evaluating and analysing the impact of these factors is critical to the realistic valuation of the entity.

6.4 METHODS OF VALUATION

There are several methods that practitioners use to value businesses. Each method has its own relevance, merits, and demerits. Normally, the final valuation of the target is arrived at by using the appropriate blend of the results available using more than one method. Though the fundamental variables of all methods might differ, they are all based on the assumption that analysis regarding strategic fit, financial logic, and industry and economy analysis have already been carried out and have been found to be favourable.

In addition, there could be a range of valuation estimates for the same company depending on the entity and the purpose for which the valuation is being done. In each case, the valuation estimates may differ. Broadly, there would be two major estimates of values: standalone value and restructured value.

Under the former estimate methodology, the value of the target is determined on a standalone basis without considering any internal, external or financial restructuring improvements. Under the latter methodology, all improvements and estimates pertaining to the company's restructured value are incorporated.

It is important to note that the estimate methodology for the input variables in the corporate valuation exercise depends upon whether one is valuing the company on a standalone basis or on restructured value. It is also interesting to note that acquirers prefer the standalone estimate methodology while target companies prefer the restructured value methodology. Since the preferences differ from one party to another, the ultimate valuation defers.

There are three basic methods of valuation:

- Asset-based valuation
- Earning-based valuation
- Market-based valuation

There are other variants of these methods:

- Book value approach
- Stock and debt approach
- Direct comparison approach
- Discounted cash flow method
- Cash flow forecast during the explicit forecast period
- Cost of capital
- Continuing value

Let us now understand some of these methods.

6.4.1 Asset-based Valuation

As the name suggests, asset-based valuation involves estimation of the value of corporate assets, as if they have been with the bidder. The assets that are valued include the net fixed assets, intangible assets, investments, current assets, and all third party liabilities.

While valuing the fixed assets, each sub-class is considered and the value of all the individual assets under each sub-class is estimated. Examples include real estate, plant and machinery, furniture and fixtures, buildings, and vehicles.

While valuing investments, the value of each and every investment is estimated either at their realizable value or its current yield. Investments are valued under the categories of listed securities, unlisted securities, inter-corporate deposits, and other investments. Current assets such as stocks and receivables are also estimated at their realizable values.

Finally, all third party liabilities are valued and deducted from the total assets to arrive at the value of the target. The liabilities included here are short-term borrowings, creditors, and contingent/deferred liabilities. They are pegged at an appropriate level to arrive at an estimated value of total liabilities of the business. Contingent liabilities are also included in the valuation, for their value sometimes becomes so significant that it may turn an acceptable proposal into a non-viable one. Hence, these liabilities should be suitably factored in. These liabilities take the form of pending litigations related to business, guarantees provided by the company, etc.

The entire valuation exercise is carried out by valuing all the assets and liabilities at their revised value or at their current yield. While the assets and liabilities are all generally taken over, the parties to the deal may also decide to knock them off at the time of agreement. In such cases, their value becomes irrelevant and immaterial.

In short, the calculation of net assets value may be carried out as under:

Net fixed assets
+   Current assets
+   Investment
+   Intangibles
−   Long-term debts
−   Short-term debts
−   Contingent liabilities

- − Accumulated losses and miscellaneous expenditure not written off, if any
- = Net assets of the company
- − Preference share capital, if any
- = Net assets for equity shareholders

When the net assets for equity shareholders are divided by the number of equity shares, one arrives at the net assets value (NAV) per share.

6.4.2 Earning-based Valuation

In this method, the future maintainable earnings (FME) of the target company are estimated after adjusting the extraordinary items, if any, such as seasonal fluctuations, contingent payments or receipts, any concessions or penalty in the past years, or any non-recurring items such as profit or loss from sale of assets, or profit, or loss from treasury function.

This method assumes that FME will continue to be available to the business till its survival, which is assumed to be infinite, based on the principle of going concern. The value of the business is arrived at using the principle of present value of perpetuity, where FME represents the perpetuity value of the business.

Accordingly, the value of the target is determined using the formula

$$\frac{\text{FME}}{r}$$

Here, r is an appropriate discount rate and normally represents the opportunity cost of the funds used by the acquiring entity.

It is a known fact that entities pursue and attain growth over a period of time, although the growth rate cannot be predicted accurately. In such cases, it is assumed that FME shall grow at the rate of g. As such, the value of the target firm is determined using the equation

$$\frac{\text{FME}}{r-g}$$

In this equation, r is the appropriate rate of discount and g is the growth rate, subject to the condition that $g < r$.

If one looks at the equations, one finds that the two crucial elements that influence the value of the entity under consideration include estimation of FME and capitalization rate. The capitalization rate is often determined using the shareholders' expected rate of return—the return expected by the equity shareholders from their investment in the company. This expected rate of return expected by the investor is crucial and not the rate of return of the business because FME represents earnings available for distribution amongst equity shareholders and not profit before tax$(1 - \text{tax})$, that is, earnings available to the business entity for servicing its debt and equity capital. One could also express this concept as the mirror image of cost of equity capital. Thus, if one is ascertaining the value of the business, then FME can be taken as $\text{PBIT}(1 - t)$, where PBIT is profit before interest and tax.

The rate can also be estimated by using the inverse of price/earning (P/E). This method focuses on the value of the company as determined in the market, based on the earnings of the company. Similarly, the capitalized value of business can also be estimated by capitalizing $\text{PBIT}(1-t)$ by cost of capital—cost of equity and debt. From the capitalized value, one needs to deduct the value of debt and the resultant figure shall be the value of the equity of the company. When the value of equity is divided by the number of shares, the outstanding one gets is the value per share. Since the value is determined on the basis of P/E, the method is also known as profit-earning capacity value (PECV) of the share.

6.4.3 Market-based Valuation

This method of valuation involves comparison of the target company's market variables and other comparables with that of the industry. The value so arrived at is termed as market-based valuation.

The most commonly used variables are as follows:

- Price/earnings
- Price/sales
- Price/assets
- Any other quantifiable variable in relation to market price per share (such as price/cash earning per share, price/operating profit per share, etc.)
- Variables for different periods (such as highest, lowest, and current)
- Fundamentals factors such as earnings, assets, or capital employed, which-ever is found appropriate

Under this method, once these variables have been calculated, appropriate weightage is assigned to each variable to arrive at the weighted average multiplier, for calcu-lating the market capitalization of the target company. The resultant figure is then divided by the number of shares outstanding to arrive at the value per share.

6.4.4 Book Value Approach

The accuracy of this approach depends on whether the net book values of the assets are closer to their market values or not. If the difference between the two values is wide, the value of the company becomes unrealistic and vice versa. Some of the factors that result in the difference in values include the following:

Inflation   Inflation becomes an influencing factor since book value is calculated using the historical cost of the asset less depreciation. This implies that inflation is ignored in the calculation of the book value. On the other hand, market value obviously includes the impact of inflation on the value of the asset.

Technological changes   Technological changes can often render certain assets obsolete and worthless well before they are fully depreciated in the books of account. This means that the books will continue to show the assets having value while the market considers their obsolete nature and treats them as worthless. This obviously results in a difference in the two values of assets.

Organizational capital   Organizational capital never gets reflected in the balance sheet of the company. It is the value that gets created when all the stakeholders such as employees, customers, suppliers, and managers have a mutually beneficial and productive relationship and collectively contribute towards the attainment of corporate objectives. This factor influences the value simply because organizational capital cannot be easily separated and eliminated from the entity as a going concern.

The crucial aspect that needs to be remembered here is that an assets' earning power is not always related to its book value. This is very true in the case of assets that are old, for the earnings of such assets are more likely to be related to its current replacement cost. Since the replacement cost becomes crucial here, companies would do well by substituting the net book value of the asset by its current replacement cost.

Entities can also ascertain the approximate fair market value of the asset by finding out what the asset would fetch if it is liquidated immediately. This value can be determined only if there is an active secondary market for the assets. In cases where there are no active secondary markets for the assets, one needs to estimate the hypothetical price at which assets may be sold. The problem with this hypothetical price is that it may not give the correct value and may finally impact the value of the target company. In addition, the liquidation approach ignores organizational capital, which is a crucial element of the business.

6.4.5 Stock and Debt Approach

This method is followed when the securities of a company are publicly traded. Here, the value can be obtained by merely adding the market value of all its outstanding securities.

While this approach is fairly straight forward, the important issue that remains to be resolved is what price one should consider for equity shares. This dilemma is on account of the volatility one sees in the price of equity shares. Experts suggest different basis for valuing equity shares. Some suggest using an average of the recent share prices instead of the price prevailing on the day of valuation. The argument given is that the value prevailing over a certain period represents a more reliable value of the shares rather than taking the value prevailing on the day when the valuation is being done.

6.4.6 Direct Comparison Approach

This method is based on the assumption that similar assets sell at similar prices. As such, one can ascertain the value of an asset by checking the price of a comparable asset in the market. This principle is commonly applied while dealing with assets such as land and building. Let us now discuss the steps on which this method is based:

Economy Analysis

This analysis involves assessing the prospects of various industries/sectors operating in the economy and gradually progressing on to the evaluation of individual companies within an industry. The analysis aims at ascertaining the GDP, annual industrial production, annual agricultural output, inflation rate, interest rates, balance of payments, exchange rates, budget of the state, and its composition.

Industry Analysis

This analysis focuses on elements such as the relationship of the industry with the economy as a whole, life cycle stage of the industry at that point, profit potential of the industry, types and nature of regulations applicable to the industry, and relative competitive advantages that the company enjoys in procurement of raw materials, production costs, marketing and distribution arrangements, and technological resources.

Company Analysis

Company analysis focuses on all aspects of the company and its business such as its product portfolio and market segments, availability and cost of inputs, technological and production capabilities, image of the company in the market, the company's distribution reach, customer loyalty, and product differentiation. In addition to these elements, the analysis also covers managerial competence and drive, quality of human resources deployed, the company's competitive position, its liquidity, leverage and access to funds, turnover margins, and return on investment.

The analysis serves the purpose only when efforts are made to look carefully at 15–20 companies in the same industry and select at least 1–2 companies that come close to the line of business, markets served, scale of operations, and other parameters of the target. Once the comparable companies are selected, the historical financial statements of the target and the comparable companies should be analysed to identify similarities and differences in various variables, so that appropriate adjustments can be made to put these companies on a comparable platform. The adjustments that may be required could include differences in inventory valuation methods, type and amount of intangible assets, and off balance sheet items.

Apply Ratios or Multiples

The ratios or multiples provide a very reliable and sound basis for decision making. The ratios commonly used cover firm value to sales; firm value to book value of assets; firm value to profit before interest, depreciation, and tax (PBIDT); firm value to PBIT; firm value to profit after tax (PAT); equity value to equity earnings (price earning multiple); equity value to net worth (market book ratio); etc.

Select Comparable Companies

This step involves deciding where the target company fits in relation to the comparable companies. This step, of course, relies on judgement.

Value the Company

Once this is done, one can apply appropriate multiples to the financial numbers of the company so that the value of the target company can be determined.

It is crucial to remember that if one employs several bases for determining the value of the target company, the estimates may be averaged to arrive at the value.

This approach has been popular with valuers because it relies on multiples that are easy to relate to and can be obtained quickly and without any difficulty. The approach is also useful when several comparable companies are traded and the market prices them correctly. One can rely on the available data and use it as the basis of valuation.

The biggest drawback of this approach is that it relies on multiples that are subjective and hence can be easily misused and manipulated. This is based on the concept that no two forms are identical in terms of risk and growth. Thus, when the multiples are manipulated, the same gets reflected through valuation errors, in terms of overvaluation and undervaluation of the market.

6.4.7 Discounted Cash Flow Method

Discounted cash flow (DCF) represents the present value of the expected cash flows generated through an asset, which are discounted at a discount rate that reflects the risk involved in earning these cash flows. It is the most preferred and acceptable method of valuation at present. The main reason behind its popularity is that it is based on fundamentals of time value of money (the value of money changes over time) and gives weightage to the future prospects of the business rather than on its historical performance.

It would be worth asking a question at this stage—why do companies purchase assets? The only logical answer is that one expects these assets to generate cash flows in the future. In that sense, one can say that the value of an asset depends on the following:

- The predictability of cash flows
- The quantum of cash flows

The argument that would get accepted in this regard without any contradictions would therefore be 'assets with more predictable and higher cash flows would command a higher value and vice versa'.

Proceeding further with the equation for valuing an asset or an entity using the DCF technique, the equation used would be

$$\text{Value of an asset or entity} = \frac{ECF_1}{(1+r)} + \frac{ECF_2}{(1+r)^2} + \frac{ECF_3}{(1+r)^3} + \cdots + \frac{ECF_n}{(1+r)^n}$$

where ECF_1, ECF_2, ..., ECF_n represent expected cash flows over a period of n years, r represents the discount rate that incorporates the risk involved in the investment, and n represents the useful life of the investment (the time frame during which the investment would generate cash flows).

The formula reiterates what we just said, that DCF is based on the future cash flow prospects of the investment and the risk involved in the asset or the business being valued—the target company. It is imperative to draw one's attention to the fact that the more certain the cash flows, the lesser is the risk involved in the investment and the higher the value, and vice versa.

Valuation through DCF The valuation of the firm using the DCF involves three basic components:

- Expected cash flows
- Discount rate
- Ascertaining the DCF

Let us understand these three elements in detail.

Expected Cash Flows

Cash flows are the earnings of the company. It is critical to remember that cash flows can be of different types. Let us briefly analyse them:

Free cash flows to the firm The after-tax operating earnings of the company are termed as free cash flows to the firm. These represent cash flows generated for all claim holders in the firm and are the pre-debt cash flows (Damodaran 2002). In other words, they represent the following:

- Operating income of the firm $(1 - \text{tax})$
- Capital expenditure – depreciation
- Changes in non-cash working capital

Free cash flows to equity The cash flows that are ascertained after deducting the cash outflows on account of all types of debt are termed free cash flows to equity. These are thus cash flows that are available for distribution among equity holders. In other words, they represent the following:

- Net income
- Capital expenditure – depreciation
- Changes in non-cash working capital + new debt raised – repayments

Nominal cash flows The cash flows that incorporate expected inflation are termed nominal cash flows. These are expressed in specific currencies and as such vary across currencies.

Real cash flows The cash flows that do not incorporate the inflation component are termed as real cash flows. Real cash flows, thus, represent the changes in the number of units sold and real pricing power.

Pre-tax cash flows The cash flows that have been discussed so far under cash flows to the firm and cash flows to the equity were pre-tax cash flows. Such cash flows are calculated after paying corporate taxes but before the tax payable by investors.

Post-tax cash flows These cash flows are arrived at after deducting the tax payable by the investors, that is, tax on dividend and capital gains for equity investors shareholders and tax on interest for debt investors. This is because all types of investors have to pay tax on their income, which includes the aforesaid taxes.

Discount Rate

The discount rate generally considers risks associated with earning that year's cash flow including cyclical movements, inflation, exchange rates, and market trends. This obviously implies that as one moves down the time graph, the uncertainty associated with forecasting the cash flow increases, resulting in higher risk. This, in turn, would affect the discount rate that would keep increasing. This changing risk variable creates various problems and complexities, and firms avoid putting it into practice. As a substitute to this, companies choose a discount rate that is higher than the normal discounting rate. As a result of this strategy, a company is able to use only one standard rate of discount for the entire analysis.

The rate of discount can be ascertained in the following alternate manners:

- For discounting cash flow available to equity holders, the discount rate used is generally equivalent to the cost of equity. The cost of equity represents the returns expected by investors, which obviously differ from investor to investor. This is taken care of by determining the cost of equity by using either a rough estimate that is immediately available as inverse of P/E for companies that are listed, or a surrogate P/E of some comparable company after considering appropriate discount for illiquidity in cases where companies are not listed.

- Another way of determining the cost of equity is by ascertaining the cost of equity using the capital asset pricing model (CAPM). In this case, historical returns and risk premium (market returns less risk-free rate of returns) are regressed to find out the degree of volatility of stock returns with risk premium and that resultant figure, which is known as beta, can be used to find the cost of equity for the given risk premium. This is the most popular method used today in spite of its in-built limitations. The output of any of the analyses results in valuation of equity.

- For discounting the cash flow available to firm, the discount rate taken is the weighted average cost of capital (WACC). It is the average of cost of debt and cost of equity determined after assigning due weightage to these elements either according to their market value or book value. The cost of debt is estimated on the basis of average coupon rates of the debt under consideration. In conditions where the interest rates fluctuate wildly, it would be appropriate to use weighted average yield to market (YTM) of debts under consideration by assigning the proportion of book values of debts as eights.

Ascertaining the DCF

Discounted cash flow involves calculating the free cash flows to the equity. The process involves a detailed analysis of future cash flows of the company for n years. The analysis includes the industry and its prospects, projected growth in the market, existing and expected market share of the company, analysis of operations of business and their sensitivity to value, scanning the external environment including regulatory framework and competitive scenario, and the impact of globalization and proposed reforms, if any. The forecast should also factor in the expected rate of inflation, exchange rate movements, and movements in the interest rates.

Once the future cash flows are reasonably estimated, one needs to ascertain the period for which the forecast has to be projected. One also needs to estimate and appropriately treat the base/current year's cash flow. Once this is done, the present value of the cash flows post the base/current year is determined.

The present value is ascertained by multiplying the estimated cash flows with an appropriate discount rate for further analysis. The process of discounting is done so that the expected risk gets reflected in the estimated cash flows. The rate of discount selected by the company should most appropriately reflect the risk involved in the business during the years for which the analysis is being done.

Thus, the discounted cash flow approach to valuing a firm involves the following steps:

- Forecast the cash flow of the explicit forecast period—the period during which a business reaches a steady state.
- Establish the cost of capital to arrive at the discount rate.
- Determine the continuing value at the end of the explicit forecast period.
- Calculate the firm value and interpret results.

6.5 IS DCF SAME IN VALUATION OF ALL INVESTMENT?

This question is often asked while one goes through the valuation process. This is driven by the belief that every asset has some intrinsic value. Though nobody tries to defy this argument, it is equally true that nobody ever gets to see the intrinsic value as it is a matter of one's own faith and belief than anything else. Therefore, companies use different approaches in valuing equity, assets, and firm through the DCF technique.

Let us now analyse the valuation techniques of the different investments.

6.5.1 Valuation of Assets

The value of an asset can be best described as the present value of the future cash flows from the use of the assets concerned. To determine the DCF of assets, all the available assets that have a useful life and are capable of generating cash flows are determined individually. This method helps the company to ascertain the cash flows of individual assets. Thus, if a company finds out that the cash flows of an asset are below the expected rate or that risk is involved, it may decide to liquidate that asset. Companies, more often than not, determine the values of assets based on the liquidation presumption, that is, assets are presumed to have been sold. If the liquidation value is in excess of the future cash flows from the use of the asset, the company may actually liquidate the assets. The logic behind this is very similar to the old saying 'a bird in hand is worth two in the bush'. It implies that if the current liquidation value exceeds the future cash flows, companies should go ahead and liquidate the assets, for the following reasons:

- It releases immediate cash into the coffers of the company, which can be used more efficiently elsewhere to increase the overall average returns of the company.
- Selling the assets immediately implies that the risk associated with future cash flow generation is avoided.

It has to be noted that the liquidation value of the assets also depends on the urgency factor. If the company shows urgency in liquidating its assets, the assets may have to be liquidated at a discount. Again, the quantum of discount would depend on the number of potential buyers for the assets, the asset characteristics, and the state of the economy (Damodaran 2002).

6.5.2 Valuation of Going Concern

We have just seen the concept of valuation of assets. When the sum total value of all the assets owned by the business is considered, we get the value of a going concern. A going concern is an entity that already owns assets that are deployed for generating cash flows. In addition, a going concern has no intentions of liquidating the assets. Thus, the only way the value can be determined is to look at the value of the assets reflected in the company's balance sheet. These are termed 'assets in place'. A going concern may also make investments in future to pursue its growth objectives. The assets so acquired are termed as 'growth assets'.

A going concern, thus, determines its value by valuing both assets in place and its future investments in growth assets. The real value of a going concern lies in its investments in the growth assets and the resultant profitability.

6.5.3 Valuation of Equity

The valuation of the equity stake in the business is called equity valuation. The cash flows that are left after debt payments and reinvestment needs are called free cash flows to equity. Similarly, the discount rate that reflects just the cost of equity financing is called cost of equity (Damodaran 2002).

The value of equity can also be determined by subtracting the value of the all the non-equity claims from the value of a going concern.

6.6 INTRODUCTION TO ACCOUNTING ISSUES

Every commercial entity maintains books of accounts that give complete details of the activities carried out on a day-to-day basis. These records are used to ascertain the profitability of the entity, and to assure the stakeholders that these affairs are being carried out in the most effective and efficient manner. Proper maintenance of records also helps in fulfilling the statutory requirements and forms the basis of transparency and fairness in the affairs of the entity.

6.7 ACCOUNTING FOR AMALGAMATIONS

The accounting issues pertaining to amalgamation as defined under the provisions of the Companies Act, 1956, or any other statute applicable to companies are dealt with under Accounting Standard (AS) 14 as evolved by the Institute of Chartered Accountants of India. The term includes absorption as well. The basic difference between the two terms, however, needs to be understood and appreciated. Amalgamation results in the emergence of a new entity and the status of the existing two or more legal entities vanishes. In absorption, one entity takes over the existing entity and as such one (or more) legal entity ceases to exist.

Accounting Standard 14, however, excludes cases where a company obtains control over another entity without impinging upon the status of each company being an independent and separate legal entity, but still deriving the benefits of 'coming together' by acting as one single 'economic entity'. The accounting treatment under such situations is covered under AS 21–Consolidation of Financial Statements (Kumar 2010).

Accounting Standard 14 also defines the terms such as transferor, transferee, and purchase consideration. Let us understand these terms:

Transferor   This represents the company which is amalgamated into another company. The selling entity is also called 'vendor company'.

Transferee   This is the entity with whom the transferor company is amalgamated. The buying entity is also called 'vendee company'.

Purchase consideration   When an amalgamation takes place, the vendee company acquires all the assets and liabilities of the vendor company. The difference between the assets and liabilities taken over represents 'net assets'. The vendee company has to pay the vendor company for the value of net assets. This amount is called *purchase consideration*. The dues are settled by issuing shares and other securities and by paying cash to the vendor company.

The amount of purchase consideration is paid to the equity and preference shareholders. When the vendee company undertakes the responsibility of settling external/third party liabilities such as loans, debentures or incurs expenses to carry out the process of amalgamation, these do not form a part of the purchase consideration.

The accounting standard talks of two methods of amalgamation—amalgamation in the nature of merger and amalgamation in the nature of purchase.

6.7.1 Amalgamation in Nature of Merger

In this type of amalgamation, there is a polling of not just the assets and liabilities but also the interests of shareholders and of the business of the two entities merging with each other.

Accounting Standard 14 prescribes fulfilment of five conditions for a merger to fall in the aforesaid category:

- All the assets and liabilities of the transferor company become the assets and liabilities of the transferee company.
- Shareholders of the transferor company holding not less than 90% of the face value of equity shares become the shareholders of the transferee company. While calculating the 90% value, shares held by the transferee plus subsidiaries of the transferee and nominees of the transferee should be excluded.
- The consideration payable to the shareholders of the transferor company should be paid through issue of shares in the transferee company. Fractional shares, if any, can however be paid for in cash.
- The transferee has the intention of carrying on the business of the transferor after amalgamation
- The assets and liabilities of the transferor company are incorporated into the balance sheet of the transferee company. In addition, the assets and liabilities should be shown using uniform accounting policies. For example, if the transferor company has been charging depreciation on straight line basis and the transferee company has been charging depreciation using the reducing balance basis, when the two entities amalgamate, the transferor's assets will have to be first adjusted under the reducing balance method and only then added to the assets of the transferee company.

In this case, the method of accounting is known as pooling of interest method. Accounting Standard 14 states that under pooling of interest method, three salient features are observed:

- When the financial statements of the transferee are prepared, the assets, liabilities, and reserves of the transferor should be recorded at the value appearing in the books of accounts and in the same form as on the date of amalgamation. Similarly, if there is any balance in the profit and loss account, the same should be aggregated with the corresponding balance of the transferee. If the books of the transferee do not have profit and loss balance, then the balance in the books of the transferor should be transferred to the general reserves. Again, if the purchase consideration is less than the paid-up capital of the transferor company, then the difference should be recorded as capital reserves.
- If the transferor company has been following a different set of accounting policies, then the same should be modified in accordance with the policies of the transferee company. The effect of any changes in the accounting policies should be reported in accordance with AS 5.
- If there is any difference in the purchase consideration and the amount of share capital of the transferor, the difference should be adjusted in reserves, and no goodwill or capital reserves should be shown in the books of accounts of the transferee.

6.7.2 Amalgamation in Nature of Purchase

In an amalgamation in the nature of purchase, one company acquires another company, as a result of which the shareholders of the company which is acquired do not continue to possess interest in the equity of the combined entity in the proportion in which they held the shares in the liquidated company. Here it is also possible that the business of the acquired entity may not be continued. This happens when even one of the conditions listed is not fulfilled.

Under this case, the method of accounting that is followed is called purchase method. Here the accounting for amalgamation is done in a manner similar to purchase of assets under normal circumstances. The salient features are as follows:

- The assets and liabilities of the transferor company are included in the financial statements of the transferee company at their values on the date of amalgamation. The non-statutory reserves, both capital and revenue, of the transferor company are not included in the financial statements of the transferee company.
- If the purchase consideration exceeds the net assets value—assets taken over minus liabilities taken over, then the excess amount is recorded as goodwill. The amount of goodwill should be amortized over a period not exceeding five years, unless a longer period can be justified.
- If, on the other hand, the purchase consideration is less than the net assets value, it is recorded as capital reserves.
- Where the requirements of relevant statute require statutory reserves of the transferor company to be recorded in the financial statements of the transferee company, the statutory reserves are credited and the amalgamation adjustment account is debited. This account should be shown under miscellaneous expenditure on the assets side of the balance sheet. If at a later stage this amount is no longer required, then a reverse entry should be passed.

6.8 PROVISIONS OF ACCOUNTING STANDARD 14

Accounting Standard 14 deals with three areas that are linked when accounting is done for amalgamation (Kumar 2010).

6.8.1 Non-cash Consideration

The purchase consideration may be discharged through cash and non-cash elements. The non-cash element includes securities or other non-cash elements. While these elements are being recorded, the following aspects have to be kept in mind:

- The non-cash component must be valued at fair value.
- In case of securities, fair value would be the value fixed by statutory authorities.
- For other assets, fair value is determined with reference to the market value of the assets.

- In case the market value of some assets cannot be reliably assessed, the assets may be valued at their respective net book value, i.e., value appearing in the books of accounts on the date of amalgamation.

6.8.2 Future Events

A merger may be concluded with consideration payable at a future date and subject to occurrence of one or more future uncertain events. In this case, if the event is probable and the amount can also be estimated, the same should be included in the purchase consideration.

On all other cases, the amount should be recorded as soon as it is determinable.

6.8.3 Treatment of Reserves

In certain cases of amalgamation, the approval of the court is necessary. In such cases, the court is empowered to impose conditions to ensure that the scheme of amalgamation is fully and effectively carried out. The order might include conditions pertaining to treatment of reserves after amalgamation. Such conditions need to be adhered to under all circumstances.

6.9 INTERNATIONAL FINANCIAL REPORTING STANDARDS 3—BUSINESS COMBINATIONS

The International Financial Reporting Standards (IFRS) uses the terms 'acquirer' and 'acquiree' instead of 'transferee' and 'transferor'. It lays down accounting principles from the perspective of the transferee or acquirer. The basic provisions of IFRS 3 are as follows:

Focus of coverage While business combinations imply combining two entities into one, IFRS 3 states that the provisions need to be applied even when a segment or a profit centre of one entity is acquired by another entity. Under IFRS 3, the acquiree company may continue to exist as a legal entity.

Types of combinations The IFRS covers transactions between shareholders of two independent entities that combine into one or between an entity and shareholders of another that result in one or more of the following:

- Purchase of equity
- Purchase of part or whole of the assets
- Assumption of liabilities
- New entity or restructuring of one or more of the combining entities

The purchase consideration may be paid through equity, cash, or both.

Measurement of cost The acquirer measures the cost of business combinations as an aggregate of the following:

- Fair values of assets taken over
- Value of liabilities assumed

- Equity instruments issued by the acquirer in exchange for control
- Any additional cost directly incurred for the business combination

Measurement of consideration The consideration is measured in terms of the carrying amount of the elements stated in the measurement of cost. If the carrying amount and the fair value differ, then the difference should be recognized as profit or loss.

Allocation of cost The cost of the business should be allocated by recognizing the identifiable assets, liabilities, and contingent liabilities that satisfy the recognition criteria—whose fair value can be determined. If under the business combination, non-current assets held for sales are also acquired, the same should be recognized at fair values less disposal costs.

The fair value of assets and liabilities are determined on the following basis:

Tangible assets Probability of future economic benefits in accruing to the acquirer and reliable measurement of fair values

Liabilities Probability of outflow of economic benefits in future and reliable measurement of fair values

Intangible assets Reliable measurement of fair values

Contingent liabilities Reliable measurement of fair values. In case the fair values cannot be measured, the cost will be recognized as goodwill.

'Negative goodwill' is not recognized by IFRS 3. Accounting for the excess of net assets acquired over the fair value of consideration paid is recognized as 'bargain purchase' and is recorded as a gain in the income statement.

Accounting for restructuring costs Restructuring costs is recognized only when the conditions for recognition are satisfied as per the accounting principles laid down in IFRS 3.

Concept of provisional fair values If at the end of the first reporting date, the acquirer is unable to determine the fair value of the assets and liabilities acquired, the same can be accounted for on the basis of provisional fair values. These are then to be crystallized over a 12-month period and are reflected as goodwill on a retrospective basis.

Measurement of goodwill Goodwill is the excess of cost of acquisition over the fair value of net assets. The amount so determined is recorded as an asset, reflecting flow of benefits in future. Goodwill is not amortized but is tested for impairment each year.

Contingent liabilities If contingent liabilities assumed and recognized at fair values subsequently become liabilities, they are to be measured higher than the following:

- Initial value at which the same was recognized
- Value if the amount had been recognized as per IAS 37

Deferred tax assets An entity may not be able to recognize a deferred tax asset pertaining to tax loss carry forward at the time of combination. If at a subsequent date the deferred tax happens to be realized, the amount so realized will be recognized as a gain in the statement of profit or loss. Similarly, goodwill, if recognized, should be correspondingly reduced by recognizing the reduction as expense in the profit and loss statement.

6.10 SOLVED EXAMPLES*

1. The balance sheet of Munna Ltd on 31 March 2008 was as follows:

Balance sheet as on 31 March 2008
Munna Ltd

Liabilities	Amount (₹)	Assets	Amount (₹)
Authorized, issued equity share capital (20,000 shares of ₹100 each)	2,000,000	Goodwill	200,000
7% 10,000 Preference shares of ₹100 each	1,000,000	Plant and machinery	1,800,000
Sundry creditors	700,000	Stock	300,000
Bank overdraft	300,000	Debtors	750,000
		Preliminary expenses	100,000
		Cash	150,000
		Profit and loss account	700,000
	4,000,000		4,000,000

Two years' preference dividends are in arrears. The company had a bad time during the last two years and hopes for better business in the future, earning profit, and paying dividend provided the capital base is reduced.

An internal reconstruction scheme as follows was agreed to by all concerned.

- Creditors agreed to forego 50% of the claim.
- Preference shareholders withdrew arrears dividend claim. They also agreed to lower their capital claim by 20% by reducing the nominal value in consideration of 9% dividend effective after reorganization in case equity shareholder's losses exceed 50% on the application of the scheme.
- The bank agreed to convert the overdraft into a term loan to the extent required for making the current ratio equal to 2:1.
- The revalued figure for plant and machinery was accepted as ₹1,500,000.
- Debtors to the extent of ₹400,000 were considered good.
- Equity shares shall be exchanged for the same number of equity shares at a revised denomination as required after the reorganization.

---

* All solved examples have been adapted from real situations and companies.

Show:

(a) Total loss to be borne by the shareholders of the organization
(b) Share of loss to the individual classes of shareholders
(c) New structure of share capital after reorganization
(d) Working capital of the reorganized company
(e) Pro forma balance sheet after reorganization

Solution

(a) Total loss to be borne by the shareholders of the organization

The amount is calculated after ascertaining the reduction in the value of the assets and liabilities. While calculating the amount, fictitious and intangible assets are written off. Preference dividend in arrears is not taken into account for the purpose of the calculation as the shareholders have decided to forego the claim. The calculation is as follows:

Assets/Liabilities	Amount (₹)	Working note no.
Goodwill	200,000	(i)
Plant and machinery	300,000	(ii)
Bad debts	350,000	(iii)
Preliminary expenses	100,000	(iv)
Profit and loss account	700,000	(v)
Total	**1,650,000**	
Less: Creditors	350,000	
Loss to be borne	**1,300,000**	

Working notes on (a):

(i)	Intangible assets written off	200,000
(ii)	Original value – new value = (1,800,000 – 1,500,000)	300,000
(iii)	Debtors as per B/S = 750,000 Less: Amount recoverable (good) 400,000	350,000
(iv)	Fictitious assets written off – preliminary expenses	100,000
(v)	Accumulated loss – profit and loss	700,000
(vi)	Dues foregone by creditors = 700,000 × 50%	350,000

Note: Money measurements are in rupees.

(b) Share of loss to the individual classes of shareholders

Since the total loss is greater than 50% of the paid-up equity share capital, preference shareholders shall bear loss equivalent to 20% of the total preference capital as given in point (ii) of the scheme.

Accordingly, loss is shared between shareholders as follows:

Capital	Amount (₹)	Working note no.
Preference shareholders	200,000	(i)
Equity shareholders	1,100,000	(ii)
Total loss as in (a)	**1,300,000**	

Working notes on (b):

    (i) Loss borne by preference shareholders
        Total preference capital $\times$ 20%
        ₹1,000,000 $\times$ 20% = ₹200,000

    (ii) Loss borne by equity shareholders
        Total loss − preference shareholders' share in loss
        ₹1,300,000 − ₹200,000 = ₹1,100,000

(c) New structure of share capital after reorganization

Capital	Amount (₹)	Working note no.
20,000 equity shares of ₹45* each fully paid	900,000	(i)
10,000 9% preference shares of ₹8 (₹10 − 20%) each fully paid	800,000	(ii)
Total capital in the new company	**1,700,000**	

Working notes on (c):

    (i) Equity share capital =
        Capital as per balance sheet − share in loss as per (b)
        ₹2,000,000 − ₹1,100,000 = ₹900,000
        * (900,000/20,000 = 45)

    (ii) Preference share capital
        Capital as per balance sheet − share in loss as per (b)
        ₹1,000,000 − ₹200,000

(d) Working capital of the reorganized company

Component	Amount (₹)	Working note no.
Stock	300,000	(i)
Sundry debtors	400,000	(ii)
Cash	150,000	(iii)
Total current assets	**850,000**	

(Continued)

Component	Amount (₹)	Working note no.
Less: current liabilities		
Sundry creditors	350,000	(iv)
Bank overdraft	75,000*	(v)
Total current liabilities	**350,000**	

Working notes on (d):

(i)	Stock—as given in the balance sheet	300,000
(ii)	Sundry debtors Amount as per balance sheet – bad debts as per scheme = 750,000 – 350,000	400,000
(iii)	Cash—as given in the balance sheet	150,000
(iv)	Sundry creditors Amount as per balance sheet – claim foregone as per scheme = 700,000 – 50% = 350,000	350,000
(v)	Bank overdraft The required current assets to current liabilities ratio needs to be 2:1 as per the scheme. The current assets as calculated above ₹850,000. Accordingly, current liabilities need to be 50% of ₹850,000, that is, ₹425,000. Of these, sundry creditors account for ₹350,000. Therefore bank overdraft will represent the difference, that is, 425,000–350,000.	75,000

* Accordingly, the remaining amount of the bank overdraft shall stand converted in term loan, that is, 300,000 – 75,000 = 225,000.

Note: Money measurements are in rupees.

(e) Pro forma balance sheet after reorganization

Balance sheet after reorganization
Munna Ltd

Liabilities	Amount (₹)	Assets	Amount (₹)
20,000 Equity shares of ₹45 each fully paid Note (i)	900,000	Plant and machinery Note (vi)	1,500,000
10,000 9% Preference shares of ₹8 each fully paid Note (ii)	800,000	Stock Note (vii)	300,000
Term loan Note (iii)	225,000	Sundry debtors Note (viii)	400,000

(Continued)

Balance sheet after reorganization
Munna Ltd   (*Continued*)

Liabilities	Amount (₹)	Assets	Amount (₹)
Sundry creditors Note (iv)	350,000	Cash Note (ix)	150,000
Bank overdraft Note (v)	75,000		
Total	**2,350,000**	**Total**	**2,350,000**

Working notes on (e):

    (i) Equity share capital as calculated in (c)
    (ii) Preference capital as calculated in (c)
    (iii) Term loan = conversion of bank overdraft
    (iv) Sundry creditors as calculated in (d)
    (v) Bank overdraft as calculated in (d)
    (vi) Plant and machinery as calculated in (a)
    (vii) Stock at original value
    (viii) Sundry debtors as calculated in (d)
    (ix) Cash at original value

2. The balance sheet of Sickness Ltd as on 31 March 2008 was as follows:

Balance sheet as on 31 March 2008
Sickness Ltd

Liabilities	Amount (₹)	Amount (₹)	Assets	Amount (₹)	Amount (₹)
Share capital: 8,000 equity shares of ₹100 each, ₹50 per share paid up		400,000	Fixed assets: Goodwill at cost Others	40,000 850,000 890,000	
			Less: depreciation	270,000	620,000
11% Preference shares of ₹100 each fully paid.		400,000	Investments		25,000
Premium received on preference shares		40,000	Stock intrade		210,000
General reserve		60,000	Sundry debtors		255,000
Current liabilities Contingent liabilities		310,000	Cash and bank balances		100,000
Preference dividends are in arrears for three years including the year ended 31 March 2006					
		1,210,000			**1,210,000**

The funds of the company are sufficient to discharge its liabilities including preference dividends in arrears. However, the company does not want to deplete its resources. It would also like to reflect the values of some of its assets in a realistic manner. The board of directors of the company decided and proposed the following scheme of rehabilitation/reconstruction to be effective from 1 April 2008.

- The cumulative preference shareholders are to be issued, in exchange of their holdings, 13% debentures of the face value of ₹100 each at a premium of 10%. Fractional holdings are to be paid off in cash.
- Arrears of preference dividends to be converted into equity shares of ₹100, ₹50 per share paid up.
- After the issue of the equity shares mentioned in (ii), the paid-up value of all the equity shares is to be reduced to ₹25 each.
- The face value of all the equity shares to be reduced to ₹50 each and the remaining unpaid portion is to be called up fully.
- Goodwill has lost its value and has to be written off. Market value of other fixed assets is determined, as on 31 March 2006 at ₹500,000.
- Investments have no market value and have to be written off.
- Stock in trade is to be valued at 110% of its book value and sundry debtors are to be discounted by 5%.

The scheme, as approved by the directors, is duly accepted by all the authorities and put into effect. During the working for the half-year ended 30 September 2008, it is noticed that the trading for the period has resulted in an increase of bank balances by ₹55,100, sundry debtors by ₹40,000, trade creditors by ₹26,000, and a decrease in stock by ₹8,000. Depreciation for the half year on fixed assets at 10% per annum to be provided. The increase in the bank balances was prior to the company paying the half yearly interest on the debentures and redeeming one half of the debentures on 30 September 2008. From this information, you are required to prepare the balance sheet of Sickness Ltd, as on 30 September 2008. In addition, show the statement showing effects of six months on the working capital.

Solution

Balance sheet after implementation of rehabilitation scheme
Sickness Ltd

Liabilities	Amount (₹)	Assets	Amount (₹)
Share capital:		Fixed assets (as given)	500,000
10,640 Equity shares of ₹50 each fully paid Note (ii)	532,000	Current assets:	
Reserves and surplus:		Stock (valued at 110%)	231,000
Share premium Note (iii)	73,610	Sundry debtors (valued at 95%)	242,250

(Continued)

Balance sheet after implementation of rehabilitation scheme
Sickness Ltd   (*Continued*)

Liabilities	Amount (₹)	Assets	Amount (₹)
General reserves	60,000	Cash and bank Note (iv)	365,960
13% Debentures Note (i)	363,600		
Current liabilities and provisions	310,000		
	1,339,210		**1,339,210**

Statement showing effects of six months on working capital:

Particulars	Amount (₹)	Particulars	Amount (₹)
Total Liabilities	1,339,210	Total assets	1,339,210
Less: reduction in debentures due to redemption	181,800	Add: increase in bank balance	55,100
Add: increase in sundry creditors	26,000	Less: debenture interest paid	23,634
	1,183,410	Less: debentures redeemed	188,800
Add: profit and loss for six months	12,466	Add: increase in debtors	40,000
		Less: decrease in stock	8,000
		Less: depreciation	25,000
	1,195,876		**1,195,876**

Balance sheet as on 30 September 2008
Sickness Ltd

Liabilities	Amount (₹)	Assets	Amount (₹)
Share capital:		Fixed assets	475,000
10,640 Equity shares of ₹50 each fully paid	532,000	Current assets:	
Reserves and surplus:		Stock	223,000
Share premium	73,610	Sundry debtors	282,250
General reserves (60,000 + 12,466)	72,466	Cash and bank Note (iv)	215,626
13% Debentures Note (i)	181,800		

(*Continued*)

Balance sheet as on 30 September 2008
Sickness Ltd   (Continued)

Liabilities	Amount (₹)	Assets	Amount (₹)
Current liabilities and provisions	336,000		
	1,195,876		**1,195,876**

Working notes:

(i) Settlement of the dues of preference share capital
Face value per preference share = 100
Premium to be charged (10%) = 10
Total payable per share = 110
Number of debentures to be allotted = 400,000/110 = 3636.3636
Debentures issued = 3636 × 100 = 363,600
Share premium = 3636 × 10 = 36,360
Cash payable (for fraction) = 0.3636 × 110 = 40

(ii) Settlement of dues of equity shareholders
Total number of equity shares = 8,000
Shares allotted for preference dividend in arrears
400,000 × 11% × 3 = 132,000
Number of shares allotted 132,000/50 = 2,640
Total shares = 10,640
Equity × share capital = 10,640 × 50 = 532,000

(iii) Share premium
Opening balance 40,000
Premium as per note (i) 36,360
Less: premium rescued to put through the scheme 2,750
Closing balance = 73,610

(iv) Cash and bank balance
Opening balance 100,000
Cash received by making shares fully paid (10,640 × 25) 266,000
Less: Cash paid as per note (i) 40
Closing balance = 365,960

3. The following are the balance sheets of RS Ltd and XY Ltd as on 31 March 2008.

Balance sheets as on 31 March 2008
RS Ltd and XY Ltd

Liabilities	RS Ltd (₹000)	XY Ltd (₹000)	Assets	RS Ltd (₹000)	XY Ltd (₹000)
Share capital: equity shares of ₹100 each fully paid up	2,000	1,000	Fixed assets net of depreciation	2,700	850
Reserves and surplus	800	–	Investments	700	–
10% Debentures	500	–	Sundry debtors	400	150

(Continued)

Balance sheets as on 31 March 2008
RS Ltd and XY Ltd   (*Continued*)

Liabilities	RS Ltd (₹000)	XY Ltd (₹000)	Assets	RS Ltd (₹000)	XY Ltd (₹000)
Loan from financial institutions	250	400	Cash and bank	250	–
Bank overdraft	–	100	Profit and loss account	–	800
Sundry creditors	300	300			
Proposed dividend	200	–			
Total	**4,050**	**1,800**	**Total**	**4,050**	**1,800**

It was decided that XY Ltd will acquire the business of RS Ltd for enjoying the benefit of carry forward of business loss. After acquisition, XY Ltd will be renamed as XYZ Ltd.

The following scheme has been approved for the merger:

- XY Ltd will reduce its shares to ₹10 and then consolidate 10 such shares into one share of ₹100 each (new share).
- Financial institutions agree to waive 15% of the loan of XY Ltd.
- Shareholders of RS Ltd will be given one new share of XY Ltd in exchange of every share held in RS Ltd.
- RS Ltd will cancel 20% holding of XY Ltd. Investments were held at ₹250,000.
- After merger, the proposed dividend of RS Ltd will be paid to the shareholders of RS Ltd.
- Authorized capital of XY Ltd will be raised accordingly to carry out the scheme.
- Sundry creditors of XY Ltd includes payable to RS Ltd ₹100,000.

Analyse the accounts of RS Ltd. Prepare a balance sheet of XYZ Ltd showing relevant working notes.

Solution

XY Ltd is a financially sick company. It is going through internal reconstruction and trying to takeover RS Ltd, which is a sound company. This is thus a case of reverse merger. RS Ltd is already holding certain shares in XY Ltd, the value of which will be reduced first; while discharging the purchase consideration, the number of shares will be reduced.

Effect of reconstruction on XY Ltd:

Share capital before reconstruction:	
10,000 shares of ₹100 each	1,000,000
After reconstruction:	
10,000 shares of ₹10 each	100,000
After consolidation:	
1,000 shares of ₹100 each	100,000

Note: Money measurements are in rupees.

Effect of reconstruction on RS Ltd:

Share held in XY Ltd before reconstruction:	
2,000 shares of ₹100 each	200,000
After reconstruction:	
2,000 shares of ₹10 each	20,000
After consolidation:	
200 shares of ₹100 each	20,000

Note: Money measurements are in rupees.

Purchase consideration:

Share capital of RS Ltd	2,000,000
Shares to be given in XY Ltd in the ratio of	1:1
Therefore shares of ₹100 each to be issued	20,000
Less: Already held	200
Net shares to be issued	19,800
Face value per share	100
Amount of purchase consideration = 19,800 × 100	**1,980,000**

Note: Money measurements are in rupees.

Analysis of the accounts of RS Ltd

Profit and loss on reconstruction:

Fixed assets	2,700,000
Investment (excluding the shares held in XY Ltd)	450,000
Sundry debtors	400,000
Bank	250,000
Total assets	**3,800,000**
Debentures	500,000
Loans	250,000
Sundry creditors	300,000
Proposed dividend	200,000
Purchase consideration	1,980,000
Total liabilities	3,230,000
Loss	**570,000**

Note: Money measurements are in rupees.

Status of shareholders:

Share capital opening	2,000,000
Reserves and surplus	800,000
Total	**2,800,000**
Less: Decline in the value of investment in XY Ltd	230,000
(Held – New shares allotted) = (2,50,000 – 20,000)	
Less: Loss as above	570,000
Equity shares in XY Ltd	**2,000,000**

Note: Money measurements are in rupees.

Shares in XY Ltd:

Opening balance	250,000
Purchase consideration	1,980,000
Less: Loss on investment in XY Ltd	230,000
Equity shares in XY Ltd	**2,000,000**

Note: Money measurements are in rupees.

Balance sheet after reconstruction/merger
XYZ Ltd

Liabilities	Amount (₹)	Assets	Amount (₹)
Share capital:		Fixed assets	3,550,000
20,800 equity shares of ₹100 fully paid (of the 19,800 shares issued for consideration other than cash)	2,080,000	(₹2,700,000 + ₹850,000)	
Reserves and surplus:		Investments	450,000
Capital reserves	160,000		
Other reserves	570,000		
Loans and advances:		Current assets:	
10% Debentures loans	500,000	Sundry debtors	450,000
(₹400,000 – ₹60,000 + ₹250,000)	590,000	(₹400,000 + ₹150,000 – ₹100,000)	50,000
		Cash and bank	
		(₹250,000 – ₹200,000)	
Current liabilities:			
Sundry creditors	500,000		
Bank overdraft	100,000		
	4,500,000		**4,500,000**

4. Chennai Ltd and Kolkata Ltd have agreed that Chennai Ltd will take over the business of Kolkata Ltd with effect from 31 December 2007. It is agreed that

- Shareholders of Kolkata Ltd holding 1 million shares will receive shares of Chennai Ltd. The swap ration is determined on the basis of 26 weeks average market price of shares of both the companies. Average prices have been worked out at ₹50 and ₹25 for the shares of Chennai Ltd and Kolkata Ltd respectively.
- In addition to (a), shareholders of Kolkata Ltd will be paid cash based on the projected synergy that will arise on the absorption of the business of Kolkata Ltd by Chennai Ltd. 50% of the projected benefits will be paid to the shareholders of Kolkata Ltd.

The following projections have been agreed upon by the management of both the companies:

Year	2008	2009	2010	2011	2012
Benefits in ₹ million	5	7.5	9	10	10.5

The benefit is estimated to grow at the rate of 2% from 2007 onwards. It has been further agreed that a discount rate of 20% should be used to calculate the cash that the holder of each share of Kolkata Ltd will receive.

(a) Calculate the cash that holder of each share of Kolkata Ltd will receive.
(b) Calculate the total purchase consideration.

Discounting factors:

Discounting rate	Year 1	Year 2	Year 3	Year 4	Year 5	Year 6
20%	0.833	0.694	0.579	0.482	0.402	0.335
18%	0.847	0.718	0.609	0.516	0.437	0.370
16%	0.862	0.743	0.641	0.552	0.476	0.410

Solution

(a) Computation of cash payment based on projected synergy benefits Present values (PVs) of future cash flows:

Years	Cash flows (₹ million)	PVIF $_{20\%}$ (₹ million)	DCF (₹million)
08	50	0.833	41.65
09	75	0.694	52.05
10	90	0.579	52.11
11	100	0.482	48.20
12	105	0.402	42.21
		Total	236.22

At the end of 2012, PV of benefits is expected to grow at 2% from 2013.

$$PV = (D_6/K_e - g) \times PVIF$$

where D_6 is the value of cash flows in the 12th year
K_e is the discounting rate, i.e., 20%
g is the expected growth rate of the company
PVIF is the present value of cash inflows
Therefore

$$(105 \times 1.02/0.20 - 0.02\ ) \times 0.402 = 239.19$$
$$\text{Total PV} = 236.22 + 239.19 = ₹475.41 \text{ million}$$
$$50\% \text{ of } 475.41 \text{ to be paid in cash} = ₹237.71 \text{ million}$$

(b) Computation of shares to be issued and total purchase consideration:
Valuation of shares of Kolkata Ltd
1,000,000 × 25 = 25,000,000
Agreed value per share = ₹50
Therefore, total shares to be issued = 500,000
Purchase consideration:

Equity shares – 500,000 @ of ₹25 at ₹50 each	25,000,000
Add cash	23,771,000
Total	48,771,000

5. Alpha Ltd and Beta Ltd were amalgamated on 1 April 2008. A new company Gamma Ltd was formed to take over the business of the existing companies. Here are the balance sheets of Alpha Ltd and Beta Ltd as on 31 March 2008:

Balance sheets as on 31 March 2008
Alpha Ltd and Beta Ltd

Liabilities	Alpha Ltd (₹ million)	Beta Ltd (₹ million)	Assets	Alpha Ltd (₹ million)	Beta Ltd (₹ million)
Share capital:			Fixed assets	120	100
Equity shares of ₹100 each	100	80	Current assets, loans, and advances	88	56.5
15% Preference shares of ₹100 each	40	30			
Reserves and surplus					
Revaluation reserves	10	8			
General reserves	20	15			
Profit and loss account	8	6			
Secured loans:					
12% Debentures of ₹100 each					

(Continued)

Balance sheets as on 31 March 2008
Alpha Ltd and Beta Ltd (*Continued*)

Liabilities	Alpha Ltd (₹ million)	Beta Ltd (₹ million)	Assets	Alpha Ltd (₹ million)	Beta Ltd (₹ million)
Current liabilities and provisions	20.4	9.5			
	208	**156.5**		**208**	**156.5**

Other information:

- 12% Debenture holders of Alpha Ltd and Beta Ltd are discharged by Gamma Ltd by issuing adequate number of 16% debentures of ₹100 each to ensure that they continue to receive the same amount of interest.
- Preference shareholders of Alpha Ltd and Beta Ltd have received same number of 15% preference shares of ₹100 of Gamma Ltd.
- Gamma Ltd has issued 1.5 equity shares for each equity share of Alpha Ltd and 1 equity share for each equity share of Beta Ltd. The face value of shares issued by Gamma Ltd is ₹100 each.

Prepare the balance sheet of Gamma Ltd as on 1 April 2008 using the pooling of interest method.

Solution

Note: Values are in ₹ million unless stated otherwise.

Computation of purchase consideration:

Particulars	Alpha	Beta
400,000 15% preference shares of ₹100 each	400	
300,000 15% preference shares of ₹100 each		300
1,500,000 equity shares of ₹100 each	1500	
800,000 equity shares of ₹100 each		800
Purchase consideration	**1,900**	**1,100**

Total purchase consideration = (1,900 + 1,100)   = 3,000
Less: preference shares issued and equity capital   = 2,500
To be written off against reserves = 3,000 − 2,500   = 500

Profit on settlement with debenture holders:
Debentures to be issued (96 + 80) × 12%/16%   = 132
Book value of debentures as on today   = 176
Profit   = 44

New totals of profit and loss and reserves:
Profit and loss (80 + 60 + 44)   = 184
General reserves (9200 + 150)   = 350
          = 534

Less difference on merger written off as per (1)   = 500
Profit and loss   = 34

While writing off the loss, one should utilize reserves before profit and loss.

Balance sheet as on 1 April 2008
Gamma Ltd

Liabilities	Amount (₹000)	Assets (₹000)	Amount (₹000)
Share Capital:		Fixed assets	2,200
700,000 15% preference shares of ₹100 each	700		
2,300,000 Equity shares of ₹100 each	2300		
Reserves and surplus:		Current assets	1,445
Reserves	180		
Profit and loss	34		
Loans:			
16% Debentures	132		
Current liabilities:	299		
Total	3,645		3,645

The valuation process is, thus, a very lengthy and tedious process, and requires that the persons given the task of determining the value of the target are familiar with the industry and its fundamentals, and have appropriate knowledge about the economy.

The accounting issues have to be handled carefully too. While consolidating the accounts post merger, the provisions of AS 14 and IFRS 3 must be adhered to.

SUMMARY

Valuation is a very critical process. Any loopholes in the process would result is either overvaluing or undervaluing the target. This would obviously affect all the stakeholders and the future prospects of the merged entity. Paying the right price for the entity taken over not only affects the financing of the project, but also its future profitability. The exercise of valuing the entity should be carried out with utmost care, for it does not just affect the present financing of the deal, but can also have serious future repercussions.

While valuation ensures that the real value of the entity gets determined, accounting issues ensure that the deal gets reflected in the most appropriate and transparent manner adhering to all the statutory provisions spelt out in this regard.

KEY DEFINITIONS

Amalgamation in the nature of merger   This is a situation where there is a polling of just not the assets and liabilities, but also the interests of shareholders and of the business of the two entities merging with each other.

Amalgamation in the nature of purchase   This is a situation where one company acquires another company, as a result of which the shareholders of the company which is acquired do not continue to possess interest in the equity of the combined entity in a proportion that they held the shares in the liquidated company.

Asset-based valuation The method involves estimation of the value of corporate assets, as if they have been with the bidder. The assets that are valued include the net fixed assets, intangible assets, investments, current assets, and all third party liabilities.

Direct comparison approach This method is based on the assumption that similar assets sell at similar prices. As such, one can ascertain the value of an asset by checking the price of comparable assets in the market.

Discounted cash flow (DCF) method DCF represents the present value of the expected cash flows generated through an asset that are discounted at a discount rate that reflects the risk involved in earning these cash flows.

Earning-based valuation Here the future maintainable earnings (FME) of the target company are estimated after adjusting the extraordinary items, if any.

Free cash flows to equity The cash flows that are ascertained after deducting the cash outflows on account of all types of debt are termed free cash flows to equity. These are thus cash flows that are available for distribution among equity holders.

Free cash flows to the firm The after-tax operating earnings of the company are termed as free cash flows to the firm. These are pre-debt cash flows generated for all claim holders in the firm.

Market-based valuation This method of valuation is the value arrived at by comparison of the target company's market variables and other comparables with that of industry.

Nominal cash flows The cash flows that incorporate expected inflation are termed as nominal cash flows. These are expressed in specific currencies and as such vary across currencies.

Non-cash consideration The purchase consideration may be discharged through cash and non-cash elements. The non cash element includes securities or other non-cash elements.

Post-tax cash flows These are cash flows arrived at after deducting the tax payable by the investors, that is, tax on dividend and capital gains for equity investor shareholders and tax on interest for debt investors.

Pre-tax cash flows Such cash flows are calculated after paying corporate taxes but before the tax payable by investors.

Real cash flows The cash flows that do not incorporate the inflation component are termed real cash flows.

Shares and debt approach This method is followed when the securities of a company are publicly traded. Here, the value can be obtained by merely adding the market value of all its outstanding securities.

Valuation It is a process of determining the monetary value of the target giving due consideration to economic and environmental factors.

Valuation of assets This term refers to the present value of the future cash flows from the use of the assets concerned.

Valuation of equity It is the valuation of the equity stake in the business. The value of equity can also be determined by subtracting the value of the all the non-equity claims from the value of a going concern.

Valuation of going concern When the sum total value of all the assets owned by the business is considered, we get the value of a going concern. A going concern is an entity that already owns assets that are deployed for generating cash flows.

CONCEPT REVIEW QUESTIONS

6.1 Explain the concept of valuation. State and explain the three fundamental concepts of valuation.

6.2 What are the factors to be considered for the purpose of valuation? Explain.

6.3 State and explain the different methods of valuation.

6.4 Is DCF the same in the valuation of all investment?

6.5 Enumerate the key features of AS 14.

6.6 What are the key features of IFRS 3?

6.7 Write notes on the following:
   (a) Asset-based valuation
   (b) Earning-based valuation
   (c) Market-based valuation
   (d) Book value approach
   (e) Shares and debt approach
   (f) Direct comparison approach
   (g) Discounted cash flow method
   (h) Expected cash flows
   (i) Methods of amalgamation as per AS 14
   (j) Pooling of interest method
   (k) Purchase method
   (l) Accounting for amalgamation under AS 14

NUMERICALS FOR PRACTICE*

1. Ram Ltd and Krishna Ltd had the following financial position as on 31 march 2010:

Balance sheets as on 31 March 2010
Ram Ltd and Krishna Ltd

Liabilities	Ram Ltd (₹)	Krishna Ltd (₹)	Assets	Ram Ltd (₹)	Krishna Ltd (₹)
Share capital:			Goodwill	500,000	100,000
Equity shares of ₹100 each	800,000	600,000	Fixed assets	400,000	700,000
General reserves	300,000	200,000	Investments at cost	300,000	200,000
Statutory reserves	–	300,000	Current assets	300,000	250,000
Sundry liabilities	400,000	150,000			
	1,500,000	1,250,000		1,500,000	1,250,000

It was decided that Ram Ltd will take over the business of Krishna Ltd on the basis of the respective share values adjusting, whenever necessary, the book value of assets and liabilities on the strength of information given as follows:

- Investments of Krishna Ltd included 1,000 shares in Ram Ltd acquired at a cost of ₹150 per share. The other investments of Krishna Ltd have a market value of ₹25,000.
- Goodwill of Ram Ltd and Krishna Ltd are to be taken at ₹400,000 and ₹200,000, respectively.
- The market value of investments of Ram Ltd was ₹200,000.
- Current assets of Ram Ltd included ₹80,000 of stock in trade obtained from Krishna Ltd which they normally sold at a profit of 25% above cost.
- Fixed assets of Ram Ltd and Krishna Ltd are valued at ₹500,000 and ₹750,000, respectively.

Suggest the scheme of absorption and prepare the balance sheet of the company after takeover of the business of Krishna Ltd.

2. The balance sheets of Big Ltd and Small Ltd as on 31 March 2008 were as follows:

Balance sheets as on 31 March 2008
Big Ltd and Small Ltd

Liabilities	Big Ltd (₹)	Small Ltd (₹)	Assets	Big Ltd (₹)	Small Ltd (₹)
Equity share capital (₹10 each)	800,000	300,000	Building	200,000	100,000
10% Preference share capital (₹100 each)	–	200,000	Machinery	500,000	300,000

(Continued)

* All numericals for practice have been adapted from real situations and companies.

Balance sheets as on 31 March 2008
Big Ltd and Small Ltd (*Continued*)

Liabilities	Big Ltd (₹)	Small Ltd (₹)	Assets	Big Ltd (₹)	Small Ltd (₹)
General reserves	300,000	100,000	Furniture	100,000	60,000
Profit and loss account	200,000	100,000	Investments 6000 shares of Small Ltd	60,000	–
Sundry liabilities	200,000	300,000	Stock	150,000	190,000
			Debtors	350,000	250,000
			Cash and bank	90,000	70,000
			Preliminary expenses	50,000	30,000
	1,500,000	1,000,000		1,500,000	1,000,000

Big Ltd has taken over the entire undertaking of Small Ltd as on 30 September 2008. On this date, the position of current assets except cash and bank balances and current liabilities were as under:

Assets	Big Ltd (₹)	Small Ltd (₹)
Stock	120,000	150,000
Debtors	380,000	250,000
Creditors	180,000	210,000

Profits earned for the half year ended 30 September 2008 after charging depreciation at 5% on building, 15% on machinery, and 10% on furniture are as follows:

Big Ltd　　₹102,500
Small Ltd　₹54,000

On 30 September 2008, both companies have declared 15% dividend for 2007–08. Goodwill of Small Ltd has been valued at ₹50,000 and other fixed assets at 10% above their book values on 31 March 31, 2008. Preference shareholders of Small Ltd are to be allotted 10% preference shares of Big Ltd and equity shareholders of Small Ltd are to receive the requisite number of equity shares of Big Ltd valued at ₹15 per share in satisfaction of their claims. Show the balance sheet of Big Ltd as of 30 September 2008 assuming that absorption is through by that date. You may take depreciation on book value for the purpose of calculating the purchase consideration.

3. It has been decided that PURU Ltd will absorb the entire undertaking of SHO Ltd and THAM Ltd. The outside shareholders in the latter companies are to be issued equity shares in PURU Ltd on the basic agreed issue price of ₹20 per share. For this purpose, the interests of such shareholders are to be determined according to the intrinsic values of the shares of the respective companies. AN Ltd is a

subsidiary of THAM Ltd and is also to be merged into PURU Ltd appropriately. The balance sheets of the companies stood as follows as on 31 March 2009:

Balance sheets as on 31 March 2009
PURU Ltd, SHO Ltd, THAM Ltd, and AN Ltd

	PURU (₹ million)	SHO (₹ million)	THAM (₹ million)	AN (₹ million)
Sources:				
Share capital: equity shares of ₹10 each	1,500	1,000	800	400
Reserves	2,000	540	702	400
Loans	1,600	900	1,000	700
	5,100	**2,440**	**2,502**	**1,500**
Application:				
Land	200	100	50	10
Buildings	500	400	100	400
Machinery	1,500	800	500	500
Other fixed assets	400	100	200	50
Investments:				
40 million shares of SHO	500	–	–	–
20 million shares of THAM	300	–	–	–
40 million shares of AN	–	–	400	–
Others	100	–	–	–
Net current assets	1,600	1,050	1,252	740
	5,100	**2,440**	**2,502**	**1,500**

For the purpose of the scheme, it is agreed to give effect to the following value appreciations of the assets of the companies to be absorbed.

Land   100%
Buildings   50%
Machinery   20%

In order to obtain the consent of the creditors of THAM Ltd, it becomes necessary to accept a claim of ₹20 million hitherto classified as contingent, 60% of the claim is accepted by THAM Ltd and the balance is to be settled by PURU Ltd.

You are required to

(a) Compute the number of shares to be issued by PURU Ltd to eligible outsiders.

(b) Show the balance sheet of PURU Ltd after the absorption.

4. AB Ltd and MB Ltd decide to amalgamate and to form a new company AM Ltd. The following are their balance sheets as on 31 March 2008:

Balance sheets as on 31 March 2008
AB Ltd and MB Ltd

Liabilities	AB Ltd (₹)	MB Ltd (₹)	Assets	AB Ltd (₹)	MB Ltd (₹)
Share capital (₹100 each)	1,000,000	600,000	Fixed assets	750,000	200,000
General reserves	100,000	50,000	Investments:		
Statutory reserves	40,000	30,000	1500 shares in MB Ltd	350,000	–
12% Debentures	300,000	100,000	4000 shares in AB Ltd	–	500,000
Sundry creditors	60,000	20,000	Current assets	400,000	100,000
	1,500,000	800,000		1,500,000	800,000

Calculate the amount of purchase consideration for AB Ltd and MB Ltd and draw up the balance sheet of AM Ltd after considering the following:

- Assume amalgamation is in the nature of purchase.
- Fixed assets of AB Ltd are to be reduced by ₹50,000 and that of MB Ltd are to be taken at ₹300,000
- 12% debenture holders of AB Ltd and MB Ltd are discharged by AM Ltd by issuing such number of its 15% debentures of ₹100 each as to maintain the same amount of interest.
- Shares of AM Ltd are of ₹100 each.

Show how the statutory reserves will be treated in the financial statements assuming the reserves will be maintained for 3 years.

5. The following balance sheets of X Ltd and Y Ltd, as on 31 March 2010, are given to you:

Balance sheets as on 31 March 2010
X Ltd and Y Ltd

Liabilities	X Ltd (₹)	Y Ltd (₹)	Assets	X Ltd (₹)	Y Ltd (₹)
Equity share capital (₹100 each)	1,500,000	500,000	Fixed assets	1,000,000	50,000
12% Debentures	–	300,000	Sundry debtors	290,000	150,000
General reserves	200,000	100,000	Stock	480,000	210,000
Profit and loss account	160,000	10,000	Investments:		
Current liabilities	200,000	90,000	1000 shares in Y Ltd	150,000	–

(Continued)

Balance sheets as on 31 March 2010
X Ltd and Y Ltd   (*Continued*)

Liabilities	X Ltd (₹)	Y Ltd (₹)	Assets	X Ltd (₹)	Y Ltd (₹)
			3000 shares in X Ltd	–	500,000
			Cash and bank	140,000	90,000
	2,060,000	**1,000,000**		**2,060,000**	**1,000,000**

Y Ltd traded in raw materials that were required by X Ltd for manufacture of its products. Stock of X Ltd includes ₹100,000 for purchase made from Y Ltd which the company made at a profit of 20% on selling price. X Ltd owed ₹40,000 to Y Ltd in this respect. It was decided that X Ltd should absorb Y Ltd on the basis of the intrinsic value of the shares of the two companies. Before absorption, X Ltd declared a dividend of 8%. X Ltd also decided to revalue the shares in Y Ltd before recording entries relating to the absorption.

Prepare its balance sheet immediately thereafter. All workings should form part of your answer.

PROJECT ASSIGNMENT

Analyse the valuation of the Reliance Power and RNRL merger. Do you think the RNRL share-holders got a fair deal? Justify.

REFERENCES

Damodaran, A., *Damodaran on Valuation—Security Analysis for Investment and Corporate Finance*, 2nd edition, John Wiley and Sons Inc., Boston, 2002, pp. 79

Kumar, M.P.V., *First Lessons in Accounting Standards*, 10th edition, Snow White Publications, Mumbai, 2010, pp. 245–246

7 Post-merger Issues

LEARNING OBJECTIVES

After studying the chapter, you will be able to understand

- the concept of integration in mergers
- the tools for integration
- post-merger growth strategies
- the human side of mergers and acquisitions

7.1 INTRODUCTION

In the earlier chapters, we have discussed the concept of mergers in great detail. Though mergers result in an increase in the new organization's resources and workforce, they do affect the efficient functioning of the newly merged entity. This transformation is a critical period for the organization and the workforce, which experiences extra pressure and responsibility in the form of problems of job security, identity crises, etc. Hence, it is important to motivate the employees and show them the brighter side of the merger and how it would benefit them.

Equally true is the fact that a merger and acquisition (M&A) may not always cause disorientation in the combined organization. There are several examples where two or more organizations have merged in a harmonious fashion, resulting in a bigger and more efficient entity.

A combined organization enjoys an edge over its competitors, and has better opportunities of growth. However, this may not be possible without paying adequate attention to the grievances and training of the workforce, alignment of diverse processes, and utilization of all the critical information. In addition, proper assessment of the time and method of the merger is highly essential to facilitate successful merger of organizations. This chapter focuses on integration issues in M&As.

7.2 CONCEPT OF INTEGRATION IN MERGERS

Integration in M&As can be summed up by the catchphrase 'make him like me'. A merger proposal involves negotiation with the target company's manager/directors to facilitate a smooth deal between the entities. Mergers and acquisitions involve bringing people and organizational structures of more than one type under single control and effect their unification. Easier said than done, this is one of the most complex tasks in the process of M&A. Along with the resources, a newly formed organization also inherits a stock of liabilities. Dealing with these issues and the integration of various processes is critical for the survival of the new organization.

Mergers and acquisitions have the potential to enhance shareholder value by creating cost advantages, increase in revenue, increase in market penetration, and/or intangible synergies, or a combination of these. Unfortunately, most organizations fail in effectively executing the integration process. They are also unable to handle the problems that can occur almost anywhere, during the prolonged process of integration.

Mergers represent important transformations in organizations that, if not properly managed, can create disruptions and destroy a firm's value. To achieve the anticipated value creation and to preserve this intrinsic value, the integration stage must be aggressively managed and the sources of value need to be focused on.

It is during this integration process that entities realize synergies that result in improved earnings and cash flow that create value. The entire process of M&A focuses on theoretical forecasting exercises until the integration process commences. It is during integration that teams are rebuilt, capabilities are developed, and people are motivated to drive the integration process.

The process involves the following aspects:

- Managing multiple cultures
- Innovating
- Building new teams
- Managing the complex change process

The objectives intended to be achieved during the process of integration include completing analytical activities not completed prior to closing, integrating the target, and rebuilding the organization into a stronger, more competitive entity that is capable of creating value. This is why it is said that an M&A is a theoretical forecasting exercise until the integration process commences.

To complicate matters further, each M&A is unique. However, there are activities that are common to most M&A integrations:

- Demonstrating a committed and open-minded leadership
- Building teams and work units
- Focusing on financial and strategic objectives
- Remaining flexible
- Providing for capable and motivated teams
- Assimilating new people and achieving cultural integration

Some common challenges that organizations face in the process of integration include the following:

- Getting employees to embrace change
- Sharing information and fostering corporate understanding

- Implementing the process and cooperating during its duration
- Setting priorities
- Combining corporate functions and internal processes
- Measuring results

Organizations can mitigate these challenges and achieve value creation by effectively using project management, performance measurement, and continuous improvement methodologies.

7.3 ISSUES INVOLVED IN INTEGRATION

It is increasingly understood that what ultimately makes mergers or alliances work are the people and the collective cultures of the companies that are merging. This calls for working towards and attaining effective post-merger integration. Corporate history shows that integration is easier said than done. When different mindsets and differing corporate cultures come together, the task becomes all the more challenging.

This fact is substantiated by a study of the Global Workshop Group titled 'Global Mergers and Acquisitions Integration' that states, 'Research evidence going back to the 1970s suggests that M&As have an unfavourable impact on profitability. They are strongly associated with lowered productivity, labour unrest, higher absenteeism, and higher accident rates. According to the study referred to, 50% to 80% of all M&As turn out to be financially unsuccessful. This includes mergers in which the two firms were rooted originally in the same national culture.'

Some related facts are as follows:

- Information published on CnetG in 2000, referring to the findings of *CEO Magazine, Business Week*, and *Fortune*, claims that '75% of mergers and acquisitions are disappointing or outright failures. 50% experience a decline in productivity in the first four to eight months. 47% of senior executives in acquired firms leave in their first year, 75% in the first 3 years.'
- Another study done by Coopers & Lybrand (1996) indicated that 85% of failed/troubled mergers are due to differences in management style and practices.
- Other statistics from KPMG (1987), Accenture (2002), and McKinsey (2006) indicate the following:
  - 50% drop in productivity in the first 6–8 months
  - 47% of top management leave within the first year
  - 62% show zero growth over a three-year period

Research also indicates that senior executives rate 'lack of understanding of the importance and difficulty of integrating cultures' as a major cause of integration failure (www.globalworkshop.com).

While statistics would make anybody believe that M&As do not add value as perceived, it would be wrong to generalize results. What one needs to understand here are the causes behind these unfavourable results. The common causes include the following:

- Failure to align leadership, management, and supervisory practices with the new combination's core values
- Absence or lack of guidance about managing the 'people factor' to maintain productivity and job satisfaction
- Failure to facilitate multi-directional knowledge transfer and organizational learning within the new combination
- Failure to redesign core work processes in a way that involves the employees
- Failure in the selection of appropriate personnel for cross-border and cross-unit assignments
- Lack of global competencies in key managers and supervisors
- Failure to re-conceptualize performance management and career planning
- Failure to align differing benefits and compensation packages
- Failure to facilitate the productivity of geographically dispersed 'virtual' teams
- Slow decision-making process
- Failure on the part of the CEO and other top-level executives to provide coaching or mentoring to subordinates in preparation for a deal

These factors infuse stress and anxiety in the combined organization and encourage power politics. They also prevent proper information-sharing. Thus, one finds all the ingredients of a system breakdown in such organizations.

7.4 TOOLS FOR INTEGRATION

The post-merger integration phase covers the operational part of the merger project. Often, this phase decides if the merger becomes a success or failure. Many of the critical success factors of the integration phase are also referred to as soft factors. Therefore, it is necessary to focus attention on the following issues (Recklies 2001):

- Communication of the new strategic objectives and the new vision of the merged organization
- Implementation of a new shared corporate and management culture
- Development of a new management structure for the new, larger organization, especially overcoming leadership problems in very large units
- Integration of formerly separate units from both former organizations
- Harmonization of management compensation and management incentive systems
- Overcoming language barriers and country-specific cultural differences
- Overcoming staff's suspicions of the other organization—the 'us vs them' syndrome
- Filling of management positions

- Allocation of responsibilities
- Knowledge transfer among units that are to be integrated
- Maintenance of customer relationships during integration phase

These arguments clearly indicate that the success of M&As is greatly influenced by effective integration. Organizations, therefore, need to take care of the factors discussed in Sections 7.4.1–7.4.6 to facilitate successful integration.

7.4.1 Mission and Vision

Research by A.T. Kearney done in the late 1990s suggested that the vision of the merged entity has a critical function in post-merger integration. It is very important for a merged company to get out of the old format and develop a new future strategy, taking into consideration the mission and vision of the merged organization as well. The new organization must exploit new opportunities and take critical decisions. However, unless the stakeholders understand the vision of the new entity, they would hesitate to invest their time, effort, and money in the entity (Recklies 2001). Therefore, it is critical that leaders decide on the new vision and values for the newly formed entity. One needs to remember that positivity in relation to a merger spreads from leaders to workers.

The term vision' is misunderstood in most organizations. In business, several concepts—from strategy to operational plans—are often interpreted as the vision of the entity. The ever-changing dynamics of the organizational environment thus make vision the most critical element, as it projects organizational thinking and aspirations. For all the merged entities, shared vision is the central element that allows them to gain the support of all the stakeholders (Recklies 2001).

7.4.2 Ensuring Communication

Poor communication, more than any other factor, is often to be blamed when an entity fails in achieving the desired results. The merging entities should practise open and clear communication with each other in terms of knowledge, information, and technical skills. It is the leader's job to bridge the gap between the employees of the merged entities. He needs to ensure that employees are introduced to each other properly and that they make a collective effort to attain the goals of the organization. Communication should not be restricted to employees alone. It should be extended to all the key stakeholders including investors, customers, suppliers, the media, and industry analysts. All of them should be well-informed about the transition happening in the merged entity.

7.4.3 Selecting the Right Leader

To speed up the process of integration, it is crucial to identify a leader quickly, but with due consideration. The right person for the task would be one who does not believe in doing the entire job by himself, but resorts to teamwork. He should be able to allocate the right jobs to the right people at different hierarchies. The success of a leader greatly depends on intelligence, fairness, and objectivity shown in selecting and handling a team. A team should include people from both the companies. A leader should evolve realistic targets and offer incentives for reaching the targets. He should leave no stone unturned to maintain the focus of the integration team on capturing value (Viscio et al. 1999).

7.4.4 Welcoming New Culture

A merged organization should not interpret cultural differences in a negative sense. On the contrary, the differences should be effectively utilized to derive value. The merging entities should ensure that integration is attained not through the prevailing organizational cultures of the merging entities, but through a culture that emphasizes performance. Performance culture can be defined as a practice that focuses and lays stress on efficiency at all levels irrespective of hierarchy. If the merged entity can promote performance culture, attaining integration is just a matter of time.

7.4.5 Team-building

Merger gives way to new teams. The teams that come into existence may have diversity in language, culture, religion, economic background, etc. Differences should not be perceived as a threat; instead, they should be looked upon as a source of value creation. The leader has to play a very important role and needs to encourage coordination and cooperation among the new team members. They should be encouraged to rise above their differences and work together for the growth of the merged organization. They should be made to focus on the new vision of the merged entities.

7.4.6 Capturing Value from Different Sources

The biggest advantage merged entities enjoy is diversity. The diverse characteristic of the workforce and value systems can be used as the basis of capturing value. Diversity provides several key sources of capturing value. Depending on the circumstances of the merger, some will be more valuable than others.

As an example, the following areas can be considered for identifying sources of value (Viscio et al. 1999):

Growth-oriented sources of value

- New products, service offerings, markets, customer segments, and distribution channels
- Enhanced market presence and market capture
- Enhanced product development efficiency, such as leveraged research and development and internal best practices
- Combined technologies or capabilities
- Leveraged sales force
- Increased capture of the value chain

Efficiency-oriented sources of value

- Integrated supply chain
- Leverage procurement volume (product and non-product)
- Production footprint optimization
- Facility optimization
- Vertical integration and de-integration
- Distribution channel optimization
- Sales force optimization
- Headquarters consolidation
- Support function consolidation such as human resources, finance, IT, etc.

Other sources of value

- Financial value such as balance sheet items, taxes, etc.
- Optimized programmes and policies, such as benefits programmes
- Rationalization and/or elimination of special programmes, projects, etc.
- Additional alliances or relationships

Organizations that can address the aforementioned issues effectively can be sure that the merging entities shall integrate successfully.

7.5 STRATEGIES FOR POST-MERGER SUCCESS

Roger Cline, Director of Hospitality Consulting Services of the erstwhile Arthur Andersen, suggested the following strategies for the success of mergers by challenging odds on the post-merger integration success (Cline 2003):

- Provide visible leadership from top management.
- Ensure that the transition follows a structured and phased approach.
- Ensure that goals are clearly defined and progress is tracked.
- Manage change from the outset.
- Use best practices to drive the creation of the new organization and its business processes.
- Use cross-functional teams to drive the merger.
- Ensure that communication is well-planned and coordinated.
- Recognize that a merger is fraught with risk—avoid taking too much for granted.
- Focus on adding value to the enterprise, while avoiding those actions that can destroy it.
- Avoid the compromises that result from playing to politics.
- Concentrate on key employee retention—some employees may not have the same roles as before, but their value should be recognized and their egos nurtured.
- Identify the leadership who will make the merger work. It is a very tough process and not always suitable for managers who have proven to be best at organic growth.

- Do not leave culture clashes left unchecked—culture can be pervasive and the differences between two merged companies can undermine the best laid plans for collaboration.
- The 'cultural migration' to the desired organizational behaviour is best achieved by a visible example along with continuous reinforcement.
- Information technology systems are frequently incompatible—it is best to come to grips with this reality sooner than later.
- Recognize the importance of the company's customers and its own people. Mergers offer great opportunity for competitors to raid the company for its best people and customers.
- Focus on the 80/20 rule—see Exhibit 7.1.
- Avoid over-analysis. When one has a tendency to over-analyse, one is influenced by the desire to be perfect. Excessive focus on perfection is generally ineffective. The delay it causes encourages resistance to change which undermines the plans that are eventually implemented.
- Finally, do not miss revenue enhancement opportunities that come through cross-selling and the development of new products and services for the expanded customer base.

Exhibit 7.1 Pareto principle or 80/20 rule

The Pareto principle was suggested by Joseph M. Juran who named it after Italian economist Vilfredo Pareto. The rule states that roughly 80% of the effects come from 20% of the causes. Pareto undertook a study in 1906 in which he observed that 80% of the land in Italy was owned by 20% of the population. He further observed that 20% of the pea pods in his garden contained 80% of the peas. The principle is applicable in business where common observation shows that 80% of sales revenue comes from 20% of the customers. Similarly, 80% of the work is done by 20% of the staff.

7.6 POST-MERGER GROWTH STRATEGIES

All merger interventions are complex change initiatives, and post-merger integration activities are the key elements of successful changes. A structural plan is required for the post-merger period. The management should be aware of all the types of outcomes. Extensive planning is required not only before the mergers, but even after the merger deals are done. Facts and research support that 70% of the outcome of a merger depends upon the way activities are handled during the post-merger period. Managements should be well prepared not only for the changes, but also for the outcome of the changes. Any ignorance on the part of companies to develop a merger integration plan, taking it for granted that after the merger other adjustments will happen automatically is a big mistake.

In this discussion, we have been stressing on the fact that the process of integration is very complex, time-consuming, and full of challenges. This is because during the process of integration one is required to carry out the following crucial activities:

- Manage expectations.
- Communicate decisions through the right channels in a timely manner.
- Give consistent messages about strategies to all stakeholders.
- Assign management change agents, so that they facilitate change and ensure that all hurdles in the process are removed.

A company that is unable to create a trusting environment falters in the very first stage, making the process difficult to complete. Creating an environment where the stakeholders feel safe and satisfied helps companies to introduce and sustain change and make it part of the corporate structure.

The post-merger growth of the entity depends on the following elements.

7.6.1 Effective Human Resource Strategies

It is the moral responsibility of the merged entities to communicate changes openly at the right time with all the levels of the organization. The reason is that the bottom of the organizational pyramid gets most affected by mergers. Employees should be effectively motivated to support the changes which arise due to mergers.

7.6.2 Social and Cultural Integration

Merged companies should take special care to promote social and cultural activities to bridge the differences across the organizations and among the employees. Questionnaires and interviews are of great help in knowing the views and ideas of the organization employees. They aid in accelerating the integration process.

7.6.3 Reliable Environment for Employees and Customers

Creation of a trusting environment and satisfaction of the customers and employees is another post-merger necessity. To make a change sustainable and make it a part of the corporate structure, a company must provide a healthy and new atmosphere to its employees and customers. Changes are not easily accepted, so it becomes very important that both employees and customers should be slowly introduced to them.

7.6.4 Well-informed Stakeholders

Stakeholders are an important part of any organization. Therefore, the merged organization must keep the stakeholders well informed about the changes that have taken place in the organization, and how the stakeholders would be positively or negatively affected due to these changes.

7.6.5 Expectations Management

The merged organization should be ready to welcome changes at regular intervals. In addition, it should be well prepared to meet the rising expectations of customers, employees, stakeholders, and the market as a whole.

7.6.6 Change Agent

An effective management is the most important change agent. The management can work as an intermediary between the pre-merger and post-merger expectations and ensure that they are met. The management should take care of the following phases of the post-merger integration:

- Identification of the strategies
- Establishment of the integration plan
- Implementation of the plan

Integration guidance and major decisions should be in line with the future vision and development strategy for a post-merger company.

7.6.7 Effective Schedule

It is very important that an effective, quick, and crisp schedule is prepared for post-merger integration. This is because a prolonged post-merger growth strategy might lead to unnecessary rise in costs, which includes time, money, and material costs.

It is very important to have an external and internal growth strategy so that there is a simultaneous growth of the merged company/organization in finance, marketing, sales, personnel matters, etc. Apart from becoming bigger in size, a merged organization should also strive to become better and more efficient in its processes.

7.6.8 Detailed Market Research

An extensive primary and secondary market research is required so that market expectations can be met effectively.

A well-managed merger can help a merged company to create opportunities for higher growth, better profitability, better efficiency, and optimum productivity. In a global and highly competitive market, the issue of post-merger growth strategies gains more importance. Irrespective of the sector in which merger happens—insurance, banking, automobile, retail, or any other sector, post-merger adjustments are crucial for sustainable and profitable growth.

7.7 HUMAN SIDE OF MERGERS AND ACQUISITIONS

A purely economical approach towards mergers fails to consider a key element—the people. A good merger can fail despite good financial or strategic sense, if the human element is ignored (Carey and Ogden 2001). In most mergers, the human side is treated very lightly without realizing that such a move could be catastrophic. By focusing on the human aspect, the risk of failure of the proposed M&A can be reduced to a great extent. Most mergers fail as the expectations of the employees, customers, and clients are overlooked. For the merged entities to work together harmoniously, it is important that the corporate culture of both the companies go hand in hand. Though inherent differences will always be there, the real challenge is in integrating these differences and pursuing the set objectives. It is important to assess the quality of people in both the entities. A successful post-merger integration process requires good governance and healthy management practices, attention to cultural profiles, and focus on individual behaviour. While cultural conflicts can have a strong negative effect on the post-merger integration process, one needs to resolve them at the earliest.

A good merger would have the following features:

- It takes into consideration the people affected by it and involves them in the process of the merger.
- It keeps the employees well-informed.
- The right people are assigned the right tasks.
- Continuous efforts are made to minimize the negative effects of the cultural differences between the employees of the merging entities.
- Continuous measures are initiated to unite people.
- Importance is given to the views and vision of executives of both the sides.
- Talent is recognized and suitably rewarded.
- Employees get continuity in employment and work in a fair environment.
- Queries are not left unanswered.
- It promotes employee satisfaction.
- An honest appraisal of the situation is done and communicated to all.
- The HR department is effective and fair to all.

Once the merger has happened, the people component becomes an important ingredient of success of the merger. The right time to give importance to people is even before due diligence. The people component should be addressed much before the deal is announced. A merger can fail if the organizations decide to quickly change the behaviours that are an outcome of gradual social developments. A holistic approach and a sustainable effort towards change is a better option. A merged organization takes it for granted that everyone is aware of the vision of the merged company. The management may interpret the vision in a different way and employees may perceive an altogether different meaning. A merger can be successful only if the management, employer, and employee have a common understanding of the vision and mission.

People issues are considered to be soft issues, but if they are ignored, an organization can lose its momentum to grow. It can lose its key talents, customers, and perhaps a significant portion of market share. The employees' productivity may also go down. Therefore, they should be given some time to adjust to the new merged atmosphere. Involving employees in cultural and social meetings is a good option before the mergers happen. Employees in both organizations should be continuously updated about changes in relation to wages, compensations, benefits, employment contracts, etc. An effective human capital programme is one in which people are involved in all the phases of M&A transactions—pre-deal, during the deal, and post-deal.

While entities pay a lot of attention to the financial elements, they are often not adequately prepared to tackle critical people issues such as retention of key talent, engaging the customer-facing workforce, communication, remuneration and rewards, and cultural integration.

An international survey of HR managers conducted by global consultant Mercer in 2009 revealed that only around 21% of companies involve HR at the strategy and planning stage of a merger, acquisition, or other similar business transaction (Isely 2009).

The focus of managers is so much on the financial imperatives that they either do not involve HR, or they do it so late that it creates a significant negative impact on the ultimate value and success of the transaction. Increasingly, managements are realizing that human capital has an enormous impact on the company's financial performance, both short- and long-term, and hence, neglecting people issues can aggravate matters and increase the risk of failure.

Mercer has identified three key factors to help companies achieve merger success, and people dimensions play an important part in each. Companies need to ask themselves questions in the following areas (Isely 2009):

Business logic Why is the deal being done and what needs to be achieved? How will we define 'success' and what are the people issues that need to be tackled to achieve success?

Price paid What is the economic baseline and what improvements in post-merger performance do we need to see? What are the people-related programmes that will have a major impact on performance?

Integration How do we translate the strategy to merge or acquire into real value? How will the new organization be established and how can we motivate people to drive sustained success?

In a nutshell, what the management of the merging entities needs to remember is that a successful M&A strategy is one where HR spans all the stages of the transaction—pre-deal strategy and planning, carrying out due diligence, and post-merger integration.

It is clear from this discussion that the process of integration is very crucial to the success of M&As. All companies carry out the process with utmost sincerity, but do not always succeed. Here the observation of Deloitte Consulting sounds very appropriate: 'It is not that companies deliberately set out to leave integrations undone. However, even the most far-sighted integration projects can fall prey to powerful external and internal pressures that prioritize speed, risk avoidance, and immediate cost synergies over the need to make long-term business investments.' (www.deloitte.com)

SUMMARY

While M&As are here to stay, the challenges involved in effectively carrying out the process remain the same, i.e., attaining effective integration of the merging entities.

Failure to integrate all elements of the two entities often results in failure. It defeats the very purpose for which the merger was sought. Managers need to realize that post-merger issues are an integral part of the process and not something apart from it. This belief is sure to change the very manner in which M&As are treated, and can surely make a difference in the success rate.

KEY DEFINITIONS

Growth strategies   Growth strategies are post-merger interventions that aim at rationalizing complex structures of the merging entities and driving change initiatives that spell success.
The following are the key areas of focus:

- Managing expectations
- Communicating decisions using the right channels in a timely manner
- Giving consistent messages about strategies to all stakeholders
- Assigning management as change agents

Human side of M&As   Human resource is the most crucial element of successful mergers. Companies often give undue importance to economic considerations and ignore the human considerations. This is where companies falter and fail to achieve the value intended through the process.
This area focuses on having informed employees, making efforts to minimize the negative effects of the cultural differences, integrating the efforts of the team, identifying the right place for the key talent, etc.

Integration in M&As   Integration in M&As is all about bringing people and organizational structures of more than one type under a single control and unifying them so that the merged entity can function smoothly. The process requires the following:

- Managing of multiple cultures
- Innovating
- Building new teams
- Managing a complex change process

Team-building   Team-building is a process of bringing together individuals possessing diversity in language, culture, religion, economic background, etc., to function as one, setting aside their differences. While the process of integration is difficult, one needs to shed the belief that it is a threat. Integration is a source of value creation.

Value creation   Diversity is one of the biggest advantages of mergers. The diverse characteristics of the workforce and value systems are the real basis of capturing value. Diversity provides several key sources of capturing value:

- Growth-oriented sources of value
- Efficiency-oriented sources of value
- Other sources of value such as the balance sheet items, taxes, optimized policies, and rationalization

CONCEPT REVIEW QUESTIONS

7.1 What do you mean by integration in mergers?
7.2 Discuss some tools of integration.
7.3 'People are an important element of a merger.' Do you agree? Discuss in detail.
7.4 Discuss some post-merger growth strategies.
7.5 A successful merger is one that concentrates on financial and strategic details. Do you agree? If not, what are the other important elements of a successful merger?

7.6 Write notes on the following:
(a) Integration in mergers
(b) Tools of integration
(c) Importance of the human element in mergers
(d) Elements of successful mergers
(e) Strategies for post-merger success

PROJECT ASSIGNMENT

Study three companies where mergers failed due to post-merger mismanagement and clearly identify the elements responsible for failure. What steps could the companies have taken to avoid the failure?

REFERENCES

Carey, D. and Ogden, D., *The Human Side of M&A—How CEOs Leverage the Most Important Asset in Deal-making*, Oxford University Press, New Delhi, 2001

Cline, R., *Strategies for Merger Success*, Arthur Andersen, New York, 2003

http://www.deloitte.com/view/en_US/us/6ef2e33d390fb110VgnVCM100000ba42f00aRCRD.htm, last accessed on 29 September 2010

http://www.globalworkshop.com/merger.html, last accessed on 23 February 2010

http://www.themanager.org/pdf/Merger_Vision.PDF, Vision as Key Factor in Merger Processes, Oliver Reck-lies, Recklies Management Project, 2001, last accessed on 29 September 2010

Isely, K., *M&A ready or not? The Human Factors*, http://www.ceoforum.com.au/articles.cfm/KarenIsely, last accessed on 29 August 2009

Viscio, A.J., Harbison, J.R., Asin, A., and Vitaro, R.P., 'Post-Merger Integration: What Makes Mergers Work?' *Strategy + Business*, 4th Quarter, 1999, http://www.strategy-business.com, last accessed on 16 May 2011

CASE STUDY

Key to Successful Integration

Abstract

The success of M&As depends on how effectively the merging entities are integrated post merger. While the process of merger is difficult, the real issues arise once the two entities merge and try to integrate. Most mergers fail as companies fail to integrate their operations. The case looks at different companies that merged, encountered integration problems, but forged a successful partnership as the integration process was well handled.

Pedagogical Objectives
- To understand and identify factors that drive a successful M&A
- To analyse the cultural issues to successful integration
- To identify the factors one needs to look at minutely to facilitate effective integration

Introduction

Mergers and acquisitions are often carried out with the objective of creating value for the stakeholders of the merged entities. The key reason behind their failure has been that the managements often look for short-term gains, overlooking the long-term benefits and issues. The analysis of M&As in developed economies shows that the strategies employed by such economies were driven by their economic and naval superiority. All the target companies identified for mergers were evaluated in terms of the acquirer's growth and development strategies. The analysis of M&As in developing countries such as India showed that such economies preferred alliances to begin with, acquired entities subsequently, and would then work towards decentralizing the power structure (Sharma 2009).

While M&As were popular, the post-merger integration often turned out to be a difficult process because one would observe tremendous cultural and social gaps between the merging entities, especially if they happened to be from developed and under-developed economies.

What Drives Mergers and Acquisitions?

Mergers and acquisitions are often finalized on the basis of strength of the balance sheet, healthy financial ratios, fit between vision and mission statements (Sharma 2009), favourable regulatory environment, growth aspirations of the acquirer, and suitability of the target in the overall growth plan of the acquirer.

Companies in developed countries have been active in the process of M&As for years now. For Indian companies, the strategy of attaining growth through M&As is very new. Liberalization of the Indian economy opened the flood gates and Indian companies went on a rampage acquiring and merging with entities across the globe. The Cerebrus Report of 2008 indicated that M&A deals in India amounted to $25.6 billion, which is more than the GDP of many developing and under-developed economies of the world. Though the figure is that mind-boggling, the success rate is far from satisfactory. This is because Indian companies continue to repeat mistakes of the past while merging. One of the common areas of default is that companies often overlook the need for improved human skill sets that are required as the merged entity grows. Companies presume that the skill sets required by the merged entity shall remain the same even after merger, which leads to innumerable problems.

Research has highlighted people-related issues, but managers fail to learn from their past mistakes. A survey of KPMG in 1999 highlighted that a successful merger requires the following elements:

• Synergy evaluation
• Selecting the right management team
• Resolving cultural issues
• Improving communication—internal and external
• Integrating the operations of the two entities

If one analyses these elements, one finds that they are all people-related issues, making cultural integration a necessity.

Issues of Cultural Integration

To understand the seriousness of cultural integration, let us consider these M&As:

Sona Group and ThyssenKrupp   Sona Okegawa Precisions Forgings Ltd of the Sona Group acquired German component giant ThyssenKrupp's precision forging business. It made Sona Okegawa Group the largest precision forging group in the world. The merger, it was expected, would create value for global customers by integrating the low cost development and engineering skills of Sona with high levels of productivity and leading technology of ThyssenKrupp.

ThyssenKrupp's unionized workforce resisted the proposal over concerns of job security. Kapur, Sona Group's Chairman, kept communicating with the workforce all along and tried to sell the idea that the attained post-merger expansion would require the existing workforce. He even assured the team that he would analyse the production processes, cultural differences, and performance of the employees at ThyssenKrupp for six months before taking a call on the organizational structure to be finalized post merger. This helped in addressing the concerns of the workforce and paved the way for a smooth integration. Thus, addressing the concerns of the workforce is the key to successful integration.

Standard Chartered Bank and American Express Bank   Standard Chartered Bank (Stanchart) acquired the private banking business of American Express Bank (Amex) in March 2008. The entire focus was put on smooth integration. To begin with, all the employees of

Amex were absorbed and HR issues such as rewards harmonization, compensation and benefits integration, job grades harmonization, and training programmes were addressed in a phased manner. These elements clearly reflected that Stanchart was keen on addressing the cultural issues to make the merger successful.

Amtek Auto and Triplex Kelton Group   Amtek acquired UK-based Triplex Kelton Group, an automotive precision machining company. Amtek had completed 13 overseas acquisitions earlier, and all were quite successful. The strategy behind the success was that they had a task force that dealt with all HR-related issues. This was supplemented by open communication with the employees on various issues of employee concern. The task force would address all the cultural issues in the early days as it believed that was the time people show maximum restrictions. As time passed by, the anxiety levels would fall and integration would be attained with ease.

Alcatel and Lucent   Alcatel was a major GSM player and Lucent a prominent CDMA player. When the two entities decided to merge, they placed HR issues on the top of the agenda and discussed salaries and benefits, designations, and other structural issues sensitively. The companies were aware that on day 1, they would have two executives heading the same function. So it was decided that the best man would continue to hold the designation, the other would be given similar options in regions such as China or Singapore, or be asked to sit back for sometime before a right opportunity was found. The HR head was blunt and stated that the company did not have solutions to every problem, so individuals having problems adjusting to the post-merger situation could take time and gradually move on. The merged entity also initiated the process of imparting specific skills training to the employees to make them understand the technologies of the companies. This step increased the comfort levels of the employees who could work on all types of projects efficiently. This obviously addressed the post-merger blues and made integration easier.

In short, mergers can become successful by addressing the following issues:

- Human issues
- Cost management strategies so as to avoid duplication of processes and activities
- Controlling the speed of integration
- Putting focus on creating value
- Facilitating compulsory retirement scheme (CRS) programmes

Discussion Questions

1. Analyse the cases mentioned with reference to the integration strategies adopted by these companies.
2. Which were the areas left unattended?
3. What consequences would the unattended areas lead to?

Reference

Sharma, A., *Post Merger Acquisitions, Challenges and Solutions—A Contemporary Perspective*, www.ezinearticles.com, pp. 1, last accessed on 22 March 2009

8

Cross-border Acquisitions

LEARNING OBJECTIVES

After studying the chapter, you will be able to understand

- the concept of cross-border acquisition (CBA)
- the need for CBA
- benefits and problems of CBAs
- the need for integration in CBAs

8.1 INTRODUCTION

The globalized business environment has encouraged companies to search for a competitive advantage that is also global in scale. Companies have been quick to respond to the needs of global customers and have started spreading their wings across continents. While deregulation, privatization, and corporate restructuring became a way of life in the 1990s, it resulted in an unprecedented surge in cross-border mergers and acquisitions (M&As).

8.2 CONCEPT OF CROSS-BORDER ACQUISITIONS

Cross-border acquisition (CBA) is the merger of companies that have headquarters in two different countries. Such acquisitions are treated differently from local acquisitions as they are governed by a different set of laws. They are also culturally very different. Some experts argue that mergers of companies with headquarters in the same country but branches across the world should also be treated as CBAs, as even these companies have to integrate operations that are spread across different countries. For example, when Boeing acquired McDonnell Douglas, the two American companies had to integrate their operations in dozens of countries across the world (Finkelstein 1999).

8.3 NEED FOR CROSS-BORDER ACQUISITIONS

The increasing number of CBAs highlights their need and relevance. According to Securities Data Corporation, more than 2,000 CBAs, worth over $252 billion, were announced in 1996. Compared to 1991, this represented a 54% increase in terms of numbers and three times increase in terms of amount (Finkelstein 1999). This figure increased to around $759 billion during 2000–09. This increase clearly indicates the increasing importance of CBAs in the global business landscape.

Every CBA involves two imperatives. First, every merger should create value. Value creation comes through synergy realization that cuts cost and facilitates competitive strategy repositioning to attain growth and increase revenues. Second, the synergy realization and competitive strategy goals cannot be achieved without focusing attention on issues relating to acquisition integration (Finkelstein 1999).

8.4 BENEFITS OF CROSS-BORDER ACQUISITIONS

Cross-border acquisitions are beneficial to both the acquiring company and the target company. The benefits are explained in Sections 8.4.1–8.4.8.

8.4.1 Expansion of Markets

Cross-border acquisitions open new markets for companies. It becomes easier for companies to enter foreign markets and sell their products once the domestic markets are saturated. This helps companies to diversify into markets that provide growth opportunities.

8.4.2 Possibility of Raising Funds Abroad

Cross-border acquisitions also enable the merging entities to tap foreign capital markets. This option ensures the availability of adequate financial resources at reasonable rates.

8.4.3 Synergistic Benefits

The acquiring company also derives synergistic benefits such as effective use of available resources, cost reduction, and reduction in labour force. Synergy increases revenue and thus profitability of the company.

8.4.4 Technology Transfer

Cross-border acquisitions facilitate the transfer of technology from one country to another, which generates benefits for the acquiring entity. It results in the receiving unit assimilating or accumulating new knowledge, thus increasing its productivity. Transfer of technology affects the productivity of the acquired company at least in two ways: generation of new products and improvement of production technology (Ravenscraft and Scherer 1987).

8.4.5 Tax Planning and Benefits

Cross-border acquisitions also result in tax benefits as the acquirer can invest the profits in acquiring another entity, which generates tax benefits because capital investments are dealt with differently. In addition, if the acquiring company takes over the losses of the target company, the same can be adjusted against the profits of the acquirer. This reduces the overall income of the acquirer and helps the acquirer to take advantage of available tax benefits.

8.4.6 Foreign Exchange Earnings

Cross-border acquisitions open new vistas of earning for the company that enters the foreign market. These foreign exchange earnings come in handy for making further acquisitions and acquiring resources and technology for the existing units. This helps the company avoid raising fresh capital from the market or borrowing additional resources. Thus the company is able to maintain its existing capital structure and generate savings, as the cost of capital remains the same.

8.4.7 Countering Recessionary Pressures

Cross-border acquisitions prove beneficial during recessionary times. Since the impact of recession is not the same globally, such companies can supplement the decline in their earnings in one country by their earnings from other markets (in other countries). Overall, the total earnings do not fall as drastically as that of companies that operate only in the local markets.

8.4.8 Greenfield Investments

Many countries encourage inflows of greenfield FDI although there are stringent restrictions imposed on foreign acquisitions. Greenfield investments are encouraged as they are seen to have a positive impact on host countries. For instance, a new research and development (R&D) capacity can be developed in the host country as it creates technological spill-over benefits such as increase in income levels and consumption levels in the local markets.

8.5 DIFFICULTIES IN CROSS-BORDER ACQUISITIONS

While an increase in the number of CBAs is often interpreted as positive, the results noticed on this front are far from satisfactory. When CBA deals are examined closely, one finds that a majority of them are not successful. A study done by economists David J. Ravenscraft and William F. Long (1993) indicated that 89 acquisitions done by American companies between 1977 and 1990 did not improve the operational performance up to one year after the acquisition.

The major problems encountered in CBAs are described in Sections 8.5.1–8.5.9.

8.5.1 Legal Problems

The two merging entities face legal problems as they operate in different countries under different legal frameworks. The acquirer has to fulfil all the legal provisions prevalent in its home country when it acquires another company. The process is made difficult by the fact that the target company may find some legal provisions of the acquirer's country incompatible, resulting in a deadlock. For example, when

Sony Corporation acquired Columbia Pictures in 1989, it had to face numerous legal problems that stemmed from the recruitment of senior management who were under contract at Time Warner (Finkelstein 1999).

8.5.2 Accounting Issues

Companies often realize that the merging entities do not have similar levels and scales of internal control. Absence of internal controls results in financial mismanagement. In addition, accounting standards differ from country to country. When the merger happens, the items of the balance sheet have to be adjusted according to the norms prevalent in the acquirer's country. This makes it difficult for both the companies, as the assets may either appear to be either overvalued or undervalued. For example, when Hindustan Lever Ltd (HLL) merged with Brooke Bond India Ltd (BBIL), the two companies had to harmonize their accounting, as both the companies were following different accounting policies and internal controls. While HLL used US GAAP standards, BBIL prepared its accounts using Indian accounting standards. These two companies are no exception to this variation. Practically every CBA confronts this issue.

8.5.3 Weak Understanding of Fundamentals of Acquired Business

The acquirer may possess a very vague understanding of the fundamentals of the acquired business. This often drives out the anticipated synergistic benefits from the merger. For example, the failure of the merger between US Railroad, Pennsylvania and New York Central (1968), AT&T and NCR, transformation of Daimler Benz into a technology group, and the merger between Deutsche Bank and Dresdner Bank (2000) were solely because the merging entities had different visions and did not make an attempt to understand the business of the target company. This resulted in non-alignment in their visions and hence the attempts failed.

8.5.4 Technological Differences

This is a big problem that companies face in cross-border deals. The technology differences make integration difficult and complex. While one company would like to introduce a superior technology, the other may feel that the consumers in their country are still not ready for such technologically advanced products. This obviously poses a challenge as the former may not like to compromise on the available superior technology like the latter. For example, Columbia Pictures was in movie production, while Sony's competencies were in the movie and television business. While Sony was innovative and believed in developing and using the latest technology, Columbia was a little slow in this respect. Each wanted to stick to its core competencies and technology, thus causing integration problems.

8.5.5 Strategic Issues

Companies entering into CBA have very important issues to resolve, such as deciding which products and services to offer, who will be responsible for making this happen, where cost savings would come from, the division of labour, and issues that would generate potential synergies. These issues often remain unresolved and lead to conflict between the merging entities (Finkelstein 1999).

In recent years, 'strategic' mergers have acquired a bad name, and some pundits have defined strategic mergers as those where the acquiring company overpays. While the price paid for a company is a critical determinant of the success of the resulting acquisition, there is no inherent reason why mergers that are strategically well-conceived should fail. The merger of British Petroleum's (BP) and Mobil's downstream operations across Europe is a case in point. The strategic logic for this deal says that size and market power are required to compete against the other major oil companies and even supermarket chains with gas pumps in Europe. Significant cost savings can be realized by eliminating duplicate facilities and employees, and by rationalizing purchasing and cutting overheads. Although this merger is not without significant integration challenges, it appears to have a solid strategic logic, and indeed is considered a blueprint for similar deals among rivals such as Shell, Texaco, and Amoco. It is also an unusual merger since BP and Mobil are only consolidating their refining and marketing operations in Europe, and remain rivals elsewhere. Nevertheless, estimates of cost savings are in the range of $500 million a year, a figure which, if maintained, will clearly make this merger a success.

8.5.6 Fundamental Differences across Countries

The merging entities also face a set of problems arising from different cultures, values, and operating styles due to their different backgrounds, external environment, and other fundamental differences across countries. These involve corporate governance, job security, regulatory environments, customer expectations, and the country's culture. These differences add to the complexity of CBAs and make the task of managers engaged in the process more difficult. For example, the employees of the merging entities might have differences in work cultures, such as employees being accustomed to easy access to top management, flexible work schedules, or even a relaxed dress code. When the two entities merge, the new management may not approve of such practices. This may cause resentment and shrinking productivity and result in conflict between the partners.

8.5.7 Tendency to Overpay

The price paid by the acquirer to the target company is a critical determinant of the success of an acquisition. But many a time an acquisition goes awry because the acquirer overpays for the target company. When the anticipated synergies do not materialize or get delayed, the acquirer feels the heat and repents on the decision to acquire. The Tatas' decision to acquire Jaguar and Land Rover brands is a good example. This deal is not one that would build economies of scale and help the Tatas reach new markets. The deal had a different motive. For the Tata group, it was a game of reaching out to a brand with some prestige value as part of expanding its global visibility. This motivated the Tatas to pay a hefty amount for the two brands, which as of now seem to be adding no great value to Tata Motors.

8.5.8 Failure to Integrate

Most CBAs run into difficulties because of failure in the integration process. This happens due to poor interaction and coordination between merging firms. For example, the merger of BP and Mobil was expected to generate market power and cost savings through consolidation of their refining and marketing operations in Europe. But integration issues remained, for the two companies merged in Europe but remained rivals elsewhere.

8.5.9 HR Issues

Employee stress and uncertainty is a major issue in CBAs. Some employees tend to leave the merged entities, and others are laid off. Several studies conducted in this area have indicated that often employees leave the company due to attractive opportunities available elsewhere. Feelings of mistrust and stress, perceived restrictions in career plans, and changes in the organizational culture are the other contributing factors. These issues act as a barrier to the success of CBAs. For example, the merger of Bridgestone and Firestone faced tremendous HR issues. The employees of Firestone had a feeling of mistrust and stress, and perceived restrictions in career plans and attacks on established cultural traditions within the merged entity. With these issues playing in their minds, Firestone workers went on a strike when Bridgestone initiated cost-cutting measures to tackle the huge losses incurred. Had the feeling of mistrust and stress been addressed, the strike could have been averted.

8.6 INTEGRATING CROSS-BORDER ACQUISITIONS

Achieving integration is the key to the success of CBAs. Integration is all about realizing the perceived benefit of a merger and putting the merged entity on the path of growth.

Integration requires the following:

* Effective interaction and coordination between merging firms
* Special attention to the HR concerns

To manage integration effectively, companies need to focus on the following considerations:

* Value creation happens only after a deal is done. All the projected synergies and benefits are realized once integration is complete.
* Integration needs to be planned before entering into a deal. Avoiding this planning due to lack of awareness regarding criticality of integration can prove to be disastrous. They have to evolve an appropriate action plan and allocate responsibilities of the various elements of the integration process to suitable persons.

- Provide training to the executives of the acquiring company in areas such as accounting standards, labour laws, environmental regulations and norms, regulation and culture of the acquiring firm's country.
- Develop a clear communication plan to keep the communication channels open throughout the integration process.
- Address the stakeholders' concerns in a proactive manner.

The acquiring company needs to remember two important facts:

- Value creation results from a combination of synergy realization such as increasing revenue, cutting costs, and attaining growth.
- Integration is the only way to achieve synergy realization and competitive strategic goals.

Cross-border acquisitions are becoming common. Globalization and liberalization have made the business environment more conducive for them. Globalization has changed the rules of the game and managers across the globe have gained confidence to compete globally. This has been supplemented by the availability of human resources and willingness to explore business opportunities beyond national boundaries.

SUMMARY

Cross-border acquisitions are becoming very popular due to their capacity to generate additional revenues. Such companies enjoy the benefits of wide market coverage and extensive growth. While CBAs are good, they do not always succeed as companies often fail to adapt to the cultural differences among different markets across the globe. However, if a company can take care of these issues that it has to confront in the foreign market, it can certainly derive the benefits of expansion in operations and synergy and stay ahead of the competitors in the long run.

KEY DEFINITIONS

Cross-border acquisition   Cross-border acquisition is the merger of companies that have headquarters in two different countries.

Greenfield projects   These are projects that are started from scratch and are initiated for the first time.

Integration   Integration means combining parts so that they work together or form a whole. In terms of mergers, it implies pursuing common goals or objectives decided by the merged entity so that they benefit both the entities. It is all about realizing the perceived benefit of a merger and putting the merged entity on the growth path.

CONCEPT REVIEW QUESTIONS

8.1   What are cross-border acquisitions? Why do companies feel the need for cross-border acquisition?

8.2   State and explain the benefits of cross-border acquisitions.

8.3   Why do cross-border acquisitions fail?

8.4   Write notes on the following:
   (a) Need for cross-border acquisitions
   (b) Integration in cross-border acquisitions
   (c) Difficulties faced in cross-border acquisitions
   (d) Greenfield projects

PROJECT ASSIGNMENT

Analyse the failure of Bharti Airtel to acquire MTN. What measures do you think they need to take before making another attempt for cross-border acquisitions?

REFERENCES

Finkelstein, S., 'Safe ways to cross the merger minefield', *Financial Times*, 1999, pp. 119–123

Ravenscraft, D.J. and Scherer, F.M., 'Life after Takeover', *Journal of Industrial Economics*, Volume 36, 1987, pp. 147–156

CASE STUDY

Sony vs Matsushita

Abstract

Cross border acquisitions pose a number of challenges, ranging from legal frameworks to cultural integration and demographic variables. This case deals with the issues that confronted Sony and Matsushita when they planned on forging an alliance to exploit the expansion opportunities available across the globe.

Pedagogical Objectives
- To understand and identify the expansion opportunities companies aim at exploiting when they go for a CBA
- To analyse different strategies adopted by Sony to enter new markets
- To identify the hurdles faced in CBA
- To recommend strategies that work in forging a successful CBA

Introduction

Cross border acquisitions (CBAs) have always posed challenges for global businesses. While CBA is a difficult process, it represents the response of the rapidly consolidating global economy to facilitate M&As beyond domestic boundaries.

Sony vs Matsushita

Masura Ibuka and Akio Morita founded the Tokyo Telecommunication Engineering Company in 1946. The mission was an intelligent initiative of forming a company that would make new technology products in indigenous ways. By 1957, the company had successfully developed the transistor, cassette recorder and pocket sized radio. It was then that the company was re-christened as Sony—derived from the Latin word 'sonus' meaning 'sound'.

In 1967, Sony formed a joint venture with CBS Records to manufacture and sell records in Japan. In 1974, Sony launched the Betamax home video cassette recorder. The product was doing well until Matsushita subsidiary JVC introduced The Video Home System (VHS). The company licensed the VHS to others, a strategy that proved profitable. However, Sony did not follow suit and kept the Betamax format to itself. Another factor that went against Betamax was that it was expensive compared to VHS. In spite of releasing a large number of library titles in the Betamax, Sony suffered. Customers were influenced by price considerations and overlooked the technological superiority of Betamax. Morita conceded this failure, saying that they had failed to put in enough efforts into making a family of products, which Matsushita did so conveniently and with greater ease. What Morita meant was that while Matsushita licensed its technology and expanded, Betamax did not do the same. As a result, Sony was unable to sell a product that was far superior to what the competitor had to offer. This embarrassment did not go well with Sony and the stage was set for an intense battle in the market with Matsushita.

Sony evolved a different strategy and decided to focus on its record library. The company was of the belief that CBS Records would act as the software for its new digital audio tape technology. Therefore, they decided to purchase CBS Records at $1.2 billion. Responding to Sony's strategy, CBS increased its price to $2 billion.

Sony's Takeover of CBS

Some highly placed employees in Sony believed that $2 billion was too much for CBS Records, but Sony went ahead with the purchase in 1988. Sony did not repent its decision as CBS Records business grew and reached $3 billion under the able leadership of Yetnikoff, who became a very important link in the decision-making chain at Sony. He suggested that Sony should acquire a studio to complement its music business.

Sony's Acquisition of Columbia

Sony kept looking for prospective targets and ultimately zeroed in on Columbia Pictures, which had two production units—Columbia and Tri-star, and a very rich library. The interesting part of the deal was that Coca Cola, which owned 49% stake in Columbia, was willing to sell its stake. The then President and CEO of Columbia, Victor Kaufman, however, decided to move out of Columbia after it was bought by Sony. Sony gave the responsibility of choosing the chief for Columbia Pictures to Mickey Schulhof, who was the chief of Sony in North America.

Schulhof shortlisted the names of Peter Guber and Jon Peters, who ran the Guber-Peters Entertainment Company. The reason for settling for these two was their involvement in one of the highest grossing Warner Brothers movie *Batman* that released in 1989. This was despite the negative impression that the two carried in Hollywood. The only hitch was that Sony had to purchase GPEC if it wanted Guber and Peters, who had entered into a five-year contract with Warner Brothers to take care of Columbia Pictures. The deal was ultimately finalized and GPEC was purchased by Sony for $200 million, a premium of 40% above its prevailing market price.

The Deal that Added Fuel to Fire

Post this deal, Columbia Pictures was sold for $27 per share. This purchase meant Sony had to borrow another $1.4 billion, and the cost kept escalating since the interest cost on these borrowings was added on. This was not the end of Sony's agony. While Guber and Peters agreed to join Sony, Steve Ross, the chief of Warner Brothers, refused to let them go, and sued Sony for breach of contract. Warner Brothers finally agreed to withdraw the case against Sony if it agreed to fulfil three demands of Warner Brothers:

- Warner Brothers gets to reclaim the portion of Burbank controlled by Columbia in exchange for the Metro-Goldwyn-Mayer (MGM) group lot.

- It gets 50% equity stake in Sony's Columbia House mail-order music club.
- It gets the rights to distribute Columbia's library over its cable network.

These demands were so futile for Sony that it was called 'Pearl Harbour Revenged'. Ultimately the settlement was made and the cost was estimated to be over $500 million. The agony of Sony did not end here. Guber and Peters added fuel to fire and embarked on a lavish spending spree, and in the process, even the MGM group went through extensive renovations, and spending on production, management, and television ballooned. While the industry average cost of a motion picture was $28 million, Sony had to spend $40 million per picture due to excessive overheads. Sony's revenues continued to be eroded by interest and goodwill charges. The box office bombing of *The Last Action Hero* starring Arnold Schwarzenegger added fuel to fire. This was followed by a string of failures that paralysed the studio. The end result of this mess was the resignation of Guber. Moreover, Sony decided to write off an amount of $3.2 billion related to Columbia Pictures, which wiped out 25% of Sony's shareholder equity. In spite of all this, Sony did not give up hope and embarked on a restructuring process.

Discussion Questions

1. Analyse the key elements of the Sony story.
2. Comment on the acquisition strategy of Sony.
3. Where did Sony go wrong in the process of acquiring Columbia?
4. What restructuring measures would you suggest for Sony?

9 Alternatives to Mergers and Acquisitions

LEARNING OBJECTIVES

After studying the chapter, you will be able to understand

- the concepts of divestitures, strategic alliances, and internal development
- the types of divestitures and the reasons behind them
- the types of strategic alliances and the reasons behind them
- the benefits and weaknesses of strategic alliances

9.1 INTRODUCTION

Companies consistently look for ways to add value to shareholders' wealth. This is done through expansion or contraction of operations. Mergers and acquisitions (M&As) tend to focus on corporate expansion, but companies are often forced to contract or downsize their operations. This occurs when they are performing poorly, the concerned line of operation no longer fits into the company's plans, or the company wants to undo a previous M&A that has failed to deliver value.

Companies have three different alternatives to M&As, apart from several corporate restructuring strategies discussed in Chapter 1 on corporate restructuring. These alternatives are divestitures, strategic alliances, and internal development. The general presumption is that corporate contraction or divestiture has a positive impact on stock prices as it helps the company to get rid of divisions that are no longer adding value and are pulling down the profits of the company. Likewise, alliances help the company to diversify into segments and markets that seem lucrative and thus have the potential to add to the profitability of the company. Companies also opt for internal change/development, which is expected to add value to the operations. All these are probable alternatives to M&As.

This chapter deals with corporate contraction and the methods deployed by a company to determine whether a particular division is worth retaining, or whether the company needs to come out of its shell and explore moving out of its core area of operations. The process is complicated since the company may have its own perspective on the matter and as the decision to adopt a particular strategy is need-driven.

9.2 CONCEPT OF DIVESTITURES

The sale of a part of a firm to another company is referred to as a divestiture. The firm that sells a part receives the payment in cash, marketable securities, or a combination of both. Divestitures are simple exit routes and do not result in the creation of a new entity. They involve simultaneous contraction (of the selling firm) and expansion (of the purchasing firm).

The primary reasons for adoption of divestitures are as follows:

- Certain (saleable) assets do not contribute to the firm's profits; rather, they put extra pressure on its resources.
- Divesting the excess assets can help a firm focus on its remaining assets, thereby increasing the overall efficiency of the enterprise.

Although most firms look forward to opportunities to expand, regulatory measures in the market often restrict such ambitions. Expansion does not always result in a more successful and profitable firm. An unsuitable expansion can adversely affect the firm's existing business. Expansions are particularly risky during recession.

In such an environment, a divestiture can be a good alternative to deal with declining demand, the need for raising funds, and the need to improve cash flows. Divestitures have always formed a small part of the net transactions. However, the early and mid-1970s witnessed a significant rise (up to 54%) in the share of divestitures (Gaughan 2007).

When market conditions started improving, divestitures again slowed down. However, the 2000s again saw an increase in divestitures as the global economy started experiencing a slowdown. Divestitures represent sell-offs of previous acquisitions. This is generally done to correct the common belief that the said acquisition has failed to add value. Research carried out by Kaplan and Weisbach covering 271 companies that had completed acquisitions between 1971 and 1982 showed that 119 of these were divested by 1982. Most of the divested entities were held for an average period of seven years. Further analysis of the motive behind divestitures indicated that diversifying acquisitions were four times more likely to be divested than non-diversifying acquisitions (Kaplan and Weisbach 1992). Another trend observed during the late 1980s was that when M&As slow down, the pace of spin-offs and divestitures increase and vice versa (Gaughan 2007).

9.3 TYPES OF DIVESTITURES

Divestitures are classified into two types—voluntary and involuntary.

9.3.1 Voluntary Divestitures

This is a process wherein the selling entity feels that a certain division is not adding to its profitability, and is diverting the company's attention from more profitable divisions. To refocus its attention on the profitable divisions, the company might decide to divest the unprofitable division. Such divestitures help the company get rid of the unprofitable division's assets and help in improving its overall profitability. They also result in increased cash flows for the company, which could be deployed towards the following:

- Expanding profitable divisions
- Distribution among the shareholders
- Repaying outstanding debt

The divestment of Raymond's synthetics division to Reliance Industries and steel business to ThyssenKrupp, and the divestment of the detergents division by Tata Chemicals are examples of voluntary divestitures.

9.3.2 Involuntary Divestitures

When a firm is compelled to divest itself off a particular asset as a result of a legal dispute, it is referred to as involuntary divestiture. For example, one of the biggest mergers in the history of railways took place in June 1983 when Santa Fe merged with Southern Pacific. However, it was followed by an antitrust petition filed against the merger. In June 1987, the Inter State Commerce Commission (ISCC) adjudged that the merger was against fair competition. It was believed that such a giant firm would reduce competition in the market. Subsequently, the ISCC ordered Santa Fe–Southern Pacific to submit a divestiture plan within 90 days. As a result, the stock prices of Santa Fe registered a steep decline and the firm became a target of a bid by the Henley Group (Gaughan 2007).

9.4 REASONS FOR DIVESTITURE

Divestitures are motivated by a variety of reasons. Some of them are described in Sections 9.4.1–9.4.7.

9.4.1 Unprofitable Division

When a particular division of a company does not contribute to profitability, the company may consider divesting it. It could be bought by another company that can make the division a productive part of its enterprise and use it to increase its own efficiency and profits.

9.4.2 Bad Fit

Sometimes businesses on sale are bought by firms with an intension to enhance their existing efficiency and productivity. However, the purchased asset may not perform as anticipated and turn out to be a bad fit. In such cases, the firm may consider divesting the unfavourable acquired business.

9.4.3 Reverse Synergy

Synergy refers to the added values that result from the combination of assets or businesses. A merger (or acquisition) produces synergy when the value of the combined entity is higher than the sum of the participating units. However, this may not always be the case. Mergers (or acquisitions) can also lead to a decline in the value of the resultant firm. That is, the value of the combined entity becomes lower than the value of the sum of its parts. Such reduction in the value is referred to as reverse synergy. The firm affected by it can choose to divest the acquired asset to generate cash inflows.

For example, United Airlines acquired Hertz, a rental car company, and Westin and Hilton International hotel chains to reap benefits of the combined enterprise. However, the acquisition resulted in reverse synergy as the stock prices of the combined entity started falling. The divestiture involved a hostile bid from Coniston Partners, a New York-based investment firm that believed that the combination of the entities had led to the destruction of value of the separate parts (Gaughan 2007).

9.4.4 Failure to Generate Hurdle Rate of Return

The hurdle rate of return is the minimum threshold that a company uses to evaluate projects or acquired targets. The hurdle rate is generally lower than the firm's cost of capital. When an acquired division fails to generate more than the expected hurdle rate, the parent company might decide to divest the division.

However, before divesting such a division, the parent company analyses the reasons behind non-generation of the hurdle rate of return, which varies with the decline in the industry, increase in cost, unionized labour force, etc.

It is often observed that the management of such companies are reluctant to sell such divisions as they feel it gives the impression of inadequate performance or acquisition of a poor target. They continue to hold on to such divisions for a longer time than justified by their performance (Boot 1992).

9.4.5 Capital Market Factors

Very often, a combined entity has business interests in diverse sectors. Such an entity fails to appeal to all types of investors, thus discouraging them from investing in the combined entity. For example, a combined entity has business interest in fast moving consumer goods (FMCG) and automobiles. Some investors might be interested in investing in FMCG, but may not be keen on investing in the combined entity for they want to stay away from automobiles and vice versa. The end result is that the combined entity carries no appeal for both categories of investors. Both categories of investors however do not mind investing in standalone entities engaged in the sector of their interest, for they have clearer identification and market segmentation. In such a situation, divestiture is the answer. The entity could divest one of the sectors, thus increasing its access to capital markets.

9.4.6 Generation of Cash Flow

A firm, particularly during a financial crisis, resorts to divestiture to generate cash flows. Firms choose to sell a division that owns long-term assets. For example, Chrysler Corporation was compelled to sell off its prized tank division in the face of imminent bankruptcy (1980). Similarly Navistar had to sell its well-performing asset Solar Turbines to Caterpillar Tractors Company to pay off part of its huge debts (Gaughan 2007).

9.4.7 Abandoning Core Business

Every business reaches a stage of maturity, which reduces growth opportunities. An entity that faces this situation diversifies into more profitable areas and finances expansion of such projects by selling off the core business. The business world is full of examples wherein companies have moved away from their core activities. Not all of these have been failures, but the shift has certainly posed a new set of challenges to the entities. Such companies enjoy a strong niche position within a larger market. However, the company may strongly feel that its need to grow is prevented by insufficient growth opportunities in its historic specialty, and it is imperative to venture into the broader arena. Some examples are as follows:

- Greyhound sold off its business just because the management felt the bus business had matured and had no growth potential (Jackson 1984).
- Dell, a $35 billion company with a $3.5 billion cash flow, started looking for growth beyond the PC segment (Zook 2004). It started exploring a range of adjacency initiatives, including low-end switches, printers, and supplies, handheld devices, and even retail kiosks. There is no doubt that a company such as Dell had hundreds of choices given its commanding position, but the company narrowed down on a few, for it felt these products would help the company to maintain the remarkable growth momentum of the past.
- Hillenbrand Industries is another classic example of this situation. Hillenbrand is in two businesses—mechanical hospital beds and caskets. Both markets have been growing at less than 5% per year with Hillenbrand having more than 70% market share in each segment (Zook 2004). The company realized that further growth in its market share was limited, and driven by hospital use and burials. So the company was forced to examine businesses that utilize its basic skills but might be several steps away from its historic cores.
- Enterprise Rent-A-Car is another example. The company enjoyed a commanding market share of replacement rentals from body shops and insurance companies. The company was encountering entrenched competitors in every direction, such as Hertz and Avis in business rentals, Alamo in leisure rentals, PHH and GE Capital in fleet leasing, etc. The company tried to venture into new businesses/locations as a result of this increasing competition. (Zook 2004).

The aforesaid examples clearly indicate that one company's adjacency is another company's core, for markets often have many related customer and product segments.

9.5 BENEFITS OF DIVESTITURES

All corporate restructuring strategies are carried out with the sole objective of creating value and attaining competitive advantage. Divestment is no different. Companies aim at drawing a number of benefits from divestment. Some are now discussed.

- Companies go in for divestiture where justification lies in increased economies of scale and economies of scope. If a steel mill owns a coal mine and also ventures into the road transport business, such an entity could make better use of its coal mine in its own operations, without depending on the road transport business. The company would do well by focusing on the coal mine and divesting its assets in the road transport business.

- Divestiture is also resorted to when companies fail to attain anticipated synergies. While these are related to the concept of economies of scale, they attempt to translate product-specific technologies to entirely different markets. For example, a manufacturer of military aircraft may purchase a company building business jets operating at a loss. This plan is driven by the fact that the company's engineering expertise could be applied to design better and therefore more profitable airplanes for the business and passenger segment of the market. The company may later realize that its expertise can be applied only in manufacturing military aircrafts and other high-speed manoeuvrability and radar-evading designs, but not for making aircraft for private operators. Thus the company is unable to apply the advantages from its knowledge of military technologies to the civilian aircraft market. In this situation, the company may not be able to exploit its strength and capitalize on synergistic benefits. It would be better for the company to divest from the civilian aircraft market.

- Divestiture is very advantageous where business cycles are involved. For example, a paper and lumber company may diversify its operations and start producing certain types of specialty chemicals. This can certainly provide the company with an alternative source of income, unlike the paper and lumber markets that are seasonal in nature. What is even more important to note is that when one sector is unprofitable, the other would provide stability in earnings. This obviously is in the interest of the company. While the industry presumes that this would coincide conveniently, it may not happen every time. If the business cycles do not coincide as presumed in the example, the company might decide to divest from one industry to stem its financial losses and generate capital to pay off its debt, if any. The decision to divest may actually increase the value of the company and it may continue to grow unabated.

- A company may also choose to divest unrelated divisions if the management believes that it can no longer administer the entity being placed on the block efficiently. For example, a steel manufacturer may decide to diversify into manufacturing final products, say automotive components, household appliances, and missiles. It is important to remember that while all the products are made out of the steel manufactured by the parent company, each division may build unique administrative organizations and reflect different cultures based on the markets they serve. The concern here is about the position of the parent company. If the parent company loses its competitive position in steel, all the divisions would suffer. If the parent company were to exit the market, it would have three functionally dissimilar companies. Over a period of time, the management may feel that its assets are not appropriately distributed and may decide to divest one of the divisions that contributes the lowest earnings in proportion to its worth and investment. The funds so realized could then be channelized into the other businesses to make them more effective and profitable.

• Companies also look at divestment as an invaluable strategy of discovering unanticipated economies and synergies through trial and error. For example, a company whose core competency lies in financial control and administrative consolidation might aim to become a fully diversified conglomerate hoping it would add to its profitability. If this does not happen, the company may divest from some of its operations and try to get into another sector.

9.6 STRATEGIC ALLIANCES

Strategic alliances refer to arrangements in which business entities join forces to form a cooperative partnership. Typically neither owns the other, though they often create a third entity (Miller and Dess 1996). In common parlance, strategic alliances are also called joint ventures. Strategic alliances, if approached realistically, can provide companies with meaningful ways of achieving growth through cooperation. It is for this reason that such arrangements are growing at a very rapid pace. For some companies, alliances have become a way of carrying on business. For example, IBM has over 400 alliances with firms ranging from Sears to Apple (Miller and Dess 1996). It is important to note that in each arrangement, the company pursues different goals. Table 9.1 substantiates this point.

Table 9.1   IBM's cooperative arrangements with different partners

IBM partners	Goal
Ferranti	Market penetration of PS/2 systems
Toshiba	Sharing of development costs
DEC, Apollo, and HP	Development of a competitive advantage over Sun and AT&T
Siemens	Sharing of R&D costs
Microsoft	Improvement in competitive position

Source: Adapted from Krubasik, E. and Lautenschlager, H., 'Forming Successful Strategic Alliances in High Tech Business', in *Collaborating to Compete: Using Strategic Alliances and Acquisitions in the Global Marketplace*, Bleeke, J. and Ernst, D., Wiley, New York, 1993, pp. 55–56

What is very important to remember is that strategic alliances make sense when each party has strengths that offset the weaknesses of the other (Schillaci 1993). For example, Dow Corning has always seen performance levels higher than those of its parents, Dow Chemical and Corning Glass (Gaughan 2007).

9.7 WHY DO COMPANIES ENTER INTO STRATEGIC ALLIANCES?

As stated earlier, strategic alliances help in offsetting the weaknesses of one entity with the strengths of the other. Harrigan (1980) has provided a detailed analysis of the goals and motives of strategic alliances, which can be classified into three categories—internal, competitive, and strategic reasons. Let us see the sub-elements under each category.

9.7.1 Internal Reasons

Companies may enter into strategic alliances for the following internal reasons:
- To spread costs and risks
- To safeguard resources which cannot be obtained through the market
- To improve access to financial resources
- To derive benefits of economies of scale
- To gain access to new technologies, customers, and innovative managerial practices

9.7.2 Competitive Goals

The following competitive goals motivate companies to enter into strategic alliances:
- To pre-empt competitors
- To create stronger competitive units
- To influence the structural evolution of the industry
- To respond defensively to blurring industry boundaries and globalization

9.7.3 Strategic Reasons

Companies may enter into strategic alliances for the following strategic reasons:
- To create and exploit synergies
- To transfer technologies and skills
- To diversify and derive related benefits

9.8 TYPES OF STRATEGIC ALLIANCES

Strategic alliances can be structured in a number of ways. Each structure generates benefits and synergies, poses challenges, and leads to conflicts. These elements need to be monitored and managed during the course of implementation of the alliance. Hermann (1994) has suggested six types of alliances that differ from one another in terms of the relationships between partners and the strategic focus of the alliance. Let us now discuss these in brief.

304 Mergers and Acquisitions

Complementary alliance Under this alliance, the partners combine their technologies to diversify their existing products/market portfolios.

Market alliance This alliance aims at combining the market knowledge of one partner with the production or product know-how of the other.

Sales alliance Here the producer and a local partner cooperate in an arrangement that is a mixture of independent representation and own branch.

Concentration alliance Here competing partners cooperate to form larger and more economical units.

Research and development alliance In a research and development (R&D) alliance, the partners aim to create synergy by making joint use of research facilities, exploiting opportunities to specialize, standardizing combined know-how, and sharing risks.

Supply alliance In a supply alliance, competitors who need similar inputs need to cooperate with one another to safeguard supplies, reduce procurement costs, or to prevent the entry of new competitors.

9.9 IMPLICATIONS OF STRATEGIC ALLIANCE

A strategic alliance can have serious and far-reaching implications on the very continuance of the alliance, if mismanaged. The partners can have misunderstandings and conflicts on account of various factors, such as those described in Sections 9.9.1–9.9.5.

9.9.1 Formal Structure of Relationship between Partners

Partners in a strategic alliance enter into a formal and well-defined relationship that can be horizontal, vertical, or neutral in nature.

A horizontal relationship is one where the partners are competitors outside the area of the proposed alliance (Buchel and Prange 1998). In spite of the alliance, the partners can have conflicts on areas such as influence of the partners on the alliance strategy, basis of profit-sharing, contribution or sacrifice made by partners, and how others view it, etc.

A vertical relationship is one where the partners share a supplier–customer relationship (Buchel and Prange 1998). The areas of conflict under this relationship include purchase and supply obligations of each partner and legal obligations of the partner's dependence of the partners on the alliance.

A neutral relationship is one where the partners come from different business areas (Buchel and Prange 1998). The areas of conflict include strategic orientation of the alliance and strategy for handling the situation when the markets converge.

Partners need to ensure that these areas of conflict are known and proper corrective measures taken at the very beginning to avoid future misunderstandings.

9.9.2 Internationality of Alliance

The alliance faces a different set of challenges and issues when the partners come from different countries. This is because of the prevailing cultural and business differences, differences in language of the two countries, difference in customer needs and consumption patterns, etc. These elements can have a very serious impact on the alliance.

9.9.3 Value Added Chains

A strategic alliance also has to deal with the challenges and conflicts that emerge as a result of its position in the value added chain. This position affects the autonomy and control relationships within the alliance. For instance, the autonomy of some partners is bound to be sacrificed if the alliance pattern is closer to the core activities of certain other partners (Gaughan 2007).

9.9.4 Profit/Ownership-related Issues

These issues affect the performance and responsibilities of the partners and determine how the alliance would grow in the future. This aspect includes elements such as structure of the contracts, profit sharing, and authority assigned dominance of a partner in the alliance.

9.9.5 Orientation of the Alliance

This element gives rise to issues and problems related to the daily operation of the alliance. The possible areas of differences between the partners include autonomy, coordination, adaptability, and responsibility-sharing among partners.

9.10 BENEFITS OF STRATEGIC ALLIANCES

Strategic alliances generate the following benefits:

- The partners can share the burden of investment required in the alliance. In addition, the partners are not required to invest in developing the entire range of capabilities required as a lot of them already exist, which the partners are willing to share.
- The alliance is able to attract funds easily as it is backed by entities that are willing to contribute in all possible ways to make the alliance successful. Alliances between large and small firms are very common.
- Alliances are very beneficial to small firms that may not have the required competencies in all areas. They depend on larger firms to perform specialized functions which are beyond the purview of the small firms. For example, Cetus, one of the leading biotech firms, entered into a number of alliances to produce and market some of the first diagnostic instruments based on biotechnology. Under the alliance, Cetus provided the bulk research, while the larger firms took care of activities such as financing, marketing, and manufacturing capabilities (Gaughan 2007).

9.11 WEAKNESSES OF STRATEGIC ALLIANCES

Strategic alliances generally suffer from strategic issues that affect overall performance of the partners. The common weaknesses include those described in Sections 9.11.1–9.11.4.

9.11.1 Harmony-related Issues

This is a major concern in strategic alliances as the expectations of the partners differ. Harmony-related issues may also arise with partners who may make unequal contributions to the alliance, but have very high expectations. These problems arise as related issues are taken very lightly in the initial stages. When harmony gets affected, it results in an atmosphere of mistrust and absence of commitment.

9.11.2 Implementation Issues

Translating a planned strategy into reality is a very difficult task. The partners who form an alliance usually agree to a certain strategy. However, they often fail to discuss its implementation, which is very complicated and poses many difficulties. The problems are further aggravated when partners are from an unfamiliar industry and lack the experience to develop a realistic industry-based strategy.

9.11.3 Problems of Coherence

The issue of coherence arises for partners who are often confronted with additional expectations which are left unexpressed. It may be because they could not be ascertained at the stage of finalizing the alliance. Sometimes, the expectations also undergo significant changes. This affects the trust and commitment of the partners and leads to destabilization and weakening of the alliance.

9.11.4 Changes in Business Environment

There is always a time lag between entering into an alliance and making it operational. During this time lag, the business environment could change, leading to new developments, new challenges, new expectations, as well as new opportunities. These new opportunities may conflict with the original goals and objectives of the alliance, resulting in a re-evaluation, re-negotiation, and redefining of the alliance. This may not always be possible as it strains the relations between the partners.

9.12 STRATEGIC MANAGEMENT OF ALLIANCES

Achieving close coordination between the partners of a strategic alliance is the biggest challenge. The alliance can grow unabated, provided the existing differences and incompatibilities are resolved effectively. These can be avoided in the following ways.

9.12.1 Clear Understanding between Partners

The partners in the alliance should establish a clear understanding on all aspects of the partnership so that conflicts are avoided. It requires a detailed discussion of the following elements (Gaughan 2007):

- Mission of the new venture
- The products/services that the venture would offer
- The markets it will operate in
- The role, responsibilities, and obligations of each partner
- The course of action to be followed in the event of differences among partners
- The procedure for dissolving the venture, if necessary

9.12.2 Avoiding Excessive Stress on Legal Contract

While entering into a contract, stating the terms and conditions of the alliance is crucial. However, laying excessive focus on the contract to make the alliance work never gives the desired result. Alliances succeed when the partners and their representatives walk that extra mile to make them work. Referring to the contract and its provisions obsessively can only spread bitterness and mistrust. As stated earlier, Dow Corning was created with a handshake and was already on the path of growth by the time the contract was actually signed between the partners (Gaughan 2007).

9.12.3 Avoiding Greed

Alliances are entered into for mutual benefits through synergies. It is important that all the partners contribute sincerely towards attainment of the objectives and mission. There is no room for greed in an alliance. For example, the aviation industry has many alliances where the partners agree to route-sharing, on the basis of routing and cost. The adoption of route-sharing strategy helps the airlines to block the competitive threat of preferential routing in the specific markets in which the airline chooses to compete. While such an alliance is expected to ensure competitive parity, in reality it may not happen. The senior partner in the alliance would like to retain a major share in this arrangement out of sheer greed, posing problems to the very continuance of the alliance.

9.13 INTERNAL DEVELOPMENT

Internal development is a strategy of building new businesses in-house, more or less from scratch. Internal development is also known as corporate entrepreneurship.

Internal development can be pursued in four different ways, as described in Sections 9.13.1–9.13.4.

9.13.1 Venture Capitalists

In this strategy, the company acts as a venture capitalist. A venture capitalist is one who provides funds for a new project, generally in a new sector. For example,

Exxon invested in 18 new ventures in 10 years from the 1980s onwards. Of these, six became very successful and Exxon subsequently bought them. The other 12 were never bought by Exxon but still represented sound financial investment as Exxon had invested $12 million in these projects and got a return of $218 million in cash or marketable securities over a 10-year period (Kanter et al. 1990).

9.13.2 New Venture Incubator

Under this strategy, the company provides not only funds for the proposed venture, but also provides low-cost space, equipment, and limited managerial support. Such entities might be started within an existing company/corporate sponsor or as an independent entity assisted by a company/corporate sponsor. New venture incubators are started when the company/corporate sponsor has extra space, idle equipment, and unused managerial skills and talent (Williams et al. 1991). While this strategy looks impressive, it poses major hindrances in the integration of the existing business with the new ventures initiated by the company. For example, Kodak pursued the new venture incubator strategy, but was unable to integrate the entities with its existing businesses and eventually discontinued the strategy (Williams et al. 1991).

9.13.3 Idea Generation and Transfer Programme

This strategy involves executing new business ideas. Once the idea starts giving results, the new entity is transferred to an established company for further development and management. The success rate of this strategy has been much higher than the two earlier options. The major criticism against this strategy is that it rarely results in the development of an entirely new business. In most cases, the new products or product refinements are confined to the existing businesses. For example, Raytheon, a company operating in the defence systems and related equipment sector, has a new product development centre that runs the idea generation and transfer programme. This centre successfully produced fifty or more patentable innovations per annum (Kanter et al. 1990).

9.13.4 Intrapreneurship

This strategy involves encouraging in-house entrepreneurial individuals or teams working to develop new ideas for the company. Companies often introduce a number of practices to spread the entrepreneurial spirit among its employees. For example, 3M has always successfully introduced practices for encouraging the entrepreneurial spirit amongst its employees (Miller and Dess 1996).

Each of the strategies discussed so far can have a lasting impact on the corporate culture, diversification, and financial performance of the company concerned.

9.14 CONCLUSION

While M&As are an important means for attaining corporate growth, they may not always be feasible and possible for a company. It is because a number of factors and environmental elements have to be evaluated before the company decides to go ahead with its M&A decisions. If the company feels that the proposed M&A may not add value, or is not feasible vis-à-vis its existing operations, alternatives have to be explored. While the synergistic benefits may not be achieved, the strategies discussed above can certainly improve the profitability of the company.

SUMMARY

To sum up, one can say that while M&As do generate benefits, they do not always succeed due to problems pertaining to integration and effective implementation. Under such circumstances, companies find it better to explore alternatives to M&As that can be implemented with limited resources and do not necessarily involve issues of integration.

KEY DEFINITIONS

Complementary alliance   It is an alliance where the partners combine their technologies to diversify their existing products/market portfolios.

Concentration alliance   Concentration alliance is one where competing partners cooperate to form larger and more economical units.

Core business   Core business is the main activity of an entity. When a business reaches a stage of maturity, it reduces growth opportunities forcing the entity to diversify into more profitable areas. Companies often finance such expansion by selling off the core business.

Divestiture   A divestiture is a sale of a portion of a firm to an outside firm. The selling firm is usually paid in cash, marketable securities or a combination of the two.

Horizontal relationship   It is a relationship where the partners are competitors outside the area of the proposed alliance.

Idea generation and transfer programme   This strategy involves executing new business ideas. Once the idea starts giving results, the new entity is transferred to an established company for further development and management.

Internal development   Internal development is a strategy of building new businesses, more or less, from scratch. Internal development is also known as corporate entrepreneurship.

Intrapreneurship   This strategy involves encouraging entrepreneurial individuals or teams working within the company to develop new ideas for the company. Companies very often introduce a number of practices to spread the entrepreneurial spirit amongst its employees.

Involuntary divestitures   Involuntary divestitures occur when a company receives an unfavourable review under any legal dispute that requires the company to divest itself of a particular division.

Market alliance   Market alliance aims at combining the market knowledge of one partner with the production or product know-how of the other.

Neutral relationship   Neutral relationship is one where the partners come from different business areas.

New venture incubator   It is a strategy where the company not only provides funds for the proposed venture, but also makes available low-cost space and equipment and limited managerial support.

Research and development alliance   In a research and development alliance, the partners aim to create synergy by making joint use of research facilities, exploiting opportunities to specialize and standardize, combining know-how, and sharing risks.

Sales alliance   A sales alliance is an arrangement where the producer and a local partner cooperate to have a mixture of independent representation and own branch.

Strategic alliances   Strategic alliances refer to joint ventures—arrangements in which business entities join forces to form a cooperative partnership. Typically neither owns the other, though they often create a third entity.

Strategic management of alliances   Effective management of alliances calls for close coordination between partners. To ensure that the alliance grows unabated, the existing differences and incompatibilities need to be resolved effectively.

Supply alliance   In a supply alliance, competitors with similar input needs cooperate to safeguard supplies, reduce procurement costs, and prevent the entry of new competitors.

Venture capitalists   This is a strategy where a company just acts as a venture capitalist. A venture capitalist is one who provides funds for new project, generally in a new sector.

Voluntary divestiture   It is a process wherein the selling entity feels that a certain division is not adding to its profitability and is diverting the company's attention from more profitable divisions. To refocus its attention on the profitable division, the company might decide to divest the division. Such divestitures help the company to get rid of the unprofitable division's assets and help in improving its overall profitability.

Vertical relationship   It is a relationship where the partners share a supplier–customer relationship.

CONCEPT REVIEW QUESTIONS

9.1   Explain the concept of divestitures. Why do companies seek divestitures?

9.2   State and explain the different types of divestitures with examples.

9.3   What are the benefits of divestitures?

9.4   What are strategic alliances? Why do companies enter into strategic alliances?

9.5   State and explain the different types of strategic alliances. What are the implications of strategic alliance?

9.6   Explain the benefits and weaknesses of strategic alliances.

9.7   What is internal development? State and explain the different strategies of internal development.

9.8   Write short notes on the following:
   (a) Types of divestitures
   (b) Types of strategic alliances
   (c) Reasons for entering into strategic alliances
   (d) Strategic management of alliances

PROJECT ASSIGNMENT

Analyse the alternative strategies adopted by the following entities:
   (a) 3M
   (b) Kodak
   (c) Raytheon

REFERENCES

Boot, A., 'Why hang on to Loser? Divestitures and Takeovers', *Journal of Finance*, September 1992, pp. 1401–1420

Buchel, B., Probst, G., and Prange, C., *International Joint Venture: Learning to Cooperate and Cooperate to Learn*, John Wiley and Sons, Boston, 1998, pp. 19–20

Gaughan, P.A., *Mergers, Acquisitions and Corporate Restructurings*, 4th edition, Wiley and Sons, Boston, 2007

Harrigan, K.R., *Managing for Joint Venture*, Lexington Books, New York, 1980, pp. 16

Hermann, R., *Joint Venture, Strategien, Strukturin, Systems and Kulturen, Dissertation*, St. Gallen, 1994, pp. 21, http://eprints.mdx.ac.uk/6518/1/Namazie-factors_affecting.phd.pdf, last accessed on 8 August 2010

Jackson, C., *Hounds of the Road: a History of the Greyhound Bus Company*. Bowling Green University Popular Press, Ohio, 1984

Kanter, R.M., Quinn, G., and North, J., 'Engines of Progress: Designing and Running Entrepreneurial Vehicles in Established Companies', *Journal of Business Venturing*, Issue 5, 1990, pp. 415–430

Kaplan, S.N. and Weisbach, M.N., 'The Success of Acquisitions: Evidence from Divestitures', *Journal of Finance*, March 1992, pp. 107

Miller, A and Dess, G.G., *Strategic Management*, 2nd edition, McGraw Hill, New York, 1996, pp. 259

Schillaci, C.E., 'Designing Successful Joint Ventures', *Journal of Business Strategy*, September 1993, pp. 59–63

Williams, M.L., Tsai, M., and Day, D., 'Intangible Assets, Entry Strategies and Venture Success in Industrial Markets', *Journal of Business Venturing*, Issue 6, 1991, pp. 315–333

Zook, C., *Beyond the Core: Expand Your Market Without Abandoning Your Roots*, Harvard Business School Press, Watertown, 2004, pp. 63

CASE STUDY

Strategic Alliance—Kingfisher and Jet Airways

Abstract

While M&As are the most preferred way for forging an alliance, they are not the only way. Companies often adopt various alternative tools to drive value. Strategic alliance is the preferred way. The case analyses the strategic alliance between Kingfisher and Jet Airways, and the legal issues the alliance ran into.

Pedagogical Objectives

• To understand and evaluate strategic alliance as an alternative strategy for joining hands
• To identify the legal hurdles the alliance faced and what went wrong in the alliance

Introduction

The civil aviation industry deals with all non-military operations, both private and commercial, which ferry passengers and cargo. The passenger services are classified into scheduled and non-scheduled services. Scheduled services are operated on regularly scheduled routes as per the time table. Non-scheduled services are services that are not scheduled, and include chartered flights.

Civil Aviation in India

Air travel has generally been perceived as a mode of transport for the rich and for international travel. The Indian civil aviation industry was no different. It had one more important characteristic—it was nationalized with no role for the private sector. It was only when the Indian skies were opened to the private sector that the industry underwent a massive change and transformation. The sector saw a number of airline companies being promoted. Today the sector no longer remains the prerogative of the government.

A large number of low-cost private airlines operate in the market today. No wonder the Indian aviation industry is one of the fastest-growing aviation industries in the world with private airlines accounting for more than 75% of the domestic aviation market as of 2006. The sector is on an upswing with a compound annual growth rate (CAGR) of 18%. The country has 454 airports and airstrips, of which 16 are designated as international airports.

The 9/11 Tragedy that Struck the Aviation Industry

The civil aviation sector was doing pretty well until the September 2001 terrorist attacks in the US. The use of commercial airplanes as assault vehicles had no precedent in aviation history.

At the time of 9/11, the industry was already in financial trouble due to the recession. The event severely compounded the industry's financial problem (www.fas.org).

Among the immediate effects of the attack on the World Trade Centre was the sudden increase in the price of oil, leading to increases in the price of aviation turbine fuel (ATF). The global economy started feeling the heat of increasing oil prices since oil prices can have serious negative effects on the growth of GDP and on inflation, as experienced in 1973–74 and 1989–90 (www.fas.org).

The 9/11 attacks compounded financial troubles that the airline industry was already experiencing before the attacks. The share prices of airlines and airplane manufacturers plummeted after the attacks. It would not be wrong to say that 9/11 had an accelerating negative effect on the global economy. Many airline companies were pushed to the brink of bankruptcy and had to shut down operations as this sector has high capital costs, high fixed costs, and razor-thin margins. Example: Midway Airlines. The matter got worse since the number of air travellers fell, revenues declined rapidly, leaving airlines with the only option of laying-off tens of thousands of employees. In a nutshell, the industry lost years of growth.

Counter Strategy of Global Airline Industry

The global airline industry which was already tremendous pressure due to recessionary trends suffered another setback on account of this tragic incident. The industry started feeling the heat because airline costs are fixed in the short-term, and any sharp reductions in revenues inevitably means large losses for the airlines. The general opinion of the airline industry was that the attacks were targeted at government policies rather than at the air transport industry. Therefore, they expected that governments would respond appropriately as long as market conditions were not restored to normality. Some felt that a few carriers should be offered specific government support; others believed that government response should aim to offer solutions to meet the common problems encountered by all air operators. The Association of Asia Pacific Airlines (AAPA) called on the region's national governments to aid the industry in its attempt to recover from the current crises by providing relief from landing fees, terminal charges, and taxes. It has also asked governments to help by promoting tourism and facilitating international air travel (Morrell and Alamdari 2002).

A number of measures were initiated by governments and airline operators across the globe to counter the situation. These included the following:

- Looking at airline mergers more favourably, and thus allowing further consolidation to take place more easily
- Help to fund the increased security measures at airports
- Financial assistance from governments, in addition to underwriting increased insurance costs
- Governmental approval for 'soft' loans
- A two-year pay freeze for executives of airlines obtaining loan guarantees
- Elimination of some unprofitable routes, and reduced frequencies on others; for example, British Airways and KLM
- Cut in all non-essential capital expenditure
- Considering investing in airlines that became available as a result of bankruptcies; for example, Virgin Express in 'Sabena' and Virgin Blue in 'Ansett'
- Adopting consolidation strategies and strategic alliances within a country

Jet Airways Arrives on the Indian Aviation Scene

Jet Airways was established on 1 April 1992, as an air taxi operator by Naresh Goyal. The commercial airline operations of Jet Airways started on 5 May 1993. The first fleet consisted of four leased Boeing 737-300 aircraft. In January 1994, the airline applied for scheduled airline status. In January 1995, after the Air Corporations Act (1953) was repealed, Jet Airways received its scheduled airline status. With a flight to Sri Lanka in March 2004, Jet Airways started its international operations as well. Jet Airways also focussed on good service and tickets were priced accordingly.

Traces of the WTC attack were seen in the strategy of Jet Airways. In April 2007, Jet Airways took over Air Sahara, which was later renamed JetLite and became the low cost carrier of Jet Airways. Two years after the inception of JetLite, Jet Airways introduced another low-cost airline to its Indian customers—Jet Airways Konnect. Started in May 2009, Jet Airways Konnect makes use of spare aircraft from Jet Airways' routes, which were continued by the parent company, due to the low passenger load factors.

Kingfisher's Grand Entry

The Vijay Mallya-promoted Kingfisher Airlines began its operations on 9 May 2005 through the lease of four Airbus A320 aircraft, with an inaugural flight from Mumbai to Delhi. In June 2005, it became the first Indian airline to order the Airbus A380. It placed orders for five A380s, five Airbus A350-800 aircraft, and five Airbus A330-200 aircraft in a deal valued at over $3 billion.

Kingfisher Airlines made a mark in the market through a trail of innovations and introduced a range of market-firsts that completely redefined the whole experience of flying. By elevating its customers to a level of being 'guests' and not just passengers, Kingfisher Airlines endeared itself to all its passengers. It also became the first Indian airline to introduce in-flight entertainment (IFE) system on domestic flights and also provided complimentary 'welcome kit' containing a pen, facial tissue, and headphone to use with the IFE system to all its passengers. The IFE was made available through an alliance with Dish TV to provide live TV entertainment to passengers. All these facilities, of course, came at a cost—comparatively higher cost of tickets—but passengers still found the airline appealing due to the quality of service.

The growth continued unabated and Kingfisher started its international operations on 3 September 2008 with a flight between Bangalore and London and later on added new international destinations, namely Hong Kong, Dhaka, Colombo, Singapore, Dubai, and Bangkok.

The 9/11 attack had an impact on Kingfisher too. The decline in passenger traffic was visible and Kingfisher also started experiencing its share of problems. As a way out of the trouble, Kingfisher Airlines and Deccan Airways decided to merge in December 2007, with Kingfisher Airlines' parent company United Breweries (UB Group) acquiring 46% of Air Deccan's parent Deccan Aviation, which possessed 52% of the total stake.

The Strategic Alliance of Kingfisher and Jet Airways:

According to estimates by the aviation industry, India-based airlines have been hit hard by falling passenger numbers, and the domestic airlines are likely to suffer combined losses amounting to $2 billion (www.dancewithshadows.com). To sail through the impact of 9/11, the Indian aviation sector also started initiating corrective measures. Rival private airlines Kingfisher Airlines and Jet Airways shocked the aviation circles by announcing a strategic alliance to tide over the crisis, in what could be described as the largest operational alliance in the aviation sector of India. These two airlines, with a collective market share of over 58%, came up with this strategy to reduce cost and enhance efficiency. The companies opted for a strategic alliance as a formal merger of the two airlines was not possible because the competition laws in India mandate that airline companies cannot have a market share of over 40% after they merge.

The alliance involved the following:

- Code-sharing on domestic and international flights
- An interline agreement
- Joint fuel management
- Common ground-handling services
- Cross-selling flights through the global ticketing system
- Cross-utilization of crew on similar aircraft types
- Use of common training facilities
- Use of frequent flyer programmes in either of the airlines

A code-sharing agreement is a commercial agreement between airlines in which airlines mutually use their two-letter identification code to book flights and sell seats under one airline's name on another carrier's flight. It results in the airlines obtaining a larger network by using fewer flights. It also facilitates flying different legs of a journey by issuing a single ticket. It benefits the airlines by facilitating joint fuel management thus reducing fuel expenses and common ground-handling. It also allows cross-selling of flight inventories using a common global distribution system platform and cross-utilization of crew on similar aircraft types and commonality. Code-sharing, it is argued, does not result in any savings or profits, but generates more traffic. This was done pending the approval from the Directorate General of Civil Aviation (DGCA) as required in India. This alliance was expected to help save at least ₹15 billion annually.

The two companies, however, clarified that the alliance would not involve an equity investment in each other's company. With a view to justifying the alliance, the airlines stated that a better understanding of the demand and supply in this capital-intensive and labour-intensive industry was the only way to improve profitability and enhance shareholder value. The alliance provided that the airlines would fly 927 domestic flights and 82 international flights a day. With the two airlines hit hard by the downturn, the companies stressed that other alliances may well be formed if airlines continue to struggle, which could lead to a drop in competition in the airfreight sector.

The capital market greeted this announcement with a bang with Jet Airways shares jumping 10% and Kingfisher by 28% even though the alliance raised quite a few eyebrows. The two companies justified their decision saying strategic alliances were a global phenomenon, although it was the first such alliance in India. The companies also defended their decision saying the alliance should not be looked upon as a cartel but a simple arrangement essentially meant to save costs as airlines are losing money. They further argued that any savings materializing through the arrangement shall be passed on to the passengers.

At this point of time, the domestic aviation industry was, on an average, losing ₹8–9 billion due to a 20%–25% gap between revenues and costs. This was because of the irrational pricing by air-carriers to tide over the recessionary pressures being felt in the industry. In addition to the synergistic benefits of the alliance, Goyal, the owner of Jet Airlines, advocated a 20%–25% increase in fares across the board to bridge the gap between input costs and revenue. His argument was based on the logic that the industry was facing a situation wherein costs were increasing while the revenues had been falling; increasing fares was the only way to recover the increasing costs and break even.

The alliance has been projected as a step that would imply the following from the passenger's perspective (Anand 2008):

- An imminent fare hike
- Better standard of services, at a cost though
- Sharing of experienced staff
- Passengers can buy Jet tickets from Kingfisher and vice-versa
- Frequent fliers of both airlines will be able to interchange their flying miles

Competition Commission of India Sees Red

The Competition Commission of India (CCI), an antitrust body, was created under the Competition Commission Act to act against formation of business 'cartels' which may hamper fair competition. The Commission felt that the Kingfisher and Jet Airlines alliance had all the elements of cartelization. So the Commission started investigations to examine the alliance between Kingfisher and Jet Airlines as it felt the code-sharing and ground handling agreement would create a monopoly in the aviation industry.

The Commission issued a show cause notice to the airlines seeking explanation on why action should not be initiated against them for the alliance, which according to CCI was a clear case of cartelization. The Competition Act provides that if the case of cartelization is proved against entities, CCI is authorized to impose a heavy fine amounting to three times the profit or 10% of the individual turnover of the firms for the period of cartelization.

Kingfisher was not pleased with this investigation, as it felt CCI had no authority to reopen the case that was closed by former antitrust regulator Monopolies and Restrictive Trade Practices Commission on 4 September 2009 or to investigate the same. Kingfisher decided to move to the Mumbai High Court against this show cause notice arguing that the alliance was formed before the Competition Act came into force, and therefore, it could not be probed under the Act. The senior counsel of Kingfisher also argued that the new rules relating to fair trade practices cannot have a retrospective effect. The CCI, however, argued that the matter was well within its jurisdiction and informed the court that Kingfisher was not cooperating in the investigation. The Mumbai High Court ruled in favour of CCI and directed Kingfisher to cooperate with the fair trade regulator in the matter.

Kingfisher felt aggrieved with the Mumbai High Court order and therefore moved the Supreme Court seeking a stay on the same. The Supreme Court, however, refused to stay the order of Mumbai High Court stating that it was analysing the Competition Commission Act, and was trying to ascertain whether the CCI had powers to initiate investigations and whether the aggrieved party could challenge the same at the show cause notice stage. It said that the Court would lay down norms for such an investigation and that Kingfisher's petition would be taken up after it pronounced its decision on another similar issue, wherein CCI had challenged a petition filed by SAIL and the Indian Railways, stating that the Competition Appellate Tribunal was overstepping its power by initiating a probe into an alleged 'cartel-like arrangement' between them.

Outcome

The strategic alliance between Kingfisher Airlines and Jet Airways did not generate the expected results, and failed to achieve tangible progress. The alliance did not make much headway initially because of internal and technical issues involved.

The alliance ran into trouble after Jet announced layoffs of up to 1,900 of its workers, leading to protests in Mumbai, where it is based, and forcing it to rescind the plan to trim its workforce. This event put Kingfisher in a fix, which distanced itself, as it did not want to be seen as a party to this act. This forced analysts to believe that the alliance was as good as buried. Three months after the plan was announced, it failed to take off as the necessary permissions sought from the civil aviation ministry were not received. The DGCA has a broad guideline for code-sharing. So any approval for code-sharing becomes arbitrary in nature. The approval it was felt may also not have been received because other airlines viewed this alliance as an attempt to kill competition and create a situation of monopolistic competition. The DGCA and Ministry of Civil Aviation did not want to get involved in a controversy and wanted to remain focused on its task of improving aviation infrastructure.

Industry analysts did not see much benefit accruing from the alliance. Even CRISIL Research felt that the alliance might mitigate some costs for the two airlines, but would not bring profits as the industry was experiencing negative growth (Sanjai 2009). The alliance could not progress beyond a tactical alliance for the two partners to the extent of sharing ground handling services, parts and airport equipment; it failed to become a tie-up for sharing routes and customers (Sharma 2010). Ernst & Young felt that such tie-ups work only when the sector has attained maturity. The Indian aviation sector was not mature enough to handle such tie-ups.

The outcome was not encouraging because the two airlines were competitors, do not offer complimentary services, and because it required both the partners to make sacrifices.

Discussion Questions

1. Do a SWOT analysis of the case.
2. Do you think the two parties should have undertaken a PESTEL analysis—an analysis of the political, economic, social, technological, and legal environment—before getting into the final analysis?
3. What elements should have been focused in PESTEL while initiating the alliance?

References

Anand, A., 'Kingfisher—Jet Alliance will not benefit you,' www.mid-day.com, last accessed on 8 August 2010

'Jet Airways, Kingfisher Airlines to code-share on domestic routes,' http://www.dancewithshadows.com/aviation, last accessed on 8 August 2010

Morrell, P.S. and Alamdari, F., 'The Impact of 11 September on the Aviation Industry: Traffic, Capacity, Employment and Restructuring,' A Working Paper under Sectoral Activities Programme, *International Labour Office*, Geneva, January 2002, pp. 20

Sanjai, P.R., 'Six months on, Jet–Kingfisher alliance set to start rolling,' *The Mint Sun*, 26 April 2009, www.livemint.com, last accessed on 8 August 2010

Sharma, P., 'A year on, Jet–Kingfisher fail to fly in formation', 16 March 2010, www.dna.com, last accessed on 8 August 2010

'The Economic Effects of 9/11: A Retrospective Assessment', *Congressional Report Service*, The Library of Congress, 27 September 2002, pp. 9 and 21, www.fas.org, last accessed on 5 August 2010

1   Hindalco–Novelis Merger

If we earn $10 for every $100 aluminium we sell, we will now be able to earn another $10 for every $100 worth of aluminium that Novelis processes into rolled products.

> —Debu Bhattacharya, MD, Hindalco Industries Ltd

Acquisitions are not geography-dependent. They depend on value-creation and will have to be in sync with existing business.

> —Kumar Mangalam Birla, Chairman, Aditya Birla Group

Introduction

In early 2007, Hindalco Industries Ltd (Hindalco), the flagship company of the Aditya Birla Group, announced that it would acquire the Canadian company Novelis. The transaction would make Hindalco the world's largest aluminium rolling company and one of the biggest producers of primary aluminium in Asia, as well as India's leading copper producer. Novelis was to be acquired in an all-cash deal valued at approximately $6 billion, including debt. Under the terms of the agreement, Novelis shareholders would receive $44.93 in cash for each outstanding common share.

The Chairman of the Aditya Birla Group, Kumar Mangalam Birla, was of the opinion that aluminium was a core business with enormous growth potential in revenues and earnings. The acquisition of Novelis was a step in this direction as it was felt that the combination would establish an integrated producer with low-cost alumina and aluminium facilities combined with high-end rolling capabilities and a global footprint.

Industry Overview

The global aluminium industry is seeing increased scope in packaging applications. The other sectors using aluminium increasingly are power, infrastructure, and automobiles. These sectors shall provide the much-needed fillip to the aluminium industry and demand is expected to grow rapidly and attain double-digit growth. Domestic and global demand will rise over a long-term period.

A number of other factors influence the market of aluminium, such as lowering of import duties, domestic realization of aluminium majors, pressure on Hindalco and Nalco, reduction in buffer on international prices, greater linkage to international prices, and volatility in financials. To negate the effect of these factors, producers have started moving downstream to mitigate higher volatility.

The key features of the industry are as follows:

- The industry is highly concentrated with only five primary plants in the country.
- All the producers use the Bayer–Hall–Heroult technology.
- The industry has a very high energy cost—40% of manufacturing cost for metal and 30% for rolled products.
- Technology cost is very high and this is the main barrier in achieving high energy efficiency.
- The main aim of the industry is energy conservation and reduced consumption.
- The industry faces stiff competition from imports.

Aluminium is a power-intensive industry with one tonne of aluminium requiring over 15,000 KW of power. Power constitutes almost 40% of the total cost of production. Hindalco enjoys an advantage in this respect with the smelters backed by captive power plants, making it one of the lowest cost producers globally.

As regards Hindalco, the following issues were found to be prominent: large upstream and midstream production, cyclical business linked to commodity prices, low cost commodity operations, proximity and good access to Asian markets. With regard to Novelis, the factors that were crucial were market leading downstream portfolio, stable cash flows, substantive proprietary technology-led operations, and leading world market position.

Hindalco—The Aluminium Giant

Hindalco, the metals flagship company of the Aditya Birla Group, is the world's largest aluminium rolling company and one of the biggest producers of primary aluminium in Asia. Its copper smelter is the world's largest custom smelter at a single location.

Established in 1958, Hindalco commissioned the aluminium facility at Renukoot in eastern Uttar Pradesh in 1962. The company grew from strength to strength through acquisitions and mergers with Indal and Birla Copper. With the acquisitions of the Nifty and Mt Gordon copper mines in Australia in 2003, its position was strengthened in value-added alumina, aluminium, and copper products.

Its aluminium units across the globe encompass the entire gamut of operations, from bauxite mining, alumina refining, and aluminium smelting to downstream rolling, extrusions, foils, along with captive power plants and coal mines. Similarly its copper unit, Birla Copper, produces copper cathodes, continuous cast copper rods, and other by-products such as gold, silver, and DAP fertilizers.

The Birla Nifty copper mine consists of an underground mine, heap leach pads, and a solvent extraction and electrowinning (SXEW) processing plant, which produces copper cathode.

The Mt Gordon copper operation consists of an underground mine and a copper concentrate plant. Until recently, the operation produced copper cathode through the ferric leach process. Nifty and Mt Gordon have entered into a long-term 'life of mine' offtake agreement with Hindalco to supply copper concentrate to the copper smelter located at Dahej, Gujarat.

A strong presence across the value chain and synergies between operations have provided Hindalco with a dominant share in the value-added products market. The ever-expanding market for value-added products and services has provided the opportunity for the launch of three new products—Everlast roofing sheets, Freshwrapp kitchen foil, and Freshpakk semi-rigid containers.

Hindalco also has a number of greenfield projects that focus on quality, safety, and environmental concerns. The projects are Mahan aluminium project at Madhya Pradesh, Aditya alumina and aluminium project at Orissa, the Utkal alumina project at Orissa, aluminium project at Jharkhand, smelter project at Hirakud, alumina project at Belgaum, and alumina refinery at Mori.

Novelis—The Canadian Giant

Novelis is a Canadian corporation formed in January 2005, as a spin-off from Alcan Inc. It is the world's leading producer of aluminium-rolled products based on shipment volume. The company produced an estimated 19% of the world's flat-rolled aluminium products, and is the biggest producer in Europe and South America, and the second-largest in North America and Asia.

Novelis has also been a world leader in the recycling of used aluminium beverage cans, with nearly 39 billion cans recycled into new can sheet to be manufactured into beverage cans in 2008. The company operates in four continents and is the only company that has the expertise to produce premium aluminium-rolled products. The company has expertise in producing end-use applications and light gauge products that include beverage and food cans, foil and packaging, transportation, electronics, construction, and industrial products. The company also operates bauxite mining, primary aluminium smelting, and power generation facilities.

Hindalco's Strategy

A business model describes how a company will operate in the market so that the pre-determined marketing goals are attained effectively. Hindalco had a very clear business model for its aluminium business. The model focused on a totally integrated business solution, keeping in mind the large size of the division.

The company pursued an objective of optimally exploiting the aluminium value chain balancing between the more volatile high-margin upstream products and the steadier low-margin downstream portfolio.

Its upstream strategy focused on continuing the existing low-cost operations and gradually progressing to new greenfield projects. This, it was presumed would further improve cost competitiveness through lower production costs; by controlling key resources, such as bauxite mines, refineries, power plants and coal; and reaping the benefits of economies of scale.

Added to this strategy is the fact that Indian bauxite is of the highest quality with high alumina content, less than 2% Boehmite content, very low reactive silica content, and negligible organic content. It also possesses a higher liquor purity and productivity that is more cost-efficient. Again large deposits of bauxite are found in a single plateau, which allows more efficient extraction. India also has abundant coal supplies, easy availability of labour, and is located in close proximity to the fast-growing markets. All these factors create the right setting for producing high quality aluminium.

The Acquisition Advantage

Hindalco's decision to acquire Novelis was influenced by the fact that Novelis had a well-diversified geographical market base, which would enhance the stature of Hindalco in the area of downstream production. The growth seen at Hindalco was the result of a well-crafted growth and integration strategy that hinged on three cornerstones—cost competitiveness, quality, and global reach. The company was also committed to the triple bottom line accountability of economic, environment, and social factors.

Novelis was the world leader in rolled aluminium products, which would help Hindalco to extend its reach in the industry. Novelis also had long-standing relationships with leading customers, which Hindalco expected to exploit. The list of customers included Agfa-Gevaert, Alcan, Anheuser-Busch, Ball, Coca-Cola, Crown Cork & Seal, Daching Holdings, Ford, General Motors, Lotte Aluminium, Kodak, Pactiv, Rexam, Ryerson Tull, Tetrapack, and ThyssenKrupp.

The fact that Novelis used advanced scientific techniques and applied knowledge to deliver innovative, customer driven products also made it a good buy. The extensive research and development capabilities ensured that Novelis was able to provide innovative production and application technologies, including breakthroughs in the following areas:

- Alloy development/optimization for improved properties such as strength, formability, corrosion resistance
- Molten metal and advanced solidification technology
- Innovative manufacturing technologies
- Advanced surface treatment and coating technologies for semi-finished products
- Modelling of forming processes for automotive sheet components and product performance for auto structure crash behaviour and beverage can down-gauging
- Development of innovative products like heat exchanger materials, automotive sheet, beverage and semi-rigid containers, etc.

Novelis also used the concept of global technology organization wherein it committed itself to providing world-leading research and technology support.

This allowed Novelis to share its knowledge and experience rapidly between teams and facilities around the globe so that innovations could be applied appropriately, and with the same speed, by customers who possess regional or worldwide manufacturing capabilities. The company collaborated very closely with customers to identify their needs in the areas of manufacturing process support, the introduction of new manufacturing technologies, and the design and development of new and improved products. The collaboration involved physical simulation of a customer's processes and products through the development of pilot line capabilities, and simulation via state-of-the-art computer-aided design and engineering.

Novelis had the technology, economic strength, commitment, and skills in the financial, environmental and social dimensions to excel as a sustainable corporation. Hindalco's acquisition made sense because of all these factors.

What Did the Deal Mean in Numbers?

The acquisition was very crucial for Hindalco and in terms of numbers it meant the following:

- The acquisition was executed through an all-cash transaction wherein Novelis was valued at approximately $6 billion, including around $2.4 billion in debt.
- The merger would establish a globally integrated aluminium producer with low-cost alumina and aluminium production facilities combined with high-end aluminium rolled product capabilities.
- The merger would ensure that Hindalco would become the biggest rolled aluminium products maker and fifth largest integrated aluminium manufacturer globally.
- Novelis, being a global leader in aluminium rolled products and aluminium can recycling, with a global market share of about 19%, would make Hindalco a major player in the market. At the time of acquisition, Hindalco held 60% share in the high-growth Indian market for rolled products, which today appears to be small.
- Hindalco has always been one of the lowest cost producers of primary aluminium in the world, but the merger would enable it to leverage its position and become a key player globally.
- Novelis, it was expected, would incur a loss of $263 million in 2006. However, it expects to make a profit of $68 million in 2007. The total free cash flow was expected to be $175 million in 2006.
- The debt component of Novelis stood at $2.4 billion and additional $2.8 billion would be added as this is the amount Hindalco would take to finance the deal. This was expected to put a tremendous pressure on profitability due to high interest burden.
- Hindalco was then planning a major expansion at an investment of Rs 250 billion. This would put a tremendous interest burden on the company.

Looking at the financial position of the two entities and their future growth plans, they would not have been able to finance the deal through a high debt mix. Let's take a look at the numbers to substantiate our argument. Novelis had a debt–equity ratio of 7.23:1, making it practically impossible for it to borrow any further.

Hindalco proposed to buy the $3.6 billion worth of Novelis's equity as follows:

- $2.85 billion through borrowing
- $300 million as debt from group companies
- $450 million from its cash reserves

The second part of the deal was the debt of Novelis of $2.4 billion. Hindalco proposed to take refinancing facility to finance these borrowings. These were ultimately to be repaid with the cash flows of Novelis.

Conclusion

Critics are of the view the numbers indicate that Novelis is a costly buy and Hindalco has taken a hasty step. At the same time they believe Novelis looks like a long-term buy. The immediate benefit seems to be Hindalco's desire to be amongst the top five aluminium manufacturing companies globally.

Discussion Question

Analyse the merger and indicate the rationale behind it.

Reference

Research reports of HSBC and KPMG, http://www.researchreports.com, last accessed on 31 March 2011

2   Tata–JLR Acquisition

Introduction

Modern organizations pursue the growth objective unabated. To attain this objective, global expansion is critical. To succeed and thrive in a competitive environment, one needs to be a global player. A company can test its potential only in the global environment, which provides opportunities for exploring new horizons and transforming entities. Tata Motors is a living example that has a number of acquisitions, subsidiaries, associate companies, and strategic tie-ups. The expansion continues with the acquisition of Jaguar Land Rover (JLR), two of the world's most respectable and iconic brands. Through this acquisition, Tata Motors has come of age and joined a league of global entities that operate in the premium global car market.

The Tata Group

The Tata Group, a 150-year old entity, owns Tata Motors, previously known as Tata Engineering and Locomotive Company. It is India's largest passenger automobile and commercial vehicle makes established in 1945. It is the fifth-largest medium and heavy commercial vehicle manufacturer in the world and is listed on both Indian bourses and the New York stock exchange. It was only manufacturing heavy motor vehicles initially. The desire to enter the small car segment motivated the Tata Group to acquire Daewoo Motors. It entered the small car segment with Indica and followed it up with Indigo, Indigo Mariner, Indigo Manza, and Nano, the world's cheapest car.

Jaguar and Land Rover

Jaguar was founded in 1922 in Blackpool as the Swallow Sidecar Company. Due to financial difficulties, it was nationalized in 1975. Later it floated as a separate company. However, even that did not improve the situation. In 1990, it was taken over by Ford for $2.5 billion.

Land Rover was founded in 1948 as a marquee of the Rover Group. It manufactured vehicles that were known for their superior on-road performance. The vehicles were used by the military for projects and expeditions. In 1994, the BMW took over the Rover Group, but could not turnaround the company. Eventually Rover was sold to Ford for $2.75 billion in 2000. The biggest challenge before Ford was to bring down the production costs and turn around the two entities. Ford failed in this attempt. Finally, the US auto major put the two marquees on the block in 2007 after posting losses of $12.6 billion in 2006. This loss was the heaviest in its 103-year history. Reports, however, indicated that the losses of Jaguar stood at $715 million, while Land Rover's profit, driven by the record sale of 260,000 vehicles, grew by 18% year-to-year growth in 2007.

The Deal

In June 2007, Ford announced its plans to sell Jaguar and Land Rover. This announcement was received well by prospective buyers such as Tata Motors, Mahindra & Mahindra (M&M), Cerberus Capital Management, TPG Capital, and Apollo Management showed interest in acquiring the beleaguered brands.

While M&M bid for the two brands for $1.9 billion, Tata Group was chosen the preferred bidder with a $2.30 billion bid and the two brands were sold.

The Real Picture

The domestic market was passing through a very difficult phase. Tata was experiencing the effects of the changes in the consumer market for cars. Tata Motors faced plummeting consumer demand, frozen credit lines, a huge debt burden, and the project to launch the world's cheapest car Nano. All this impacted the performance, which showed a drop in passenger vehicles to 41,287 units, a drop of 14.14%. This fall forced the company to cut production across different categories.

The quest for bringing out the world's cheapest car was also on. The company had spent approximately $430 million on developing the Nano. A sum of Rs 20 million was invested on the plant in Singur, West Bengal, which ran into trouble due to widespread protests by farmers. The plant had then to be shifted to Gujarat. All this happened around the same time when Tata Motors has decided to buy the two brands. Tata went ahead with the purchase of the two brands because it felt that there were strategic reasons behind purchasing the two brands:

- Long-term strategic commitment to the automotive sector
- Opportunity to participate in two fast growing auto segments viz. luxury cars and all terrain vehicles
- Sharing of best practices in manufacturing and quality assurance systems
- Benefits from component sourcing, design services, and low cost engineering

Synergies Expected from the Deal

The deal was expected to generate a lot of synergies such as good brands, customer preferences for the well-known car brands, growing Indian car market, product being taken over by Tata Group, and increasing consumption ability of Indian customers. Added to these were the following synergies.

Cost synergies   The following cost synergies were expected to be generated:

- Tata Motors noted that the purchasing basket offered a bigger opportunity for cost reduction for high-end products such Land Rover; material costs and not manpower was the key to better margins. The group started focusing on managing material and sourcing costs to improve margins.
- Tata Group has a rich ecosystem of joint ventures with leading players in the auto ancillary space. This, it was felt, could be leveraged to the projects advantage.
- Tata Steel–Corus is the leader in automotive grade steel in the European markets with 16% of its revenue coming from this division. It enjoyed 'Q1' supplier status with Ford to supply steel for Jaguar and Land Rover.
- Tata Consultancy Services was also expected to contribute effectively by providing services such as engineering design, manufacturing solutions, and sourcing solutions. The automotive division accounted for 15% revenues with some of its major customers being Chrysler, Ford, and General Motors.
- INCAT, part of the Tata Group, would bring synergistic benefits for it was good at providing services such as supplier programs, consulting services, and global sourcing. It had a clientele list that consisted of Chrysler, Ford, General Motors, Honda, and Nissan.

Revenue synergies   It was expected that in the long run Tata Group and Tata Motors should help Jaguar/Land Rover diversify their geographic dependence from the US where it had 30% of the volume and Western Europe where it had 55% of volume.

Financing the Deal

The deal was priced at $2.3 billion. The amount was financed by raising a bridge loan of $3 billion through a syndicate of banks. An additional amount of $0.70 was raised for engine and component supply, contingencies and working capital. Tata Motors raised a bridge loan of $3 billion through a syndicate of banks. The loan was raised through Tata Motors UK, a special purpose vehicle and a 100% subsidiary of Tata Motors. The interest on the bridge loan was linked to LIBOR (London inter bank offer rate). Tata also proposed to raise around $500–600 million through an international issue.

The amount was repaid in following manner:

- ₹1.92 billion underwriting agreement with JM Financial Consultants
- ₹1.75 billion was raised through a deposit scheme from the public
- Additional subscriptions by promoter companies' such as Tata Sons, Tata Capital, and Tata Investment Ltd
- £1 billion aid package by the British Government (out of a total of £2.3 billion)

This was the first time that an Indian company had issued shares with differential voting rights. The manner in which the funds were to be raised for the deal is shown here.

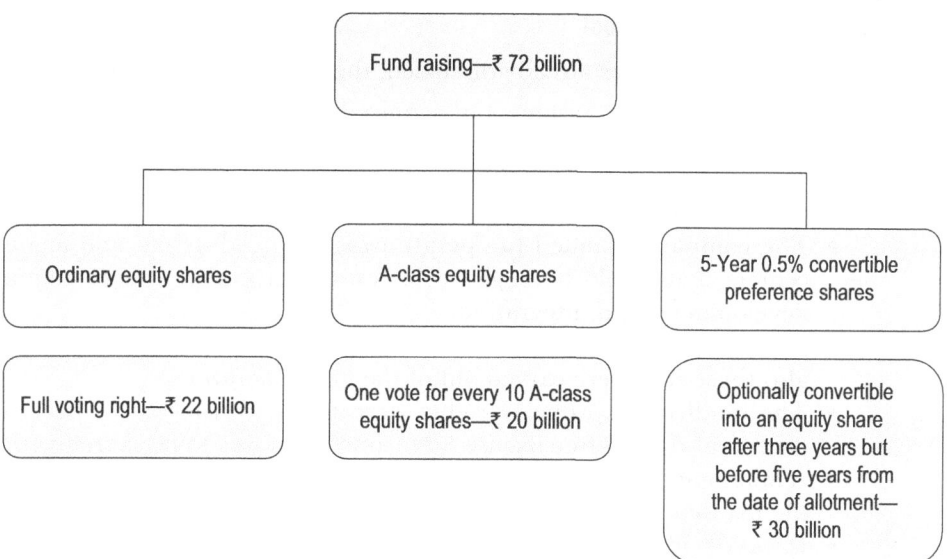

Post-merger Initiatives

The company was aware of the fact that the post-merger integration would be a big challenge. The cash flows had to be taken care of as the company had borrowed huge amounts and the burden of repayment would be tremendous. In view of this, a number of cost rationalization initiatives were taken to improve cash flows:

- It was decided that all the three UK assembly plants shall work on single shifts and downtime basis.
- The payment terms for the suppliers were extended from 45 to 60 days in line with industry standards.
- The receivables were reduced by £133 million from 38 to 27 days.
- The inventory was reduced by £217 million between June 2008 and March 2009 and from 70 to 50 days.
- The following labour actions were initiated:
  - Voluntary retirement was given to 600 employees.
  - Agency staff was reduced by 800.
  - Leaves were offered to 300 workers of Bromwich and Solihull plant.
  - Additional 450 job cuts were announced including 300 managers.
- An agreement was entered into with unions to implement pay freezes and longer working hours. This was anticipated to be equivalent to approximately 20% reduction in labour costs.
- Attention was paid to achieving engineering and capital spending efficiencies.
- Fixed marketing and selling costs were reduced in line with sales volume.
- A reduction in all other non-personnel related overhead costs was planned.

Other Facts about the Deal

In addition to the facts already discussed, the following facts need mention:

- Tata Auto Comp Systems Ltd acquired the business and initially JLR was to be operated independently of the partner.
- The three plants in the UK were all well invested and were to continue their operation in the same manner.
- The company planned to operate two advanced design and engineering centers that would be engaged in testing, prototype design engineering, development, and integration.
- The company decided to continue with the national sales units of JLR and also those that were carved out of the Ford operations.
- The intellectual property rights were to be transferred to JLR and the perpetual royalty free license on technologies was to be shared with Ford.
- A minimum guarantee amount of $1.1 billion was sanctioned to help manage the tax that would arise going forward.
- It was decided that Ford Motor Credit would continue to support the sales of JLR for the next 12 months.
- It was decided that Ford will contribute $600 million towards pension fund.

Benefits Anticipated Post Merger

Tata Motors had gone ahead with the acquisition for it anticipated lot of synergies from it. Even though critics felt that Tata was pursuing a costly buy, the company went ahead with it. The anticipated benefits were as follows:

- Tata was keen on making a global impact and thought the two brands would give better value in future.
- Tata had been eyeing the European market for long. This acquisition, it was thought, would ease the entry of Tata into the European market.
- The deal would reduce Tata's dependence on the Indian market which accounted for 90% of its sales. The market would undergo a major shift with the increase in the sales in emerging markets and reduced dependence on mature markets. This would provide an opportunity to spread its business across different customer segments.
- The price of the vehicles starts from Rs 6.3 million and goes up to ₹ 9.3 million. This it is felt would be Tata's answer to brands such as BMW, Audi, and Mercedes.
- JLR had many new models lined up for the next three years, and these were expected to result in a surge in profits.
- The companies have a very strong R&D culture and facilities, which would help the company bring about radical improvements and introduce new models with ease.
- The brands also enjoy component sourcing, engineering, and design benefits.

Problems Post Merger

The merger was carried out meticulously, but the response of the market was not very positive. The market felt that the price paid for the acquisition was on the higher side. The following problems were experienced post merger:

- The share price of Tata Motors dropped post merger.
- The rights issue planned to raise funds to finance the acquisitions failed to raise interest.
- The acquisition resulted in a huge debt burden on the company.
- The sales volume of the vehicles decreased by 35.2%.
- The consumer experienced a lot of difficulties in getting loans for purchasing the vehicles.
- The pace of change was very slow because there was no operational freedom.
- The global premium car market continued to be in a depressed state and this affected the sales of JLR.
- For the fiscal year ending March 2009, JLR lost $504 million and Tata Motors reported a net loss of $67 million for the quarter to ending June.
- Tata's core commercial vehicles market in India also suffered from slower sales and this further added to the losses of Tata Motors.
- The manufacturing cost in Britain was very high, which created a great deal of pressure and affected the bottom line of the company. The company was forced to, therefore, eliminate more than 2,200 jobs.

Conclusion

The performance of JLR has been impressive with sales clocking 21,134 vehicles in 2009, higher by 33% over 2008. Of these, the sale of Jaguar was 4,794, an increase of 5%, while the sale of Land Rover was 16,340, an increase of 45%. While the sales figures have been impressive, one should not forget that Tata Motors is vulnerable as the competition in the domestic market is getting stiff. Foreign vehicle makers such as Daimler, Nissan Motor, Volvo, and MAN AG are striking local alliances for a bigger presence in the Indian market. Tata also has to counter competition from Maruti Suzuki, Hyundai, Renault, and Volkswagen. The only way to counter this increasing competition lies in delivering good quality at reasonable cost.

Discussion Question

Analyse the case and do a SWOT analysis.

3

RIL and RPL

Introduction

Mergers have not been confined to any specific sector. The rationale behind mergers is known, and thus every entity that merges looks for synergistic benefits and the hidden value that is presumably released after the merger. One such merger that has made waves in the market is RIL and RPL. The case aims at looking at the issues involved in the merger.

Reliance Industries Ltd

Reliance Industries Ltd (RIL) is India's largest private sector enterprise with strong financials. Its revenue exceeds $33 billion, exports are about $21 billion, and earnings before interest, tax, depreciation, and amortization (EBITDA) is over $5 billion. Of its revenue, 98% comes from refining and petrochemicals, its core business.

The net sales of RIL in 2007 was $269 billion, net worth $190 billion, total assets $299 billion, and net profit $179 billion. The net profit increase has been greater than 20% per annum in any 5-year period since 1977. The company has not been affected by business cycles and has shown unabated growth (See Appendix I).

No wonder these figures sound like a dream, one that everyone aims to achieve. This makes RIL India's most valuable company having a world-class, complex refinery.

RIL Refinery—The Success Mantra

In 1999, RIL commissioned a large, world-class, complex refinery in record time at a competitive capital cost. This refinery created industry benchmarks. The refinery was so versatile and robust that it successfully processed over 80 heavy/sour crude variants from across the world. It consistently demonstrated higher gross refining margins (GRMs) compared to global benchmarks. This enviable track record has continued over decades and there is no halt in the commitment to excel in everything that the company does.

In average capacity utilization during the period of 2001–08, the company left everyone behind. The refineries in the Asia Pacific region attained 86% capacity utilization, Europe attained 86%, and North America attained 88%, compared to 99% achieved by RIL.

RPL—The Investor's Delight

Reliance Petroleum Ltd (RPL) is a refinery set up in a record time of 36 months. The progress was for the world to see. The refinery has a crude processing capacity of 580,000 barrels per day. It is among the top 5% refineries globally with a capacity to process ultra-heavy crude having a complexity index of 14 and an average API (American Petroleum Institute) rating of 24. The refinery, possessing a Nelson Complexity Index of 14, ensured regular supply of ultra-clean fuels to meet the world's evolving needs. The focus of the refinery was on high growth transportation fuel. What differentiates the refinery from others is it has the lowest US $/complexity barrel cost among the refineries built recently.

This world-class refinery, with minimal project risk, commenced refining operations on 25 December 2008 and the first batch of products was exported in January 2009.

RIL–RPL Merger Rationale

While RPL was capable of delivering superior returns, RIL saw a rationale in merging the entity with itself. The rationale was driven by the following factors:

- Unlocking synergies such as crude sourcing, product placement, and supply chain optimization, through combined operations
- Greater flexibility in operations and planning that would facilitate expansion of refined product range
- Optimization of the secondary process units and infrastructure of the refinery
- Accretive nature of earnings per share (EPS)
- Efficient utilization of cash flows
- The experience of integrated energy companies that consistently get higher valuations vis-à-vis pure refineries

Reliance Industries Ltd was very sure that the merger would enhance its competitiveness in the energy value chain and increase both its productivity and profitability by taking care of the cyclical fluctuations in the market and delivering superior products with higher margins. In addition to this the shareholders of RIL would benefit greatly from the merger without any execution risk as the refinery was fully functional and profitable (Appendix II).

Financials

The two companies decided the appointed date would be 1 April 2008. The swap ratio was decided to be 1 share of RIL for every 16 shares of RPL. The RPL shares already held by RIL were to be cancelled and no fresh treasury stock was to be created. It was decided that RIL will issue 60.92 million shares to RPL shareholders. As a result of this, the equity base of RIL would increase by 4.4% from ₹15.74 billion shares to ₹16.43 billion. To accommodate this issue, the promoter's holding in RIL was to be reduced from 49% to 47%, and the shareholding pattern underwent a change. The merger of RIL and RPL would result in the creation of the world's largest shareholder family of around 3.7 million shareholders (Appendix III).

Impact of Merger

The merger earned RIL a position among the top private sector refinery companies. As a result of this merger, RIL will own two of the world's three largest and most complex refineries and the world largest producer of ultra-clean fuels at a single location. The merger would place RIL among the world's 50 most profitable companies and the five largest producers of polypropylene (Appendix IV).

Reliance Petroleum Ltd had a Nelson Complexity of 14.7 against RIL, which had 11.7. The merger would thus give the merged entity an extra gross refining margin to the extent of $2 per barrel. This would certainly generate synergy in terms of increasing capacity and savings in overhead cost.

Conclusion

The RIL–RPL merger would result in India's largest ever merger. The merger would enhance the value for shareholders of both the companies. The merger would ensure that the consolidated company would be a world class, complex refinery with minimal residual project risk, while complementing RIL's product range.

Annexure I   RIL's growth since IPO in 1977

Variables	FY 1977–78 ($ million)	FY 2002–03 ($ million)	FY 2007–08 ($ million)	CAGR in the last 31 years (%)	CAGR in the last 5 years (%)
Turnover	76	13,701	34,713	22	20
Net profit	3	864	3,804	26	35
Cash profit	5	1,593	6,282	26	32
Total assets	38	13,422	37,348	25	23
Net worth	11	6,387	20,311	27	26
Exports	7	2,424	20,811	29	54
Market cap*	11	8,129	39,507	30	37

Note: 1. Data as on March 31 each year
           2. Market cap data as on 27 February 2009

Source: RIL Annual Reports, 2002–03 and 2007–08, http://www.ril.com/html/investor/investor.html, last accessed on 31 March 2011

Annexure II   Current valuations

Particulars	PER ($ million)		EV/EBIDTA ($ million)		PBV ($ million)	
	CY 09/FY 08	CY 10/FY 11	CY 09/FY 09	CY 10/FY 11	CY 09/FY 09	CY 10/FY 11
Reliance Industries	**9.7**	**7.9**	**7.5**	**6.1**	**1.5**	**1.2**
Reliance Petroleum	**7.0**	**5.0**	**6.1**	**4.4**	**2.3**	**1.7**
Asian refineries	9.9	7.4	6.5	4.1	1.3	1.1
European refineries	10.7	9.5	4.7	4.5	0.7	0.6
US refineries	8.8	6.6	4.7	3.6	1.4	0.9
Global refining average	**9.8**	**7.8**	**5.3**	**4.1**	**1.1**	**0.9**
Asian integrated	11.4	9.2	6.6	5.1	1.2	1.1
European integrated	13.6	9.8	5.8	4.5	1.6	1.5
US integrated	16.9	8.9	5.7	4.0	1.5	1.4
Global integrated companies	**14.0**	**8.3**	**6.0**	**4.5**	**1.4**	**1.3**
Premium over pure refineries (%)	**43**	**19**	**14**	**11**	**28**	**49**

Note: PER = Price–Earnings ratio; EV = Enterprise value; EBIDTA = Earnings before interest, depreciation, tax, and amortization; PBV = Price by volume chart

Source: Bloomberg analyst research based on 27 February 2009 prices, http://www.ril.com/, last accessed on 31 March 2011

Annexure III   Distribution of RIL shareholding

Particulars	Dec 2008 (%)	Post merger (%)
Promoter group	49.0	47.0
Held by RIL subsidiaries	6.0	5.7
Banks and financial institutions	6.5	6.9
Mutual funds	2.5	2.7
FIIs	15.5	15.1
GDRs	3.7	3.6
Public	16.7	19.0
Total	100.0	100.0

Source: RIL Annual Report, 2008–09, http://www.ril.com/html/investor/investor.html, last accessed on 31 March 2011

Annexure IV   Five largest producers of polypropylene

Company	Location	CDU capacity (kbpsd)	Nelson Complexity Index
BP	Texas City	433	14.2
RIL SEZ	Jamnagar	580	14.0
RIL EOU	Jamnagar	660	11.3
Citgo	Lake Charles	320	11.2
Exxon Mobil	Baytown	428	10.9
Exxon Mobil	Beaumont	320	10.8

Note: CDU stands for crude distillation unit.

Source: International Energy Agency, http://www.iea.org/, last accessed on 25 December 2010

Discussion Question

Analyse the merger of RIL and RPL and comment on the synergies the merger would generate.

References

RIL Annual Reports, 2007–08 and 2008–09, http://www.ril.com/html/investor/investor.html, last accessed on 31 March 2011
RPL Annual Report, 2007–08, http://www.ril.com/html/investor/investor.html, last accessed on 31 March 2011

4 Procter & Gamble and Gillette

Introduction

Mergers and acquisitions (M&As) have been the buzz word in the last two decades. Not that there were no mergers happening earlier, but the last two decades have seen the numbers swell. The M&A activity has not remained confined to any particular industry, but has been quite widespread. One such M&A has been that of Procter & Gamble and Gillette. It has been the biggest merger in the history of consumer goods, and has changed the equations in the market.

Procter and Gamble—A Look into the Past

Procter & Gamble Home Products Ltd was incorporated as a 100% subsidiary of the Procter & Gamble Company, USA, in 1993 with the divestment of the detergents business. This was followed by a number of products such as Pantene Pro-V, Head & Shoulders shampoo and Tide detergent powder—the largest selling detergent in the world. This expansion continued when in June 2000 it launched Pantene Lively Clean stating that its unique pro-vitamin formula cleans oil-build up, dirt and grime in just one wash, delivering lively, free-flowing and sparkling-clean hair. This was followed with New Ariel Power Compact detergent claiming that its new global technologies breathe new life into clothes, by removing dinginess and restoring the original colour of the fabric. The product expansion continued with a wide variety of products being introduced in the market.

Gillette India—The Man's World

Gillette India Ltd (GIL) was one of the premier FMCG (fast moving consumer goods) companies in India. It made a name for itself in the Indian market with products such as Gillette Mach3, Gillette Turbo, Oral-B, and Duracell. The company has constantly worked to bring out high quality, value-added products for the consumer.

Gillette India Ltd was launched in 1985 as Indian Shaving Products Ltd. Later, the name of the company was changed to Gillette India Ltd. Gillette India offers a range of products for the consumer, ranging from 7 O'Clock Ejtek PII Shaving System, shaving creams, Gillette Presto Ready Shaver, 7 O'Clock Ready II, Oral-B, Gillette Sensor Excel Shaving System, shave foam, shave gel, aftershave splashes, deodorants, and conditioners. The company figured among the top 100 Indian companies in market capitalization very soon because of overwhelming response from the consumers.

The Growing Strength of Retailers

The consumer goods industry grew rapidly from the 1950s through the 1980s, after which the growth slowed down. Slow sales growth, increasing cost of inputs, emergence of private labels, lower margins, difficult price negotiations, and the increasing diversity of channels, choices, and consumer types posed many difficulties for the $2 trillion plus industry. Retailers such as Wal-Mart, Kmart, and Sears Roebuck did everything possible to exert their purchasing power over suppliers to achieve lower prices. The main players who competed in the consumer goods industry were renowned names such as P&G, Colgate-Palmolive, L'Oreal, Kimberly Clark and Masco, Gillette, Revlon, Henkel, and Reckitt-Benckiser in the household and personal products category; Nestle, Unilever, Pepsico, ConAgra Foods, and Sara Lee dominated the food products segment; Johnson & Johnson was a big player in the healthcare category. The increasing competition had made promotional offers a norm in the industry and advertising and marketing costs increased due to stiff competition.

In 1999, P&G had approached Gillette with a takeover proposal, but Gillette had turned down the offer. When P&G approached Gillette again in November 2004, the company showed interest in the offer, raising eyebrows in the market. Very few realised that the offer was a compulsion rather than choice, because marketing pressures forced companies to diversify. Consolidation was perceived to be the only way to survive the difficult times. The merger was also necessitated by the fact that consumer goods companies wanted to be at par with retailers, who had acquired considerable bargaining power.

The only fear was the concern about P&G handling the risk accompanying the merger, for it had not undertaken such a big merger in its 168-year-old history. Integration was expected to be a huge challenge for the workforce as the cultures differed immensely. The merger would also call for a massive layoff across countries.

The Merger

Cincinnati-based P&G announced its decision to acquire Boston-based Gillette for $57 billion, setting the stage for becoming the world's largest consumer products company with annual sales of $60.7 billion. The new company would overtake Unilever, which had sales of $48.25 billion in 2003. The company would become a $21-billion brand with a market capitalization of $200 billion after the merger. The CEOs of both the companies felt that the deal was a friendly move, which would benefit both of them equally. The analysts also favoured the deal as they felt the merging companies had many similarities in corporate history— they were both more than a century old, had billion-dollar brands, and were pioneers in consumer product marketing initiatives. The merger was based on a different model where the focus was on innovation rather than on scale. It was a unique case of acquisition by an innovative company to expand its product line by acquiring another innovative company.

The Deal

The deal had the following features:

- P&G would pay $0.975 for each share of Gillette, valuing the acquisition at a 20% premium.
- P&G agreed to pay Gillette 40% in cash and 60% in stock.

The shareholders of P&G were a little apprehensive that the deal would dilute the company's share prices. To avoid this, P&G promised to buy back its shares, worth $18–$22 billion, over the next 12–18 months. Critics felt that the 20% premium paid by P&G for Gillette's stock would make it difficult for the company to pay dividends to shareholders.

Why Gillette?

This was a question in the mind of every individual, irrespective of whether he/she was involved in the deal. The answer was not difficult to find:

- P&G was strong in women's personal care products while Gillette's strength was in men's grooming category.
- Gillette's stock had climbed 50% since 2003 on account of jump in profits on premium products. It was estimated that the acquisitions would add about 20% to P&G sales and the long-term sales would grow by an estimated 5–7% a year. This would increase the operating margin by 25% by 2015 from 19% in 2003.
- The companies also expected cost savings of $14–16 billion from combining back-office operations and exploring new growth opportunities.
- The merger would provide the companies with the resources needed for intensive collaborative of supply chain initiatives in a more cost-effective way.
- The merger would also bring down the advertising and media costs owing to greater bargaining power.
- Gillette, it was felt, would give exposure to P&G in emerging economies such as India and Brazil, while P&G would distribute Gillette products in China.
- The acquisition would give P&G the much-needed boost to further strengthen its product categories where at present it has negligible presence.
- The deal would help Gillette in improving its inventory days.

Given these reasons, it was surely going to be a win–win situation for both the companies.

The Concerns

The merger raised certain concerns and analysts felt that the product overlaps would make it difficult for the merged company to set prices. Again, the strong overlaps in toothbrushes and toothpaste would mean the regulators would seek some divestitures. Another view was that the company would overcome the regulatory hurdles because the products were sold to different customers. In addition, creating regulatory hurdles would prevent US companies from expanding, as it would make them vulnerable to foreign competition. Objections were expected from the European Union antitrust regulators as the deal would give the merged company added strength in the overseas market.

Another fear was that P&G would face the risk of not being able to concentrate on its functioning due to the demands of the integration effort. It was felt that the formulation of country-specific strategies for the combined firm could take considerable time. Critics also pointed out that P&G already had some in-process integration of Wella, Germany's leading cosmetic supplier that it had acquired in 2003, which could divert the management's attention and energies away from the current integration.

Integration Issues

The integration of P&G and Gillette necessitated by the acquisition was a big challenge. It was expected that the merger would result in around 6,000 job cuts, equivalent to 4% of the two companies' combined workforce of 140,000. This was required to eliminate management overlaps and consolidate business support functions. Fortunately, the two entities did not face cultural problems because of their geographical proximity. Another matter of concern was that P&G was considered a promote-from-within company, and already had a lot of executive talent at the top. Therefore, absorbing Gillette's management to their satisfaction could be difficult. P&G's ability to handle this massive cultural assimilation would decide the success or failure of this acquisition. Finally, there were brands that overlapped with each other's product portfolio.

Future Outlook

In spite of all the concerns and problems anticipated, the two companies went ahead with the merger. The two entities took the bold view that problems would remain, and that they should not worry too much about them. Rather than foreseeing too many problems in advance and worrying about their solutions, they decided to cross the bridge when they came to it.

The merged entity was expected to face pressure from competitors in the industry, but the only way to handle it was by launching new products and or strengthening the supply chain relationships. P&G–Gillette, it was felt, could be a transformative deal for the industry because of Gillette's growth potential. Analysts forecast that this deal could lead to further consolidation in the industry.

Conclusion

The two companies finally decided to work together and explore the growth the industry had to offer, rather than worrying too much about what critics had to say and what regulators felt. The merged entity is doing well and growing with every passing day.

Discussion Question

Critically analyse the merger. What were the concerns raised in the merger? What solutions do you feel would be needed to address the concerns?

 **Due Diligence Checklist**

Step 1: Collection of Documents/Information from the Management

1. Memorandum and articles of association of the entity
2. Financial statements consisting of balance sheet, profit and loss account, schedules, cash flow statement, notes to accounts, auditor's report and director's report for the last three or five years
3. Projected business and income scenario
4. Foreign collaboration agreements
5. Technical collaboration agreements
6. Intellectual property rights—copyrights, patents, and trade marks
7. Pending litigation details with estimated financial liability
8. Licenses, quota rights, etc.
9. Government approvals including environmental clearances
10. Correspondence with government authorities
11. Marketing network details with feasibility studies
12. Brand and goodwill valuation
13. Internal audit reports
14. Tax assessments and tax audit reports for the last three or five years
15. Loan agreements and charge certificates
16. Corporate guarantees given
17. Lease agreements
18. Shareholding details
19. Technical feasibility reports
20. Pending contracts/orders in hand
21. Internal control systems and processes
22. Statement of inventory for the last three or five years
23. Dealership and franchisee agreements
24. Employee contracts
25. Payroll liability
26. Status of statutory dues including labour dues
27. Titles and ownership of property and assets
28. Status of contingent liabilities
29. Sales and purchase agreements
30. Pricing policy
31. MOUs and shareholders' agreements
32. Joint venture agreements

33. Subsidiary and associate company details and financials
34. Warranty agreements
35. Insurance policies
36. Cenvat credit on capital goods
37. ESOPs and sweat equity shares
38. Segment information
39. Information technology systems
40. IT security measures
41. Minutes of board and committee meetings

Step 2: Assemblage of Information from Independent Sources

1. Industry data
2. Independent search of title deeds
3. Market reports and studies
4. Customer reports
5. Product feasibility report
6. Past litigation record and orders
7. Prosecution of company and directors for offences for non-compliance of laws
8. Procurement of certified copies of financial statements and other documents
9. Search report for charges and mortgages
10. Credit report from bankers/financial institutions

Step 3: Review of Documents/Information

1. Over valuation of assets
2. Undervaluation of liabilities
3. Hidden liabilities
4. Product warranties/claims
5. Financial liability arising out of pending litigation
6. Guarantees/comfort letters/letters of credit given
7. Statutory dues liability including interest and penalty
8. Non-recoverable assets
9. Bad and doubtful debts
10. Likelihood of accrual of contingent liabilities
11. Over valuation of intangible assets
12. Technological obsolescence
13. Tax liabilities in future
14. Status of labour management agreements with reference to retrenchment
15. Slow-moving, non-moving, and obsolete inventory
16. Valuation method of inventory
17. Compliance of various laws
18. Compliance of accounting standards
19. Intellectual property restrictive covenants

20. IT security measures
21. Identification of items not disclosed
22. Correctness of financial figures
23. Quality of management and leadership
24. Research and development programmes
25. Market reputation
26. Governance policies

B Draft Scheme of Amalgamation

In this Scheme, unless inconsistent with the subject or context:

(a) "The Transferor Company" means ABCD Limited, an Existing Company under Section 3 of the Companies Act, 1956, having its Registered Office at _____, in the State of _____.

(b) "The Transferee Company" means WXYZ Limited, a Company incorporated under the Companies Act, 1956, having its Registered Office at _____, in the State of _____.

(c) "The Act" means the Companies Act, 1956.

(d) "The Appointed Date" or "The Transfer Date" means April 1, 2005.

(e) "The Effective Date" means the date on which the last of the approvals hereinafter provided will have been obtained. However, for the purposes of Income Tax Act, the Effective Date shall be April 1, 2005, and for the purposes of allotment of shares of Transferee Company, the Board of Directors of the Transferee Company may fix the date.

(f) "The Scheme" means the Scheme of Amalgamation of ABCD Limited with WXYZ Limited as contained herein, or as sanctioned by the _____ High Court, with modifications, if any.

(g) For the purpose of this Scheme, the Undertaking of the Transferor Company shall include all rights and privileges, powers and authorities, and all properties, movable and immovable, real or corporeal, incorporeal in possession or reversion, present or contingent, of whatsoever nature and wheresoever situated including in particular all licenses permits, quotas, approvals, rights, claims, leases, tenancy rights and liberties, patents, trade marks, and import quotas held by the Transferor Company to which the Transferor Company is entitled, and all debts, liabilities and duties of the Transferor Company and all other obligations of whatsoever kinds including liabilities in respect of the employees of the Transferor Company agreed to be taken over by the Transferee Company, with regard to the payment of gratuity, pension benefits, provident fund or compensation in the event of voluntary retirement or retrenchment.

Share Capital

A. Transferor Company

On March 31, 2005, the Authorised Share Capital of the Transferor Company is ₹1,00,00,000 (Rupees One Crore) divided into 1,000,000 equity shares of ₹10 each and ₹10,00,000 (Rupees Ten Lakhs) divided into 1,00,000 preference shares of

₹10 each. The issued Capital is ₹_____ (Rupees _____)
divided into _____ equity shares of ₹10 each and the subscribed and
paid-up Capital is ₹_____ (Rupees _____) divided into
_____ equity shares of ₹10 each.

B.   Transferee Company

On March 31, 2005, the Authorised Share Capital of the Transferee Company is
₹20,00,00,000 (Rupees Twenty Crores) divided into 2,00,00,000 equity shares of
₹10 each and _____ Preference Shares of ₹_____ each.
The issued Capital is ₹_____ (Rupees _____) divided into
_____ equity shares of ₹10 each and the subscribed and paid-up Capital
is ₹_____(Rupees _____) divided into _____ equity
shares of ₹_____ each.

The Scheme of Amalgamation

1. (a) The Undertaking of the Transferor Company and particularly the immovable
        property incapable of passing by manual delivery including licences, permits, quo-
        tas, incentives, subsidies, approvals, rights, claims, leases, tenancy rights, liberties,
        patents, trade marks and import quotas shall under the provisions of Sections 391
        and 394 of the Act and pursuant to the Orders of _____ High Court
        without any further act or deed but subject to the charges affecting the same as on
        the Effective Date, shall be transferred to and vested in the Transferee Company
        so as to become the Undertaking and property of the Transferee Company from
        the Appointed Date. Provided, however, that such charge shall not extend over
        or be deemed to be extended over any of the assets of the Transferee Company
        already owned and held by the Transferee Company.
    (b) With effect from the Appointed Date, all debts, liabilities, duties and obligations
        of the Transferor Company (hereinafter referred to as "the said liabilities")
        shall, pursuant to the Order under Section 394 of the Companies Act, 1956, of
        _____ High Court and without further act or deed be transferred
        or deemed to be transferred to and vested in and assumed by the Transferee
        Company so as to become the debts, liabilities, duties and obligations of the
        Transferee Company.
    (c) Upon this Scheme becoming effective, the items appearing as Reserves and
        Surplus in the books of the Transferor Company as at the Appointed Date shall
        become the corresponding reserves and surplus of the Transferee Company.
2. If any suit, appeal, or other proceedings of whatever nature (hereinafter called the
    "proceedings") by or against the Transferor Company be pending, the same shall
    not abate, be discontinued or be in any way prejudicially affected by reason of the
    Transfer of the undertaking of the Transferor Company or of anything contained
    in the Scheme, but the proceedings shall be continued, prosecuted and enforced by
    or against the Transferee Company in the same manner and to the same extent as
    they would or might have been continued, prosecuted or enforced by or against the
    Transferor Company if the Scheme had not been made.

3. The transfer of undertaking under Clause 1 hereof and the continuance of the proceedings by or against the Transferee Company under Clause 2 hereof, shall not affect any transactions or proceedings already concluded by the Transferor Company, in the ordinary course of business on or after the Transfer Date to the end and intent that the Transferee company accepts and adopts on behalf of itself all acts, deeds and things done lawfully and executed by the Transferor Company in regard thereto as having been done or executed on behalf of the Transferee Company.

4. As from the Transfer Date, the Transferor Company shall be deemed to have carried on and to be carrying on its business for and on behalf of and on account of and in trust for the Transferee Company until such time that the amalgamation becomes effective in terms of the Scheme.

5. As from the Transfer Date, the Transferor Company shall carry on the business of the Transferor Company until the amalgamation becomes effective, with utmost prudence and shall not without concurrence of the Transferee Company alienate, charge or otherwise deal with the property or assets of the Transferor Company or any part thereof, except in the ordinary course of business.

6. With effect from the Transfer Date and up to and inclusive of the Effective Date, all the profits and incomes accruing or arising to the Transferor Company or expenditure and losses incurred or arising as the case may be by the Transferor Company shall, for all purposes, be treated and be deemed to be and accrue as profits or income or expenditure or losses, as the case may be of the Transferee Company.

7. Subject to the other provisions contained in the Scheme, all lawful contracts, deeds, bonds, agreements and other instruments of whatever nature to which the Transferor Company is a party subsisting or having effect immediately before the amalgamation shall be in full force and effect against or in favour of the Transferee Company and may be enforced as fully and effectively as if instead of the Transferor Company, the Transferee Company had been a party thereto.

8. (a) All employees of the Transferor Company in the employment of the Transferor Company on the Effective Date, shall, as from the said date become the employees of the Transferee Company on the basis that their services have not been interrupted by the vesting of the undertaking of the Transferor Company in the Transferee Company under the Scheme and that the terms and conditions of service applicable to them immediately after the Effective Date will not be in any way less favourable to them, than those applicable to them immediately before the Effective Date.

(b) As far as the Provident Fund, Gratuity Fund, Superannuation Fund or any other Special Fund created or existing for the benefit of the employees of the Transferor Company are concerned, upon the Scheme becoming effective, the Transferee Company shall be substituted for the Transferor Company for all the purposes whatsoever related to the administration or operation of such Schemes or Funds or in relation to the obligation to make contributions to the said Funds in accordance with provisions of such Schemes or Funds according to the terms provided in the respective Trust Deeds or other documents. All the rights, duties, powers, and obligations of the Transferor Company in relation to such Schemes or Funds shall become those of the Transferee Company. The services of the employees of the Transferor Company will be treated as being continuous for the purposes of the aforesaid Schemes or Funds.

9. (a) Upon the Scheme become effective, in consideration of the transfer to and vesting of the undertaking of the Transferor Company in terms of the Scheme, the Transferee Company shall, with any application being made by the shareholders of the Transferor Company, issue and allot to the equity shareholders of the Transferor Company, equity shares in the Transferee Company in the proportion of 1 (one) share of the face value of ₹10 each of the Transferee Company, credited as fully paid up for every 25 (twenty five) fully paid up equity shares of the face value of ₹10 each, held by the equity shareholders of the Transferor Company on such date as the Board of Directors of the Transferee Company may decide.

(b) As a result of the issue and allotment of the share Capital of the Transferor Company in the manner specified in sub-clause (a) to this Clause hereinabove, if any equity shareholder of the Transferor Company becomes entitled to any fraction of equity shares of the Transferee Company, no such fractional coupon shall be issued in respect of or representing such equity shares of the Transferee Company, but such fractional coupon shall be consolidated into whole equity shares and the Board of Directors of the Transferee Company, or a Committee thereof may allot any one or more of such consolidated shares to any nominee(s) as the Board of Directors or the Committee may their absolute discretion deem fit for the purpose of holding and selling of such consolidated equity shares. Every such sale of the consolidated equity shares shall be at such price or prices as may be approved by the Board of Directors or the Committee and upon receipt of the purchase price in respect of such sale (provided the Board of Directors or the Committee approved the purchaser), the Board of Directors or the Committee shall allot the equity shares to the approved purchaser/s. the total net sale proceeds of such consolidated equity shares (after defraying therefrom all costs, charges, and expenses of sale) shall be distributed and divided among those equity shareholders of the Transferor Company as would otherwise have been entitled to such fractions of the equity shares of the Transferee Company in proportion to their respective interest in such fractions.

(c) Equity shares so allotted by the Transferee Company to the shareholders of the Transferor Company will in all respects rank pari-passu with the existing equity shares of the Transferee Company for dividend, voting, and other rights.

(d) Every shareholder of the Transferor Company shall surrender to the Transferee Company for cancellation, the relevant share certificate(s) held in the Transferor Company and thereupon the Transferee Company shall issue the certificate(s) for the shares in the Transferee Company he or she may be entitled to.

10. The _____ equity shares of ₹_____ each, paid up, in the Transferor Company are held by the Transferee Company. The said _____ equity shares shall be transferred by the Transferee Company before the date of allotment of shares by it pursuant to Clause 9 hereof, to such party/parties as the Board of Directors of the Transferee Company may think fit.

11. Upon the Scheme becoming effective, the Main Objects of the Memorandum of Association of the Transferor Company shall form part of the Main Objects of the Memorandum of Association of the Transferee Company.

12. On the Scheme being agreed to by the requisite majorities of the members of the Transferor Company and of the members of the Transferee Company, the Transferor Company and the Transferee Company shall with reasonable despatch, apply to the High Court of Judicature at Mumbai for obtaining sanction to this Scheme of Amalgamation under Section 391 of the Act and for an Order or Orders under Section 394 of the Act for carrying this Scheme into effect and for dissolution of the Transferor Company without winding up as also any Order or Orders as may be necessary and appropriate under the Act.

13. The Scheme is conditional upon and subject to:

    (a) The Scheme being agreed to by the respective requisite majorities of the members of both the Companies as are referred to in clause 12 hereof and the requisite Order or Orders referred to in Clause 12 being obtained;

    (b) Such other sanction and approvals as may be required by law in respect of the Scheme being obtained.

14. This Scheme, although to come into operation from the Appointed Date, shall not become effective until the date on which the certified copies of the Orders under Sections 391 and 394 of the Act shall be duly filed with the Registrar of Companies, Maharashtra State, Mumbai.

15. In the event of any of the approvals or conditions required to be obtained or fulfilled are not obtained or complied with on or before December 31, 2005, or within such further period or periods as may be agreed upon by and between the Transferor Company and the Transferee Company (through their respective Board of Directors) the Scheme shall become null and void and in that event no rights or liabilities whatsoever shall accrue to or be incurred inter se between the Transferor Company and the Transferee Company.

16. All costs, charges, and expenses of the Transferor Company and the Transferee Company respectively in relation to or in connection with the negotiation leading up to this Scheme or carrying out and completing the terms and provisions of this Scheme shall be borne and paid by the Transferee Company.

17. For the purpose of giving effect to the Scheme, the Board of Directors of the Transferee Company or any Committee thereof, is authorized to give such directors as may be necessary or desirable and to settle as they may deem fit, any question, doubt or difficulty that may arise in connection with or in the working of the Scheme including with regard to issue and allotment of Equity Shares under Clause 9 hereof, to the members of the Transferor Company and to do all acts, deeds and things necessary for carrying into effect the Scheme.

18. A copy of the order of the _____ High Court sanctioning the Scheme of Amalgamation shall be filed by the Transferor Company and the Transferee Company with the Registrar of Companies, _____, within one month from the date the Order is received by the Transferor Company and the Transferee Company.

Draft Scheme of Demerger

SCHEME OF ARRANGEMENT & DEMERGER BETWEEN ABCD LIMITED AND WXYZ LIMITED AND THEIR RESPECTIVE SHAREHOLDERS AND CREDITORS

(Under Sections 391 to 394 read with Sections 100 to 103 of the Companies Act, 1956)

1. Preamble

(a) ABCD LIMITED is a Company incorporated under the provisions of the Companies Act, 1956 having its registered office at _____ _____.

(b) ABCD LIMITED has 2 main divisions, namely; (a) ABCD Products Division with factory located at _____ and (b) DEF Division with factory located at _____ _____.

(c) The (a) ABCD Products Division is engaged in the business of manufacturing & trading in all kinds of _____; and (b) the DEF Division is engaged in the business of manufacture, assembling and sale of all kinds of _____.

(d) WXYZ LIMITED is a company incorporated under the Companies Act, 1956 having its registered office at _____ and is engaged in the business of manufacture and sale of various kinds of _____ _____.

(e) As a measure of corporate restructuring, more efficient use of existing resources, operation on a broader scale, increasing efficiency in business operations and to realise the potential for further growth, ABCD LIMITED has decided to demerge its DEF Division. The proposed demerger will enable ABCD LIMITED to concentrate on its core business, i.e., ABCD Division and to combat fierce competition arising out of entry of global players. The demerger will provide a specialized DEF business to WXYZ LIMITED, which in turn shall be able to chalk out a growth plan thereby increasing profitability of the Division.

(f) ABCD LIMITED proposes by this Scheme of Arrangement to separate the DEF Division by demerging it to WXYZ LIMITED and restructure the respective companies ABCD LIMITED and WXYZ LIMITED post demerger.

(g) To give effect to the said proposal, the Scheme of Arrangement & Demerger is presented for approval of the Honourable High Court at Delhi.

2. Definitions

In this Scheme unless repugnant to the meaning or context thereof, the following expressions shall have the following meaning:

(a) "The Act" means the Companies Act, 1956.

(b) The "Appointed Date" means April 1, 2005, the date with effect from which the scheme of Arrangement and Demerger shall be applicable.

(c) "Court" means the Honourable High Court of Judicature at Delhi.

(d) The "Effective Date" means the date by which last of the approvals specified in this Scheme shall have been obtained.

(e) The "DEF Division" means the unit of ABCD LIMITED at .... (Delhi) and shall also include:

   (i) all the assets whether moveable or immoveable, tangible or intangible including all rights, title, interest, covenant, undertakings, liabilities including continuing rights, title and interest in connection with the land and the buildings thereon whether leasehold or otherwise, plant and machinery whether leased or otherwise, together with all present and future liability including contingent liabilities and debts appertaining thereto, of the Transferor Company of all of which relate to the DEF Division, as more fully set out in the Schedule I hereof. In particular, the details of the material parcels of land are included in Schedule II hereof.

   (ii) All permits, quotas, rights, industrial and other licences, branches, offices, depots and godowns, trade marks, trade names, know-how and other intellectual property, patents, copyrights, privileges and benefits of all contracts, agreements and all other rights including lease rights, licenses, powers and facilities of every kind, nature and description whatsoever pertaining to the DEF Division as set out in Schedule III hereof.

   (iii) All permanent employees of ABCD LIMITED engaged in or in relation to DEF Division at the factory, branches or other offices;

   (iv) All earnest moneys and/or security deposit paid by ABCD LIMITED in connection with or relating to the DEF Division;

(f) "Record Date" means the date to be fixed by the Board of Directors of ABCD LIMITED for the purpose of determining the member of ABCD LIMITED to whom the shares of WXYZ LIMITED will be allotted pursuant to this Scheme.

(g) "Scheme" means this scheme of Arrangement and Demerger in its present form submitted to the Court for sanction or with any modification(s) approved or imposed or directed by the Court.

(h) "ABCD LIMITED" or "The Transferor Company" means ABCD LIMITED, incorporated under the Companies Act, 1956 having its registered office at _____.

(i) "WXYZ LIMITED" or "The Transferee Company" means WXYZ LIMITED, the Transferee Company, incorporated under the Companies Act, 1956, having its registered office at _____.

3. **Share Capital**

    (a) Existing Share Capital of ABCD LIMITED

        (i) Authorised Share Capital   ₹3,60,00,000.00
            36,00,000 Equity Shares of ₹10 each

        (ii) Issued Share Capital   ₹3,23,80,140.00
            32,38,014 Equity Shares of ₹10 each

        (iii) Subscribed and paid up Capital   ₹3,17,07,750.00
            31,70,775 Equity Shares of ₹10 each fully paid up

    (b) Existing Share Capital of WXYZ LIMITED

        (i) Authorised Share Capital   ₹............

        (ii) Issued Share Capital   ₹............
            .... Equity Shares of ₹10 each

        (iii) Subscribed and paid up Capital   ₹............
            .... Equity Shares of ₹10 each fully paid up

4. **Transfer of DEF Division**

    (a) The DEF Division of ABCD LIMITED shall be demerged and transferred to and vested in or be deemed to be transferred to and vested in WXYZ LIMITED in accordance with Section 2(19AA) of the Income tax Act, 1961 and in the manner enumerated in ensuing paragraphs.

    (b) With effect from the Appointed Date, the DEF Division shall, without any further act or deed, be transferred to and vested in or be deemed to have been transferred to and vested in WXYZ LIMITED for all the estate and interest of ABCD LIMITED, subject to existing securities, charges and mortgages, if any subsisting thereon in favour of banks, financial institutions, as may be modified, re-adjusted, apportioned or re-allocated by them.

    (c) All debts, liabilities, contingent liabilities, duties, and obligations of ABCD LIMITED relating to the DEF Division as on the Appointed Date, whether provided for or not in the Books of Accounts of ABCD LIMITED, whether disclosed or undisclosed in the Balance Sheet of ABCD LIMITED shall, without any further act or deed, be the debts, liabilities, contingent liabilities, duties and obligation of WXYZ LIMITED and WXYZ LIMITED undertakes to meet, discharge and satisfy the same.

    (d) WXYZ LIMITED undertakes to pay, discharge and satisfy all debts, liabilities, duties and obligations of ABCD LIMITED relating to DEF Division as on the Appointed Date and all liabilities, debts, duties, obligations relating to the said division which may accrue or arise after the Appointed Date.

    (e) It is expressly clarified that with effect from the Appointed Date, all taxes, duties, excess payable by Transferor Company relating to the DEF Division and all or any refunds/credit including MAT credit/claims relating thereto shall be treated as the liability or refund/credit including MAT credit/claims, as the case may be, of Transferee Company.

(f) Transferor Company shall permit Transferee Company to use its brand "PQR" and corporate logo as a part of its brand name and marketing/promotional material for products, namely Assemblies, subject to such terms and conditions as may be agreed to between Transferor Company and Transferee Company.

5. Contracts, Deeds, Bonds, and Other Instruments

(a) Subject to the other provisions contained in this Scheme, all contracts, deeds, bonds, agreements, and other instruments of whatever nature relating to the DEF Division to which ABCD LIMITED is a party subsisting or having effect immediately before the arrangement shall remain in full force and effect against or in favour of WXYZ LIMITED and may be enforced as fully and effectually as if instead of ABCD LIMITED, WXYZ LIMITED had been a party thereto.

(b) With effect from the Appointed date, all permits, quotas, rights, industrial and other licences, branches, offices, depots and godowns, trade marks, trade names, know-how and other intellectual property, patents, copyrights, privileges and benefits of all contracts, agreements and all other rights including lease rights, licenses, powers and facilities of every kind, nature and description whatsoever pertaining to the DEF Division of ABCD LIMITED to which ABCD LIMITED is a party or to the benefit of which ABCD LIMITED may be eligible and which are subsisting or having effect immediately before the Effective Date, shall be and remain in full force and effect in favour of or against WXYZ LIMITED as the case may be, and may be enforced as fully and effectually as if, instead of ABCD LIMITED, WXYZ LIMITED had been a party or beneficiary or obligee thereto.

(c) With effect from the Appointed Date, any statutory licenses, no objection certificates, permissions or approvals or consents required to carry on operations in the DEF Division of ABCD LIMITED shall stand vested in or transferred to WXYZ LIMITED without further act or deed, and shall be appropriately mutated by the statutory authorities concerned therewith in favour of WXYZ LIMITED upon the vesting and transfer of DEF Division of ABCD LIMITED pursuant to the scheme. The benefit of all statutory and regulatory permissions, factory licenses, environmental approvals and consents including the statutory licenses, permissions or approvals or consents required to carry on the operations of the DEF Division shall vest in and become available to WXYZ LIMITED pursuant to the scheme.

(d) The WXYZ LIMITED, at any time after the coming into effect of this Scheme in accordance with the provisions hereof, if so required under any law or otherwise, will execute deeds of confirmation or other writings or arrangements with any party to any contract or arrangement in relation to the DEF Division of ABCD LIMITED to which ABCD LIMITED is a party in order to give formal effect to the above provisions. WXYZ LIMITED shall, under the provisions of this Scheme, be deemed to be authorized to execute any such writings on behalf of ABCD LIMITED and to carry out or perform all such formalities or compliances referred to above on part of ABCD LIMITED.

6.   Legal Proceedings

All legal or other proceedings including any suits, appeals, arbitrations, execution proceedings, references, review, revisions, writ petitions, if any, by or against DEF Division of ABCD LIMITED under statute, whether pending on the Appointed Date or which may be instituted in future in respect of any matter arising before the Effective Date and relating to the DEF Division (including those relating to any property, right, power, liability, obligation or duties of ABCD LIMITED in respect of the DEF Division) shall be continued and enforced by or against WXYZ LIMITED only. If proceedings are taken against ABCD LIMITED, ABCD LIMITED will defend the same as per advice of WXYZ LIMITED at the cost of WXYZ LIMITED and the latter will reimburse and indemnify ABCD LIMITED against all liabilities and obligations incurred by ABCD LIMITED in respect thereof.

7.   Transferor Company's Staff, Workmen, and Employees

(a) All permanent employees of ABCD LIMITED engaged in the DEF Division at its factories, branches and other offices and elsewhere and who are in the employment of ABCD LIMITED shall stand transferred to WXYZ LIMITED with continuity of service and on the same terms and conditions on which they are engaged as on the Effective Date by ABCD LIMITED. WXYZ LIMITED shall undertake to continue to abide by any of the Agreement/Settlement etc. entered into by ABCD LIMITED in respect of DEF Division with any Union/employees of DEF Division. WXYZ LIMITED agree that the service of all such employees with ABCD LIMITED up to the Appointed Date shall be taken into account for purposes of all retirement benefits for which they may be eligible in ABCD LIMITED up to the Effective Date. WXYZ LIMITED further agree that for the purpose of payment of any retrenchment compensation, gratuity and other terminal benefits such past services with ABCD LIMITED shall also be taken into account and agrees and undertakes to pay the same as and when payable.

(b) WXYZ LIMITED undertakes that the existing Employees Welfare measures including funds, trusts and arrangement, organised and created by ABCD LIMITED for its employees of DEF Division shall be continued for the benefit of such employees, including employees who may join WXYZ LIMITED after the Appointed Date on the same terms and conditions and with effect from such day WXYZ LIMITED shall make the necessary contributions for such employees taken over by WXYZ LIMITED until WXYZ LIMITED constitutes its own arrangements and obtains necessary approval for the same.

8.   Conduct of Business by Transferor Company Till Effective Date

With effect from the Appointed Date and up to and including the Effective Date:

(a) Transferor Company shall be deemed to have been carrying on and to be carrying on all business and activities relating to the DEF Division of Transferor Company for and on behalf of Transferee Company.

(b) All income, expenditures including management costs, profits accruing to Transferor Company and all taxes thereof or losses arising or incurred by it relating to the DEF Division of Transferor Company shall, for all purposes, be treated as the income, expenditures, profits, taxes or losses, as the case may be, of Transferee Company.

(c) ABCD LIMITED hereby undertakes up to and including the Effective Date to carry on its business with proper prudence and without the prior written consent of WXYZ LIMITED not to alienate, charge or otherwise deal with or dispose off the DEF Division or any part thereof (except in the usual course of business) or undertake substantial expansion of its existing business pertaining to the DEF Division.

9.   Issue of Shares by the Transferee Company

(a) Upon the Scheme being sanctioned by the Honourable High Court of Delhi and it becoming effective and the transfer of the DEF Division, becoming effective in terms of the Scheme, WXYZ LIMITED shall without any further application or deed, issue at par and allot on proportionate basis to each member of ABCD LIMITED, whose name is recorded in the Register of Members of SPML on the Record Date or his/her heirs, executors, administrators or the successors-in-title, as the case may be, _____ Equity shares of ₹_____ each in WXYZ LIMITED credited as fully paid-up in the ratio of for every _____ fully paid-up equity shares of ₹_____ each held by each such member of ABCD LIMITED. The paid-up share capital of ABCD LIMITED shall stand reduced to the extent of net value of assets (including reserves) and liabilities being transferred to WXYZ LIMITED.

(b) The reduction of capital as mentioned above in this Scheme of Arrangement shall be effected as a part of this composite Scheme itself and not under a separate process in terms of Sections 100 to 103 of the Act as the same does not involve either diminishing of liabilities in respect of unpaid share capital or any paid up capital.

10.   Dividends, Profits, Bonus/Rights Shares

(a) ABCD LIMITED shall not declare any dividend for the period commencing from and after April 1, 2005 without the written consent of the Transferee Company.

(b) Subject to the provisions of the Scheme, the profits of the ABCD LIMITED for the period beginning from April 1, 2005 shall belong to and be the profits of the Transferee Company and will be available to the Transferee Company for being disposed of in any manner, as it thinks fit, including declaration of dividend by the Transferee Company in respect of its financial year ending 31st March, 2005 or any year thereafter.

(c) ABCD LIMITED shall not issue or allot any Rights Shares or Bonus Shares, out of its Authorised or unissued Share Capital for the time being.

11. Term Loan and Bank Borrowings/Facilities

(a) ABCD LIMITED has obtained term loans and bank borrowings/facilities from banks and financial institutions in respect of the DEF Division against the security of the assets of the said division created as per the details given in the annexure hereto.

(b) Pursuant to the scheme, WXYZ LIMITED agrees and undertakes to pay the said term loans and bank/borrowings/facilities with interest cost, charges and expenses as remain due up to the Transfer date, pertaining to the DEF Division vested in it under the scheme and comply with all terms and conditions on which such loans have been granted with such modification as the aid institution/banks may stipulate.

(c) The securities created by ABCD LIMITED in favour of any of the financial institutions/banks as mentioned hereinabove for the amounts of their outstanding loans, borrowings/facilities on the movable and immovable properties of the DEF Division, will continue to be in full force and effect and shall remain binding on WXYZ LIMITED for the amount of debt, liabilities, and obligations.

(d) All loans raised after the Appointed Date but before the Effective Date and used and liabilities incurred by ABCD LIMITED after the Appointed Date but before the Effective Date for operations of the DEF Division shall be discharged by WXYZ LIMITED.

12. Applications to High Court

On the Scheme being agreed to by the requisite majorities of the members of ABCD LIMITED and the members of WXYZ LIMITED, both ABCD LIMITED as well as the WXYZ LIMITED shall respectively with all reasonable dispatch, make applications/petitions to the Court for sanctioning this Scheme of Arrangement under Section 391 of the Act read with Section 100 to 103 and other applicable provisions of the Act for carrying this Scheme into effect. It is hereby clarified that submission of the Scheme to the Court and to any authorities for their respective approvals is without prejudice to all rights, interests, titles and defences ABCD LIMITED and WXYZ LIMITED have or may have under or pursuant to all applicable laws.

13. Modifications/Amendments to the Scheme

ABCD LIMITED and WXYZ LIMITED may in their full and absolute discretion, assent from time to time, on behalf of all persons concerned to any modifications or amendments to the Scheme or agree to any terms and/or conditions which the Court and/or any other authorities under law may deem fit to approve of or direct or impose or which may otherwise be considered necessary or desirable or appropriate by them in the best interest of the members for settling any questions or doubt or difficulty that may arise, whether by reason of any order of the Court or of any directive or orders of any other authorities or otherwise howsoever, arising out of, under or by virtue of this Scheme and for the implementation and/or carrying out of the Scheme, or in any matter connected therewith and to do all acts, deeds, matters, and things and take all such steps as may be necessary, desirable or expedient for putting the Scheme into effect. The aforesaid powers of ABCD LIMITED and WXYZ LIMITED may be exercised by their respective Boards, a committee or committees of the concerned Board or any Director authorized in that behalf by the concerned Board.

14. Scheme Conditional on Approvals/Sanctions

The Scheme is conditional upon and subject to the following approvals/permissions and the Arrangement shall be deemed to be completed on the Effective Date.

(a) The approval of the Scheme by the requisite majorities of such classes of persons of ABCD LIMITED and WXYZ LIMITED, as may be directed by the Court on the applications made for directions under Section 391 read with section 100 to 103 of the Act for calling meetings and necessary resolutions being passed under the Act.

(b) The sanctions of the Court of the Scheme of Arrangement under Sections 391 and 394 of the Act read with Section 100 to 103, in favour of ABCD LIMITED and WXYZ LIMITED and to the necessary Order or Orders under Sections 391, 392 and 394 of the Act.

(c) The approvals of public financial institutions, banks and creditors wherever necessary, under any contract entered into with them by ABCD LIMITED and WXYZ LIMITED.

(d) The Sanction or Approval under any law of the Central Government or any other agency, department or authorities concerned in respect of any of the matters in respect of which such sanction or approval is required.

(e) The Scheme shall be subject to such modifications as the Court while sanctioning such arrangement of ABCD LIMITED with WXYZ LIMITED may direct the Scheme once sanctioned will be binding on all concerned.

(f) Notwithstanding anything contained hereinabove, the Scheme shall also become effective in terms of and upon the fulfilment of requirements of any other law that may be brought into force on this behalf before the Scheme otherwise becomes effective as hereinbefore provided.

15. Effect of Non-receipt of Approvals/Sanctions

In the event of any of the said sanctions and approvals referred to in clause 14 above not being obtained and/or the Scheme not being sanctioned by the Court and/or the order or orders not being passes as aforesaid, the Scheme of Arrangement shall become null and void and shall stand revoked, cancelled and be of no effect, and in that event no rights and liabilities whatsoever shall accrue to or be incurred by parties *inter se*, save and except in respect of any act or deed done prior thereto as is contemplated hereunder or as to any right, liability or obligation which has arisen or accrued pursuant thereto and which shall be governed and be preserved or worked out as is specifically provided in the Scheme or may otherwise arise in law. ABCD LIMITED and WXYZ LIMITED shall bear their own costs, charges and expenses in connection with the Scheme unless otherwise mutually agreed.

16.   Expenses Connected with the Scheme

(a) All costs, charges and expenses in connection with the Scheme and of carrying on or completing the terms and provisions of the Scheme including any incidental charges shall be borne and paid by ABCD LIMITED and WXYZ LIMITED in equal shares.

(b) In the event of non-fulfilment of any or all obligations under the Scheme, by either ABCD LIMITED or WXYZ LIMITED, the non-performance of which will put the other company under any obligation, such defaulting company will indemnify all costs/interests etc. to the other company, subject to a specific provision, if any, to the contrary under the Scheme.

(c) All costs, charges, taxes including duties, levies and all other expenses, including legal expenses, if any (save where expressly provided otherwise) of ABCD LIMITED or WXYZ LIMITED respectively in relation to or in connection with this Scheme including negotiation leading up to the Scheme and for carrying out and completing the terms and provisions of this Scheme and/or incidental to the completion of arrangement of ABCD LIMITED in pursuance of this Scheme shall be borne and paid equally by ABCD LIMITED and WXYZ LIMITED.

17.   Resolution of Doubts/Differences

If any doubt or difference or issue shall arise between the parties hereto or any of their shareholders, creditors, employees and/or any other person as to the construction hereof or as to any account or apportionment to be taken or made of any asset or liability transferred under this Scheme or as to the accounting treatment thereof or as to anything else contained in or relating to or arising out of this Scheme, the same shall be decided by the mutual agreement between the Board of Directors of ABCD LIMITED and WXYZ LIMITED whose decision shall be final and binding on all concerned.

Draft of Forms as per Companies Act, 1956

FORM NO. 31

(See Rule 65)

[Heading as in Form No. 1]

Company Petition No. .... of 20.......

A. B. & Co. Ltd—Petitioner

Form of Minute

The capital of A. B. & Co. Ltd is henceforth ₹........ divided into .... shares of ₹........ each, reduced from ₹........ divided into .... shares of ₹........ each. At the date of the registration of this minute, ... shares numbered .... etc., have been issued and are deemed to be fully paid [and the remaining .... shares are unissued].

[Note: 1.   The words "and reduced" are to be added only where the order so directs.]

    2.   If all the shares of a class are not issued, the minute should state the serial numbers of the issued shares. Partly paid shares should also be distinguished by their serial numbers and the amounts paid thereon should be stated. The serial numbers of shares with calls in arrears and of forfeited shares should also be stated.

FORM NO. 32

(See Rule 65)

[Heading as in Form No. 1]

Company Petition No. .... of 20......

A. B. & Co. Ltd—Petitioner

Notice of Registration of Order and Minute

Notice is hereby given that the order of the High Court at .... (or the district court of ....) dated the .... 19......., confirming the reduction of the capital of the above-named company from ₹........ divided into .... shares of ₹........ each, to ₹........ divided into .... shares of ₹........ each and the minute approved by the court showing, with respect to the share capital of the above company as altered, the several particulars required by the above Act, were registered by the Registrar of Companies on the .... day of .... 19.......

Dated ....

(Sd.) ....

Advocate for the Company

FORM NO. 33

(See Rule 67)

[Heading as in Form No. 1]

Company Application No. .... of 19.......

.... Applicant(s)

Summons for Directions to Convene a Meeting Under Section 391

Let all parties concerned attend the Judge in Chambers on .... (day), the .... day of .... 19....... at .... o'clock in the .... noon on the hearing of an application of the above named company (or of the applicant(s) above-named) for an order that a meeting (or separate meetings) be held at .... of [here enter the creditors or class of creditors e.g., debenture holders other secured creditors, unsecured creditors, etc., or the members or class of members e.g., preference shareholders, equity shareholders, etc. of which class or classes, the meetings have to be held] of the above company, for the purpose of considering, and if thought fit, approving, with or without modification, a scheme of compromise or arrangement proposed to be made between the company and the said [here mention the creditors or class of creditors or members, or the class of members] of the said company.

And that directions may be given as to the method of convening, holding and conducting the said meeting(s) and as the notices and advertisements to be issued.

And that a Chairman (or Chairmen) may be appointed of the said meeting(s), who shall report the result thereof to the Court.

Advocate for the applicant(s)

Registrar

The affidavit of .... will be used in support of the summons.

[Note: Where the company is not the applicant, the summons should be served on the company, or where it is being wound-up, on its liquidator].

FORM NO. 34

(See Rule 67)

[Heading as in Form No. 1]

Company Application No. .... of 19.......

.... Applicant(s)

Affidavit in Support of Summons

I, ... of etc., solemnly affirm and say as follows:

1. I am the managing director/secretary/a director/............/of the said company, (or an auditor of the said company authorised by the directors to make this affidavit, or liquidator of the said company in liquidation).

   [where the application is not by the company or its liquidator, but by a member or creditor, the above paragraph should be suitably altered].

2. The company was incorporated on .... 19....... The document now produced and shown to me is printed copy of the memorandum and articles of association of the said company, and also contains copies of all the special resolutions which have been passed and are now in force.

3. The registered office of the company is situated at ....

4. The capital of the company is ₹........ Divided into .... [here set out the classes of shares issued and the amounts paid up on each share].

5. The objects of the company are set out in the memorandum of association annexed hereto. They are briefly (here set out the main objects in brief).

6. The company commenced the business of .... (e.g., Hides and skins, etc.,) and has been carrying on the same since ....

7. [here set out in separate paragraphs the circumstances that have necessitated the proposed compromise or arrangement, the objects sought to be achieved by it, the terms of the compromise or arrangement, and the effect, if any, of the compromise or arrangement on the material interests of the directors, managing director, or the manager of the company, and were the compromise or arrangement affects the interests of the debentures holders, its effect on the material interests of the trustees of the

debenture truest deed. A copy of the proposed compromise or arrangement should be marked as an exhibit and annexed to the affidavit.]

8. [here set out the class of creditors or members with whom the compromise or arrangement is to be made; where the arrangement is between the company and its members, it should be stated whether any creditors or class of creditors are likely to be affected by it].

9. It is necessary that a meeting (or meetings) of the creditors/members (if the meeting is to be only of a class of creditors or a class of members, it should be so stated) should be called to consider and approve the proposed compromise or arrangement.

10. It is suggested that the meeting (or meetings) may be held at the premises of the registered office of the company or at such other place as may be determined by the court, and on such date(s) and at such time(s) as this court may direct; and that a chairman may be appointed for the meeting (or for each of the meetings) to be held.

11. It is suggested that notice of the proposed compromise or arrangement and of the meeting may be published once in (here set out the newspapers) and in such manner as the court may direct.

12. It is prayed that necessary directions may be given as to the issue and publication of notices and the convening, holding and conducting of the meeting(s) proposed above.

Solemnly affirmed, etc.

(Sd.) X. Y ....

Before me

(Sd.) ....

Commissioner for oaths

FORM NO. 35

(See Rule 69)

[Heading as in Form No. 1]

Company Application No. .... of 19......

.... Applicant(s)

Before the Hon'ble Mr Justice ....

Dated ....

Order on Summons for Directions

Upon the application of the above-named company* (or, the applicant(s) above named) by summons dated the .... day of .... 19......., upon hearing Shri .... advocate for the company [Or (where the company is not the applicant) upon hearing the advocate for the applicant(s) and the advocate for the Company], and upon reading the affidavit of .... filed the .... day of .... 19....., and the exhibits therein referred to (Exhibit .... being a copy of the proposed compromise or arrangement).

It is ordered:

That a meeting (or, separate meeting as hereinafter set out) of (here set out the class or classes of creditors and/or members of whom the meeting or meetings have to be held), of above company shall be convened and held at .... on .... (day), the .... day of .... 19......., at .... o'clock in the ...... noon, for the purpose of considering, and if thought fit, approving, with or without modifications, the compromise or arrangement proposed to be made between the said company and (here set out the class or classes of creditors or members as the case may be) of the said company.

[Note: If separate meetings of different classes of creditors and/or members are to be held, state the date, time and place of each of such meetings as fixed by the Judge, in separate paragraphs.]

That at least 21 clear days before the day appointed for the meeting (or the first of the meetings, an advertisement convening the same and stating that copies of the said compromise or arrangement and of the statement required to be furnished pursuant to Section 393 and forms of proxy can be obtained free of charge at the registered office of the company or at the office of its advocate, be inserted once in the .... Gazette and once in each of ......(here set out the newspaper or newspapers).

That, in addition, at least 21 clear days before the meeting (or the first of the meetings) to be held as aforesaid, a notice convening the said meeting at the place and time aforesaid, together with a copy of the said compromise or arrangement, a copy of the statement required to be sent under Section 393, and the prescribed Form of proxy, shall be sent by pre-paid letter post under Certificate of posting addressed to each of (here mention the class or classes of creditors or members whose meeting or meetings are to be held) at their respective registered or last known addresses.

That the advocate for the company above-named does, within 3 days from this date file in court the form of the advertisement, the notice and the statement to accompany the notice, and the same shall be settled by the Registrar of this Court.

That Shri ...., and failing him, Shri ...., shall be the Chairman of the meeting to be held on .... as aforesaid.

That the Chairman appointed for the meeting do issue the advertisement and send out the notices of the meeting (s) referred to above.

That the quorum for the said meeting(s) shall be ....

That voting by proxy be permitted, provided that a proxy in the prescribed form duly signed by the person entitled to attend and vote at the meeting, is filed with the company at its registered office at .... not later than 48 hours before the meeting.

That the value of each member or creditor shall be in accordance with books of the company, and, where the entries in the books are disputed, the Chairman shall determine the value for purposes of the meeting.

And it is further ordered that the chairman does report to this Court the result of the said meeting within .... days of the conclusion of the meeting and the said report shall be verified by his affidavit.

Dated this .... day of .... 19.......

(By the Court)

Registrar

Note: 1. Where separate meetings are to be held, the provisions should be repeated in respect of each of such meetings.

2. Where the Court directs the company or its Liquidator or any other person to issue the advertisement and notices, suitable alteration should be made.

*Where the application is by a liquidator of the company substitute the words "liquidator of the above company in liquidation" for the word "company" wherever necessary.

FORM NO. 36

(See Rule 73)

[Heading as in Form No. 1]

Company Application No. .... of 19.......

.... Applicant(s)

Notice Convening Meeting

To

....

....

Take notice that by an order made on .... 19......., the Court has directed that a meeting of (here mention the class of creditors or members of whom the meeting is to be held) of the company be held at .... on the .... day of .... 19......, at ....o'clock, for the purpose of considering, and if thought fit, approving, with or without modification, the compromise or arrangement proposed to be made between the said company and (here mention the class of creditors or members with whom the compromise or arrangement is to be made) of the company.

Take further notice that in pursuance of the said order, a meeting of (here mention the class of creditors or members of whom the meeting is to be held) of the company will be held at .... on .... (Day), the .... day of .... 19......., when you are requested to attend.

Take further notice that you may attend and vote at the said meeting in person or by proxy, provided that a proxy in the prescribed form, duly signed by you, is deposited at the registered office of the company at .... not later than 48 hours before the meeting.

This court has appointed Shri ...., and failing him, Shri ...., to be the Chairman of the said meeting.

A copy each of the compromise or arrangement, the statement under Section 393 and a form of proxy is enclosed.

Dated this .... day of .... 19.......

Chairman appointed for the meeting

(or as the case may be).

[Note: All alterations made in the form of the proxy should be initialled.]

FORM NO. 37

(See Rule 73)

[Heading as in Form No. 1]

Company Application No. .... of 19.......

.... Applicant(s)

Form of Proxy

I, the undersigned [an unsecured creditor], of the above company hereby appoint C.D., of etc., and failing him X. Y., of etc, as my proxy, to act for me at the meeting of [unsecured creditors] to be held at .... on the .... day of .... 19......., at ..... o'clock in the .... noon, for the purpose of considering and, if thought fit, approving, with or without modification, a compromise or arrangement proposed to be made between the said company and its unsecured creditors] and at such meeting and any adjournment thereof, to vote for me, and in my name .... [here, if 'for', insert 'for'; if 'against', insert 'against', and in the latter case, strike out the words below after 'compromise or arrangement'] the said compromise or arrangement either with or without modification as my proxy may approve.

[strike out what is not necessary]

Dated this .... day of .... 19.......

Signature ....

Address ....

FORM NO. 38

(See Rule 74)

[Heading as in Form No. 1]

Company Application No. .... of 19........

.... Applicant(s)

Notice Convening Meeting of Creditors/Shareholders, etc.

Notice is hereby given that by an order dated the .... 19........ the court has directed a meeting (or, separate meetings) to be held of [here mention 'debenture holders', or 'first debenture holders' or 'second debentures holders' or 'unsecured creditors' or 'secured creditors' or 'preference shareholders' or 'equity shareholders' as the case may be whose meeting or meetings have to be held] of the said company for the purpose of considering, and, if thought fit, approving with or without modification, the compromise or arrangement proposed to be made between the said company and (here mention the class of creditors or members with whom the compromise or arrangement is to be made) of the company aforesaid.

In pursuance of the said order and as directed therein, further notice is hereby given that a meeting of (here set out the class of creditors or members whose meeting has to be held) of the said company will be held at .... on (day), the .... day of .... 19........, at .... o'clock in the .... noon at which time and place the said (here mention the class of creditor or members) are requested to attend.

[Where separate meetings of classes of creditors or members are to be held, set them out separately with the place, date and time of the meeting in each case.]

Copies of the said compromise or arrangement, and of the statement under Section 393 can be had free of charge at the registered office of the company or at the office of its advocate Shri .... at ....

Persons entitled to attend and vote at the meeting (or respective meetings) may vote in person or by proxy, provided that all proxies in the prescribed form are deposited at the registered office of the company at .... not later than 48 hours before the meeting.

Forms of proxy can be had at the registered office of the Company.

The Court has appointed Shri .... and failing him, Shri ...., as Chairman of the said meeting (or several meetings). The above-mentioned compromise or arrangement, if approved by the meeting, will be subject to the subsequent approval of the Court.

Dated this .... day of .... 19.......

Chairman appointed for the meeting

(or as the case may be)

FORM NO. 39

(See Rule 78)

[Heading as in Form No. 1]

Company Application No. .... of 19.......

.... Applicant(s)

Report by Chairman

I, E.F., the person appointed by this Hon'ble Court to act as Chairman of the meeting of [the debenture holders or first debenture holders or second debenture holders or unsecured creditors or secured creditors or preference shareholders or equity shareholders] of the above-named company, summoned by notice served individually upon them and by advertisement dated the .... day of .... 19....... and held on the .... day of .... 19....... at ...., do hereby report to this Hon'ble Court as follows:-

1. The said meeting was attended either personally or by proxy by (here state the number of creditors or the class of creditors or the number of members or the class of members as the case may be, who attended the meeting), of the said company entitled together to .... (here mention the total value of the debts, or debentures, where the meeting was of creditors, and the total number and value of the shares, where the meeting was of members, of those who attended the meeting).

2. The compromise or arrangement was read out and explained by me to the meeting and the question submitted to the said meeting was whether the (here state the class of creditors or members, as the case may be) of the said company approved of the compromise or arrangement submitted to the meeting and agreed thereto.

3. The said meeting was unanimously of the opinion that the compromise or arrangement should be approved* and agreed to/or the result of the voting upon the said question as follows:

   The under-mentioned [here mention the class of creditors or members who attended the meeting] voted in favour of the proposed compromise or arrangement being adopted and carried into effect:

Name of creditor (or member)	Address	Value of debt (or No. of preference or equity shares held)	Number of votes
1.			
2.			
3.			
etc.			

The under-mentioned [Here mention the class of creditors or members who attended the meeting] voted against the proposed compromise or arrangement being adopted and carried into effect:

Name of creditor (or member)	Address	Value of debt (or No. of preference or equity shares held)	Number of votes
1.			
2.			
3.			

Dated this .... day of .... 19........

(Sd.) E.F. ....

Chairman

*If the compromise or arrangement was approved with modifications, it should be so stated and the modifications made should be set out, and also the particulars of the voting on the modifications.

FORM NO. 40

(See Rule 79)

[Heading as in Form No. 1]

Company Petition No. .... of 19.......

connected with

Company Application No. .... of 19.......

A. B. & Co. [Ltd] (in liquidation, by its liquidator*

.............................) Petitioner

Petition to Sanction Compromise or Arrangement

The petition of A. B. & Co. [Ltd]., (*in liquidation, by its liquidator) the petitioner above-named is as follows:

1. The object of this petition is to obtain sanction of the Court to compromise or arrangement whereby (here set out the nature of the compromise or arrangement).

2. The company was incorporated under the .... Act .... with a nominal capital of ₹........ divided into .... shares of ₹........ each, of which .... shares were issued and ₹........ was paid up on each share issued.

3. The objects for which the company was formed are as set in the company's memorandum of association. They are in brief (Set out the principal objects).

4. [Here set out the nature of the business carried on by the company, its financial position and the circumstances that necessitated the compromise or arrangement and the benefits sought to be achieved by the compromise or arrangement and its effect].

5. The compromise or arrangement was in the following terms:

[Here set out the terms of the compromise or arrangement].

6. By an order made in the above matter on .... 19......, the petitioner was directed to convene a meeting of [Here set out the class of creditors or members of whom the meeting was to be held] of the company for the purpose of considering

and, if thought fit, approving, with or without modifications, the said compromise or arrangement, and the said order directed that E. F., or failing him, X. Y., should act as Chairman of the said meeting and should report the result thereof to this Court.

7. Notice of the meeting was sent individually to the [here mention the class of creditors or members to whom the notice was sent] as required by the order together with a copy of the compromise or arrangement and of the statement required by Section 393 and a form of proxy. The notice of the meeting was also advertised as directed by the said order in (here set out the newspapers).

8. On the .... 19......., a meeting of (here mention the class of creditors or members whose meeting was convened) of the company duly convened in accordance with the said order, was held at .... and the said E. F. acted as the chairman of the meeting.

9. The said E. F. has reported the result of the meeting to this Hon'ble Court.

10. The said meeting was attended by (here set out the number of the class of creditors or members, as the case may be, who attended the meeting either in person or by proxy), and the total value of their [here mention debts, debentures or shares, as the case may be is ₹............ [In the case of shares, the total number and value of the shares should be mentioned. The said compromise or arrangement was read and explained by the said E. F., to the meeting and it was resolved unanimously [or by a majority of .... votes against .... votes] as follows:

    [Here set out the resolution as passed.]

11. The sanctioning of the compromise or arrangement will be for the benefit of the company.

12. Notice of this petition need not be served on any person.

The petitioner therefore prays:

(a) That the said compromise or arrangement may be sanctioned by the Court so as to be binding on all the [here set out the class of creditors or members of the company on whom the compromise or arrangement is to be binding] of the said company and on the said company.

(b) Or, such other order may be made in the premises as to the Court shall seem fit.

Verification, etc.

Petitioner

[Note: The affidavit in support should verify the petition and prove any matters not proved in any prior affidavit, such as advertisement, holding of meetings, posting of notices, copies of compromise or arrangement and proxies, etc., and should exhibit the report of the Chairman and verify the same.]

Note: If the company is being wound-up, say so.

Note: If any modifications were made in the compromise or arrangement at the meeting they should be set out in separate paragraph.

*To be inserted where the company is being wound-up.

FORM NO. 41

(See Rule 81)

[Heading as in Form No. 1]

Company Petition No. .... of 19........

connected with

Company Application No. .... of 19........

A. B. & Co., [Ltd] (*in liquidation, by its liquidator) petitioner

Before the Hon'ble Mr Justice ....

Dated ....

Order on Petition

The above petition coming on for hearing on .... upon reading the said petition, the order dated .... where by the said company (or, liquidator of the said company), was ordered to convene a meeting (or separate meetings) of the creditors/debenture holders/preference shareholders/equity shareholders of the above company for the purpose of considering, and if thought fit, approving with or without modification, the compromise or arrangement proposed to be made between the said company and .... and annexed to the affidavit of .... filed the .... day of .... 19......., the .... Gazette dated .... and the (here mention the newspaper) dated .... each containing the advertisement of the said notice convening the said meeting (s) directed to be held by the said order dated .... 19......., the affidavit of .... filed the .... day of .... 19......., showing the publication and despatch of the notices convening the said meeting(s), the report(s) of the Chairman/Chairmen of the said meeting(s) (respectively) dated .... as to the result of the said meeting(s), (and upon hearing Shri .... advocate for .... etc.) and it appearing from the report(s) that the proposed compromise and arrangement has been approved** .... (here state whether unanimously or by a majority of not less than three-fourths in value of the creditors or class of creditors or members or class of members as the case may be, present and voting in person or by proxy).

This Court doth hereby sanction the compromise or arrangement set forth in para .... of the petition herein and in the Schedule hereto, and doth hereby declare the same to be binding on .... (here enter the class of creditors or members on whom it is to be binding) of the above-named company and also on the said company (and its liquidator*)

And this Court doth further order:

[Here enter any directions given or modifications made by the Court regarding the carrying out of the compromise or arrangement.]

That the parties to the compromise or arrangement or other persons interested shall be at liberty to apply to this Court for any directions that may be necessary in regard to the working of the compromise or arrangement, and

That the said company [or the liquidator of the said company] do file with the Registrar of Companies a certified copy of this order within 14 days from this date.

Schedule

Scheme of compromise or arrangement as sanctioned by the Court.

Dated this .... day of .... 19.......

(By the Court)

Registrar

*To be inserted where the company is being wound-up.

**Where the compromise or arrangement has been approved with modifications, it should be so stated.

FORM NO. 42

(See Rule 84)

[Heading as in Form No. 1]

Company Petition No. .... of 19.......

*Application No. .... of 19.......

.... Applicant

Before the Hon'ble Mr Justice ....

Dated ....

Order Under Section 394

Upon the above petition [and application] coming on for further hearing on ...., upon reading, etc., and upon hearing, etc.

This Court Doth Order

1. That all the property, rights and powers of the transferor company specified in the first, second and third parts of the Schedule hereto and all the other property, rights and powers of the transferor company be transferred without further act or deed to the transferee company and accordingly the same shall pursuant to Section 394(2) of the Companies Act, 1956, be transferred to and vest in the transferee company for all the estate and interest of the transferor company therein but subject nevertheless to all charges now affecting the same [other than (here set out any charges which by virtue of the compromise or arrangement are to cease to have effect)]; and

2. That all the liabilities and duties of the transferor company be transferred without further act or deed to the transferee company and accordingly the same shall pursuant to Section 394(2) of the Companies Act, 1956, be transferred to and become the liabilities and duties of the transferee company; and

3. That all proceedings now pending by or against the transferor company be continued by or against the transferee company; and

4. That the transferee company do without further application allot to such members of the transferor company as have not given such notice of dissent as is required by

clause .... of the compromise or arrangement herein the shares in the transferee company to which they are entitled under the said compromise or arrangement; and

5. That the transferor company do within 14 days after the date of this order cause a certified copy of this order to be delivered to the Registrar of Companies for registration and on such certified copy being so delivered the transferor company shall be dissolved** and the Registrar of Companies shall place all documents relating to the transferor company and registered with him on the file kept by him in relation to the transferee company and the files relating to the said two companies shall be consolidated accordingly; and

6. That any person interested shall be at liberty to apply to the Court in the above matter for any directions that may be necessary.

Schedule

Part I

(Insert a short description of the freehold property of the transferor company.)

Part II

(Insert a short description of the leasehold property of the transferor company.)

Part III

(Insert short description of all stocks, shares, debentures, and other charges in action of the transferor company.)

Dated this .... day of .... 19.......

(By the Court)

Registrar

*To be inserted where an application is made.

**Where the Court directs that the transferor company should be dissolved from any other date, the clause should be altered accordingly.

Draft Resolution of the Board Approving the Scheme of Amalgamation

"RESOLVED pursuant to the provisions of Sections 391 to 394 and other applicable provisions, if any, of the Companies Act, 1956 and subject to the approval of the members/creditors and approval by the High Court of Delhi at New Delhi, the Scheme of Amalgamation in terms of the draft produced at the meeting duly initialled by the Chairman for the purpose of identification, be and is hereby approved for amalgamation of the company with XYZ Limited with effect from 1st April, 2005 being the 'Appointed Date'."

"RESOLVED FURTHER that Mr _____ and Mr _____, Directors of the company be and are hereby severally authorized to sign any application, affidavit, petition, or any other document as may be required to be signed in connection with the approval of the Scheme. They are further authorized to do all such things, deeds, and acts as may be deemed necessary and expedient in connection with the approval of the Scheme, for and on behalf of the company."

"RESOLVED FURTHER THAT Mr _____ and Mr _____, Directors of the company be and are hereby authorized to appoint and engage any advocate or firm of advocates and solicitors to represent the company for approval of the Scheme."

Index